East Coast Pilot

Published by
Imray Laurie Norie & Wilson Ltd
Wych House St Ives
Cambridgeshire PE27 5BT England
☎ +44 (0)1480 462114
Email ilnw@imray.com
www.imray.com
2024

All rights reserved. No part of this publication may be reproduced, transmitted or used in any form by any means – graphic, electronic or mechanical, including photocopying, recording, taping or information storage and retrieval systems or otherwise – without the prior permission of the publishers.

1st edition 2005
2nd edition 2008
3rd edition 2011
4th edition 2015
5th edition 2019
6th edition 2024

© Garth Cooper and Dick Holness 2024
Garth Cooper and Dick Holness have asserted their rights to be identified as the authors of this work in accordance with the Copyright, Designs and Patents Act 1988.

© Plans Imray Laurie Norie & Wilson 2024

© Photographs Garth Cooper, Dick Holness, Claire Frew, John Langrick and Roger Gaspar.
© Aerial photographs Dick Holness, unless otherwise credited.

ISBN 978 178679 451 2
British Library Cataloguing in Publication Data.
A catalogue record for this book is available from the British Library.

PLANS
The plans in this guide are not to be used for navigation. They are designed to support the text and should at all times be used with up to date navigational charts.

This product has been derived in part from material obtained from the UK Hydrographic Office with the permission of the UK Hydrographic Office, Her Majesty's Stationery Office.

© British Crown Copyright, 2019. All rights reserved.
Licence number GB AA - 005 - Imrays

Without in any way limiting the Authors' (and publisher's) exclusive rights under copyright, any use of this publication to 'train' generative artificial intelligence (AI) technologies to generate text is expressly prohibited. The Authors reserve all rights to license uses of this work for generative AI training and development of machine learning language models.

THIS PRODUCT IS NOT TO BE USED FOR NAVIGATION
NOTICE: The UK Hydrographic Office (UKHO) and its licensors make no warranties or representations, express or implied, with respect to this product. The UKHO and its licensors have not verified the information within this product or quality assured it.

CAUTION
While every care has been taken to ensure accuracy, neither the Publishers nor the Authors will hold themselves responsible for errors, omissions or alterations in this publication. They will at all times be grateful to receive information which tends to the improvement of the work.

SUPPLEMENTS AND UPDATES
This pilot book will be amended as and when necessary through corrections and updates published on www.eastcoastpilot.com. These may be read and downloaded free of charge. Printed copies are also available on request from the publishers at the above address.

Printed in Malta by Gutenberg Press Ltd

EAST COAST PILOT

Great Yarmouth to Ramsgate

Garth Cooper & Dick Holness

Imray Laurie Norie & Wilson

CONTENTS

The authors *vi*
Acknowledgements *vi*
Introduction *iv*
Supporting website *viii*
Symbols used on charts *x*
Abbreviations *xi*

Small craft symbols *xi*
General information *1*
IALA buoyage system *5*
Tidal stream diagrams *6*
Index *254*

Chapter 3, Southwold

1 Great Yarmouth *10*	11 River Blackwater *104*
2 Lowestoft *16*	12 River Crouch *124*
3 Southwold *24*	13 River Roach *138*
4 Rivers Ore and Alde *30*	14 Canvey and Leigh *150*
5 River Deben *40*	15 River Thames *160*
6 Harwich Harbour *52*	16 River Medway *184*
7 River Orwell *60*	17 The Swale *210*
8 River Stour *74*	18 North Kent Coast *230*
9 Walton Backwaters *80*	19 Ramsgate *242*
10 River Colne *90*	20 Thames Estuary Passages *248*

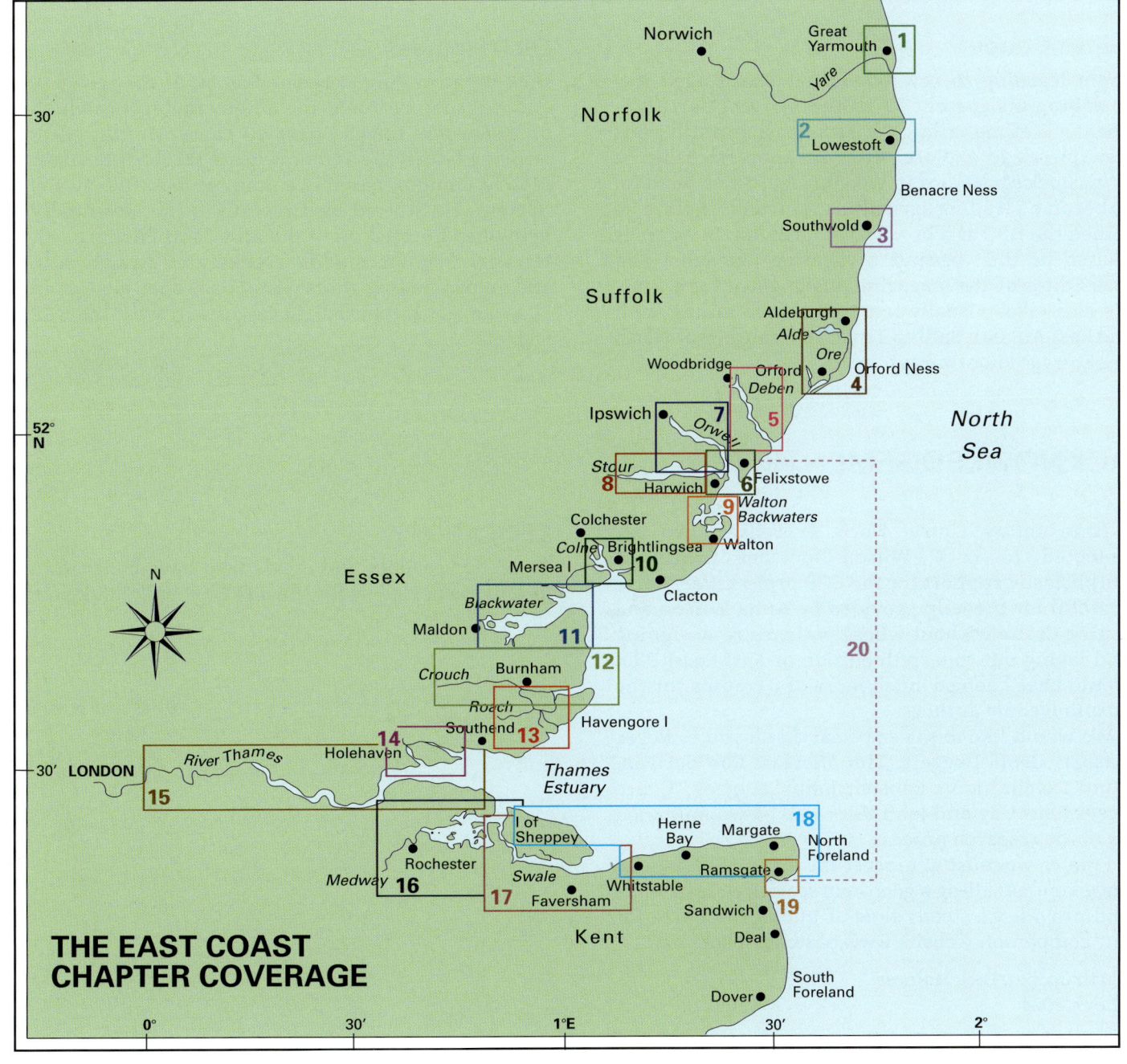

THE EAST COAST CHAPTER COVERAGE

THE AUTHORS

Garth Cooper

From learning to row on Barton Broad aged five to sailing his current 33-footer, *Morven*, Garth has spent a lifetime sailing the East Coast and still finds new places to explore. After an apprenticeship at Whisstock's boatyard in Woodbridge, Garth went on to become a leading agricultural journalist before he joined the BBC as a broadcast journalist. In a career switch he then became a yachting journalist and was Editor of the magazine *Anglia Afloat* for a time. He also takes visually impared people sailing with the East Anglian Sailing Trust. He is author of *North Sea Passage Pilot* (Imray).

Dick Holness

Dick began sailing at Herne Bay SC at the age of 12 and was soon bitten by the dinghy racing bug which occupied him for the next 40 years. He turned to cruising late in life and now has a 36' shoal-draught Moody, *Cantata*, based in a mud berth off the Swale, in Kent. He started writing late in life, eventually being headhunted on to the *East Coast Pilot* project. He adores quiet muddy creeks and swatchways, and enjoys finding short cuts. His proper job was in IT so he 'got lumbered', as he puts it, with the ECP website.

ACKNOWLEDGEMENTS

Within Imray Laurie Norie & Wilson, we are indebted to Lucy Wilson for her continued enthusiastic support for the ECP project. We're also grateful for the help provided by Anna Wilson and Emilie Crabb without whose patience re-designing and laying out this sixth edition of *East Coast Pilot* would have been so much more of a trauma for the curmudgeonly authors.

We would like to say a special thank you to Roger Gaspar, Geoff Doggett, Tim Thomas, Rob Scriven, Tony Lavelle, John Ranson, John Langrick, Claire Frew, John Udy and John Kerr – all of whom joined us in the research process.

Finally, we must not forget the many readers who have kept us sailing a good course with a clean wake and provided a steady flow of pilotage updates for our companion website www.eastcoastpilot.com

Garth Cooper, Dick Holness
March 2024

DEDICATION

To all our readers and crews who have believed in us and supported us for the last 20 years, thank you.

INTRODUCTION

FULLY REVISED SIXTH EDITION

Welcome to the sixth edition of *East Coast Pilot*. It doesn't seem that long ago when Colin Jarman, Dick Holness and I met in Maldon for a working lunch and agreed to take on this project. That was in 2004 and we tramped the East Coast and laid the foundation for what is today the most popular and successful yachtsman's guide to the waters of the East Anglian coast and Thames Estuary. Sadly, Colin died in 2016 after a long battle with cancer, but he did see his creation blossom.

2023 was a year of contrasts; June was flaming hot, while July, our target month to be afloat was abysmal with high winds and rain galore. Despite this we managed to get out and about visiting just about every port, creek and potential mooring hole on the East Coast and in the process, catching up with old contacts and making new friends, who've helped make putting this new edition together a real joy. Thank you.

Keep up to date

Large numbers of you regularly visit our dedicated website at **www.eastcoastpilot.com** to download updates. By incorporating these into your copy of the book, you will keep it current and ensure that you get full benefit from it as you pilot your boat around the East Coast and Thames Estuary. However, when we fully research the area afresh, as we have for this new edition, we always find even more changes, and these are incorporated now, but may not have been published on the website.

ECP is an evolving project, in previous issues we have extended the area of coverage to include Great Yarmouth in the North, we've expanded the tidal stream diagrams to give more information on each one and have used larger photographs with more overlaid tracks and annotations to make it easier for the pilot approaching a strange port or harbour. In this edition we introduce major changes at Great Yarmouth, Lowestoft, the Deben, the Colne and the Thames.

Shoal draught

We occasionally use the description 'shoal draught' and it's as well to understand what we mean by the term. For us a shoal draught lies between 3ft 6in and 4ft or 1-1·2m. This is important, because boat sizes (and draughts) are commonly increasing, but many creeks and anchorages are becoming shallower. Beware!

Accuracy and updates

The East Anglian coast and Thames Estuary is an area of huge and frequent change. We have done

The popular destination of Heybridge Basin on the River Blackwater

our best to ensure accuracy at the time of writing, but even by the time of publication there will have been changes, particularly to the entrance channels in river mouths like the Ore and Deben. We must, therefore, caution you to watch for changes and alterations, particularly those shown on **www.eastcoastpilot.com** and to exercise seamanlike common sense, always referring to the most up-to-date charts and published corrections.

The advice and guidance in ECP are given in good faith and is as accurate as we can make it but neither the authors nor the publisher can accept responsibility for any errors or omissions in the published material.

Electronic chart plotter displays

Chart plotters are widely used, but the temptation to rely on them not only for position fixing but also for pilotage is a bit risky, especially if the power goes down.

The authors base their navigation on paper charts, updated at regular intervals, but find that a modern plotter is a valuable aid to pilotage. However, if you are using paper charts in parallel with either a chart plotter or the Imray Navigator app, it is quite

INTRODUCTION

Keeping your *East Coast Pilot* up to date

We believe that East Coast Pilot remains unique among pilot books in having its own dedicated website, www.eastcoastpilot.com, created and maintained by the authors, as the primary vehicle for providing updates.

Generally, we show changes on the website soon after learning of them, although we sometimes take a few days to verify the information if we are unsure of the source.

By using a website to provide this information, we can afford to be generous with words, chartlets and pictures – we can give full descriptions of the changes and provide visual evidence as well, for example a photo of a new approach buoy or changes to a marina entrance.

Apart from pilotage changes and updates, we also aim to keep you abreast of other information that may affect you as you cruise the area. We do this through a News section where items are left available to read until they are no longer current. Everything else is left on the website until the next edition is published.

We also offer e-newsletters – distributed by email, a few a year – designed to call your attention to Updates and News that we have put on the website. These are completely free, just part of the service, and you can easily sign up for them via the button on the website. There are just over a 1,500 subscribers and the considerable feedback tells us how useful these emails are to ECP readers.

You can also follow us on Facebook ('East Coast Pilot') and X (Twitter) @eastcoastpilot, where we also broadcast news of changes.

We are delighted when readers get in touch and we do encourage you to tell us if you find that features we have described have changed. You can contact us by email through the website and you will usually get a quick response if we're not away sailing.

Incidentally, something we do not do on the website is provide Notices to Mariners or chart changes that are readily available from the UKHO or other publishers, although we will bring them to your attention if they are important. (Relevant NtMs can quickly be found at www.crossingthethamesestuary.com.)

For those without ready access to the internet, updates for this sixth edition are also available in paper form on request from the publisher. This is an abbreviated version of the fuller descriptions published on the website and without any photos, but will still be right up to date, because it will be printed from the website at the time of the request. Again, we believe this to be a unique feature of ECP.

We do urge you to use these facilities, via the internet or by requesting regular updates from Imray, to keep your East Coast Pilot up to date.

Through the website we can even supply you with an ECP 'community' burgee, so stand up and be counted – join the ECP Users' Community!

The ECP website helps keep your book up to date

'Rolling Roads'

Most chapters in this book have at least one 'rolling road' diagram to assist pilotage.

Read each rolling road from the bottom upwards.

The long blue arrow through the middle of the diagram shows which buoys are to be left to port and which to starboard.

Distances between buoys/waypoints are also given.

The angled short blue arrows tell the helmsman the general direction to take when passing a particular buoy, until the navigator works out the exact new course.

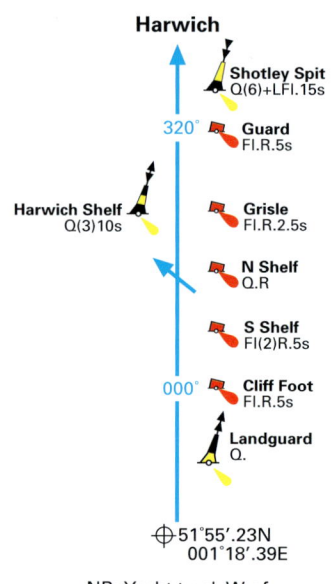

NB: Yacht track W of deep water channel

Introduction

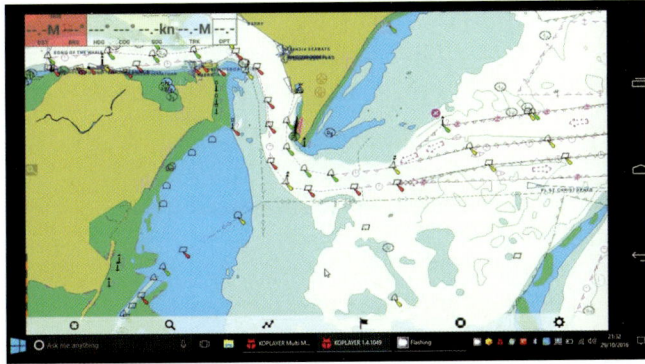

possible for the two systems to be at odds if you have not kept a perfect record of all updates and Notices to Mariners (NtMs).

It is appealing to think you can perhaps find the way up an unmarked creek by following the dotted line on the plotter display that indicates where the deepest water was when the survey was last done but remember that gutways move and many such creeks won't have been surveyed in detail for many years.

Before plotters, we might have approached such a shallow creek challenge by gently weaving from side to side and watching the echo sounder – and that is still a sensible method.

The plotter can be a valuable aid, but it is just that – an aid.

Honorary Port Pilots

With the second edition of ECP we introduced Honorary Port Pilots (HPPs) who helped us gather updates and offered local, on-the-spot advice to readers who contacted them. Some of these have now stepped down, having perhaps moved away or even given up boating, and we took this opportunity to review the concept. In some places we know that the harbour staff or their equivalent are helpful and friendly, making HPPs less needed than they once were, so we now have a shorter list — Matt Smy (Orford and Ore/Alde entrance), John White (Deben), Alec Moss (Walton Backwaters), Nigel Harmer (Blackwater), Rob Scriven (Canvey), and Simon Smedley (Conyer and Swale), Geoff Doggett (Lowestoft and Yarmouth).

The contact details of these HPPs are listed in the relevant information boxes at the beginning of each chapter and are also listed at www.eastcoastpilot.com. Don't be shy; they are willing to help first timers (and some old hands too), with planning a trip into their area.

QR codes

QR codes – the black and white chequerboard patterns printed in some of the information boxes – allow you to use a smartphone or tablet (with the appropriate free app on it), to scan them and link directly to the chosen website wherever you have internet access. It's easier and quicker than trying to type in the web addresses, particularly when butting into a Wallet chop!

Iconic Thames barges moored alongside Maldon's Hythe Quay

INTRODUCTION

SYMBOLS USED ON CHARTS

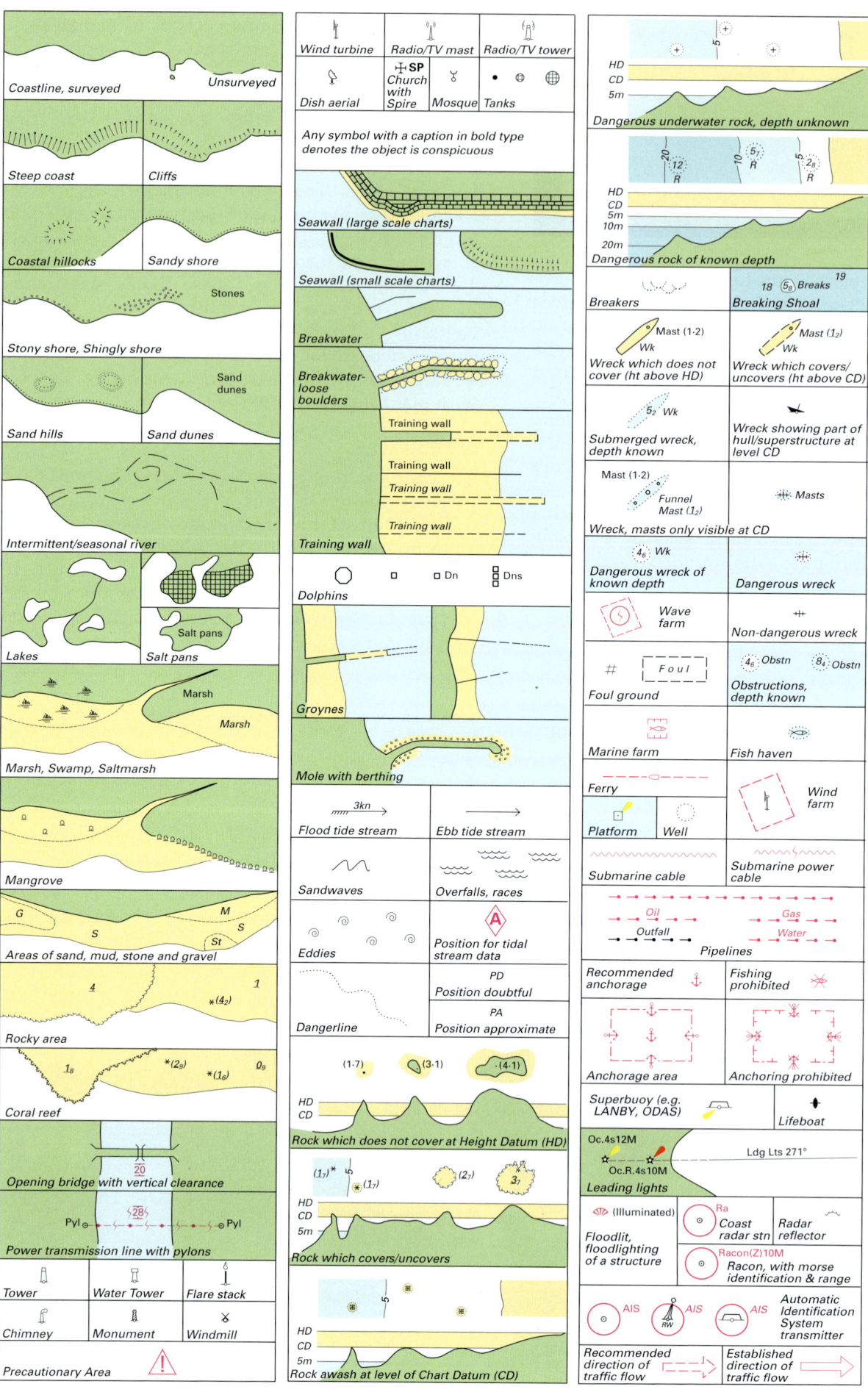

x • East Coast Pilot

Small craft symbols

ABBREVIATIONS

Bn	Beacon	NCM	North Cardinal Mark (eg beacon)
By	Buoy	NE	Northeast or Northeastwards
CC	Cruising Club	NEly	Northeasterly
CG	Coastguard	NW	Northwest, Northwestwards
Ch	Channel	NWly	Northwesterly
Conspic	Conspicuous	Oc	Occulting light
DSC	Digital Selective Calling	ODAS	Ocean Data Acquisition System
E	East, Eastwards, Easterly	PAYG	Pay as you go
ECB	East Cardinal Buoy	PH	Port Hand
ECM	East Cardinal Mark (eg beacon)	PHB	Port hand Buoy
F	Fixed light	PHM	Port Hand Mark (eg beacon)
Fl	Flashing Light	PLA	Port of London Authority
Ft	Foot, feet	Pt	Point
G	Green	PWC	Personal Water Craft (jet ski)
H	Hour, eg H +15 is 15 minutes past the hour	Q	Quick flashing light
hr	Hour, Hours	R	Red
HW	High water	S	South, Southwards, Southerly
HWN	High water Neaps	s	second(s)
HWS	High water Springs	SC	Sailing Club
IDM	Isolated Danger Mark	SCB	South Cardinal Buoy
IQ	Interrupted Quick flashing light	SCM	South cardinal Mark (eg beacon)
Iso	Isophase light	SH	Starboard Hand
Kn	Knot, knots	SHB	Starboard hand Buoy
L.Fl	Long Flash	SHM	Starboard Hand Mark (eg beacon)
LNG	Liquefied Natural Gas	S'ly	Southerly
LOA	Length Overall	SW	Southwest, Southwestwards
LPG	Liquefied Petroleum Gas	SWB	Safe Water Buoy
LW	Low Water	SWly	Southwesterly
LWN	Low water neaps	SWM	Safe Water Mark
LWS	Low Water Springs	TSS	Traffic Separation Scheme
M	Mile (Nautical mile)	UKHO	United Kingdom Hydrographic Office (the admiralty)
m	metre	UTC	Universal Time Corrected (same as GMT - Greenwich MeanTime)
MHWS	Mean High Water springs	vert	vertical
min	minute	VQ	Very quick flashing light
mins	minutes	VTS	Vessel Traffic Service
MLws	Mean Low Water Springs	W	West, Westwards, Westerly; White
MMSI	Maritime Mobile Service Identity	WCB	West Cardinal Buoy
MSI	Maritime Safety Information incl. inshore waters forecast, gale warnings and navigational warnings	WCM	West Cardinal Mark (eg beacon)
Mo	Morse	Y	Yellow
N	North, Northwards, Northerly	YC	Yacht club
NCB	North Cardinal Buoy		

SMALL CRAFT SYMBOLS

- Visitor's mooring
- Visitor's berth
- Yacht marina
- Public landing
- Slipway for small craft
- Water tap
- Fuel
- Pump-out facilities
- Customs
- Public house, inn, bar
- Restaurant
- Yacht or sailing club
- Toilets
- Public car park
- Hard standing for boats
- Launderette
- Caravan site
- Camping site
- Nature reserve
- Harbour master
- Travel hoist

- Public telephone
- Post office
- Building
- Airport
- Flagpole/flagstaff
- Castle/fort
- Hospital
- Notice board
- Wooded
- Beacon (with various topmarks)
- Mooring Buoy
- Crane
- Chimney
- Radio/TV mast
- Water tower
- Tower
- Monument
- Wind turbine

INTRODUCTION

LIFE-SAVING SIGNALS

SOLAS CHAPTER V REGULATION 29

To be used by Ships, Aircraft or Persons in Distress when communicating with life-saving stations, maritime rescue units and aircraft engaged in search and rescue operations.

Note: All Morse Code signals by light (below).

1. SEARCH AND RESCUE UNIT REPLIES

YOU HAVE BEEN SEEN, ASSISTANCE WILL BE GIVEN AS SOON AS POSSIBLE

Orange smoke flare

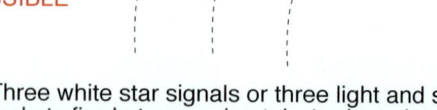
Three white star signals or three light and sound rockets fired at approximately 1 minute intervals

2. SURFACE TO AIR SIGNALS

Note: Use International Code of Signals by means of light or flags or by laying out the symbol on the deck or ground with items that have a high contrast background.

Message	International Code of Signals			ICAO
I require assistance	V	❌	...—	V
I require medical assistance	W	◩	.— —	X
No or negative	N	▦	—.	N
Yes or affirmative	C	☰	—.—.	Y
Proceeding in this direction				↑

3. AIR TO SURFACE REPLIES

MESSAGE UNDERSTOOD

Drop a message. OR Rocking wings. OR Flashing landing or navigation lights on and off twice. OR T — OR R .—.

MESSAGE NOT UNDERSTOOD

Straight and level flight. OR Circling. OR R .—. P .——. T —

4. AIR TO SURFACE DIRECTION SIGNALS

SEQUENCE OF 3 MANOEUVRES MEANING PROCEED IN THIS DIRECTION

Circle vessel at least once. Cross low, ahead of vessel rocking wings. Overfly vessel and head in required direction.

YOUR ASSISTANCE IS NO LONGER REQUIRED

Cross low, astern of vessel rocking wings.

Note: As a non preferred alternative to rocking wings, varying engine tone or volume may be used.

5. SURFACE TO AIR REPLIES

MESSAGE UNDERSTOOD - I WILL COMPLY

Change course to required direction. 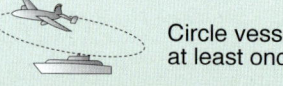 OR T — OR  Code & answering pendant "Close Up".

I AM UNABLE TO COMPLY

International flag "N". OR N —.

6. SHORE TO SHIP SIGNALS

SAFE TO LAND HERE

Vertical waving of both arms, white flag, light or flare

OR K —.—

LANDING HERE IS DANGEROUS ADDITIONAL SIGNALS MEAN SAFER LANDING IN DIRECTION INDICATED

Horizontal waving white flag, light or flare. Putting one flare/flag on ground and moving off with a second indicates direction of safer landing.

OR

S ... Landing here is dangerous.
R .—. Land to right of your current heading.
L .—.. Land to left of your current heading.

GENERAL INFORMATION

Chart datum

The charts are based on UK Hydrographic Office (Admiralty) data and, therefore, drawn to Lowest Astronomical Tide (LAT). This means, that they show a 'worst case scenario' and that there will normally be more water in an area than is shown.

The horizontal datum is WGS84, which complies with modern GPS equipment.

Courses and bearings

We have applied the general pilot book convention of providing courses and bearings in degrees True but have used the qualifiers 'about' or 'approximately'. This is because it is the skipper/navigator's responsibility to confirm such courses and bearings regarding tide, wind and sea conditions as well as applying corrections unique to the boat.

We also believe that to steer a course in a seaway to within ±10° is acceptable; to steer within ±5° is good; to steer a precise course of (say) 241° is impossible. That impossibility makes it reasonable to quote a course of 'about 240°' and let the reader make the necessary corrections.

Distances

Readers asked for a simple table of distances as an indication of the mileage between landfalls. We turned to that excellent passage planner *Crossing the Thames Estuary* by Roger Gaspar (Imray). Roger kindly let us use the data he'd developed and helped us with additional material. We highly recommend *Crossing the Thames Estuary* as a planning companion to ECP.

Tides

In the first four editions we based all tides on HW Dover, but now refer to the nearest standard port, be that Dover, Sheerness, Walton or Lowestoft. Differences in time are given before (-) or after (+) in hours and minutes, e.g. HW Sheerness +0120 is 1hr 20mins after HW Sheerness.

Landfall waypoints

To provide a starting point for the pilotage notes, we have selected a point in the offing and called it the Landfall Waypoint. It is a point in clear water, which we feel can be approached safely and from which pilotage can reasonably begin. You are strongly

DISTANCE TABLE (miles)

	Lowestoft	Southwold	Ore entrance	Deben entrance	Harwich Harbour (Landguard SHM)	Brightlingsea	Maldon	Burnham-on-Crouch	Queenborough	Tower Bridge (Thames)	Ramsgate
Lowestoft	0										
Southwold	10	0									
Ore entrance	30	10	0								
Deben entrance	35	26	5	0							
Harwich Harbour (Landguard SHM)	40	27	12	5	0						
Brightlingsea	62	52	38	33	22	0					
Maldon	70	62	44	39	31	15	0				
Burnham-on-Crouch	73	64	44	35	32	19	25	0			
Queenborough	83	73	49	47	43	30	35	25	0		
Tower Bridge (Thames)	112	103	81	78	73	60	67	51	40	0	
Ramsgate	76	66	52	46	44	54	60	50	35	62	0

INTRODUCTION

advised to plot the waypoint and decide for yourself whether you wish to use it.

You may well decide on another position nearby. Do not just put our chosen waypoint into your GPS and passage plan without checking it and agreeing with it.

Chart lists

We have given the numbers of paper charts covering a specific area published by Imray and the Admiralty (UKHO). We have not attempted to list electronic charts, because there are too many permutations of publisher, plotter and 'packages' and compiling the list would waste valuable sailing time.

Coastguard

HM Coastguard coverage of the East Coast Pilot area is shared between Humber and Dover Coastguard Operations Centres (CGOCs), with London specifically responsible for the River Thames.

There is no firm dividing line between the coverage of the two CGOCs, but in general Dover is responsible southwards from the Blackwater and Humber is responsible northwards from the Deben, with both covering the Wallet and Harwich approaches.

When calling the Coastguard, it is best to use the appropriate MMSI from a DSC VHF set; with non-DSC sets, a CGOC can be contacted via Ch 16 using 'UK Coastguard' as the call sign. Whichever CGOC is available, according to workloads, will reply using its own call sign which should be used for the rest of the conversation.

Humber and Dover both pre-announce MSI (Maritime Safety Information) broadcasts on VHF Ch 16, specifying the channels on which they will be made. London CGOC does not make MSI broadcasts.

London Coastguard

DSC MMSI 002320063 ☏0208 312 7380. Covers area from Shell Haven Point (N bank) and Egypt Point (S bank) to Teddington.

Dover Coastguard

DSC MMSI 002320010 ☏01304 210008. Covers Dover Strait and southern Thames Estuary south of Blackwater Estuary. MSI announcements on Ch 16 at 0110, 0410, 0710, 1010, 1310, 1610, 1910, 2210 UTC. MSI aerials Bawdsey Ch 62, Walton Ch 63, Shoeburyness Ch 63, Bradwell Ch 64.

Humber Coastguard

DSC MMSI 002320007 ☏01262 672317. Covers area from Deben entrance northwards. MSI announcements on Ch 16 at 0150, 0450, 0750, 1050, 1350, 1650, 1950, 2250 UTC. MSI aerials Lowestoft Ch 62, Caister Ch 64.

The apparent gap will be covered by whichever CGOC has the capacity to handle the incident. They will work the incident to its conclusion.

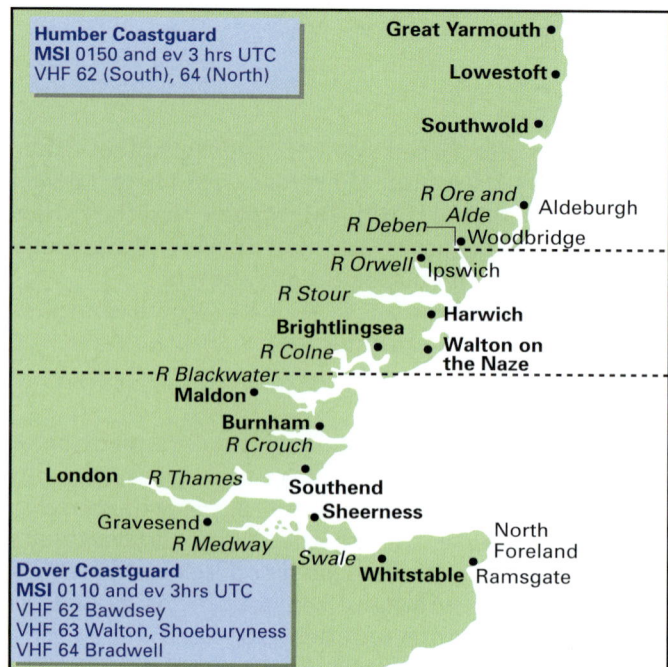

National Coastwatch Institution (NCI)

www.nci.org.uk

NCI stations are now equipped to use VHF Ch 65, a channel for their dedicated use in communication with seafarers on a variety of non-emergency routine tasks. Skippers of leisure craft can use it for radio checks if they need to (rather than calling the Coastguard) or to request local information, such as actual weather and sea state conditions. Note that not all NCI stations are open every day, and those that are open generally operate for daylight hours only.

Any other communications, most especially those of an emergency nature, must still be made with the CG via DSC and/or Ch 16.

NCI stations on the coast covered by ECP are as follows, from north to south:

Cromer	☏01263 519751
Mundesley	☏01263 722399
Gorleston	☏01493 440384
Canvey Island	☏01268 956370
Felixstowe	☏01394 802143
Southend	☏01702 593152
Whitstable	☏01227 314554

In addition, a new Coastwatch station has opened at Pakefield, Suffolk, by the newly formed Sea Safety Group. Contact ☏07522 483022.

Danger – pot markers

Poorly marked crab and lobster pots are an annoying feature of the Thames Estuary. It requires a very sharp lookout to spot small floats or empty drinks containers, which may be half submerged in a strong tide. At night it's impossible to see them until it's too late.

All of this makes motoring or motor sailing a time for extreme caution, especially at night. Indeed,

Wind farms and commerce

Cruising down the Ore

such is the problem that it may sometimes be wise to take a longer route or remain further offshore to be sure of going around infested areas.

Areas to beware of are off the North Foreland, around the Naze and towards Harwich, off Felixstowe S of the Deben entrance, East Lane (S of Ore entrance), Aldeburgh and Sizewell – there are even scattered pots in Harwich Harbour and the approaches to Lowestoft.

ECP strongly supports the campaign to get pots more clearly marked.

Medical help

For emergency medical help make a VHF call to the Coastguard when at sea or ☎999 by phone when in harbour.

For non-emergency help and advice, when in harbour, call the NHS ☎111, available 24hr.

Riding lights

The International Regulations for Preventing Collisions at Sea, 1972 (ColRegs), require vessels of more than 7m length to display a black ball during the day and an all-round white light at night when riding to an anchor.

In these days of crowded anchorages and heavy traffic, our advice would be for ALL vessels including those on moorings, to display these signals, particularly at night, when crew are on board.

Wind farms and commerce

Large wind farms are now a fact of life in the outer extremities of our waters. The nearest to shore are Scroby Sands off Great Yarmouth and the Gunfleet Sands off Clacton. The London Array is in the very middle of the Thames Estuary, while the Gabbards affect those of us who aim to venture across the North Sea. The Kentish Flats wind farm has been expanded and needs care to pass in the shallows off the North Kent coast. The Thanet wind farm stands off the North Foreland.

The Thames Estuary is the most crowded sailing area in the UK after the Solent. It has a charm and character that makes it unique, but the commercial traffic using the Thames is so continuously heavy

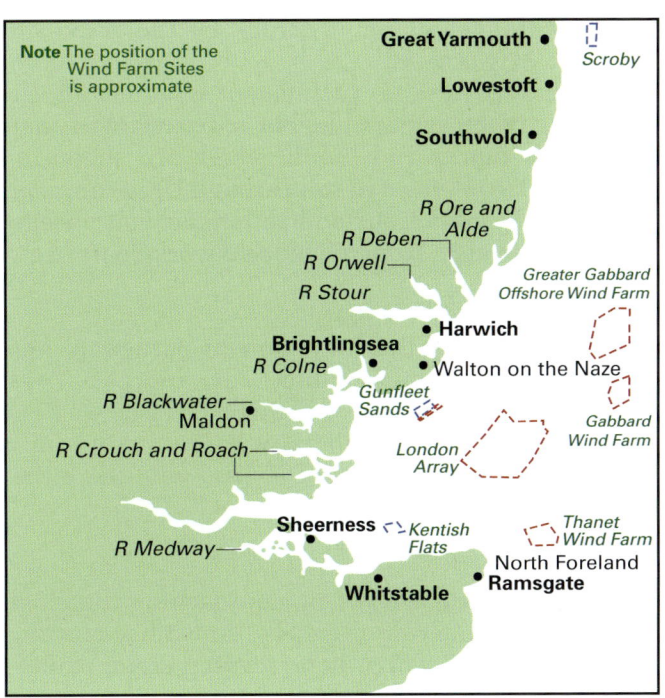

East Coast Pilot • 3

INTRODUCTION

that the Port of London Authority (PLA) is the largest port authority in the country. Felixstowe is the largest container port in the UK, one of the busiest in Europe, and accommodates the very largest cargo ships in the world. The Thames Estuary is the funnel through which much of this shipping travels to reach either Harwich in the N section or the Thames in the S.

The Estuary is becoming even more crowded with expansion of the container port at Felixstowe and the London Gateway in the Thames itself. There is also a rising demand for yachting facilities and, moreover, the explosion in wind farm developments with increasing traffic in the form of large barges used to install and maintain them and fast craft that service them.

As if all that wasn't enough, craft wishing to leave to the N of our area, say beyond Lowestoft or across to the North Dutch or Friesland coasts, will eventually run the gauntlet of a new massive multi-thousand tower wind farm stretching from just S of Lowestoft to as far N as the Dogger Bank with a width greater than half that of the southern North Sea.

To aid ship safety, the towers in all wind farms are painted yellow up to 12m above sea level and the corner towers, plus those at some key points down the sides of the farm, have yellow flashing lights, also at 12m. Red lights on the tops of the towers flash Morse 'W'. There is, however, doubt that at this height any of these lights will be visible to crews of recreational craft navigating in fog or dirty weather. The farms emit sound signals in fog.

Generally, the rotor tip clearance is 22m above MHWS and at this height 96 per cent of yachts will, if forced into the arrays, pass underneath without being struck by a rotor. Unfortunately, on the Gunfleet, just off Clacton, the clearance is only 20m, bringing the percentage of yachts able to go through without danger of being struck by the rotor tips down to 88 per cent.

General advice to yachtsmen is to avoid the farms as much as possible, but to be aware of their positions, marks and lights, which are shown on current charts. You can sail through UK windfarms in the right conditions and so long as you observe rules on distance from towers and work boats.

Caring for wildlife

In Spring 2023 the Government issued a new Marine and Coastal Wildlife Code, and East Coast Pilot supports the aims of the new code, as we hope most of our readers will as well. The main aim is to minimise disturbance of coastal wildlife, either from land or sea.

Be aware

You can disturb wildlife by approaching too close, moving, or touching them; by crowding, circling, separating, or chasing them; feeding them; making unnecessary noise; or damaging or changing their habitats. If animals are repeatedly disturbed, it can lead to stress, injury or even death; displace them from favourite habitats; disrupt their pattern of life (migration, breeding, resting, and feeding) and make them vulnerable to predators.

Give them space

Give wildlife plenty of space. Aim to stay at least 100 metres away if you can. Boat engines of all types create enormous sound in the water, be aware that close in shore and in estuaries there may be animals such as seals in the water or hauled up on the shore (Walton Backwaters is a case in point). If you are lucky enough to attract a pod of porpoises or dolphins to ride your bow wave, then hold a steady speed and course and let them go when they want to. Marine and coastal wildlife code. Download from www.gov.uk/government/publications/marine-and-coastal-wildlife-code-advice-for-visitors.

CLEAN SEAS

At *East Coast Pilot* we are deeply committed to environmental stewardship. As members of the boating community, we all have a pivotal role in safeguarding our rivers and seas. By adhering to environmental best practices, we contribute to the enduring health and vitality of these ecosystems; behaviour that not only benefits us, the users, but also the diverse wildlife and habitats that depend on these water bodies.

 A noteworthy endeavour in this mission is The Green Blue, a nationwide environmental programme established by the Royal Yachting Association and British Marine. This initiative is dedicated to fostering sustainable practices among the recreational boating community across coastal and inland waters. For resources and guidance on making your water-based activities more environmentally sustainable, visit **www.thegreenblue.org**.

Seals basking in the shallows of Oakley Creek, Walton Backwaters

IALA buoyage system

INTERNATIONAL PORT TRAFFIC SIGNALS (IPTS)

		MAIN MESSAGE	
1	🔴🔴🔴 Flashing	Serious emergency - all vessels to stop or divert according to instructions	
2	🔴🔴🔴	Vessels shall not proceed	
3	🟢🟢🟢	Vessels may proceed; One-way traffic	Fixed or slow occulting
4	🟢🟢⚪	Vessels may proceed; Two-way traffic	
5	🟢⚪🟢	A vessel may proceed only when it has received specific orders to do so	
		EXEMPTION SIGNALS AND MESSAGES	
2a	🟡🔴🔴🔴	Vessels shall not proceed, except that vessels which navigate outside the main channel need not comply with the main message	Fixed or slow occulting
5a	🟡🟢⚪🟢	A vessel may proceed only when it has received specific orders to do so, except that vessels which navigate outside the main channel need not comply with the main message	

COMMON SOUND SIGNALS

Morse code

•	I am turning to starboard
• •	I am turning to port
• • •	My engines are going astern
• • • • •	I am uncertain of your intentions

In restricted visibility, repeat at intervals of not more than 2 minutes

—	I am making way through the water
— —	I am underway, but stopped
— • •	I am restricted in my ability to manoeuvre or sail
• — •	Vessels at anchor or aground

A short blast is 1 second; a long blast is 4-6 seconds

IALA BUOYAGE SYSTEM REGION A

Lateral marks
Port hand
All red
Topmark (if any): can
Light (if any): red

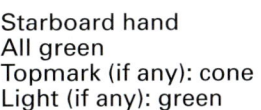

Starboard hand
All green
Topmark (if any): cone
Light (if any): green

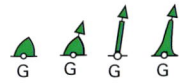

Preferred channel to port
Green/red/green
Light (if any): Fl(2+1)G

Preferred channel to starboard
Red/green/red
Light (if any): Fl(2+1)R

Isolated danger marks
(stationed over a danger with navigable water around)
Black with red band
Topmark: 2 black balls
Light (if any): Fl(2) (white)

Special mark
Body shape optional, yellow
Topmark (if any): Yellow X
Light (if any): Fl.Y etc

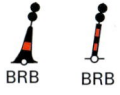

Safe water marks
(mid-channel and landfall)
Red and white vertical stripes
Topmark (if any): red ball
Light (if any): Iso, Oc, LFl.10s or Mo(A) (white)

Emergency Wreck Marking buoy
Yellow and blue vertical stripes
Topmark: upright yellow cross
Light (if any): Fl.Bu/Y.3s

Cardinal marks

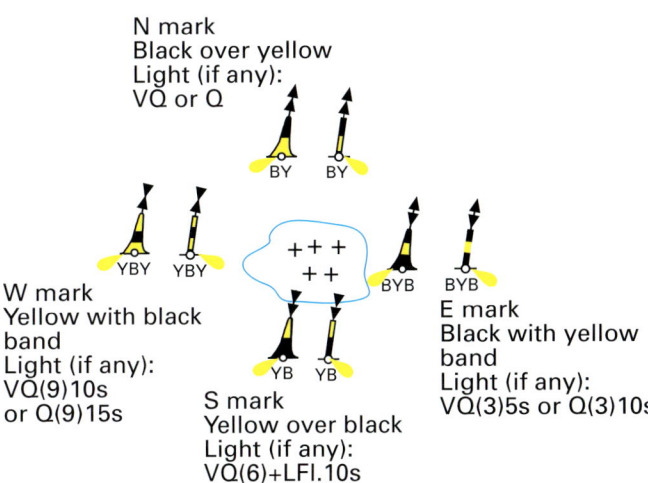

N mark
Black over yellow
Light (if any): VQ or Q

W mark
Yellow with black band
Light (if any): VQ(9)10s or Q(9)15s

S mark
Yellow over black
Light (if any): VQ(6)+LFl.10s or Q(6)+LFl.15s

E mark
Black with yellow band
Light (if any): VQ(3)5s or Q(3)10s

INTRODUCTION

THE BEAUFORT SCALE

The Beaufort scale, which is used in Met Office marine forecasts, is an empirical measure for describing wind intensity based on observed sea conditions.

TIDAL STREAMS

The figures against the arrows in the diagrams overleaf denote mean rates in tenths of a knot at neaps and springs. Thus 06,11 indicates a mean neap rate of 0·6 knots and a mean spring rate of 1·1 knots.

Specifications and equivalent speeds

Beaufort wind scale	Mean wind speed (Knots)	Mean wind speed (ms-1)	Limits of wind speed (Knots)	Limits of wind speed (ms-1)	Wind descriptive terms	Probable maximum wave height	Probable maximum wave height (m)	Seastate	Sea descriptive terms
0	0	0	<1	<1	Calm	-	-	0	Calm (glassy)
1	2	1	1-3	1-2	Light air	0.1	0.1	1	Calm (rippled)
2	5	3	4-6	2-3	Light breeze	0.2	0.3	2	Smooth (wavelets)
3	9	5	7-10	4-5	Gentle breeze	0.6	1.0	3	Slight
4	13	7	11-16	6-8	Moderate breeze	1.0	1.5	3-4	Slight - Moderate
5	19	10	17-21	9-11	Fresh breeze	2.0	2.5	4	Moderate
6	24	12	22-27	11-14	Strong breeze	3.0	4.0	5	Rough
7	30	15	28-33	14-17	Near gale	4.0	5.5	5-6	Rough-V. rough
8	37	19	34-40	17-21	Gale	5.5	7.5	6-7	V.rough - High
9	44	23	41-47	21-24	Strong gale	7.0	10.0	7	High
7.0	10.0	7	High	25-28	Storm	9.0	12.5	8	V. high
10	52	27	48-55	25-28	Storm	9.0	12.5	8	V. high
11	60	31	56-63	29-32	Violent storm	11.5	16.0	8	V. high
12	-		64+	33+	Hurricane	14+	-	9	Phenomenal

TIDAL DIFFERENCES ON DOVER AND SHEERNESS

Location	Dover	Sheerness
Allington Lock	+0210	+0054
Broadstairs	+0037	-0053
Burnham-on-Crouch	+0115	-0015
Canvey	+0125	-0005
Chatham	+0140	+0010
Colne	+0050	-0040
Gravesend	+0200	+0030
Great Yarmouth	-0200	-0330
Harty Ferry	+0120	-0010
Harwich Haven	+0040	-0050
Herne Bay	+0110	-0020
Ipswich	+0115	-0015
London Bridge	+0252	+0122
Lowestoft	-0133	-0303
Maldon	+0130	+0000
Margate	+0045	-0045
Mistley Quay	+0105	-0025
Orford Haven	+0010	-0120
Orford Quay	+0100	-0030
Paglesham	+0110	-0020
Pin Mill	+0100	-0030
Queenborough	+0130	+0000
Ramsgate	+0030	-0100
Sheerness	+0130	+0000
Slaughden	+0155	+0025
Snape	+0225	+0055
Southwold	-0105	-0235
Stone Point	+0040	-0050
Waldringfield	+0100	-0030
Whitstable	+0135	+0005
Woodbridge	+0105	-0025
Woodbridge Haven	+0025	-0105
Woolwich Ferry	+0225	+0055

Tidal Streams

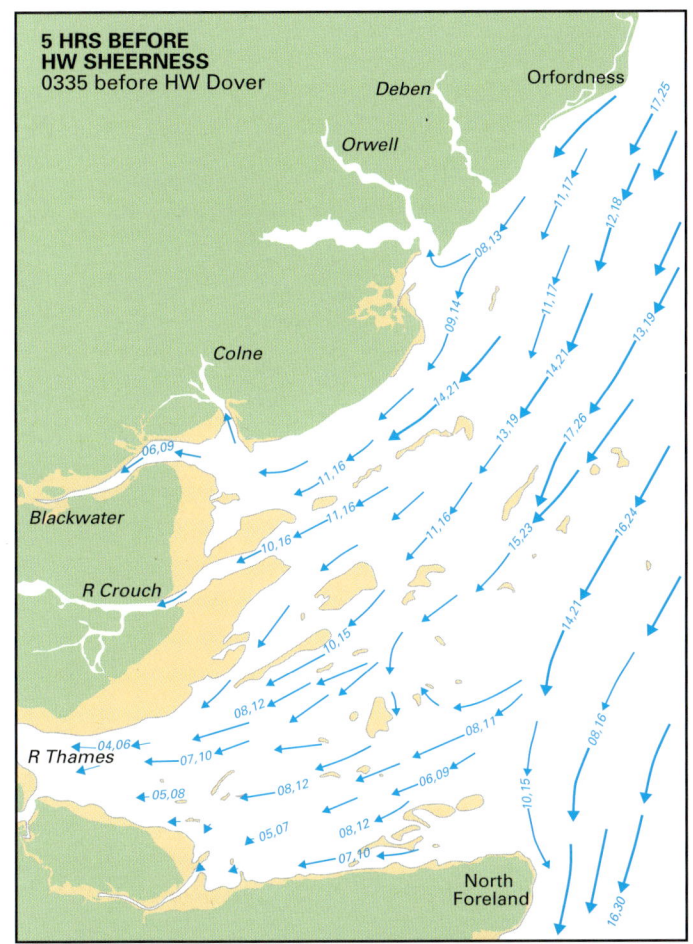
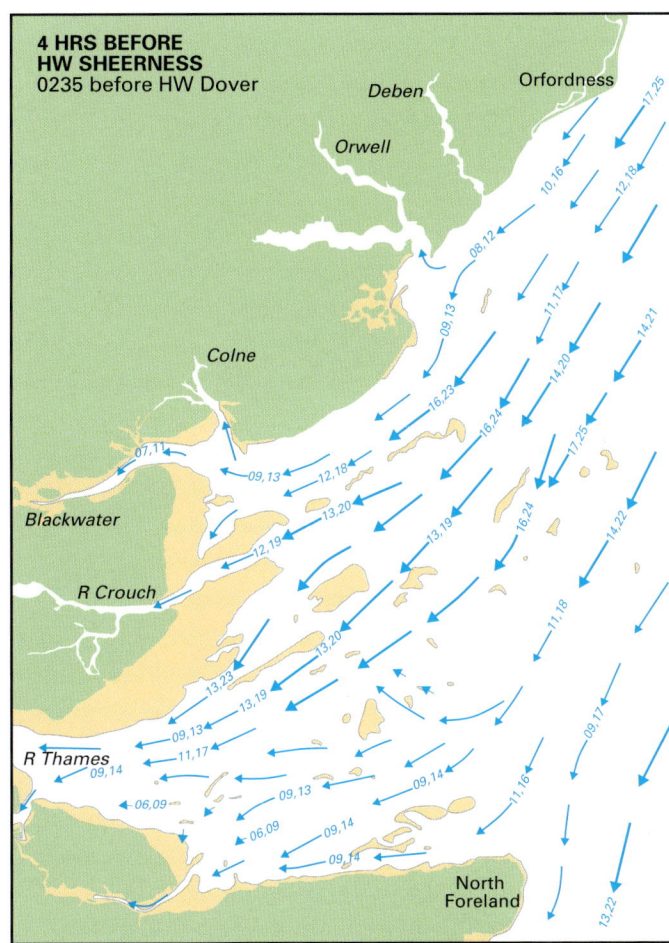
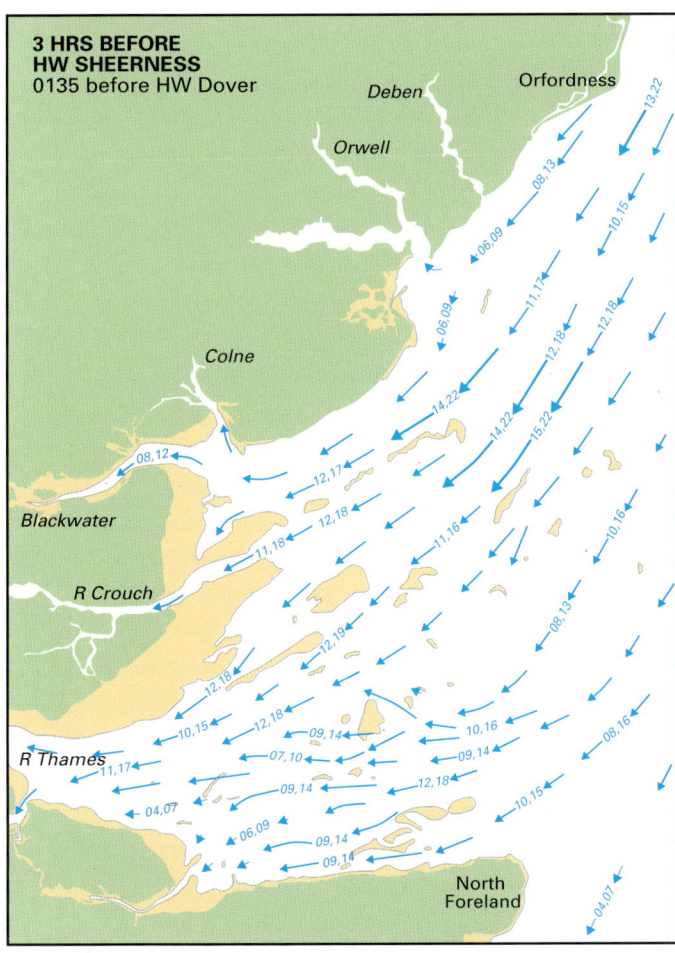
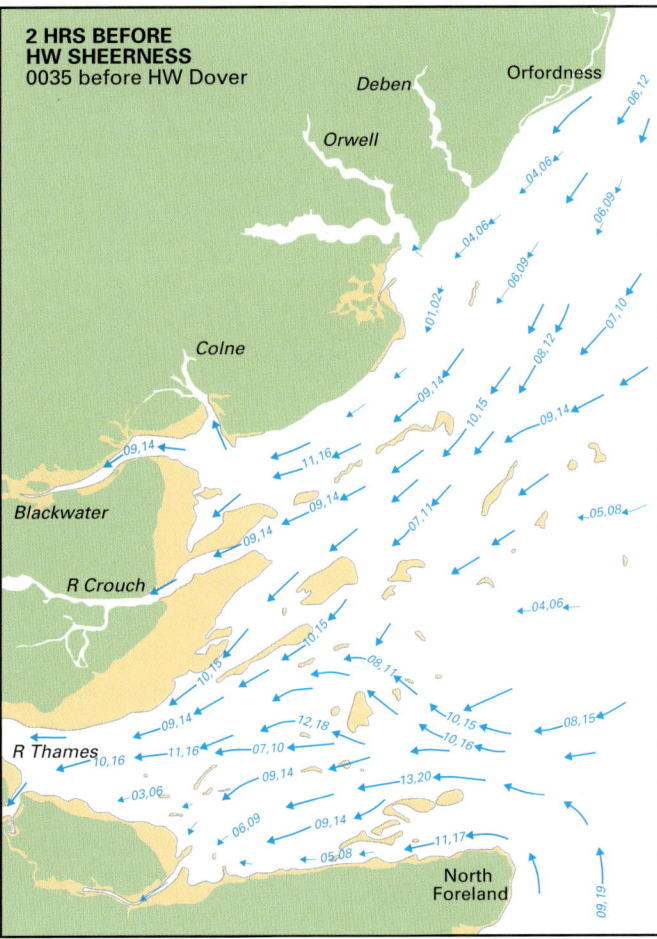

East Coast Pilot • 7

INTRODUCTION

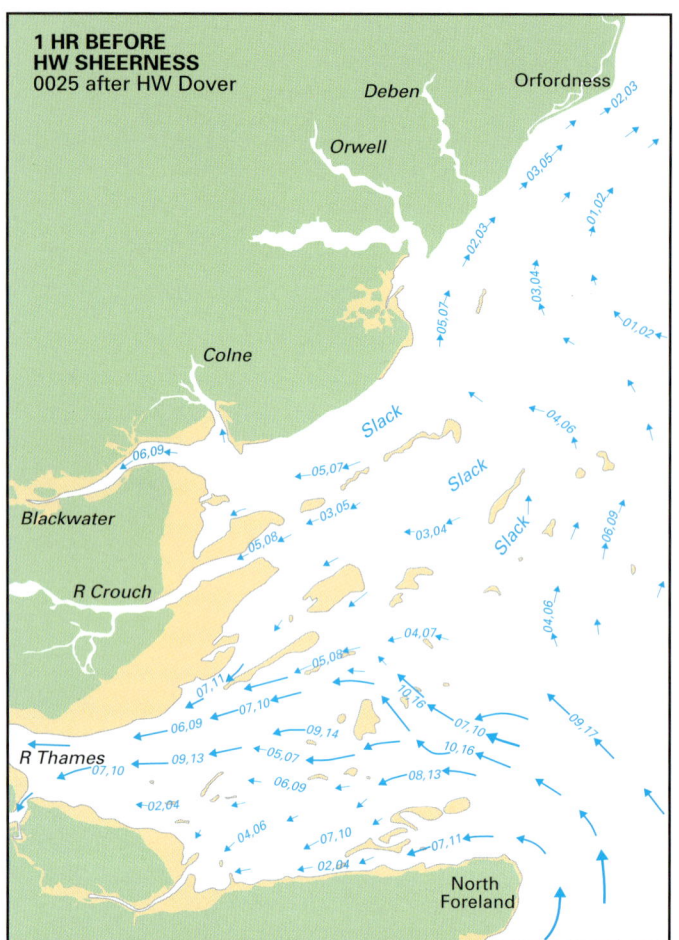

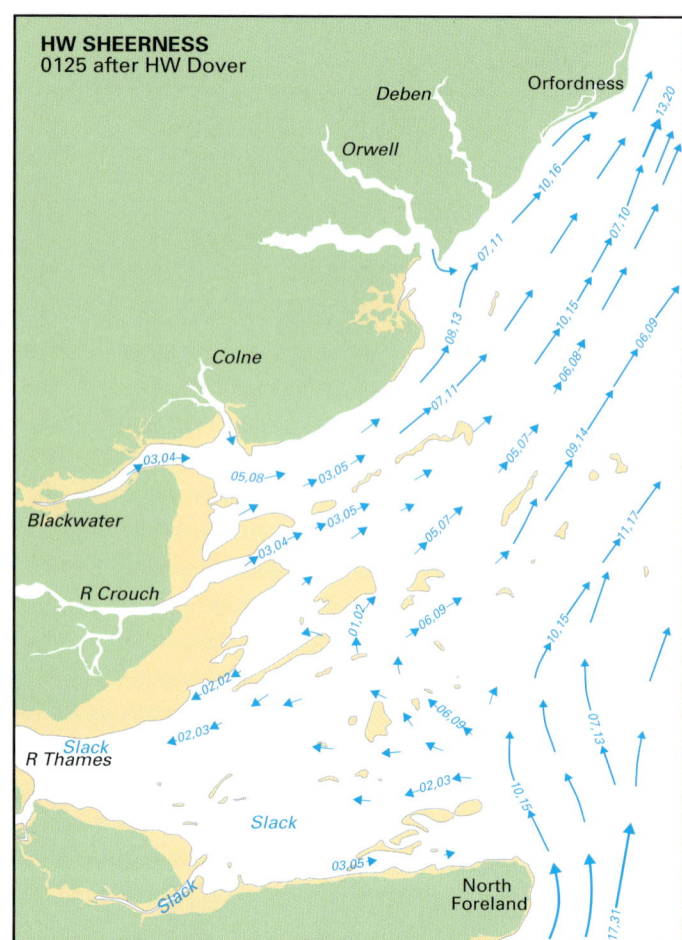

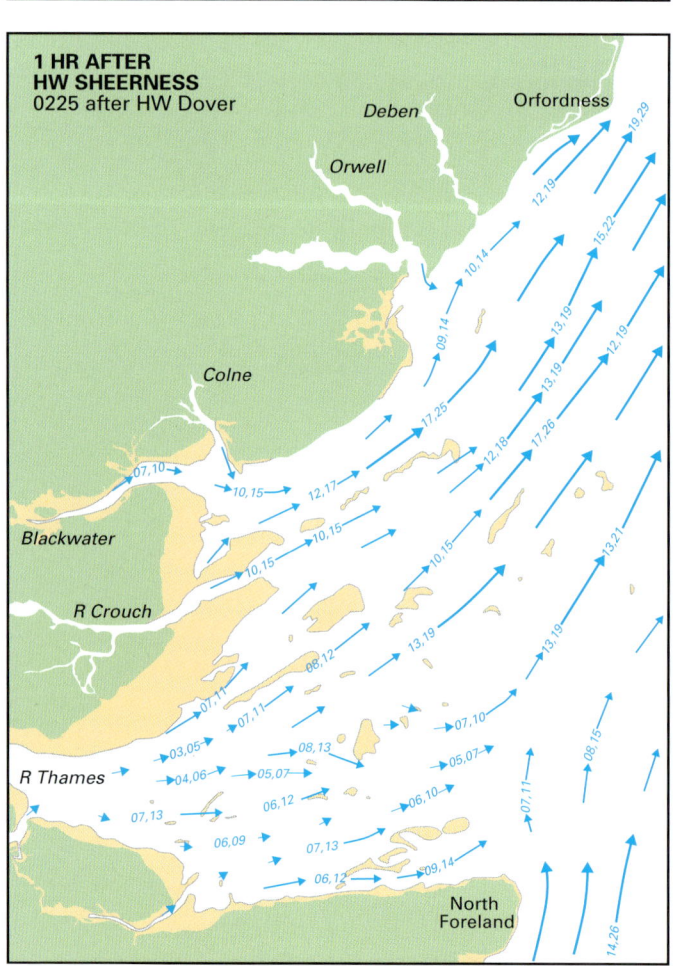

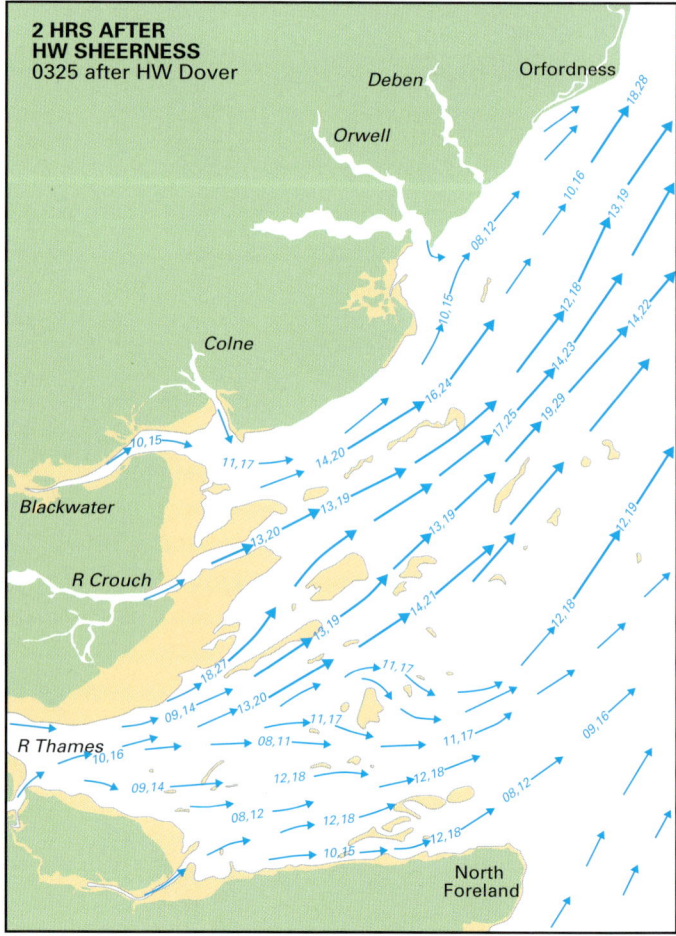

Tidal streams

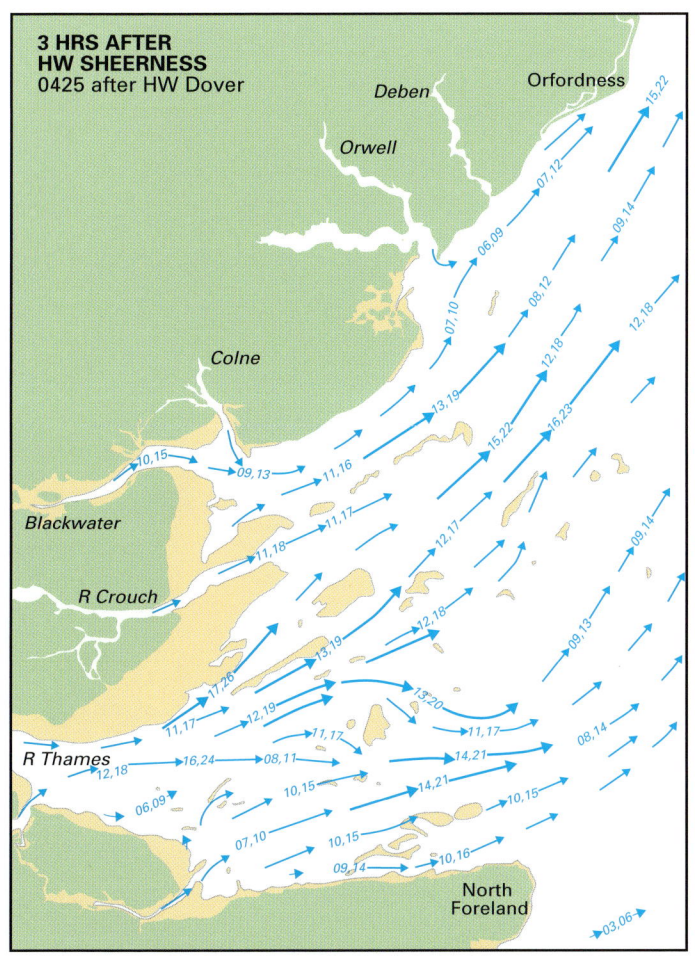

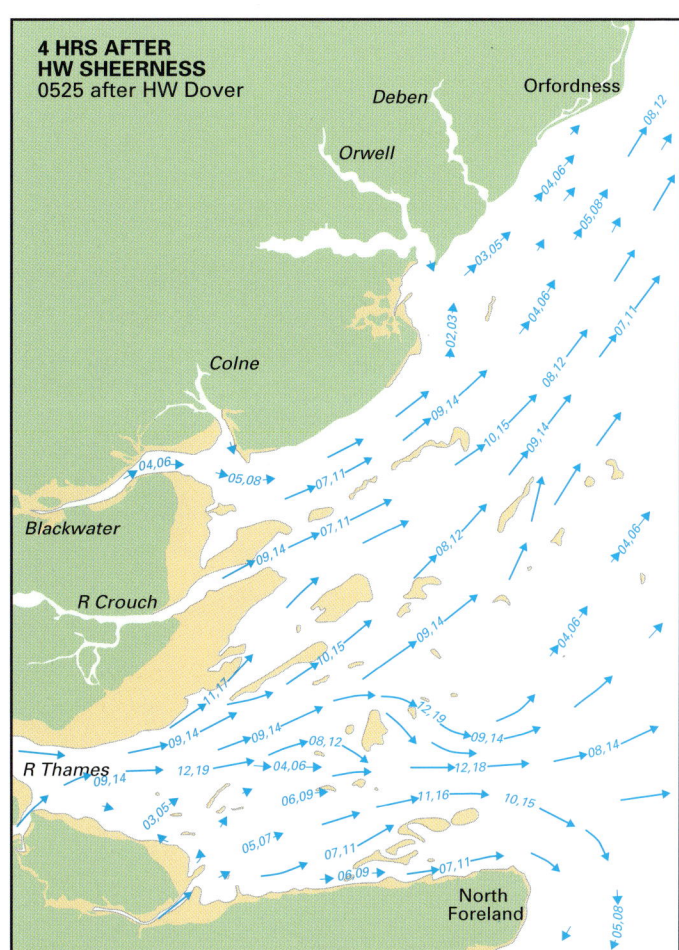

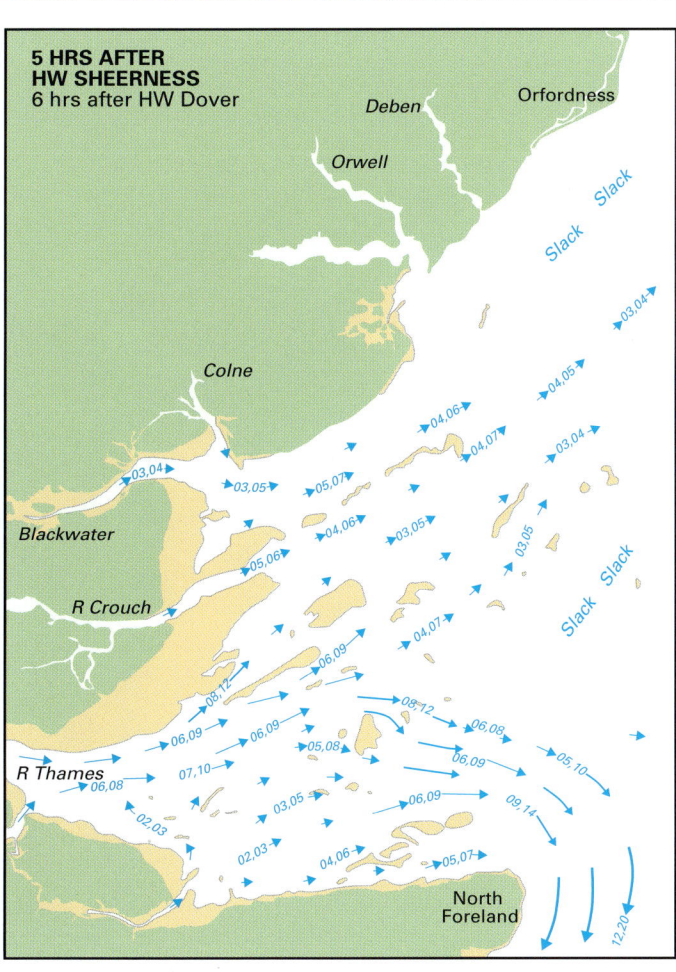

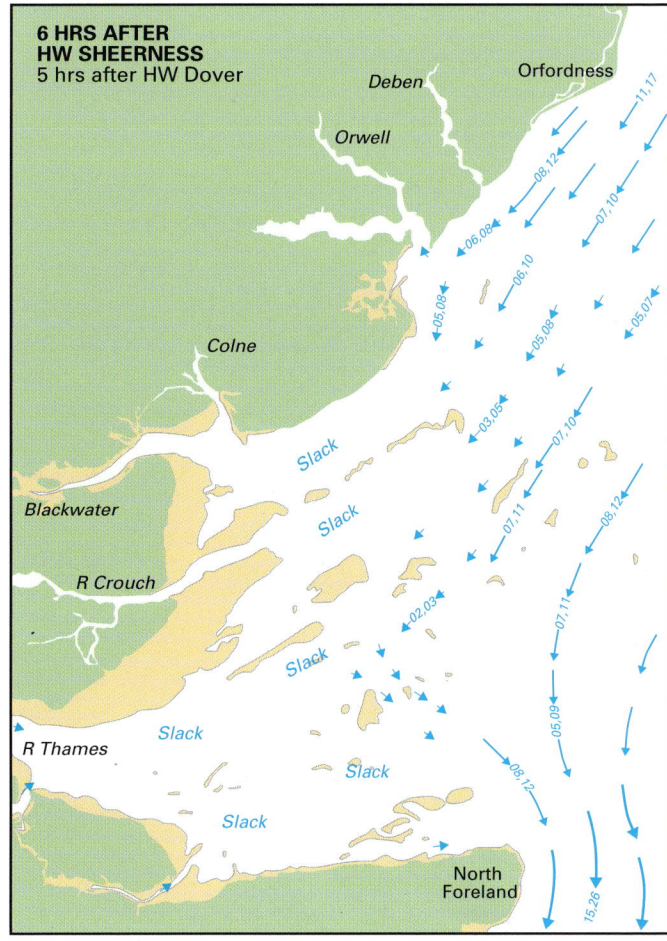

1. GREAT YARMOUTH

1. GREAT YARMOUTH

⊕ **Landfall waypoint**
52°34'·34N 001°45'·19E ½M E of entrance

Charts
Imray C28
Admiralty 1543 1534

Tides
HW Lowestoft -0035

Contact
Harbourmaster Gary Doyle
VHF Ch 12 Callsign *Yarmouth Radio*
☎ 01493 335511
greatyarmouthmarine.services@peelports.com
www.peelports.com/media/4198/visiting-small-craft-information-sheet-march2017-1.pdf

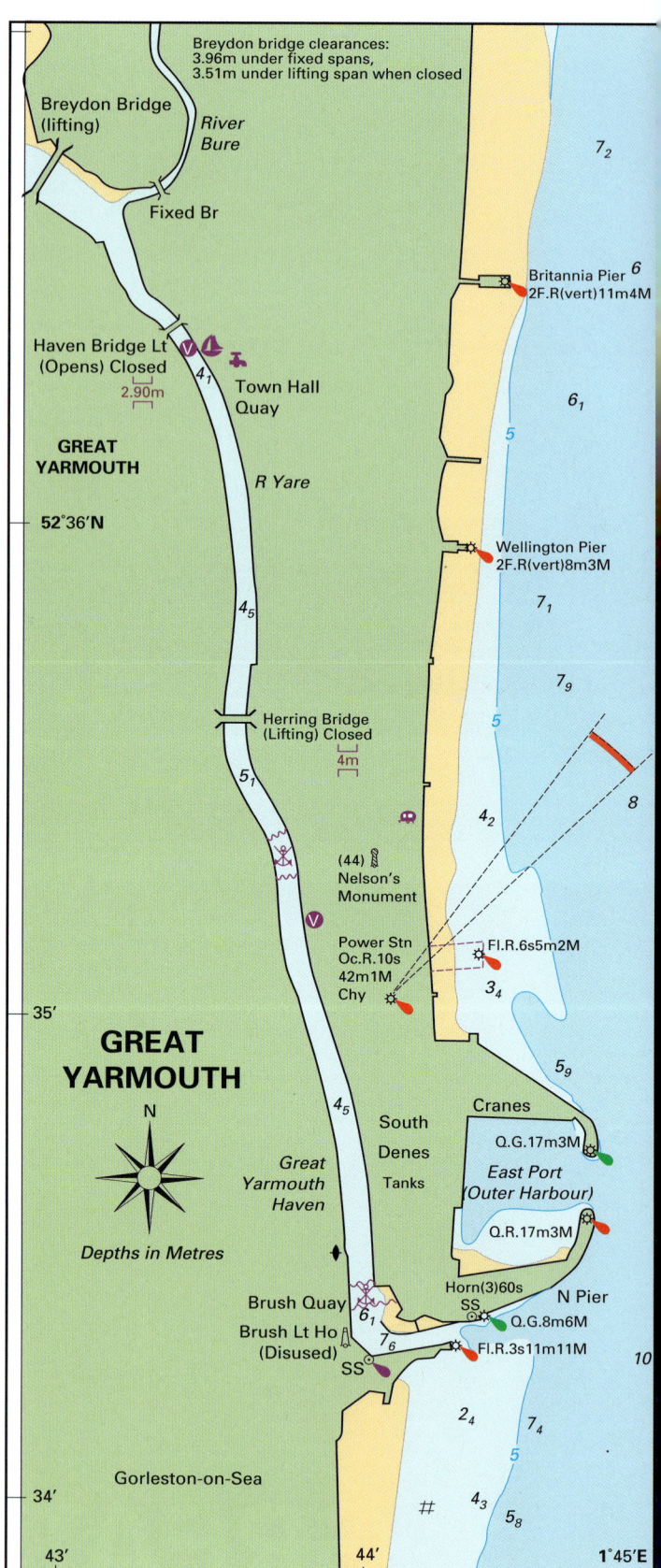

Entry to the Outer Harbour is strictly prohibited

Great Yarmouth is part of the Peel Ports Group of ports and is a predominantly commercial operation. There are no leisure craft facilities, other than a stopover area S of the Haven bridge for craft wishing to pass through to the Broads. Transit between the Broads and the sea is tolerated but visiting by yacht is not encouraged; indeed, the port's website makes a point of recommending yachts transit the Broads via Lowestoft. All leisure craft entering the harbour will be charged £20 each transit and overnight mooring will incur a £21.50 fee but boats waiting a pre-booked bridge lift will not be charged. Yachts passing through into the broads will not pay.

To further complicate matters for visitors there's the new Herring Bridge over the river, approximately halfway between the Haven Bridge and the entrance. Lifts must be booked in advance and there are waiting pontoons either side for small craft to moor up to while waiting. Vessels will also have to contact bridge control on entry to the harbour and at points up or down river so progress is monitored.

Great Yarmouth Harbour is a long, narrow concrete channel running from the entrance at Gorleston to Breydon Bridge, the second of two bridges that give access to the northern Broads via Breydon Water. The harbour was built down either side of the River Yare, which runs in an NNW to SSE direction with the man-made entrance flanked by Gorleston Pier to the S and the S retaining wall of the commercial Outer Harbour on the N side. The entrance opens due E and is narrow.

Within a short distance from the pier heads the river turns through 90° to starboard, so visitors are faced by a high blank reinforced concrete wall almost immediately after entering. The bend is blind to traffic in both directions, so it is vital to obey the port control lights mounted on a lattice tower on the N side of the entrance. Beware strong cross currents that can set you against the N pier.

Watch out too for wind farm and oil rig support and supply vessels, which use the space in the entrance to turn around and go astern into their berths further upstream.

Great Yarmouth

Vessels approaching Great Yarmouth from the N should not enter the first entrance they come to as this is the Outer Harbour also known as East Port, which is not open to leisure craft, now being a centre for installation barges and support vessels for the Gabbard and new Anglia One wind farms as well as grain ships. Instead, they must pass this entrance and follow the S wall of the Outer Harbour until the entrance to Yarmouth harbour itself opens.

There is little to commend Yarmouth as a leisure port and we don't recommend it as a port of last resort, because a strong N-S tidal flow, coupled with anything up to 6kn of river ebb, gets piled up by strong winds with any E in them. Indeed, it is not advisable to enter with a small yacht in anything over F5. Fortunately, there are no inshore sand banks to worry the careful sailor, although some shoaling can occur in the entrance during strong easterlies with depths reduced by as much as a metre.

The close approach to the harbour entrance is in clear, deep water with depths ranging from 7m to 17m. The entrance is somewhat sheltered by the southern extremity of the Scroby Sands with the deepwater Holm Channel forming a NW–SE gap between the S tip of the Scroby and the N tip of the Holm Sand.

From E Aim for the S Corton (Q (6)+L.Fl.15s (bell)) SCB and turn NW up the Holm Channel until the entrance is abeam, then turn due W to enter.

From N Enter Caister Roads by passing (in close order) the Hemsby (Fl.R.2·5s) PHB and the N Scroby NCB (VQ). The Scroby Sands wind farm opens to port. Continue past East Port while opposite the Great Yarmouth entrance, turn to starboard and head due W to enter.

From S Pick up the E Barnard ECB (Q(3)10s) S of Lowestoft, follow the Stanford Channel and continue N past the entrance to Lowestoft Harbour. Ensure you keep to port of two cardinal buoys about ½M off the end of Lowestoft Ness (an SCB (Q(6)+L.Fl.15s (bell)) and an ECB (VQ(3)5s (bell)) marking a charted obstruction. Follow the coastline N until opposite the Yarmouth entrance.

At night the entrance is marked on the S side by a red light (Fl.R.3s11m6M) erected on the red brick building on the seaward end of Gorleston Pier, at a height of 11 metres and with an arc of visibility of 115° from 235° through to 350° from seaward. The N side of the entrance is marked with a green light (Q.G.8m6M) 150 metres NE of the Gorleston Pier entrance light, at a height of 8m with an arc of visibility 098° from 176° to 078° from seaward.

Gorleston Pier and Brush Bend Lights: At the eastern extremity of Gorleston Pier are two all-round vertical fixed red lights two metres apart, with an additional six sets of lights, of the same characteristic, along the northern edge of the Pier, up to and around Brush Bend.

North Training Wall and Skeleton Works lights and marks: The extreme end of the training wall (at

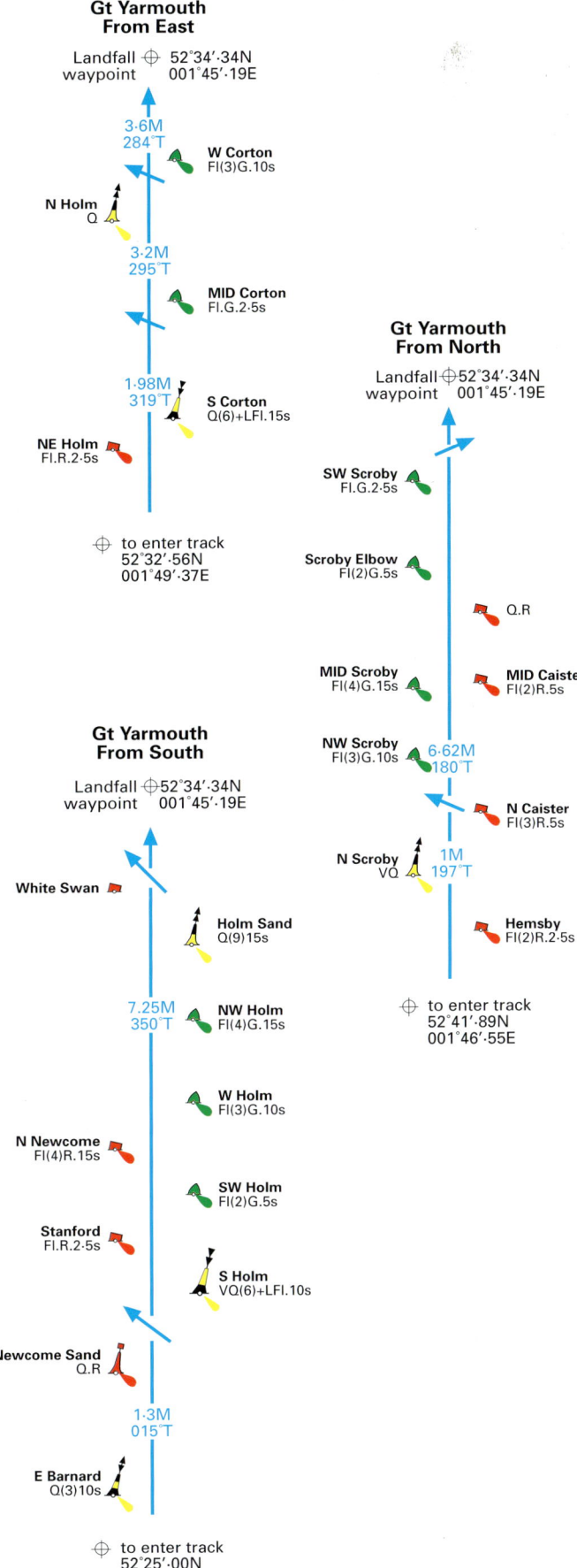

Looking N, Haven Bridge in the foreground with Breydon Bridge and Breydon Water in the background. Waiting craft moor alongside the quay to stbd

the start of the Outer Harbour south breakwater) is highlighted with illuminated white painted panels. Along the Training Wall and Skeleton Works there are five poles each displaying two all-round vertically mounted fixed green lights (2 F.G. (vert)), the outermost light is opposite the end of Gorleston Pier and the innermost light marks the end of the Skeleton Works. The Training Wall and Skeleton Works are downlit throughout their length.

Marine Services controls the port operations on VHF Ch 12 with the call sign Yarmouth Radio. Contact should be made prior to entry or departure and, if outward bound from the Broads, when passing through Haven Bridge. You can also contact them by phone or email.

Marine Services ☎01493 335511
GYMarineServices@PeelPorts.com
www.peelports.com/port-locations/great-yarmouth

Small craft must comply with the Port Traffic Signals displayed at the harbour entrance on a lattice tower on the N side. These are IALA signals showing 3 Fl.R for harbour closed and do not proceed until instructed, 3Fl.G proceed, G/W/G proceed only when told to. For leaving harbour, 3R(vert) means no vessel should proceed down river of the RNLI station sited just above the entrance bend on the Gorleston or W side. These outbound signals are sited on a tower at Brush Bend at the root of Gorleston Pier.

Vessels required to wait outside for an outbound vessel must stay clear of the port entrance, to give departing ships adequate room to manoeuvre.

A good time to enter the river is at slack low water which occurs approximately 90 minutes after high or low water.

Charges

Yachts are liable for tolls, (£20 entry, £21.50 for a pre-booked berth) but waivers are in place for vessels visiting the Norfolk Broads.

Berths

Small craft moorings are available on Hall Quay, just south of Haven Bridge on the E side of the river (opposite the red brick Town Hall building). There are mooring tails to help mooring. Vessels should moor adjacent to the access ladders. (Beware small boys throwing stones!)

There's a minimum depth of at least 3m alongside the berths on Hall Quay at MLWS. You should also allow for the strong tide when turning into the moorings and take care not to be swept into the Haven Bridge on the flood. The Hall Quay berths are close to the town centre. A five-minute walk along Regent Road will take you to the Market Place.

Bridges

For much of 2023 the bridges at Yarmouth were out of action. Breydon Bridge and Haven Bridge are now fully operational. Vessels will be grouped together

Great Yarmouth

Berthing on Hall Quay can be uncomfortable

Looking S, and rising above the early morning murk is the new 'Herring' bascule bridge dominating the skyline

on lifts whenever possible. When craft are to transit the bridge in opposite directions, those vessels going 'with the tide' will be given priority.

HAVEN BRIDGE
Bookings ☎01493 335522 or email
greatyarmouthoperations@peelports.com
Callsign *Haven Bridge* on VHF Ch 12

The Bridge is only manned ten minutes before a lift and vessels waiting for an opening should seek advice from the Bridge Master if in any doubt.

BREYDON BRIDGE
Bookings ☎01493 651275 or email
greatyarmouthbreydon.bridge@peelports.com
Call sign *Breydon Bridge* on VHF Ch 12
Lifts for weekends should be booked by 16:00 on Friday or on the previous working day in the case of Public Holidays.

Breydon Bridge is manned from 0800 to 1700 during winter months and from 0600 to 2200 or sunrise to sunset (whichever is the shorter) during the summer months, from Easter until the end of October. The new Herring bascule bridge is manned 24/7 but priority is given to road traffic and is closed to ships during rush hour. Booking a lift is essential. There are waiting pontoons each side of the bridge.

Requests to lift the Haven Bridge between sunset and sunrise incur a charge of £200.

Passing through the port

All three bridges have river traffic control lights on the bridge buttresses. These traffic signals are not exhibited constantly but are switched on approximately 10 minutes before a planned lift and are initially switched to red (stop) in both directions.

Small craft that can pass under Breydon Bridge without needing a lift should use the side spans, which have a greater air draught clearance. Vessels requiring a Breydon Bridge lift pass through the centre span. The bridge operators will advise if there is two-way traffic.

Mariners should be careful when approaching either of the bridges not to be set onto them, as tides can be strong and, at the Haven Bridge, the rates can exceed 3kn.

Outbound vessels should obey the IALA traffic signals exhibited at Brush Bend, where the channel turns sharply E towards the entrance and, if a stop signal is shown, hold their vessel north of the stop sign that is displayed on the W bank to N of the RNLI lifeboat station.

Vessels navigating through the port should be aware of large vessels manoeuvring or swinging in the narrow channel. There is a maximum speed limit of 7kn, although a slower speed may be appropriate.

Wind and tide

The tidal range within the harbour is approximately 2m and tidal flows can be swift, particularly during spring tides when rates can rise to 4kn, however, during certain wind and weather conditions, tidal flows can reach 5-6kn. Slack water at the harbour entrance is approximately 90 minutes after HW/LW, but this may vary with weather conditions.

At the entrance to the harbour sea conditions can become confused with wind over tide, particularly on the ebb or with wave reflection from the pier structures.

Inside the harbour, there is generally good shelter, however wind over tide with N or S winds can cause uncomfortable conditions on the berths at Hall Quay and fenders and fender boards should be carefully adjusted.

Waverney Dock (fishing boats)

Helipad

2. LOWESTOFT
Lowestoft is a growing yachting centre

2. LOWESTOFT

⊕ Landfall waypoint
52°28'·18N 001°46'·06E
⅓M E of entrance

Charts
Imray C28, 2000
Admiralty 1535, 1543

Tides
HW Lowestoft

Contact
Harbourmaster Mike Dunn
☎ 01502 572286
Lowestoft Port Control VHF Ch 14
Callsign *Lowestoft Port Control*
lowestoftportcontrol@abports.co.uk

Port Control Lights
Three vertical reds – Do not enter
Green, white, green vertical – Clear to enter (or depart) on specific orders from Port Control.

Before entering or leaving, request permission on Ch 14. Small craft and yachts without VHF may take the green, white, green signal as clearance to go ahead, but with extreme caution and navigational courtesy; those vessels in the Yacht Basin must contact the Port Control before departure.

Mariners should note that both Port Control, which is located at the harbour bridge, as well as departing vessels within the Outer Harbour basin, have extremely limited vision to the N of the entrance piers and should navigate accordingly.

Main hazards

Shifting sand banks make it imperative for the first time or occasional visitor to stay in the marked channels. With wind against tide, heavy seas can build off the entrance, which is quite narrow and marked by two Pagoda lighthouses on the pier ends.

The entrance tends to get choppy in anything over F5, and downright rough in F7 or more, especially with wind against the tide, which sets strongly across the entrance. With care it can be entered in almost any weather and along with Harwich can be considered a port of last resort.

The whole Lowestoft approaches area is under almost continuous survey, because of the formation of sand waves, which can give rise to rough waters in certain conditions, and continually moving sand banks. A 2023 survey found a reduction of depth of 0.5m some 700 metres N of the entrance in position centred on approx. 52° 28.555'N, 001° 45.936'E.

Once inside the harbour watch out for low flying helicopters. There's a helipad on the buttress between the outer harbour and Waveney Dock. You may be asked to stand off if one is landing or taking off.

Landmarks

Half a mile N of the entrance stands Gulliver, the tallest and most E'ly wind generator on the English mainland, which makes a good landmark, being visible from well out to sea. From N or NE the white-painted Lowestoft Lighthouse on top of the cliffs N of the harbour is also conspicuous and a good mark to aim for. Inland from Gulliver stands a complex of pale coloured factories.

Two white pagoda-shaped lighthouses on the pier heads distinguish the harbour entrance itself. The S

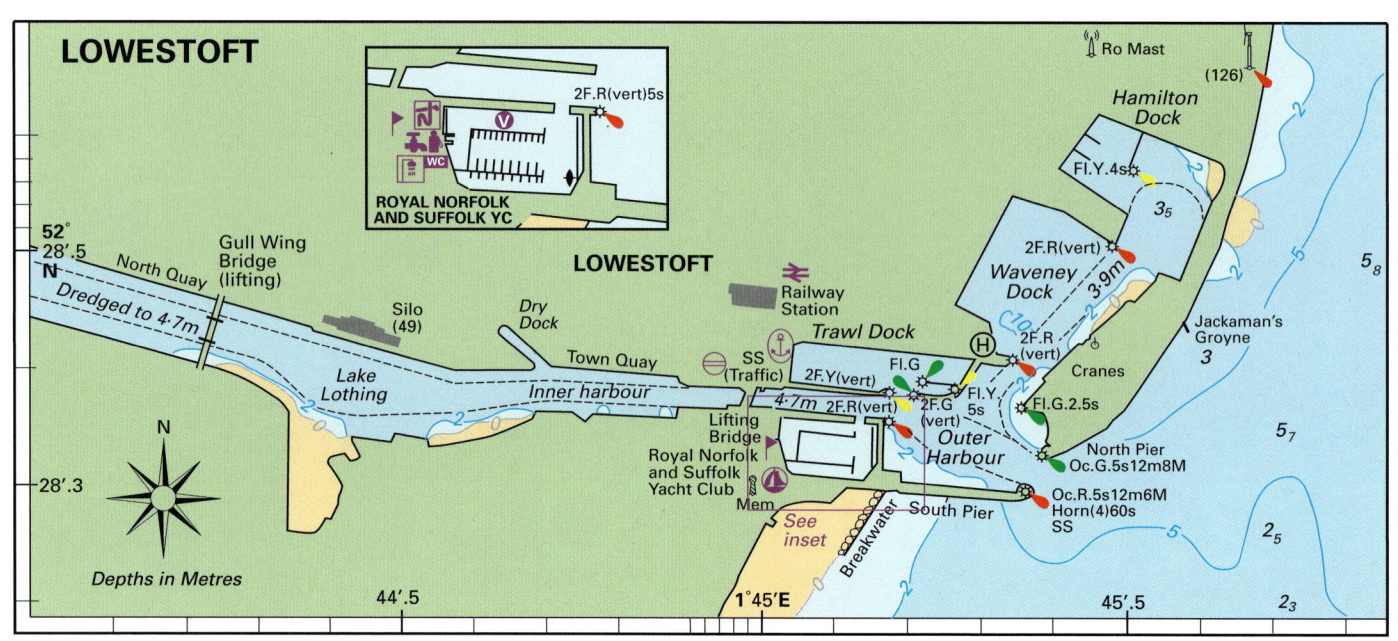

Approaches

pier is canted to face NE so that the prevailing swell from SW doesn't drive into the harbour. Immediately N of the entrance can sometimes be seen a gas rig accommodation platform under construction or repair or at other times it is possible to see huge blades from wind turbines in for repair, jutting up against the skyline.

Most of the town is low lying, but a good reference point is the top of the grain silo N of, and behind, the harbour. Because of the offset of the entrance, this silo will appear at first to be S of the harbour.

Recently two white pagoda-shaped structures on yellow masts have been erected in shallow water, close to the beach S of the entrance as future homes for kittiwakes. They have no pilotage significance other than being additional landmarks approaching the harbour, particularly from the S. (We understand two more are planned offshore at Sizewell.)

Kittiwake hotels

Approaches

From E Aim for the S Holm SCB (VQ(6)+LFl.10s) before turning NW up the Stanford Channel towards the harbour, passing between Stanford PHB (Fl.R.2·5s) and SW Holm SHB (Fl(2)G.5s). On reaching the N Newcome PHB (Fl(4)R.15s) turn due W towards the entrance piers with their twin white pagoda lighthouses.

In fair weather and calm conditions and with a sufficient rise of tide, many skippers will take a more direct route W from E Newcome to N Newcome, crossing the Holm Sand tail in about 3·5-4m of water, and then on into the harbour, keeping clear of two wreck or foul ground buoys just N of the entrance.

From S Pick up the East Barnard ECB (Q(3)10s) on the 10m contour marking the edge of the Newcome Sand. To the N lies the Newcome Sand PHB (Q.R), which marks the N extremity of the sands and is the S gate to the Stanford Channel, along with S Holm SCB (VQ(6)+Fl. 10s) which marks the S extremity of the Holm Sand.

Follow the Stanford Channel, passing between Stanford PHB (Fl.R.2·5s) and SW Holm SHB (Fl(2)G.5s). On reaching the N Newcome PHB (Fl(4)R.15s) turn due W towards the entrance piers with their twin lighthouses. Do not be tempted to cut the corner from the S Holm direct to the S pier, because it shoals to 1·9m at LAT and any onshore wind cuts up a nasty, short, steep sea.

From N Keep within sight of the shore in the buoyed channel through Corton Roads and inside the Holm Sand until abreast the entrance piers.

Watch out for a pair of cardinal buoys about ½M off the end of Lowestoft Ness – ECB (VQ(3)5s Bell) and SCB (Q(6)+L.Fl.15s Bell). They mark a charted obstruction, so do not try to pass between them.

The South Pier shows a set of international port control lights: G over W over G meaning clear to enter; 3 vert R meaning do not enter. Seek permission on

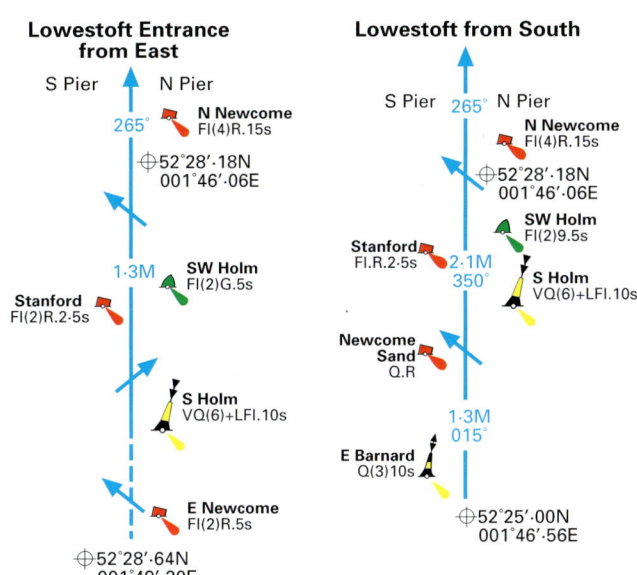

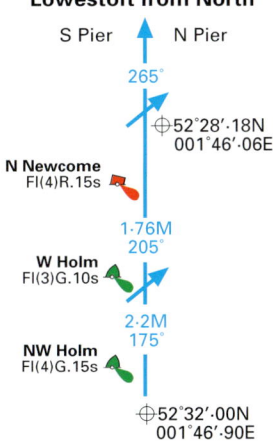

Ch 14 from Lowestoft Port Control to enter. Both pier heads are lit; the North Pier (Oc.G.5s 8M), the South Pier (Oc.R.5s 6M). Beware an eddy in the entrance between the two piers.

At night a good guide to finding the entrance is the white sector of the Kirkley Light (Oc. WRG. 10s 17m10M) to the south the entrance itself.

2. LOWESTOFT

Lowestoft harbour is being revitalised

Entry

The entrance is narrow (maximum commercial ship beam is 22m) and canted at an angle so that vessels leaving or entering cannot see each other. This makes it essential to call Lowestoft Port Control for permission to enter. The narrowness and angle of the entrance prevents very heavy S swells driving in, but it's open to NE winds and seas.

Strictly observe the Narrow Channels Rule 9(b) of the ColRegs - *'a vessel of less than 20 metres in length or a sailing vessel shall not impede the passage of a vessel which can safely navigate only within a narrow channel or fairway'*. There is a minimum of 4·3m of water, although 6m is more generally found.

Once inside, the harbour opens out into a series of basins.

LOWESTOFT HARBOUR

The harbour entrance widens into the main or outer harbour, from which several lesser basins branch off.

There is a shallow area in the SW corner of the outer harbour. Off to starboard is the entrance to the Waveney and Hamilton Docks, neither are available to leisure craft. Up river to starboard is the entrance to the Trawl Dock where there's a waiting pontoon for the Lowestoft Harbour bridge, the dock is silting up and yachts may ground at the E end of the pontoon. Smack in the middle of the harbour on the W buttress to the Waveney (Fish) Dock is a busy heliport, with priority given to low-flying helicopters and you may be asked to stand off when flying is taking place.

Opposite the Trawl dock, to port, is the yacht basin at the head of which stands the Royal Norfolk and Suffolk YC (RN&SYC). The RN&SYC marina has visitors' berths on the N side of the first linear pontoon and on the W of the cross pontoon in front of the clubhouse. It is essential to call the club's harbourmaster on Ch 80 (call sign Royal Norfolk Harbourmaster) for directions before entering.

Yachts over 12m LOA should lie against the large bumper tubes against the outer wall (to starboard inside the entrance) and guard against warps chafing on the rough stone quay. Enter with care because boats may be manoeuvring inside.

Be aware too that there's a shallow sand bar on the corner of the starboard (W) entrance buttress, especially at lower stages of the tide. On leaving, obey the light signals on the E side of the marina entrance (green, white, green – go with caution; three reds – do not go). Port Control must approve departure (Ch 14).

The Lowestoft lifeboat is also moored in this basin alongside the pontoon where the ex-trawler *Mincarlo* is worth a visit.

Just up river from the RN&SYC marina is the Lowestoft Harbour Bridge. Passage through is free, but opening times are strictly observed (see page 21). Yachts waiting to go up river can get permission to wait in the Trawl Dock if they can't get into the marina. Do not approach the bridge unless the green light on the N wall is showing.

Lowestoft Harbour Bridge

The harbour is the mouth of the River Waveney

ROYAL NORFOLK & SUFFOLK YC NR33 0AQ

Contact
VHF Ch 80
☎01502 566726 (0730–1930)
Callsign *Royal Norfolk*
Harbourmaster admin@rnsyc.net
Marina stuart@rnsyc.net
www.rnsyc.net
Facilities WC, showers, launderette, WiFi
Fuel Diesel from berth below marina office at head of marina alongside the slip
Electricity On pontoons
Water On pontoons
Launching slip (trailers)
Launching crane (2½T)
Pump-out Berth near slipway
Pressure wash Coin-operated at head of slipway
Provisions Shops nearby
Pubs/restaurants Bar/restaurant on site and in town
Local services Include chandler, electronics, engineer, rigger and sailmaker (ask at club)
Transport Rail station 10 mins, buses
Taxi ☎01502 515151, 801066, 740740

The Royal Norfolk and Suffolk YC

Lowestoft Harbour Bridge

The Lowestoft Harbour Bridge, between the outer and inner harbours, is only opened on demand to commercial shipping and then not between 0815 and 0900, 1230 and 1300, 1700 and 1730 to allow commuter traffic unimpeded access.

Small craft may pass through at the time of opening for commercial shipping, so long as Port Control has agreed beforehand. If yachts give at least 20 minutes notice of passage, the bridge can be opened for them at 0300, 0500, 0700, 0945, 1115, 1430, 1600, 1900, 2100 and midnight on weekdays and 0300, 0500, 0700, 0945, 1115, 1430, 1600, 1800, 1900, 2100 and midnight at weekends and Bank Holidays. Call Port Control on Ch 14 or ☎01502 572286.

Approaching the bridge from the E there are traffic lights on the N quay.

Small craft and yachts in a flotilla should make every effort to keep together and pass through the bridge as quickly as possible, bridge operators are instructed not to wait for stragglers. Once the bridge has been lifted the red lights on the east and west side may both be switched to green, allowing inwards and outwards movements at the same time. Boats must not proceed if the lights remain red, or until instructed by the bridge operator, keeping clear of vessels using the main channel.

With the bridge down there is 2·2m clearance at MHW springs (approximately 2·4m on the tide gauge) with a reduction of 0·5 metres for the arch sides. Vessels able to drop masts and aerials and which can pass under the bridge, may do so, once they have received permission from Port Control

There is a pontoon in the SE corner of the Trawl Dock (opposite RN&SYC) to use while waiting for the bridge. Be careful of ground though after half tide falling at the E end of the pontoon.

The inner harbour and Lake Lothing

Above the road bridge is the Inner Harbour, which swells out into Lake Lothing. It's here that a major development, the installation of a third crossing over the Waveney is nearing completion (Nov 2023). The Gull Wing bridge opens early summer 2024.

Waiting pontoons are being installed. The channel is buoyed and dredged to 4·7m up to a point abreast the Lowestoft Cruising Club pontoons on the starboard hand. It shelves to 1·8m from there to the Carlton Road railway swing bridge.

Opposite Lowestoft CC is the Lowestoft Beacon Marina. Although the general environment is that of an industrial area, visitors are welcome at all Lowestoft's yacht basins, which are in the forefront of the redevelopment of Lowestoft into a major yachting centre.

Close by the Carlton Road rail bridge on the S bank is Lowestoft Marina, a small friendly 40 berth marina right at the gateway to the Suffolk Broads.

LOWESTOFT CRUISING CLUB — NR32 3LY
Contact
☏ 07900 446909
www.lowestoftcruisingclub.co.uk
Facilities WC, showers
Water On pontoons
Electricity At each berth
Slipway
Mast crane On quayside
Berths To book, phone Andrew Pearson, LCC moorings officer, ☏ 07900 446909 or email moorings-officer@lowestoftcruisingclub.co.uk
There are 70+ berths in finger boxes. Visitors should use the E end hammerhead or empty berths on the S side of the main pontoon with a green triangle indicating they are vacant then call the berthing officer.
Provisions Banks, pubs
Transport Trains 10 minutes walk
Taxi ☏ 01502 515151, 801066, 740740.

LOWESTOFT BEACON MARINA — NR33 9NB
Contact
VHF Ch 80
Callsign *Lowestoft Beacon Marina*
☏ 01502 580300 (0730–1930)
https://www.beaconmarinas.co.uk/our-marinas/lowestoft-beacon-marina/
(also www.transeuropemarinas.com)
Facilities WC, showers, launderette, WiFi (PAYG)
Water On pontoons (use own hose)
Electricity On pontoons
Fuel Diesel (on hammerhead of pontoon A)
Gas Ask in office
Pub/restaurant The Third Crossing ☏ 01502 583596
Boat hoist 70-T (out of hours by arrangement)
Workshop
Engineers, riggers, electronics and chandlers/support services Contact marina office
Boat sales ☏ 01502 580300
Transport Trains to Norwich and Ipswich, buses
Taxi ☏ 01502 515151, 801066, 740740

The inner harbour and Lake Lothing

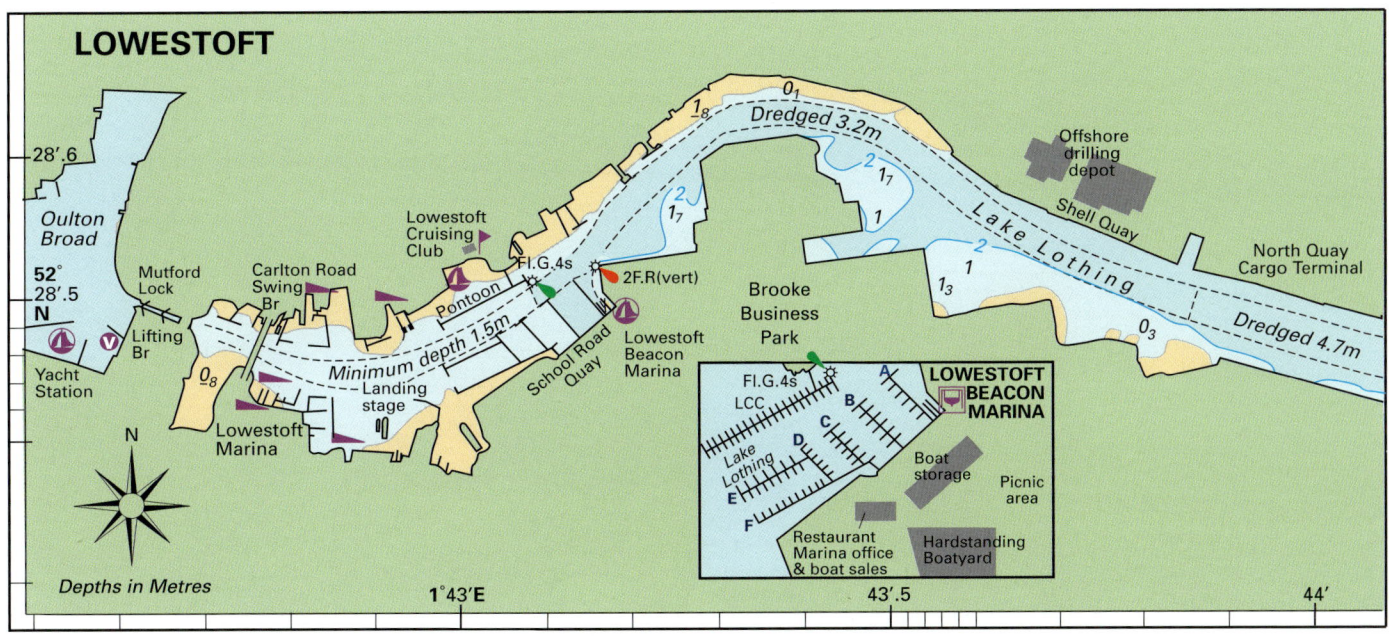

LOWESTOFT MARINA
NR33 9NQ

Contact
℡ 01502 588811 / 07972779371
(call Anthony at least two days before arrival)
enquiries@lowestoftmarina.net
www.lowestoftmarina.net

Facilities WC, showers, laundry, disabled facilities, free WiFi, CCTV
Water On pontoons
Electricity On pontoons
Transport Trains to Norwich and Ipswich, buses
Taxi ℡ 01502 515151, 801066, 740740

Mutford Lock

Lowestoft is the preferred gateway to both the S and N Broads. To make the final transition from Lake Lothing into Oulton Broad itself, boats pass through (in order from the E) Carlton Railway Bridge, Mutford Road Bridge and Mutford Lock.

It is advisable to book transits 24 hrs in advance with the lockmaster. VHF Ch 73 or 14, ℡ 01502 531778 (Lock) or 01502 574946 (Yacht Station). The lock is operated by the Broads Authority and is 22m long and 6·5m wide with a minimum 2m depth (plus state of tide). There is a fee for each lock transit or day return.

The bridges and lock open on request during the following hours daily: April to October 0800–1700. November to March 0800–1200. The lock is crowded at weekends and bank holidays.

Lowestoft Harbour Bridge – commercial ships have right of way

East Coast Pilot • 23

3. SOUTHWOLD

Southwold is a bustling mix of leisure and inshore fishing boats

3. SOUTHWOLD

⌖**Landfall waypoint**
52°18'·78N 001°40'·54E About ½M SE of entrance

Charts
Imray C28
Admiralty 2695

Contact
Harbourmasters Peter Simmons and Gerry Hilder
☎01502 724712
(0800 – 1700 , 0800 – 1800 at peak periods and 0800 – 1600 Oct to Mar)
VHF Ch 12
Callsign *Southwold Port Radio*
www.eastsuffolk.gov.uk/visitors/southwold-harbour

Tides
HW Lowestoft +0105

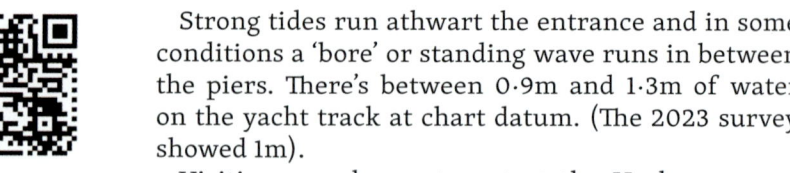

Main hazards

There are shifting sand banks close to and within the entrance. There is a sand bar that extends NE of the N pier. With wind against tide heavy seas can build up off the entrance and the depth over the bar can alter drastically after E gales.

Do not attempt an entrance during strong E or NE winds, especially if they are blowing against the tide.

Strong tides run athwart the entrance and in some conditions a 'bore' or standing wave runs in between the piers. There's between 0·9m and 1·3m of water on the yacht track at chart datum. (The 2023 survey showed 1m).

Visiting vessels must contact the Harbourmaster (Ch12) for entry and berthing instructions before approaching the entrance and again before leaving their berth for departure.

Landmarks

The town of Southwold lies 1M N of the harbour entrance, which is the mouth of the River Blyth. A white lighthouse (Fl.10s.37m24M, MMSI 992351019) stands in a prominent position on top of the low cliff on which the town stands. Also prominent is a Norman-style church built by wealthy local wool merchants. The seafront is marked by rows of colourful beach huts and, further inland, at the back of the marshes, is a large conspicuous concrete water tower.

Approach

From any seaward direction there is clear and deep water to within a short distance of the entrance. Along the coast in both directions the depth runs

Southwold

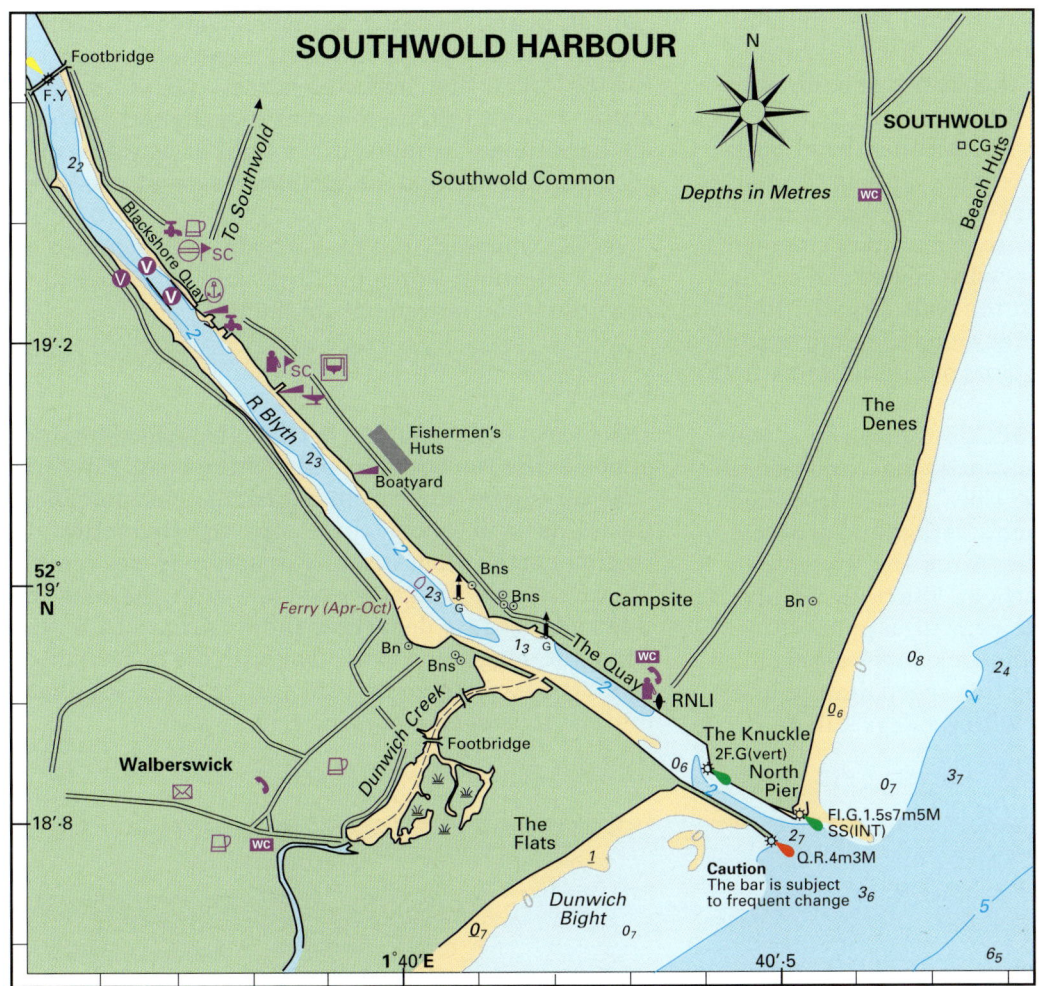
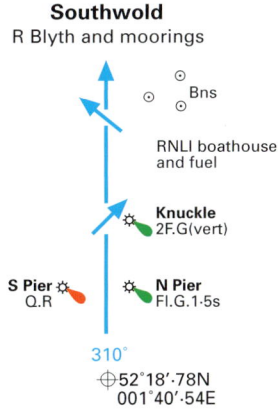

from 5m close in to 10m or more ½M out. There are no off-lying marks or buoys, so aim for the landfall waypoint. From there the entrance bears about 310°.

Entry

Entry signals

Three vertical F.R. lights or, during daylight, two red flags, mounted on a pole at the end of the N Pier, indicate 'harbour closed'. If displayed, contact Southwold harbourmaster or, if outside the listening hours of 0800–1700, contact Humber Coastguard for advice. Three vertical greens or no flags means it's clear to enter.

Entrance is best attempted from 30 min before HW or, if there is sufficient depth, near LW when the coastal tide cross stream is at its slackest. HM will advise on depths over the bar. HW at the harbour bridge is about half an hour after HW at the bar.

The North Pier is marked with a light (Fl.G.1·5s) and the South Pier with a Q.R. Do not stray into the bay N of the North Pier where the water is shallow, and the sand bank keeps moving.

Enter along the centreline of the channel parallel to the S pier. The entrance is narrow, 36m, and the stream runs hard both ways, reaching 3-4kn on flood and 5-6kn on ebb. In addition, the coastal tide flows at right angles across the entrance, both rising (southward) and falling (northward) at anywhere between 2·5 and 4kn.

Keep to the middle of the piers as far as the Knuckle (2F.G.(vert)), at the landward end of the N pier, marked with a 4kn (through the water) speed limit sign mounted on a post, which is in turn mounted on an iron frame jutting out into the entrance.

Southwold harbour entrance

3. SOUTHWOLD

Just past this, turn hard to starboard and aim to be close alongside and parallel to the concrete retaining wall on the starboard side of the river just before the RNLI station and RIB launching crane.

Follow this wall almost to its end then head back into the middle of the river. Keeping close to the wall avoids sand and shingle that's building up on the S side of the channel but take care to maintain steerage way above the tidal flow, otherwise eddies can swing the boat and push her against the wall. Usually there is at least 2m of water at low tide along the wall. At the far end of the wall, a sand spit juts out into the stream to catch the unwary.

Despite the sign on the Knuckle indicating a 4kn speed limit, the Harbour Authority has imposed a maximum speed limit of 'dead slow'. This is described as the minimum speed at which steerage and progress can be maintained and applies from the Knuckle to the bridge at the top of the harbour. The bridge, which carries a yellow light on the central support, links Southwold with nearby Walberswick on the other side of the river. Vessels exceeding this speed limit will be considered as not complying with ColRegs Rule 6.

All skippers are requested to navigate with caution and to avoid excessive wash, especially near the rowing ferry that operates across the River Blyth about 3 cables from the entrance to the harbour during summer months, it has right of way. Warning signs are positioned 100m either side of the ferry crossing.

Vessels moving in the harbour are required to keep a listening watch on Ch 12 and to report their intentions and movements to the HM.

Berthing

There are eight visitor berths alongside stagings opposite the Harbour Inn pub, where boats can form rafts up to two abreast, in occasional circumstances the HMs will allow three up; the reduction in staging berths is because the structure is weakening. Shorelines are obligatory to cope with the 6kn ebb tide and, because departure should always be on the flood, the suggestion is to moor with the boat heading down the harbour so that she can be eased out ahead into the stream and motored cleanly away.

The River Blyth meanders through marshes to join the sea at Southwold Harbour

Southwold Harbour

Fuel berth serves red diesel

There's usually around 2m of water at low tide and the bottom is hard and steeply shelving. There are ladders on the staging and the harbour authority thoughtfully supplies fender boards to straddle the piles. Remember to leave them behind on departure.

A further four visitor berths, up to 11 metres each, are available alongside two floating pontoons adjacent to the Harbour Office. Waveney District Council installed new pontoons on the Walberswick side of the river opposite the pub, where a further six craft can be moored. They have no water or electric services and deeper draught boats can ground especially at the upriver end. Recently the Council purchased a pair of deep water moorings nearer the bridge. Should all the visitor berths be fully booked, phone HMS back downstream on the N shore who may be able to find you a space Harbour Marine Services ☎01502 724721.

Take care turning around in the harbour. There are stagings on both sides of the river, but just up river of the new visitors' pontoons the S bank is clear, and it is recommended that bigger boats should turn here, using full power plus propeller kick to turn tightly in the space. A local trick is to put the boat's stem into the muddy bank opposite and let the tide swing her round, but it takes some courage to do it first time.

Above the moorings is a low bridge taking the footpath from Southwold across to the village of

SOUTHWOLD HARBOUR   IP18 6TA

Contact
Harbourmasters ☎01502 724712 (0800- 1700)
VHF Ch 12
Callsign *Southwold Port Radio*
Out of hours call Humber Coastguard on VHF Ch 16
southwoldharbour@eastsuffolk.gov.uk

Access 24hr depending on tide, draught and weather

Berthing On stagings and floating pontoons adjacent to Harbour Office and on S bank. Additional berths can be arranged with Harbour Marine Services ☎01502 724721

Facilities WC, showers, caravan site near harbour entrance, accessed with mooring receipt)

Slipways At boatyard and SC

Electricity Connection points on staging. (Pontoon connections at top of staging gangway use long leads)

Water Taps and hoses on the staging

Gas Ask at chandler

Boatyard/Repairs HMS (Harbour Marine Services) ☎01502 724721 30-T travel-hoists and large slip, full services www.southwoldboatyard.co.uk

Fuel Arrange with HM. Fuel station close to lifeboat station on N entry wall

Chandler Next to boatyard at seaward end of foreshore www.shop@harbourmarine.co.uk

Club Southwold SC www.southwoldsc.org

Phone At pub. Emergency phone at RNLI station

Provisions Some from café near chandler. Shops 1M in town

Pub/restaurant The Harbour Inn ☎01502 722381, Sole Bay Fish Co. Restaurant ☎01502 724241 and in town

Taxi ☎01502 723400

Walberswick. Boats have been known to end up against the bridge, carried there by the strong tide. The bridge is lit with a yellow light on the centre support and great care needs to be taken at night or in bad weather when manoeuvring in its vicinity.

Beware of the low bridge at the top of harbour

Southwold ferry

4. RIVERS ORE & ALDE

The entrance to the River Ore in 2023

4. RIVERS ORE & ALDE

⊕ **Landfall waypoint**
52°01'·56N 001°28'·20E Within sight of Orford Haven SWB

Charts
Imray 2000, C28
Admiralty 5607, 2052 and 2695

Tides
Orford Haven Bar Walton -0028
Orford Quay Walton +0040
Slaughden Walton +0105
Iken Cliff Walton +0130

ECP Honorary Port Pilot
(Orford and Ore / Alde entrance)
Matt Smy ☏07528 092635 or VHF Ch 08/16
orfordhaven@eastcoastpilot.com
www.aldeandore.org

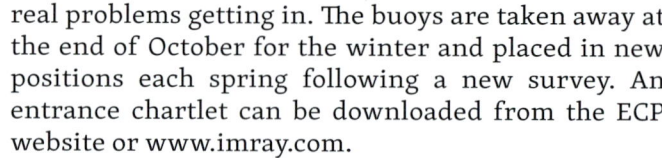

Main hazards

Rather as with the Deben entrance, there are a lot of gloomy reports about going into the Ore and Alde. True, the entrance to the Ore and Alde is subject to quite major changes from time to time, especially following E gales, but with careful planning, a cautious approach and taking note of the latest information available via **www.eastcoastpilot.com** and perhaps a call to Orford HM Matt Smy (see box details), you should have no real problems getting in. The buoys are taken away at the end of October for the winter and placed in new positions each spring following a new survey. An entrance chartlet can be downloaded from the ECP website or www.imray.com.

Ideal time to enter the Ore is about 2hr before HW.

Streams in the river run strongly at up to 5kn on spring floods and over 6kn on the ebb.

Entry should not be attempted in strong SE or E winds when seas can break heavily.

Landmarks

Sadly, we no longer have Orfordness Lighthouse as a prominently conspicuous land mark as it has been demolished; it was especially useful coming down the coast from the N or from seaward, while the bluff of Bawdsey Cliff, topped with a lattice CG radio tower, marks the S end of Hollesley Bay. We do not recommend entry to the Ore after dusk.

Approaching the Landfall Waypoint, the hamlet of Shingle Street peeps out from behind the steep gravel bank due W. To the S stand three Martello towers: the one furthest S stands on the N end of Bawdsey Cliffs, the middle one has a distinctive glass pagoda-like top and the northernmost stands W from the Orford Haven buoy at the S end of the hamlet of Shingle

The Ore entrance 2023 Weir Oxley *Credit* John Ranson

32 • East Coast Pilot

Rivers Ore & Alde

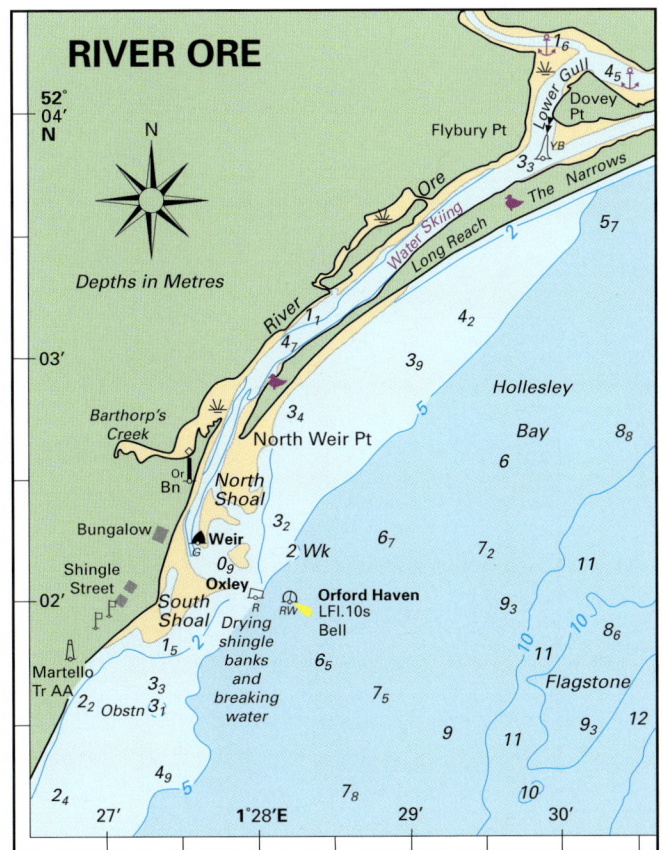

The Orford Haven offing buoy is the start of the entry track

Give Weir a fairly wide berth keeping to the centre of the channel

Street. A row of white painted ex-coastguard cottages is prominent to the N of the hamlet and marks the entrance, which is difficult to identify until close in as the shingle banks extending S from Weir Point visually merge with the shingle of the W bank.

Entry

From N Crossing Hollesley Bay pass the Ness in about 8m of water and about a cable (200 yards) off the shingle and set a course of roughly 235° towards the Orford Haven SWB (RW L.Fl.10s), which should keep you well clear of the Whiting Bank that runs on your port side roughly parallel with the coast.

From N & S There's clear and deep water to within a short distance of the entrance. Along the coast in both directions the depth runs from 5m close in to 10m or more only ½M offshore.

From the Orford Haven SWB aim due W for the Oxley PHB (unlit) and then keep to port of the Weir SHB (unlit), which comes into view ahead as you pass Oxley. Best water is about 50 metres N of the Oxley which sets across the shingle bank on the flood tide. The whole of Hollesley Bay is flat.

Keep in the centre between the shoals and turn up river passing the Weir (SHB). Stay in the middle as the river narrows opposite Weir Point where two spurs have extended out from either side. Here also are a series of exposed hard London Clay ridges, which rise vertically on the W bank close by Barthorp's Creek. Do not hug the W bank, as opposite Weir Point, you'll likely run into a collapsed concrete gun emplacement that slipped down the shingle.

With wind against tide, heavy seas build up off the entrance and the depth over the bar can alter drastically after SE gales. If you are unsure of the conditions call up Orford HM Matt Smy to obtain the latest available information about the entrance before attempting it and avoid it entirely in strong onshore winds.

TWO RIVERS

Although one long river, navigable from the entrance right up to Snape Bridge, alongside the famous Snape Maltings concert hall, it's a waterway with two names. From the entrance to about 1M above the village and quay at Orford it's the Ore; from this point in Halfway Reach up to Snape it's the Alde. (Above Snape and up to its headwater at Dennington near Framlingham it again becomes the Ore and is navigable only by dinghy)

The Ore

For much of its length, the Ore divides around Havergate Island, a bird sanctuary that's home to a great variety of wading and marsh birds, including one of the biggest breeding colonies of avocets in Britain. Landing is prohibited.

Having successfully negotiated the entrance to the Ore, the first major landmarks are the incinerator chimney and buildings of HMP Hollesley Bay on the W bank. There is a short drying creek called Barthorp's Creek in the W bank, which was used by barges taking produce from the prison farm to London.

4. RIVERS ORE & ALDE

The Ore divides round Havergate Island bird sanctuary

The rather featureless Long Reach is a straight stretch of water running NE inside Orford Ness and is a favourite area for water skiing. At the top end of the reach is an unlit SCB marking the S end of Havergate Island. Leaving the buoy to starboard leads you into the Lower Gull where there is a good anchorage under the port bank.

Butley River

The Butley River branches off NW just beyond the Lower Gull anchorage, but there's a sand spit jutting out from the W bank and the entrance to the creek is well over against the N shore.

The channel is marked with withies topped with old paint cans and there are oyster beds in the top half of the creek above the ferry landings, but there's a good anchorage in a little over 2m at LW in the lower reaches of the creek below the disused Boyton Dock.

Keep well N of this can topped withy at the entrance to the Butley River

34 • East Coast Pilot

You can also find good holding ground above the Dock, where the river turns due N for ½M before curving to starboard towards Gedgrave Cliffs, which is about as far as a sea going yacht of any noticeable draught will want to venture. From here on up the riverbed is home to oysters and anchoring is forbidden. Down river of the Cliffs are several moorings and it takes a bit of care to wend your way through them. Just before the moorings two long jetties stick out from either side into the river from which an occasional foot ferry operated by volunteers carries walkers and cyclists across. Medium draught boats can anchor in the stream between the top of the moorings and Gedgrave Cliffs, but above here the river virtually dries to a trickle.

Butley River to Orford

Past the Butley River entrance, the river Ore briefly runs SE then NE through Long Gull and turns E into Short Gull before joining once more with the other branch that flows S of Havergate Island through Main Reach. There's a good anchorage in Abraham's Bosum, just upriver of the Butley River, and in both Gulls under the lee of Havergate Island. Main Reach is virtually a straight cut through the marshes and forms a shorter, but less interesting, route to Orford. Deeper water in this reach is to be found on the E side. There are gradually sloping mudflats extending from the Island.

There's up to 2m in mid-channel opposite the old Boyton Dock

ORFORD

Approaching Orford from S, the 90ft high Norman Keep, which is all that remains of the once royal castle, stands out to the left of the village, while in the centre is the church proud on the crown of the hill.

The main channel is clearly marked by two lines of moorings each side of the river. On the outer trot of starboard-hand moorings are five laid for visitors, each with an orange or pink pick-up buoy marked 'single visitor'. To find a vacant mooring is sometimes difficult and if you do pick up one other than a visitor-marked mooring, leave someone aboard, don't leave the boat unattended and don't raft up either. Call the Orford HM as you approach the lower moorings and seek advice.

Don't anchor within the area of the moorings, where the bottom is foul, and don't anchor between

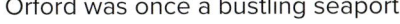

Orford was once a bustling seaport

4. RIVERS ORE & ALDE

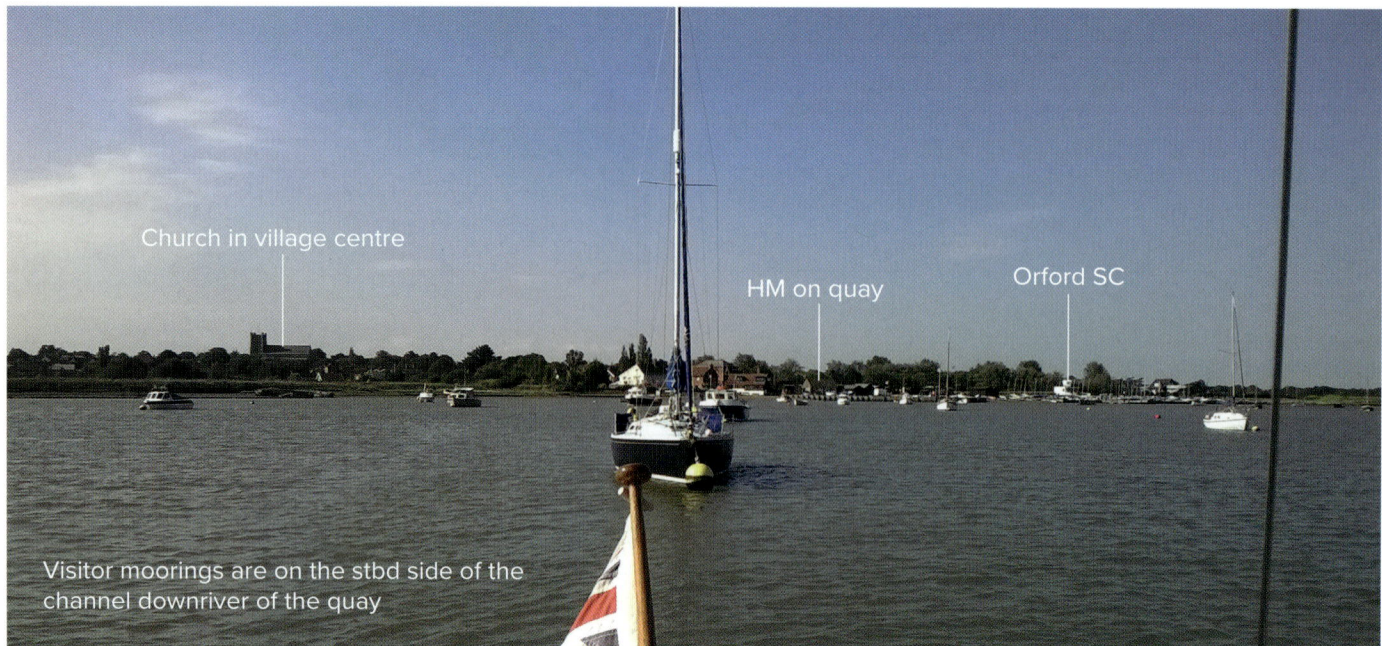

the two danger signs either side of the river at the N end of the moorings. These mark pipelines laid in the riverbed taking services to the National Trust buildings on Orford Ness. It's best to anchor well above the main areas of moorings and go ashore by dinghy but be careful of the swiftly flowing tide. You can stay for a short time alongside the quay, up to an hour or so either side of HW but watch for the ferry that runs from the quay across to the landing stage on the Ness; other riverboats also use the quay.

Continuing up river from Orford, the next prominent feature is the nest of large radio transmitter masts now used by Radio Caroline to beam programmes into Europe, to starboard. The National Trust owns the marshes surrounding them and landing is strictly forbidden.

It is here, at Pigpail Sluice, that the Ore becomes the Alde.

In Tudor times Orford was a major coastal trading port

ORFORD   IP12 2NU

Contact
Harbourmaster and Quay Warden ☎01394 459950
☎07528 092635
VHF Ch 08 or 16
Callsign *Chantry* (0930–1700 in season)
orfordquayuk@gmail.com

Water From standpipes on the quay
Provisions In village
Pubs/restaurant Several in the village
Post office/stores opposite King's Head
Scrubbing posts Near quay
Telephone Cardphone in car park at back of Orford SC
Slipway At quay, fee pay. Club slipway at Orford SC
Club Orford SC ☎01394 450997 or 450976
www.orfordsail.org.uk
Transport Buses to Ipswich and surrounding area
Taxi ☎01394 459447

The Alde

Under its new name, the river continues in a winding, but generally N direction through flat marshland up to Slaughden Quay, which is on the outside of a hairpin bend inland. The first prominent landmark is a Martello Tower on the starboard side where the shingle bank between the river and the sea is hardly more than 50 yards wide. The tower is known as 'CC'.

Slaughden Quay

Slaughden is sited on the apex of the bend in the river, which, having run NNE, now swings almost due W, as it heads inland.

A good anchorage can be found in the bay 150 yards S of Aldeburgh Yacht Club, between the designated visitor moorings and the Martello Tower.

Slaughden Quay

North Sea · Radio TRX aerials · Bawdsey Cliffs · Orford · Shingle St · River Alde · Martello Tower CC

Looking S as the Alde wriggles its way inside Orford Ness

Aldeburgh · Demon Boats · North Sea · Slaughden SC · Upson's Boatyard · Aldeburgh YC · Slaughden Quay

East Coast Pilot • 37

4. RIVERS ORE & ALDE

SLAUGHDEN QUAY (ALDEBURGH)   IP15 5NA

Contact
Harbourmaster Contact Brian Upson ☎01728 453047
Boatyards Upson's Boatyard ☎01728 453047
Aldeburgh Boatyard (Demon Yachts) ☎01728 452019
matthew@demonyachts.co.uk
www.demonyachts.co.uk
Fuel Diesel from Upson's Boatyard, petrol in Aldeburgh town
Chandler Upson's and Aldeburgh Boatyards
Rigger Aldeburgh Boatyard
Visitors' moorings Contact Upson's Boatyard ☎01728 453047 or David Cable ☎01728 452569.
Electrical and mechanical engineer Upson's Boatyard
Slipway Upson's Boatyard
Facilities (All at Aldeburgh YC) WC, showers, telephone
Club Aldeburgh YC ☎01728 452562 www.aldeburghyc.org.uk Slaughden SC ☎01728 454335 or 07715 953149 when open www.slaughdensailingclub.co.uk
Bar/food Aldeburgh YC (hours vary)
Pubs/restaurants Several in town
Water Standpipe on quay and Aldeburgh YC pontoon
Provisions Aldeburgh (about 1M)
Transport Buses
Taxi ☎01728 833621 and 452142

From Slaughden up to Westrow Point the river is lined on either side with moorings and, at the point itself, is crossed by an underwater power cable. Above that, the river turns NE in Island Reach and good places to anchor can be found between Cob Island to port and the Old Brickyard Dock to starboard or round the corner in Collier's Reach.

The steel post on the end of Cob Island has a distinctive swan emblem as a topmark. The best water is well over to starboard and well clear of the long spit that juts out from Cob Island. There is a line of small boat moorings round the outer edge of the bend.

At Cob Island the river swings W and widens out into a shallow lake with the winding channel marked by withies. Here too the character of the river changes with well wooded rolling countryside interspersed with arable fields and church steeples reaching skyward, all so characteristic of the Suffolk countryside.

Deep draught boats can find good holding in Colliers Reach, so crews can mount a dinghy excursion through the winding

The Cob on a post at the end of Cob Island is a PHM

The Alde wends it way W to head of navigation at Snape

River Alde

The water front at Snape, with the world famous Maltings concert hall behind

waterways to Snape. Shoal draught boats can anchor off Iken Church, The Oaks and Iken Cliffs in 1m and 2m of water at low tide, but care is needed as several moorings have been laid in these holes. Landing on the Iken shore is restricted and there's only a footpath along the bank to Snape.

Above Iken Cliffs the river winds N and finally NW to the quay and bridge at Snape where the world famous Snape Maltings concert hall stands. It is possible to lie alongside the quay, but it dries at low tide and fender boards are recommended, because the face of the quay is quite rough. Do not moor outside a barge or other flat-bottomed boat, because the ground here slopes and if the inner boat slides, the outer could be pushed over. For a panoramic view of the upper Alde, it's well worth a stroll up to the crossroads on the 'hill' in Snape.

General advice about the upper reaches

When planning a trip up river above Cob Island, aim to begin as early on the flood as possible. By doing so, the channel can be picked out more easily and the channel markers understood. Note these markers are withies, with port hand marks topped with red cans and the starboard withies have branched tops and occasional green cans. They tend to come and go from season to season, so once the mud is covered, there may be no marks to guide you or they may be confusing. Starting early may also make a stop at Snape for lunch and a drink at the Plough and Sail ☎ 01728 688413 www.theploughandsailsnape.com, possible before hurrying back down to deeper water.

Looking back down the Alde from Snape

5. RIVER DEBEN

The Deben entrance is subject to continuous change
Credit John Ranson

5. RIVER DEBEN

⊕ **Landfall waypoint**

51°58'·15N 001°23'·20E Close Woodbridge Haven SWB

Deben Entrance

Buoy positions may change seasonally

Charts

Imray 2000, C28

Admiralty 5607, 2693

Tides

Woodbridge Haven HW Walton −0002
Waldringfield HW Walton +0020
Woodbridge HW Walton +0040

ECP Honorary Port Pilot

John White ☏01394 270106, 07803 476621 or VHF Ch 08 Callsign *Odd Times*
deben@eastcoastpilot.com
www.debenestuarypilot.co.uk

Deben offing buoy

HMCG aerial is useful landmark offshore

Hazards

Big changes to report at the entrance to the Deben. Most agree for the better this time. The entrance closed at the bottom end over winter of 2022 and cut through as expected further up the shingle nearer to the Bawdsey shore. It's now almost a straight run through from the offing buoy towards the up-river Martello Tower, with plenty of water but it's a bit narrow so take care, especially off Knoll Spit where there's a pinch point. Prudent seamanship and carefully following the buoys and entering at the right state of the tide, will ensure you have no real problems getting in or out. It's essential to obtain the latest information from **www.eastcoastpilot.com** which carries a chartlet drawn from the latest Trinity House survey, the specialist Deben and Ore website or the Woodbridge Cruising Club's website.

www.debenestuarypilot.co.uk
www.woodbridgecruisingclub.org

The Woodbridge Haven SWB is at 51° 57'.992N 001° 23'.628E (2023). It is essential the first-time visitor should locate this mark and enter from there and not be tempted to follow others taking shorth cuts. It pays too, to check current information before approaching the entrance and we suggest calling the Felixstowe Ferry HM and ECP HPP, John White, for pilotage or advice (see contact details in Felixstowe Ferry or River Deben information panels).

The ideal time to enter is about HW-2½ hr. Streams in the river mouth are quite strong. Entry should not be attempted in strong SE or E winds or at night. Unless you have considerable spare engine power don't try entering against the ebb either, which can run at up to 5kn on springs.

Landmarks

The tall lattice frame of the CG radio tower at Bawdsey is the best landmark when approaching from a distance to the entrance to this most beautiful river. The entrance lies between Bawdsey Manor, visible in the trees on the E bank and two Martello Towers on the W side of the river.

Entry

From the Woodbridge Haven SWB (Mo(A)15s) steer a course that leaves the Mid Knolls SHB to stbd followed in close order by the West Knolls PHB to port, which marks the spit on the S shingle bank, and the Knoll Spit PHB which marks the nasty spit on the down-river side of the gate formed with the Deben SHB.

Beware of very strong cross currents as you cross The Knolls, especially on the S going flood, which can push boats onto the S-side shingle spit.

As you pass through the 'gate' formed by the Knoll Spit PHB and the large Deben SHB set a course straight up the middle of river, keeping over towards the Bawdsey bank while passing the end of the Felixstowe Ferry landing. There's not a lot of water off the Ferry point and the tide runs very hard just there.

After passing the Felixstowe Ferry Sailing Club on the W bank keep over to the Bawdsey side for the deeper water and slightly less fierce current. The relatively narrow entrance channel between the shingle banks then opens out into Felixstowe Ferry itself.

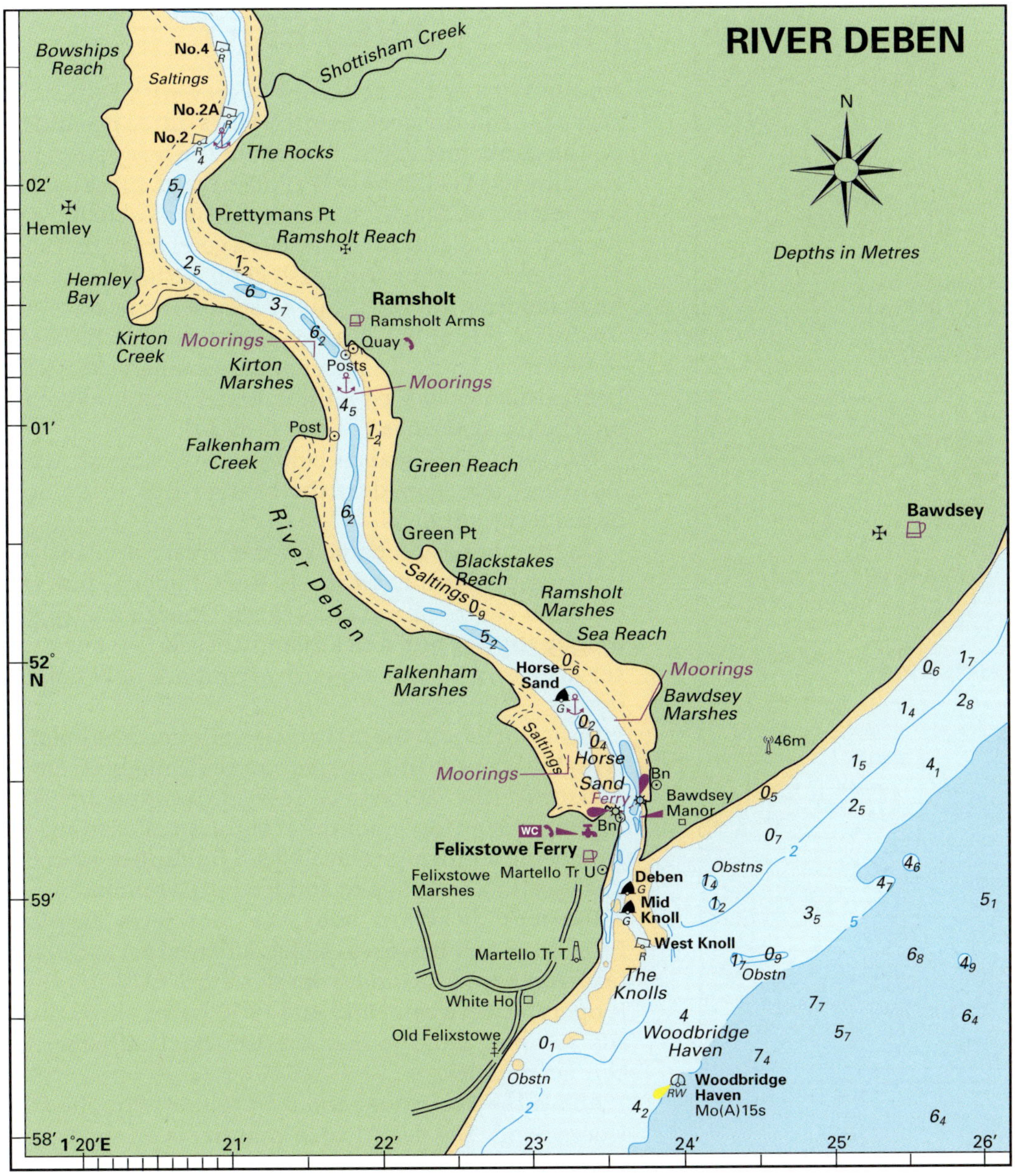

River Deben

Left Passing the SHB Deben turn up the middle of the river

Below Yachts coming out between the Mid Knoll PHB and the Deben SHB

5. RIVER DEBEN

FELIXSTOWE FERRY

On the W bank lies Felixstowe Ferry with Felixstowe Ferry SC and the grey painted HM's office prominent on the bank, just down river from the ferry steps and the slipway to Felixstowe Ferry Boatyard. Close by is an assortment of shacks, mostly used by local fishermen for gear storage, although one is a good fresh fish shop and there's another fresh fish shop at the head of the ferry landing. There's a pair of scrubbing posts on the upstream side of the slipway. There is no public access to the river; launching licences are available from the boatyard office or East Suffolk Water Ski Club (details on a board at the head of the slipway).

The Ferry Café stands behind the boatyard, while Winkles Café, owned by the boatyard, is at the head of the ferry jetty.

On the opposite bank of the river, at Bawdsey, is Bawdsey Manor, which is now a school but was once the centre of radar research. There's a jetty and dinghy slipway and a clean sandy beach. The one-time servicemen's houses along the front are now holiday homes.

Do not anchor in the main channel where the holding is highly suspect and the tide runs extremely strongly. A visit to either Felixstowe Ferry or Bawdsey involves finding a mooring – call the HM for an allocation – or anchoring a mile up river in good holding mud in Sea Reach with a long trip to and fro in the tender.

The local boatyard runs the foot ferry between Felixstowe and Bawdsey, which will also act as a water taxi to get crews to and from the shore between runs. It operates between 1000 and 1800 hours throughout the summer months (see the information panel for contact details).

Above the Ferry, just about in mid-stream, lies the Horse Sand. The deep-water channel is on the E side, while the shallower channel on the W side is crammed with moorings. This channel has silted up in recent years restricting the size of boats it can accomodate.

Felixstowe Ferry is a busy place

44 • East Coast Pilot

Ramsholt

Approaching Ramsholt from the Ferry

FELIXSTOWE FERRY — IP11 9RZ
(Ferry boatyard)

Contact
Harbourmasters John White and John Barber
☎01394 270106 or 07803 476621 or 07780 735604
VHF Ch 08
Callsign *Odd Times*
Water taxi VHF Ch 08, Callsign Deben Ferry or
☎01394 282173
Facilities WC behind FFSC
Water From standpipe by the boatyard
Chandler At boatyard (limited stock)
Provisions Shops in Old Felixstowe 2M
Pubs/restaurant Ferry Boat Inn ☎01394 284203
Ferry Café ☎01394 276305, fish & chips and all-day breakfasts
Winkles Café ☎07947 100242
Repairs Felixstowe Ferry Boatyard ☎01394 282173
www.felixstoweboats.co.uk
Crane At head of slip. Contact boatyard
Scrubbing posts Close to slip. Contact Harbourmaster
Slipway Contact Harbourmaster
Club Felixstowe Ferry SC ☎01394 283785,
www.ffsc.co.uk
Telephone Payphone near Ferry Boat Inn
Visitors' moorings Contact Harbourmaster
Taxi ☎01394 284000, 271116

There are moorings on the E of the Horse so keep outside (E) of these. The N end of the Horse is once again marked by a PHB.

The stretch of water above the last of the moorings and almost as far as the next bend in the river is the only section to which a universal 8kn speed limit does not apply. It is a designated water ski and speedboat area and on the W bank is a pontoon.

The river is clearly defined by the banks here and any buoys are racing marks for either FFSC or the upriver Waldringfield SC. This section of the river is also the least exciting visually where it runs between high sea defence banks through Falkenham Marsh to port and low-lying arable land to starboard.

At Green Point, where the river turns N and the view of Ramsholt opens out, the Deben reveals its true character with gently rolling slopes covered in woodland and well-tended farmland.

Note all the buoys above Felixstowe Ferry are unlit.

RAMSHOLT

Ramsholt stands on the E bank and consists of an old stone barge jetty and a pub, the Ramsholt Arms IP12 3AB ☎01394 411209, plus a red telephone box. There are no services there, but it's a pleasant spot to stretch the legs and 'take refreshment'. For information about moorings contact the new HM Ian Moore ☎07510 444462. There are over 200 moorings at Ramsholt and the fairway is sometimes difficult to identify, but there is good holding in the middle, if you wish to anchor, so long as you don't mind the wash from passing craft.

The red telephone box behind the Ramsholt Arms is a key feature of the place

5. RIVER DEBEN

The Rocks is a popular weekend anchorage

THE ROCKS

Above Ramsholt, the channel swings gently NW round Kirton marshes, where the drying Kirton Creek joins the river, before heading NE round Prettyman's Point into an area below Ramsholt Woods known as The Rocks, because the riverbed is strewn with them. A recent feature has been the laying of several moorings at the upper end of anchorage. There is a low sandy cliff forming a sheltered anchorage with a beach for swimming and picnicking, but it's often crowded at weekends. There are no roads or facilities and visitors are requested not to cut down trees to make fires.

Opposite the Rocks is the first of the river buoys, which continue right up to Melton.

The first four buoys are PHBs marking the edge of mudflats extending out from the W shore, pushing the channel well over to the E side of the river until it sweeps back to the W side above No.1 SHB below Waldringfield. Give Nos.4 and 6 a good berth, because the mud and sand spit they mark is growing.

WALDRINGFIELD

No.1 SHB marks the downstream extremity of Stonner Island where the main channel bears to port and is marked by triple lines of moorings all the way through Waldringfield itself.

There are no designated visitor moorings, however the owners of Waldringfield Boatyard (Woodbridge Boat Co.) have a novel scheme, using clients' vacant moorings, to each of which is attached a 12ft orange-painted rowing boat with Visitor clearly marked on the sides; oars and rowlocks are attached. Alternatively, ask the HM if he has a spare mooring. (There are no official mooring fees, but a donation is gratefully received for local sailing charities). Anchoring in the main channel is not recommended, because it is quite narrow, there is much traffic, the bottom's foul and the holding's suspect. Generally, moorings will take boats up to 35ft (10·4m). In both cases be prepared to be disappointed as the allocation of moorings is virtually full of permanent residents.

If no vacant mooring is available, go up as far as No.3 SHB, at the top of the moorings, and anchor roughly in line with it and No.5 the next buoy up on the bend. Again, such is the pressure for all-tide moorings that this area is now being populated with moorings as well, so be careful anchoring and use a trip line for safety.

There is clean landing on the beach at Waldringfield near the HM's hut and there are some pretty walks around the area, but services are limited. There is a pontoon jetty reaching out from the boatyard to which dinghies can be moored during a stroll ashore or a drink or meal at the Maybush, and a river trip boat moors across the end of the pontoon.

WALDRINGFIELD   **IP12 4QZ** (Boatyard)

Harbourmaster Tony Lyon ☎07925 081062
waldringfieldhm@btinternet.com

Boatyard Waldringfield Boatyard ☎01473 736260
VHF Ch 80 www.waldringfieldboatyard.co.uk

Water From taps at boatyard quay or outside sailing club

Fuel Diesel and petrol in cans from garage 1M up the Woodbridge road

Boat repairs Slipway and 40T crane

Scrubbing posts In front of sailing club (care with bilge keels)

Facilities Public phone box near inn. Toilets in boatyard, code on payment of mooring fee

Pub/restaurant The Maybush ☎01473 736215
www.debeninns.co.uk/maybush

Club Waldringfield SC ☎01473 736633

Provisions None

Transport Occasional bus or taxi into Woodbridge or Martlesham

---

Waldringfield is attractive but has few facilities

WOODBRIDGE

Above Waldringfield the river becomes increasingly attractive with wooded banks. It also shallows and, below half tide, great care is needed not to ground. From No.3 SHB, at the N end of Stonner Island, the river runs into a bay at the N end of which are The Hams, brown cliffs with a fine sandy beach, while to the S a promontory called The Tips marks the downriver extent of the bay. A spit from the opposite, W, bank is marked by Nos.8 and 10 PHBs. Landing at The Tips is possible, but only for a short period either side of HW.

The river swings over to the other shore just above The Hams and then straightens for the run up past Methersgate on the starboard side. There's another stone jetty here, Methersgate Quay, which was originally used for loading local farm produce into barges, but now landing is not allowed. However, you can pick up a vacant mooring in deepish water on this reach.

From the Quay and No.12 PHB, almost all the way to Woodbridge, the river is marked with both buoys and moorings. There are now so many moorings that it takes considerable care to identify the main channel. At No.14 PHB the river turns 90° to port in Troublesome Reach and heads W towards Kyson Point, which also marks the entrance to Martlesham Creek (drying), before swinging 90° back N again. The saltings that caused these violent changes in direction were cut through in the 1890s to accommodate barges. The cut, called Loder's Cut, can be used by shallow draught (max 1·5m) craft at about HW ±1hr.

There is a small boatyard, Martlesham Creek Boatyard, on the S bank of the W-running Martlesham Creek with pontoons, which dry out, and fresh water and power, plus showers and toilets. The yard can launch boats up to 10 tons and offers boat repairs and both inboard and outboard engine servicing. It is a popular spot for live-aboards.

MARTLESHAM CREEK BOATYARD   IP12 4PQ
☎ 01394 384727
www.martleshamboatyard.co.uk

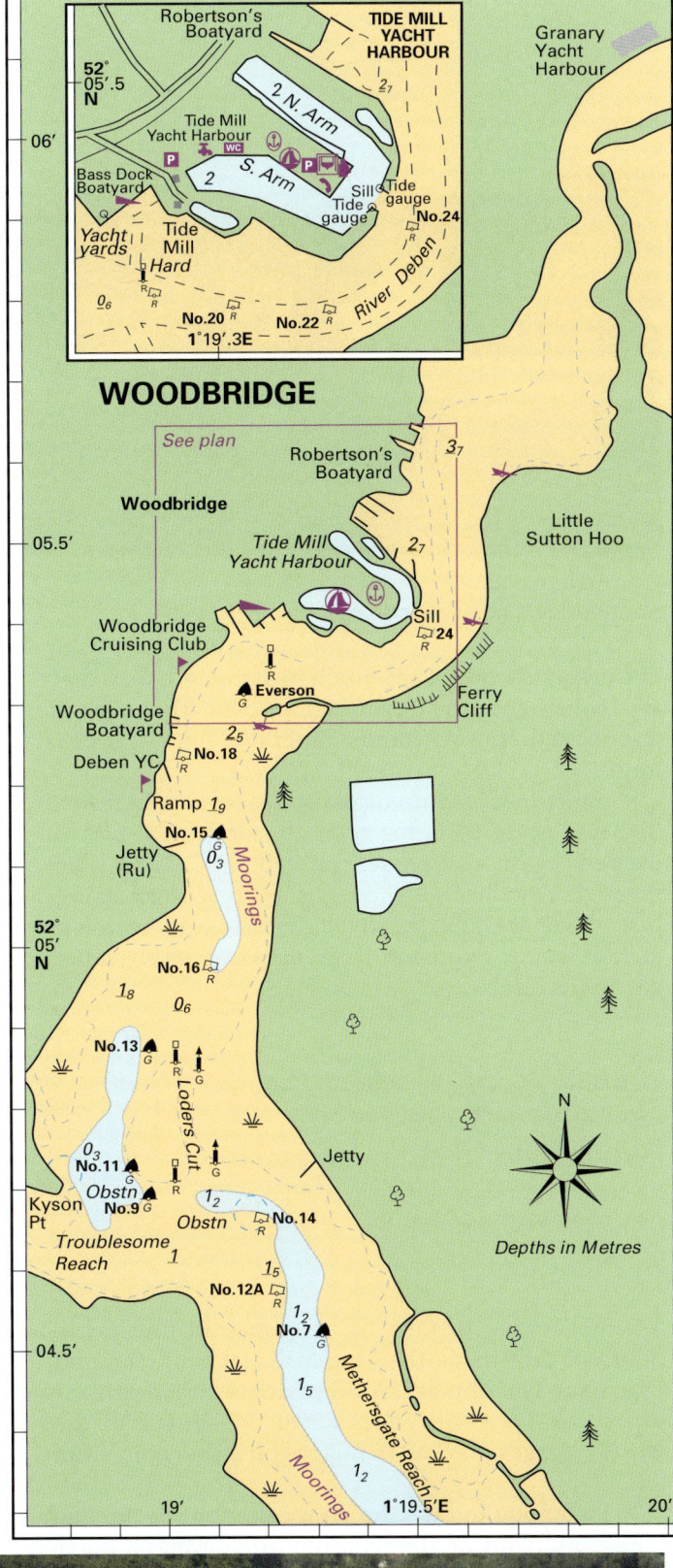

Looking up Martlesham Creek from Kyson Point towards Martlesham Boatyard

5. RIVER DEBEN

Woodbridge's busy waterfront

The creek is buoyed for much of its length and there are moorings at the upper end for boats that can take the ground. The bottom is generally good east coast mud.

Roughly half way up Granary Reach, between No.13 SHB and No.16 PHB, the river almost dries at LW, but deepens again as it passes the Deben YC. From there, through Woodbridge and right up to Wilford Bridge, just above Melton, the river dries to a mere trickle at low water, exposing large areas of lovely, black, glutinous mud.

DEBEN YC ☎01349 385400
www.debenyachtclub.co.uk

WOODBRIDGE CC ☎01394 386737
www.woodbridgecruisingclub.org
Facilities WC, showers, bar (at weekends only).

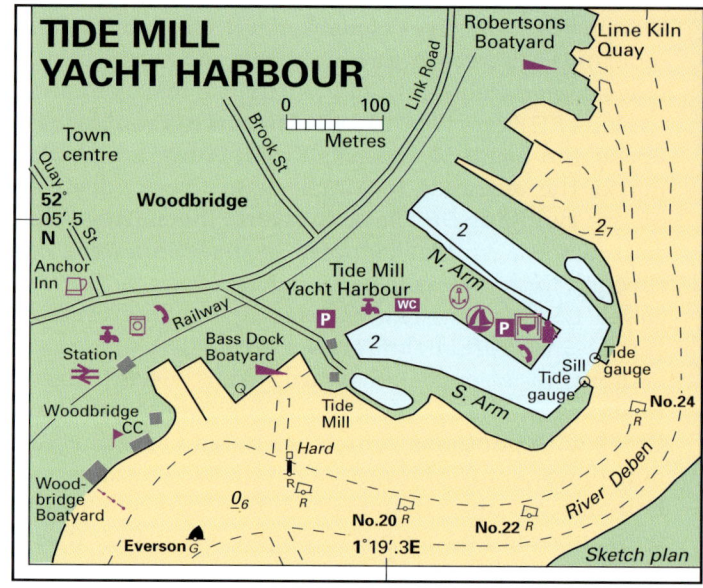

Boats unable to take the ground can find a least depth of 2m inside the Tide Mill Harbour, the main marina at Woodbridge. A sill restricts either entrance or exit to HW ±1½hr. Depth over the sill is indicated by tide gauges marked in metres on either side of the sill.

Those happy to take the mud can moor at the quay along the front of the old Tide Mill Granary, berths must be booked through Woodbridge Town Council in advance Customer Services ☎01394 383599 (£13 per 24hrs, max stay 5 nights.) Sadly, the opportunity to take a mud berth in Bass' Dock isn't possible any more as the dock is full of live-aboard craft. The old Whisstock's Boatyard has been redeveloped into modern flats and shops. The old Ferry Hard stretching right down to the middle of the river bed has been abandoned and now lies under a foot of mud, the end is still marked by a post (PHB). (At low water springs you could wade across in calf-deep water.)

Woodbridge is an historic town with a good shopping centre and easy access by bus, taxi or train to Ipswich and onward. Much of the surrounding countryside is well worth a visit and the Sutton Hoo Viking burial site is a major attraction.

Opposite the entrance to the Tide Mill the river narrows under a wooded bank. There are several moorings that can be temporarily picked up while waiting for the tide to give enough clearance over the Tide Mill sill.

Woodbridge

Woodbridge Tide Mill Marina

5. RIVER DEBEN

Past the marina the river swings W and opens out into a marshy bay on the W side. This used to be a good place for over-wintering in mud berths but has been sanitised to accommodate several large live-aboard vessels. Here also is Robertson's Boatyard and the remains of an old Lime Kiln and attendant quay.

Further up river lies the Granary Yacht Hbr (Melton Boatyard) marina and, next door upriver, Larkman's laying up yard. There is a well-buoyed, if rather tortuous, channel right up to the yards, with Wilford Bridge, the point of final navigation on the Deben, a straight run further on. Melton Boatyard's pontoon moorings are dredged to 2m while Larkman lifts boats over the river wall at spring high tide. Anyone staying in the Tide Mill Marina should consider taking the dinghy and exploring the upper reaches and even ducking under Wilford Bridge into some pretty countryside up to Ufford. Remember though, the river virtually dries at low water, the mere trickle left being almost fresh water.

TIDE MILL YACHT HARBOUR IP12 1BP
Contact VHF Ch 80
Callsign *Tide Mill Yacht Harbour*
Harbourmaster Ross Copsey
☎ 01394 385745
info@tidemillyachtharbour.co.uk
www.tidemillyachtharbour.co.uk
(includes useful daily predictor of heights over the sill)
Access HW±1½hr
Facilities WC, showers, launderette, WiFi (only close to the HM's office, and for emergencies)
Water On pontoons
Electricity On pontoons (adaptor required from office)
Gas Calor and Gaz
Telephone At railway station
Boat repairs 16T crane, 35-T boat hoist, full service workshop
Fuel Diesel on berth at entrance
Chandler (A few basic mechanical and maintenance items, on site)
Sailmaker Suffolk Sails ☎ 01394 386323 outside marina gates
Rigger Evolution Rigging ☎ 01473 655089
Brokerage Howard Ford Marine Sales ☎ 01394 385577
Provisions In town, 10 minutes
Pubs/restaurants In town
Transport Train station close by, buses
Taxi ☎ 01394 333888

BOATYARDS AROUND WOODBRIDGE
Woodbridge Boat Company ☎ 01394 385786
www.woodbridgeboatyard.com
Crane, slipway, boat repairs, specialists in classic yachts

Robertson's ☎ 01394 382305 Alan Fuller
info@robertsons-boatyard.co.uk
www.robertsons-boatyard.co.uk
Access HW±1·5hrs
Boat repairs Two slipways, 14-T hoist, crane, rigging, boat repairs (specialists in wooden boats)
Facilities WC
Water On quay
Electricity On quay

Granary Yacht Hbr ☎ 01394 386327 Simon Skeet
info@meltonboatyard.co.uk
www.meltonboatyard.co.uk
Berthing By prior arrangement
Access HW ±2hr (at springs), HW ±1 (at neaps)
Boat repairs Specialists in steel and aluminium, 40-T hoist
Small chandlery, 30-berth marina
Café Deben Cafe, on HMS Vale
☎ 01394 358643

Larkman's Boatyard Melton ☎ 01394 382943 (Steve Larkman) www.larkmansboatyard.co.uk
larkmansboatyard@btconnect.com
Boat repairs and wintering yard (250 spaces with chandler
Crane 15-T crane for lifting boats over sea wall
Limited facilities

Keep a sharp look out for wild water swimmers

Woodbridge

The upper reaches of the Deben

Wilford Bridge, the end of navigation

East Coast Pilot • 51

Felixstowe Container Port

6. HARWICH

Trinity House Quay

6. HARWICH HARBOUR

⊕ **Landfall waypoint**
51°55'·23N 001°18'·39E SW of Landguard NCB (Q) on recommended yacht track

Charts
Imray 2000, C1, Y16
Admiralty 5607, 1491, 2693

Tides
Walton HW +0005

Harbourmaster
Will Barker ☏01255 243030
www.hha.co.uk/leisure

Harwich Port Control Ch 71

Callsign *Harwich VTS*

HARWICH AREA CONTACTS

Harwich Haven Authority ☏ 01255 243030
Harwich Harbour Control (VTS) ☏ 01255 243000

PORT CONTROL

Harwich Harbour is accessible at all times and is one of only two ports of last resort on this stretch of coast – the other being Lowestoft. In recent years major construction work has extended the quay frontage on the Felixstowe side to accommodate the world's largest container ships; along with a massive multimillion pound scheme to dredge the harbour and approach channel to take them. **It is imperative that small craft keep clear of the main shipping channels and berthing manoeuvres of container ships.** The harbour authority maintains a round the clock radar and radio watch (on Ch 71) and all yachts are requested to listen on this channel from Landguard to Fagbury, on the River Orwell, and to past Erwarton Ness beacon on the Stour. Call on Ch 71 in an emergency only, such as being unable to get out of the way of an announced shipping manoeuvre. Harwich VTS ☏01255 243000.

The authority also produces an excellent free yachtsmen's guide detailing the recommended yacht tracks, which is available from local marinas and chandlers or by writing to:
Harwich Haven Authority,
Harbour House,
The Quay, Harwich CO12 3HH
☏01255 243030
The guide is also available at www.hha.co.uk

Landmarks

On the E side of Harwich Harbour is Felixstowe Container Port, the largest in the UK and following extensions to the Felixstowe quays is bigger and busier than ever. The most prominent landmarks are the huge blue cranes that stretch the length of the Trinity and Felixstowe South Quays, all along the E side of the harbour.

On a clear day, from the Landfall Waypoint, the disused lighthouse on the Dovercourt Beach is visible, looking rather like a pale coloured, over large dovecote on stilts at the back of the beach. The tall steeple of Harwich Town church, together with the white roof of the Ro-Ro shed on the end of Harwich Quay make good aiming points. On the E side of the entrance is a south cardinal beacon (SCM) on the tip of Landguard with, just inland, the lower fortifications of Landguard Fort, as well as one of the several radar towers (white) that are dotted about the harbour.

Main hazards

Big ships and ferries.

The recent extension of Felixstowe South Quay, on the E side of the harbour, has resulted in an almost uninterrupted quay face from Landguard Beach to the N end of Trinity Quay opposite Babergh PHB in the mouth of the Orwell. From several miles out to sea the veritable forest of blue container cranes makemakes the harbour conspicuous and at night the loom of the powerful work lights can be spotted 20M out to sea. Beware of big ships swinging round to face seawards when berthed.

There are areas of shallow water in the harbour that need care and attention, including the Harwich Shelf on the W side of the entrance and the Shotley Spit, which is marked by Shotley Spit SCB (Q(6)+LFl. 15s) in the centre of the harbour.

Felixstowe Container Port accommodates the largest container ships in the world

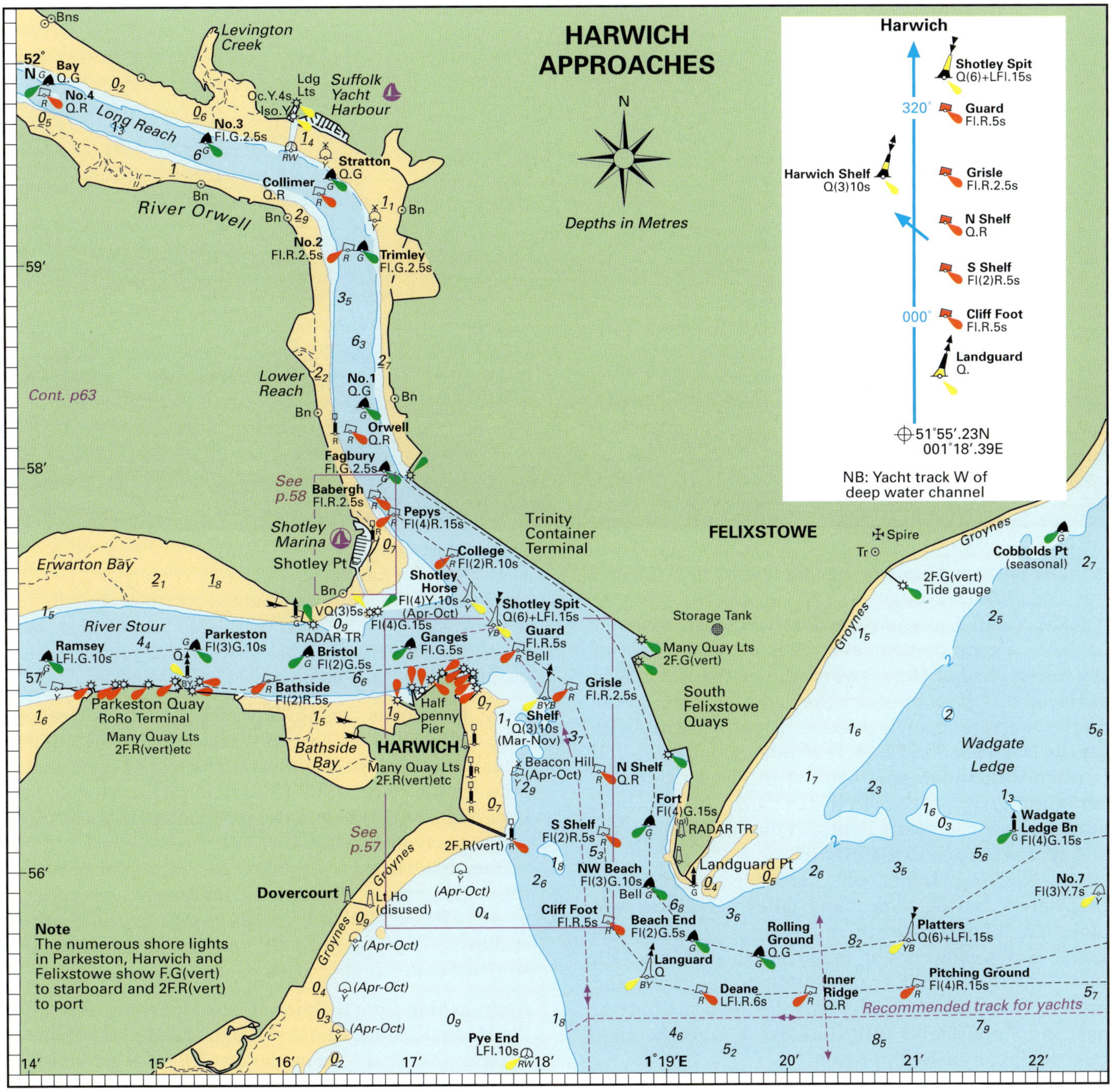

Harwich Harbour

Approaches

The approaches to Harwich are well marked. In particular, the deepwater shipping channel is heavily buoyed, but, because of the number, tonnage and size of shipping using the channel, there are recommended yacht entry tracks shown on charts, which must be used. All of them converge on the Landfall Waypoint,

At the entrance to the harbour, beware the Cliff Foot Rocks patch E of the end of Blackman's Breakwater on the W side of the approach. The bottom is foul at LW and there are strong eddies. Further in, keep to starboard of the seasonal (March to November) Harwich Shelf ECB (Q(3)10s), which marks the E limit of the Harwich Shelf, which at LWS all but dries in the centre.

Blackman's Groyne on the W of harbour entrance; avoid a rocky patch off the end where there's a back eddy and poorly marked lobster pots

East Coast Pilot • 55

6. HARWICH HARBOUR

roughly halfway between the Landguard NCB (Q) and Pye End SWB (L.Fl.10s).

Once round Landguard and squaring up to enter harbour, a good point to aim for is the white roof of the Ro-Ro shed at the seaward end of the Navy Yard at Harwich. About opposite the Redoubt Fort marked on the chart, turn a few degrees to starboard and aim for the Harwich Shelf ECB. It's quite a small buoy and is often difficult to spot against the background of ships and quays. Although lit (Q(3)10s), it's drowned at night by the working lights on the container quays and care is needed to identify it.

The working lights on the quays and ships themselves can be seen many miles out to sea and make a night entrance difficult, especially from the N and E. If in serious doubt, make S to the Medusa SHB (Fl.G.5s), which lies E from Walton on the Naze, and return N towards Harwich using the Medusa Channel past the Stone Banks PHB (Fl.R.5s). It adds distance but can be the easier approach.

Despite the background light pollution problems, Harwich is an all-weather, all-tide, 24hr, remarkably easy harbour to enter.

From seawards There are two routes into Harwich from seawards: N and S. In daylight and after a North Sea crossing, yachts can aim for the Cork Sand Bn (Fl(3) R.10s) or the nearby Cork Sand Yacht Bn NCM (VQ) and, keeping S of the deep water channel, proceed to pass well to port of Landguard NCB (Q) to keep well clear of the bend in the shipping channel. Or they can aim for Medusa SHB (Fl.G.5s) then up the Medusa Ch close past Stone Banks PHB (Fl.R.5s) to join the recommended yacht track at the Landfall Waypoint.

From N Perhaps having departed the Rivers Ore and Alde or Deben, pass close to Wadgate Ledge SHM (Fl(4) G.15s) and cross the deep-water channel at right angles between the Platters SCB (Q(6)+L.Fl.15s) and the Rolling Ground SHB (QG) to join the recommended yacht track coming in from E.

Harwich Haven Authority recommends crossing the deepwater channel between waypoints 51°55'·83N 001°20'·29E on the N side of the channel and 51°55'·23N 001°20'·39E on the S side, to give the shortest right-angle crossing.

Approaching from S Follow a course of about 345° from the Medusa SHB (Fl.G.5s) through the Medusa Channel to pass close to the Stone Banks PHB (Fl.R.5s) and join the recommended yacht track at the Landfall Waypoint or, at most, three cables S of Landguard NCB (Q).

Yachts approaching Harwich from almost due E and from the direction of the Galloper will have to negotiate the Sunk Gyratory System. Navigate in this area using only the latest charts on which the system's buoyage and traffic separation lanes are marked. It will pay you to give Sunk VTS a call on VHF Ch 71 to let them know your position and projected track before entering the system. If you have an AIS transceiver switched on they'll pick you up anyway.

Close approach (pilotage) to Harwich Harbour will be by either the S route through the Medusa Channel or the N route via Cork Sand Yacht Bn.

Inside the Cork Sand to the E and the shipping channel to the N and extending SW into Dovercourt Bay are several yellow seasonal racing marks, which have no navigational significance.

Harwich Shelf ECM guards a large shallow patch in the middle of the harbour

Harwich Yacht Clubs

Entry

Progress through the harbour must be via the recommended yacht tracks shown on current charts. Keep a sharp lookout for pilots and other working boats crossing between Harwich and Felixstowe. At the Guard PHB (Fl.R.5s Bell) either turn W along the Harwich waterfront to reach the moorings at Halfpenny Pier or cross the mouth of the Stour to Shotley Spit SCB (Q(6)+L.Fl.15s).

At Shotley Spit, turn W either towards Shotley Marina or to proceed on up the River Stour, keeping to the Shotley side until clear of Parkeston Quay, or continue N from Shotley Spit into the River Orwell. Keep close watch on the depth anywhere near Shotley Spit.

HARWICH

Halfpenny Pier

The only facilities for yachts at Harwich are at Ha'penny Pier. From the Guard PHB make W past the Ro-Ro terminal and Ha'penny Pier lies to port. The approach is clear but beware of swells from passing ships while going alongside. The gate at the top of the gangway between the leisure vessel pontoons and Ha'penny Pier itself is locked daily at 1730 for security reasons. Access between 1730 and 0900 is only possible using a code obtained from the Pier Master (PM). The office is located at the entrance to Ha'penny Pier (see Halfpenny Pier box for details).

Harwich Yacht Clubs

There are two yacht clubs based at Harwich: Harwich Town SC, which is a dinghy racing club with a clubhouse overlooking the main harbour, and Harwich and Dovercourt SC, which is a cruising club. Its headquarters are at the top of Gashouse Creek, a drying gutway between the Trinity House jetty and Bathside Bay.

There is a foot ferry between Harwich Town, Felixstowe (Landguard beach) and Shotley Marina.

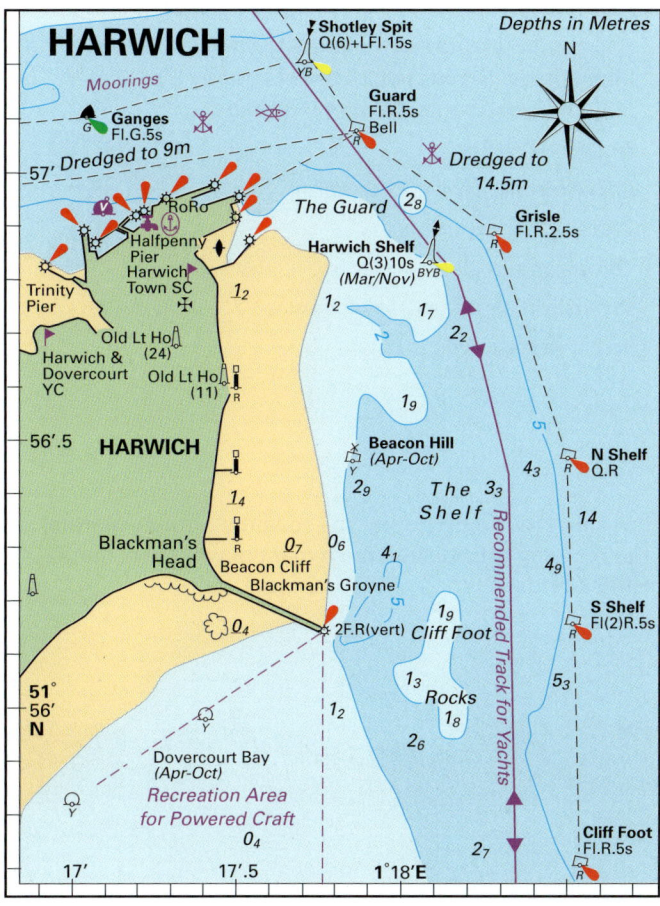

6. HARWICH HARBOUR

HALFPENNY PIER · CO12 3HH

Contact
Pier Master ☎01255 243030 or 07748 154039 (phone manned until 2100)
www.hha.uk/mooring
Pier manned by PM 0800-1100 and 1300-1800 including weekends and bank holidays, April-October

Berth Alongside pontoons. (20m LOA limit) Watch for wash from passing ships. No charge between 0900-1600, but charges apply overnight

Facilities Water (from tap on inside wall of sea wall), and electricity on pier (in emergency only, from PM's office); WC and showers via coded lock, see PM

Provisions In town

Pubs/restaurants café at root of pier; many more nearby in town

Sailmaker Dolphin Sails ☎01255 243366

Transport Trains, buses

Taxi ☎01255 506070240042, 01255 551111, 01255 506070

Note Harwich Navy Yard has no facilities for yachts. The pilots and harbour launches use it

HARWICH AND DOVERCOURT SC

Contact via website: www.hdsc.org.uk
Clubhouse on landing barge (LBK6) alongside quay. Bar open Friday evening and Saturday and Sunday lunch times. 5 mins walk from Ha'penny Pier. Gates may be locked outside opening hours

Access HW±3hr

Facilities WC (when club open)

Water On quayside

Telephone In club

Provisions In nearby town centre

Pubs, restaurants In town

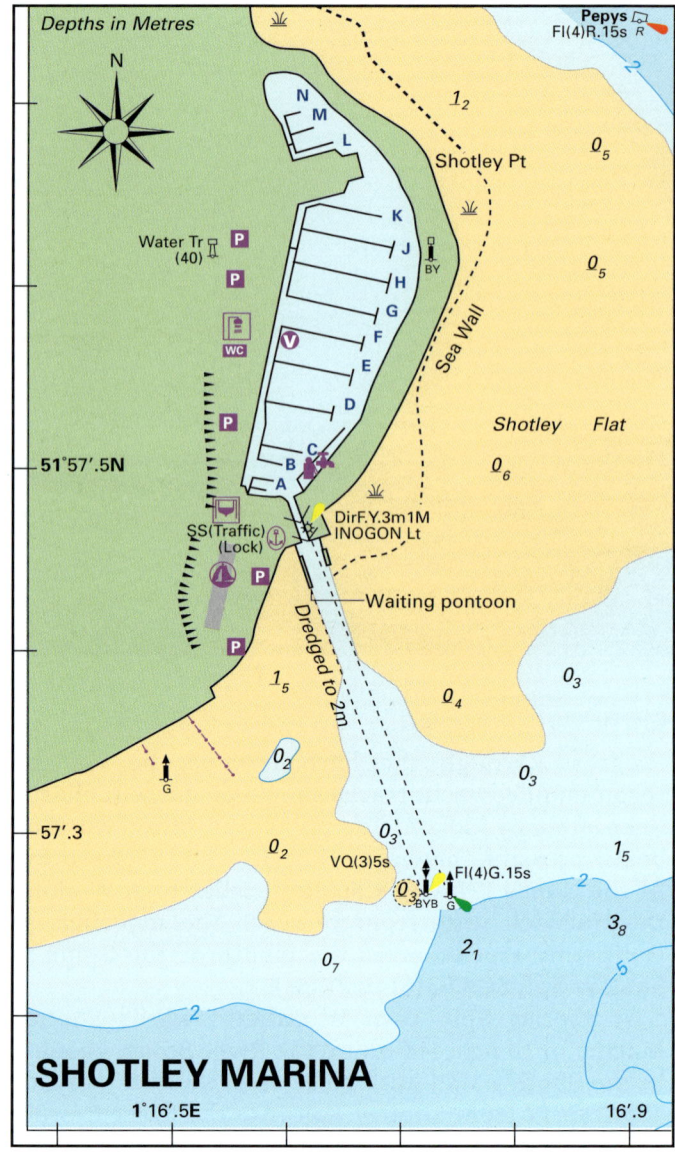

SHOTLEY MARINA

Shotley Marina is easily identified by the word Marina painted on top of its workshop building and visible across the harbour. On reaching the centre of Harwich Harbour close to Guard PHB (Fl.R.5s Bell), a low building will be seen off the port bow, which carries the word 'Marina' in large letters. It's at Shotley Marina. A prominent landmark behind the marina is the recently refurbished main mast of the old HMS *Ganges* naval training base behind the marina. It is also marked by major construction works taking place on the bank behind the marina.

Looking NW from Shotley spit towards Shotley Marina; the recently refurbished main mast of what was once HMS *Ganges* stands proud behind it

Shotley Marina

[Aerial photo of Shotley Marina with labels: Ganges, Shipwreck Chandler Broker, HM and lock control, Shower block, Visitors, Orwell, Fuel berth, INOGON, Waiting and ferry pontoon, Shotley Point Marina]

Entry to Shotley is via a dredged channel (2m at MLWS) and a lock providing 24hr access. Approach from Shotley Spit SCB, running parallel to the deep-water channel towards Ganges SHB (Fl.G.5s). When close to this buoy, turn to starboard and pass between a pair of top-marked beacons, which are lit Fl(4)G.15s on the starboard hand and VQ(3)5s on the port hand ECM. From these beacons, the channel into the lock runs on a bearing of about 340°.

Locking into the marina is governed by traffic lights (red and green) and there is a waiting pontoon and a strict rota of vessels by the HM via VHF (Ch 80).

There is a waiting pontoon to port of the entrance, ideal for crew changes or short stays, which is also used by the harbour ferry, to port on the outside of the entrance. There is an INOGON directional leading light mounted on the starboard lock knuckle with lit arrows, sometimes hard to see in bright sunlight, to keep approaching craft on line up the narrow approach channel. If the arrows point to the left, steer to port, or if they point to the right, steer to starboard, to maintain your track up the channel. Inside the lock are floating bumpers with cleats and grab lines on top. Beware a nasty cross current across the entrance.

SHOTLEY MARINA   IP9 1QJ
Contact ☏01473 788982
VHF Ch 80
Callsign *Shotley Marina*
www.shotleymarina.co.uk
reception@shotleymarina.co.uk
Max size (lock) 20m x 6·5m x 2·2m, (berth) 20m on hammerhead only
Facilities WC, showers and baths, launderette, WiFi
Water On pontoons
Electricity On pontoons (adaptor supplied)
Gas Calor and Gaz. Ask at chandlery
Chandler On site ☏01473 788982 (opens on demand)
Fuel Diesel from berth immediately to starboard inside lock (24hr)
Provisions From local shop/PO in village 30 min walk

Museum *HMS Ganges* on site
Clubs Shotley Point YC, Victory Hse, www.shotleypointyc.org
Shotley SC, www.shotleysailingclub.co.uk (clubhouse next to Bristol Arms)
Bar/restaurant and B&B The Shipwreck ☏01473 788865; Bristol Arms (10 min walk) ☏01473 787200 (check hours for both)
Boat repairs Shotley Marine Services ☏01473 788982. 40-T boat hoist, 20-T crane
Transport Foot ferry to Harwich and Felixstowe ☏01728 666329, customerservice@harwichharbourferry.com www.harwichharbourferry.com.
Bus service from Shotley Gate (10 min walk) to Ipswich.
Taxi ☏01473 222222, 407777, 255555

7. RIVER ORWELL

Head of navigation Ipswich Wet Dock

7. RIVER ORWELL

⊕ **Landfall waypoint**
51°55'·20N 001°18'·50E
SW of Landguard NCB on recommended yacht track

Charts
Imray 2000, C28, Y16
Admiralty 5607, 1491, 2693

Port Authority
ABP (From Fagbury to Ipswich Wet Dock)
Ipswich harbourmaster ☎01473 231010
Ipswich lockmaster ☎01473 213526 (VHF Ch 68)

Callsign *Prince Philip Lock*

VHF Channels
Monitor port operations Ch 71 from Pye End to Fagbury
Monitor port operations Ch 68 from Fagbury to Ipswich

Tides
Harwich HW Walton +0005
Ipswich HW Walton +0025

Hazards

The Orwell is an attractive and popular destination for cruising yachts. It carries a busy mix of commercial and leisure traffic, everything from general cargo boats to Thames Barges, East Coast smacks and several hundred small craft, all bustling about day and night. The danger for visiting yachtsmen is the commercial traffic, which is quiet and a sharp lookout must be kept astern. Ships are constrained by their draught and yachts must keep well clear. If a ship is manoeuvring near the docks or navigating one of the bends in the river, it's essential to keep well clear.

The port authority (ABP) has warned of the danger of wash and the subsequent draw down effect from passing ships in the river at LW, especially at LWS. They are particularly concerned about possible swamping of tenders or the temporary grounding of yachts on the margins of the main channel and urge great caution together with the wearing of lifejackets when going to and from moorings and the shore.

If anchoring anywhere in the Orwell, keep clear of the main channel. Remember to display a black ball during the day and a riding light at night, but it is also advisable to do the same if lying to a mooring, because it tells the skippers and pilots of passing ships that there are people on board. This advice is the result of some 'incidents' between ships and moored and anchored yachts in the past.

The river is subject to an 8kn speed limit decreasing to 6kn above Woolverstone.

The Orwell – lower reaches

The River Orwell, or the Ipswich River as it's often known locally, is attractive and remarkably unspoilt, yet increasingly commercial. It is 9M from the end of the Trinity Quay at Harwich to the lock gates into Ipswich Wet Dock and getting on for ½M wide in places at HW.

Because of the commercial shipping, the main channel has been dredged to a depth of 5·6m at LW and is about 400m (2 cables) wide. Gently rising mudflats merge into either narrow sandy beaches or heavily wooded banks on either side.

Entering the Orwell from Harwich Harbour, stay W outside the dredged channel, leaving the Guard PHB (Fl.R.5s Bell) to starboard and, after crossing the narrowest part of the deep water channel, leave the Shotley Spit SCB (Q(6)+L.Fl.15s) also to starboard, then leave the Shotley Horse buoy (Fl(4)Y.10s) close to port. This buoy is a yellow turning mark that allows yachts to turn in deep water without having to go round Shotley Spit SCB and stray into the main harbour channel. From Shotley Horse make about NW towards the College PHB (Fl(2)R.10s).

Leave College close to starboard. It marks the W edge of the deep-water channel opposite the Trinity container berths and is there for big ships. There's plenty of depth between the buoy and the Shotley Spit, which runs out from Shotley Point (roughly half way along the marina retaining wall) to Shotley Spit SCB. If a big ship is manoeuvring on the up-river Trinity Berth, keep to port of the Pepys and Babergh PHBs to remain clear of the main channel.

The changeover from Harwich Harbour Authority to Associated British Ports is at the Fagbury SHB

The Orwell wends its way inland from Fagbury to Ipswich

Shotley Point Marina · Suffolk Yacht Harbour · River Orwell · Trinity Quay

River Orwell

(Fl.G.2·5s) off Fagbury Point, close N of the container berths. Nearby is a clearly marked underwater cable, which must be avoided if anchoring to await the tide.

The river is well buoyed and generally there is plenty of room and water outside the channel to avoid large vessels (which have total right of way and often use their horn to assert it). Remember most of them must do 8-10kn just to maintain steerage way in what is quite a winding and confined channel.

The deep water channel has been pushed further over to the Shotley bank by developments and

Suffolk Yacht Harbour

extensions of the Trinity Quay and a PHB, Babergh (Fl.R.2·5s), has been installed between the Pepys and Orwell PHBs, almost opposite the first SHB, Fagbury (Fl.G.2·5s). Once past the end of Trinity Quay you are in the Orwell proper.

To port, a little N of Shotley Marina, the river opens out into a gentle bay, called Stone Heaps, the name being a legacy from the old barging days, which offers a good anchorage, if a little rough when ships pass. The holding is good, water is plentiful at all states of tide and a shingle beach offers clean landing for a walk round the back of the marina to Shotley.

Trimley Marshes

Trimley Marshes lie on the E side behind a raised flood protection bank. Once a marshy bird sanctuary, they have been excavated and flooded by breaching the sea wall to make a proper wetland for wading birds. A walk along the wall with binoculars is always rewarding for birdwatchers.

Landing is possible at HW on a sandy beach backed by cliffs. It's a popular place to picnic and swim, but the bay is also a designated speedboat and water-ski area.

The downriver end of Trimley Bay is marked by the Trimley SHB (Fl.G.2·5s) and on the opposite (W) side of the channel is No.2 PHB (Fl.R.2·5s), which marks the start of the NW bend in the river round Collimer Point.

Off Collimer Point is a PHB marked Collimer (Q.R) and a SHB marked Stratton (Q.G). On the W bank also is the remnants of a tide gauge giving the depth of water over the natural riverbed, do not try passing inshore of it or you will pile into the remains of one of the many old barge hards once in regular use on the river. The river turns NW at this point.

Suffolk Yacht Harbour (SYH)

The first major landing point on the river is at Suffolk Yacht Harbour, a few hundred yards down river from the entrance to Levington Creek (drying) on the starboard bank. The entrance to the marina is a well dredged, 30m wide by 2m deep (at LWS) channel, marked with a SWB at the start of the approach then port and starboard hand posts with fluorescent topmarks along the channel.

Tides set across the channel and care is required not to be pushed onto the posts, especially at springs. They are substantial steel tubes and will do serious damage to topsides.

At night there are leading lights (outer Iso.Y and inner Oc.Y.4s); the lower light is on a post behind and slightly to port of the visitor's berths and the upper on a taller post near the head of the West Dock, their transit gives an approach up the starboard side of the entrance channel (see chartlet) from the SWB. Changes to the security lighting in the marina have made them easier to distinguish at night.

Visitors' berths and the HPYC race office lie directly opposite the entrance with the fuel berth just to their starboard. To port is the "public" slipway and the entrance to the West Harbour used by large yachts.

Suffolk Yacht Harbour

Suffolk Yacht Harbour has 24 hr entry

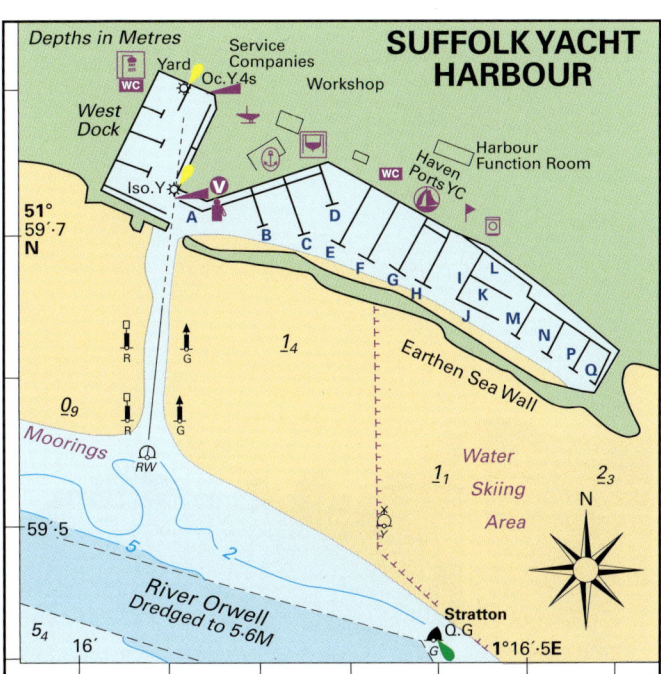

SYH is in an isolated location, 1M from the nearest bus stop to Ipswich and Felixstowe, but food and drink are available to visitors in the marina aboard LV87, the lightship home of the Haven Ports YC (for availability see club website at www.HPYC.com) There is also the Ship Inn at the village of Levington 1M away and the Harbourside Kitchen café alongside the marina entrance. There are two chandleries, one of which, Classic Marine, specialises in equipment for classic yachts.

Levington Creek

Leaving SYH and travelling up river, the next buoy, No.3 SHB (Fl.G.2·5s), lies off the entrance to Levington Creek. Visitors can pick up a vacant mooring and, approaching HW, take a dinghy up to the old barge quay at the top. From there it's a short walk to the Ship Inn at Levington. The channel in the creek is marked with withies but watch out for old iron posts and strapping near the quay.

Above Levington Creek, almost as far as the high-level Orwell Road Bridge, both shores of the river are lined with moorings between the deep-water channel and the drying banks.

Nacton

The Nacton Foreshore runs between Levington Creek and Nacton Quay, the next major landmark on the N side. The flat mud runs up into a narrow sandy beach, popular for picnics and teaching youngsters to swim, because the water gets very warm as it comes in over the mud in mid-summer. It's a good place to see cormorants standing on mud humps at LW with their wings held spread out to dry.

Long Reach and Butterman's Bay

Long reach is the wide section of the river running from Collimer to No 4 PHB (Q.R.) and Bay SHB (Q.G.) the entrance to Butterman's Bay, the reach up to Pin Mill. Off Long Reach to W is Colton Creek opposite Levington Creek, where there are several yacht moorings on both sides of the channel and a

SUFFOLK YACHT HARBOUR   IP10 0LN

Contact
VHF Ch 80
Callsign *Suffolk Yacht Harbour*
Harbourmaster ☎ 01473 659465/240
enquiries@syharbour.co.uk
www.syharbour.co.uk

Access 24hr
Facilities WC, showers, launderette, WiFi
Water On pontoons, use own hoses
Electricity At each berth
Fuel Diesel and petrol from berth at entrance
Chandlery and Classic Marine On site
Provisions Some from chandler, pre-order through Harbourside Kitchen (tel 07786 935472)
Gas Flo-Gas and Camping Gaz
Boat repairs Slipways (two), 75-T and 30-T hoists, 20-T crane
Scrubbing posts At head of West Dock, turn to port at entrance
Shipwrights On site
Sailmaker On site
Electrical engineers On site
Rigger On site
Mechanical engineer On site
Electronics On site
Brokerage on site
S/S Fabricators on site
Sea School on site
East Anglian Sailing Trust on site
Club Haven Ports YC (in old light vessel in marina)
☎ 01473 659658 www.hpyc.com
Pub/restaurant Ship Inn, Levington (1 mile)
☎01473 659573, Harbourside Kitchen, on site
www.harboursidekitchen.co.uk

7. RIVER ORWELL

Iconic East Coast watering hole, Pin Mill

recognised anchorage for sailing barges. During the summer there's often one or more of these stately craft anchored there.

At the top end of Long Reach, nestling under the end of a wooded cliff, sits a prominent, solitary white cottage, called Clamp House, which is reputed to have been a smuggler's den. No.4 PHB (Q.R) is directly opposite the cottage on the W side of the deep-water channel and, opposite that, the Bay SHB (Q.G). Upriver from both these buoys are double and triple rows of moorings, with a wide-open space in the lines of moorings under the trees on the S side, which is a good anchorage, sheltered from S and SW winds. On the S bank, lies one of the jewels of East Coast sailing, Pin Mill.

PIN MILL

Much has been written about Pin Mill and the famous boatbuilding yards of Harry King and Fred Webb, though even more column inches have probably been given over to the riverside pub the Butt and Oyster, which has one of the finest views of the river in both directions from the bar window.

Visitors to Pin Mill should look for several moorings with small orange pickup buoys with "visitor" painted on them. There are signs on the buoys giving you further information on using them. Getting ashore at Pin Mill requires a dinghy and a pair of boots, because there's a lot of mud, especially at LWS. A long hard is laid out from the shore almost to LW mark, so landing is possible at most states of the tide, but, if you go ashore at LW or early on the flood, pull the dinghy all the way up. There's a small rill – the Grindle – that runs down the upstream (W) side of the hard, enabling dinghies to float a long way up.

Similarly, if landing at HW or on the ebb, be prepared for a long drag back down. A vacant mooring may usually be used for an hour or two, if one can be found, but for longer stays, call King's Boatyard ☎01473 780258. A drying pontoon runs out in front of the yard.

PIN MILL IP9 1JW

Moorings
Contact King's Boatyard, operators of Tony Ward Moorings Ltd, ☎01473 780258; 07867 640650; or 07714 260568 (for visitor mooring enquiries) www.kingsboatyard.co.uk

Pub/restaurant Butt and Oyster ☎01473 780764

Provisions From shop in Chelmondiston. Early closing Wednesdays

Water Tap at Pin Mill SC

Boat repairs Two boatyards:
FA Webb ☎01473 780291
Harry King & Sons ☎01473 780258

Scrubbing post Contact King's Boatyard

Club Pin Mill SC ☎01473 780271 www.pmsc.org.uk

Woolverstone

Pin Mill is a small, unspoilt hamlet that lies in a steep valley running back from the shoreline up to the nearby village of Chelmondiston, from which buses run regularly to and from Ipswich. There's a grocer, butcher and Post Office in Hollingsworth's Store ☎01473 780225 at 'Chelmo', as it's known locally. Pin Mill Sailing Club ☎01473 780258 welcomes visiting yachtsmen. Next to the Butt and Oyster is the start of the Arthur Ransome's Walking Trail.

The barge hard and posts are still used by Thames barges and almost invariably there is one being worked on at weekends.

From Pin Mill, the river turns more N up Potter Reach and then back NW at Hall Point between the Park Bight SHB (Q.G) and the No.6 PHB (Q.R) into Cathouse Reach with the channel tucking under the wooded slope that shelters Woolverstone Marina and the Royal Harwich YC from SW winds.

Opposite Woolverstone Marina is the Cathouse SHB (Fl.G.2·5s).

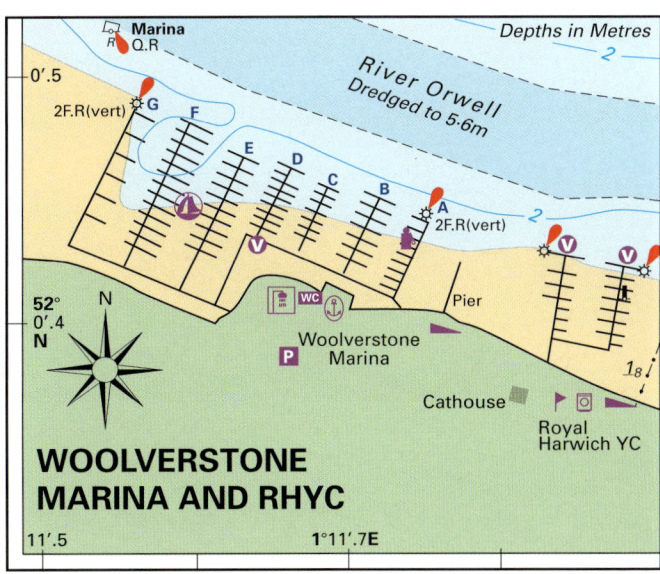

WOOLVERSTONE

The clubhouse of the Royal Harwich YC, which has its own jetty and 55 deep water pontoon berths on the S bank, is the next port of call. During the summer the club welcomes visitors, who can use the showers, bar and restaurant in the clubhouse.

Arriving from Harwich, the first pontoon is 'A', while pontoons B and C are within the marina pond, with D the row nearest the Orwell Bridge. Berth 1 is the first berth inside the hammerhead for each row.

If arriving out of hours, please tie up to one of the hammerheads and enquire at the bar.

Snuggled into the trees between the club and the adjacent Woolverstone Marina lies the fabled Cathouse, another smugglers' den. It is said that, when the coast was clear, a lamp was shown, but when the Revenue men were prowling, a white cat sat in the window as a warning. The Cathouse was recently purchased by Woolverstone Marina owners MDL.

Next door, up river, is Woolverstone Marina, an open-river 235-berth marina with pontoons held by

Royal Harwich YC and marina

7. RIVER ORWELL

Woolverstone Marina

massive piles driven into the riverbed in a deep pool S of the main channel. Its situation under the wooded shore is attractive, but it suffers from strong tidal streams through the berths and almost constant swell from passing traffic. The fuel berth is situated on the hammerhead of the first pontoon. Alongside it is a wide slip called the Cathouse Hard, also belonging to the marina.

The marina also has 45 swinging moorings in the river and runs a water taxi service on demand.

ROYAL HARWICH YC — IP9 1AT

Contact
RHYC office ☎ 01473 780319
Berth Master VHF Ch 77
Ian MacLean ☎ 07742 145994
(voicemail checked daily if unattended).
Alternatively, call the RHYC office
www.royalharwichyachtclub.co.uk

Visitors' berths By arrangement
Access 24hr
Facilities WC, showers, laundry (in clubhouse)
Water On pontoons
Electricity On pontoons
Bar/Restaurant In clubhouse (Check opening hours via website)
Slipway (dinghies only)

WOOLVERSTONE MARINA — IP9 1AS

Contact
VHF Ch 80
Callsign *Woolverstone Marina*
Harbourmaster ☎ 01473 780206, ☎ 07803 968209
woolverstone@mdlmarinas.co.uk
www.mdlmarinas.co.uk/marinas/mdl-woolverstone-marina/

Access 24hr
Visitors' berths As available. Swinging moorings with taxi service
Facilities WC, showers, laundry, WiFi
Water On pontoons
Electricity On pontoons
Fuel Diesel from fuel station on pontoon A hammerhead
Gas Ask at office
Engineer On site
Brokerage on site
Pub/Restaurant On site (closed 2023, check reopening)
Provisions Shops in Chelmondiston (see Pin Mill details)

Ostrich Creek

The Orwell High Level Bridge spans the river just before Ipswich

From Woolverstone up river, leave the No.7 SHB (Q.G) to starboard and the Marina PHB (Q.R) to port into Downham Reach. Here the channel begins to narrow markedly with unspoilt Suffolk parkland to be seen on either shore. Up ahead and spanning the river is the high level Orwell Road Bridge.

On the W shore of Downham Reach stands Deer Park Lodge, nestling in the woods with its own landing stage, and then the Stoke SC clubhouse and moorings providing a foreground to a Victorian folly. Called Freston Tower, the folly was reputedly built by one of the Paul family (famous for their barge fleet) as a garden dining room for entertaining guests to fine food and wine and views of the company's vessels plying up and down the river. Others say it was built for the education of their daughter with one floor for each day of the week.

The channel here is quite narrow but extremely well buoyed. When a ship is sighted, keep just outside the line of buoys on either hand until she passes. At the bridge itself, the channel narrows down to 92m (300ft) between the artificial islands that protect the bases of the eight piers carrying the bridge. The air draught is 43·07m (141ft) at LWS (128ft – 38M at HWS). Do not attempt to pass under the bridge at the same time as a ship, whatever her size.

Ostrich Creek

Once through the Orwell bridge – and do look up when passing under it, the deck is made in two sections with a considerable gap between them – there is a SHB E Fen (Fl.G.5s) marking the E side of the channel between the bridge and the downriver end of the Cliff Quay complex. Opposite is the West Power PHB (Fl.R.5s) and this should be left very close to starboard to stay just W of the deep water channel and clear of the shipping activities at Cliff Quay. About ¼M further N is the No.12 PHB (Q.R) that also marks the entrance to Ostrich Creek where both Fox's Marina and the Orwell YC are found.

Enter Ostrich Creek from the No.12 PHB, passing between the posts topped with R and G markers. The Orwell YC, on the N shore, has some drying moorings and water can be obtained from the clubhouse or from a floating pontoon. Fuel and oil are available at a garage adjacent to the clubhouse. There's a regular bus service into the centre of Ipswich.

Orwell YC www.orwellyachtclub.org.uk

Entering Ostrich Creek

7. RIVER ORWELL

Fox's Marina

Opposite Orwell YC, on the downriver side of Ostrich Creek, lies the 100-berth Fox's Marina and Boatyard, which has one of the largest chandlers on the East Coast, plus a club and a restaurant. Fuel and water are available from the clearly marked fuel berth, on the left as you go in.

FOX'S MARINA   IP2 8SA

Contact
VHF Ch 80 Callsign *Fox's Marina*
Harbour Master Lee Gilson/Peter Dyson (weekends)
Mon-Fri (12.30) ☎01473 689111 Fri (12.30) – Sun)
☎07515 051439
foxs@foxsmarina.com
www.foxsmarina.com
Access 24hr, dredged to 3m MLWS
Boat sizes Max 25m LOA, draught 3m
Facilities WC, showers, WiFi (free)
Water On pontoons

Electricity On pontoons
Chandler On site ☎ 01473 688431
Gas Ask at Chandlery
Fuel Diesel from fuel berth on S side of entrance
Club Fox's Marina YC www.fmyc.org.uk
Pub/Restaurant On site
Provisions Shops nearby
Boatyard Boat repairs and all services on site up to 70-T, masts to 110ft

Fox's Marina and Boatyard and Orwell YC

Ipswich Wet Dock

Ipswich Wet Dock

Although there are several buoys on the approach to the lock gates into the Ipswich Wet Dock, there is deep water from quayside to quayside and sufficient lighting to see when going in at night. Call *Prince Philip Lock* on VHF Ch 68 from about buoy No.9 (below the Orwell Bridge) to enter.

Although originally designed for commercial shipping, the lock has been refurbished and fitted with rope travellers on the high wall on the port side and a floating pontoon to starboard (when going in) for yachts to moor against as they progress through (you will need to set fenders low for this pontoon). On the very rare occasion that a ship or large vessel (a sail training ship for example) passes through they have priority and the pontoon is slipped and towed out while the vessel locks through.

Approaching the lock there is a waiting pontoon to starboard, just upstream of Cliff Quay, if you face a long wait – most boats prefer to jill about – a lot of ducks and gulls use the pontoon with clear consequences. The lock holds up to 20 x 9·75m yachts at a time, but usually it takes between six and 12.

Visual signals for entering or leaving the lock, which opens virtually on request, are a set of red and green traffic lights located above the Orwell Navigation Service's building on the E (or starboard) side of the lock.

There are big changes afoot at Ipswich. The port's owners, ABP have bought Neptune Marina with the aim of amalgamating it with the newly retitled Ipswich Beacon Marina. It is all part of a plan for the major redevelopment of the port. Although facilities at "Neptune" remain for the present until the marina is absorbed into an expanded Beacon Marina, all business and booking is done through the Beacon Marina office, now sited opposite I and J pontoons next door to the Last Anchor restaurant.

Visitor moorings are allocated near the facilities building, which is round the bend to port and several

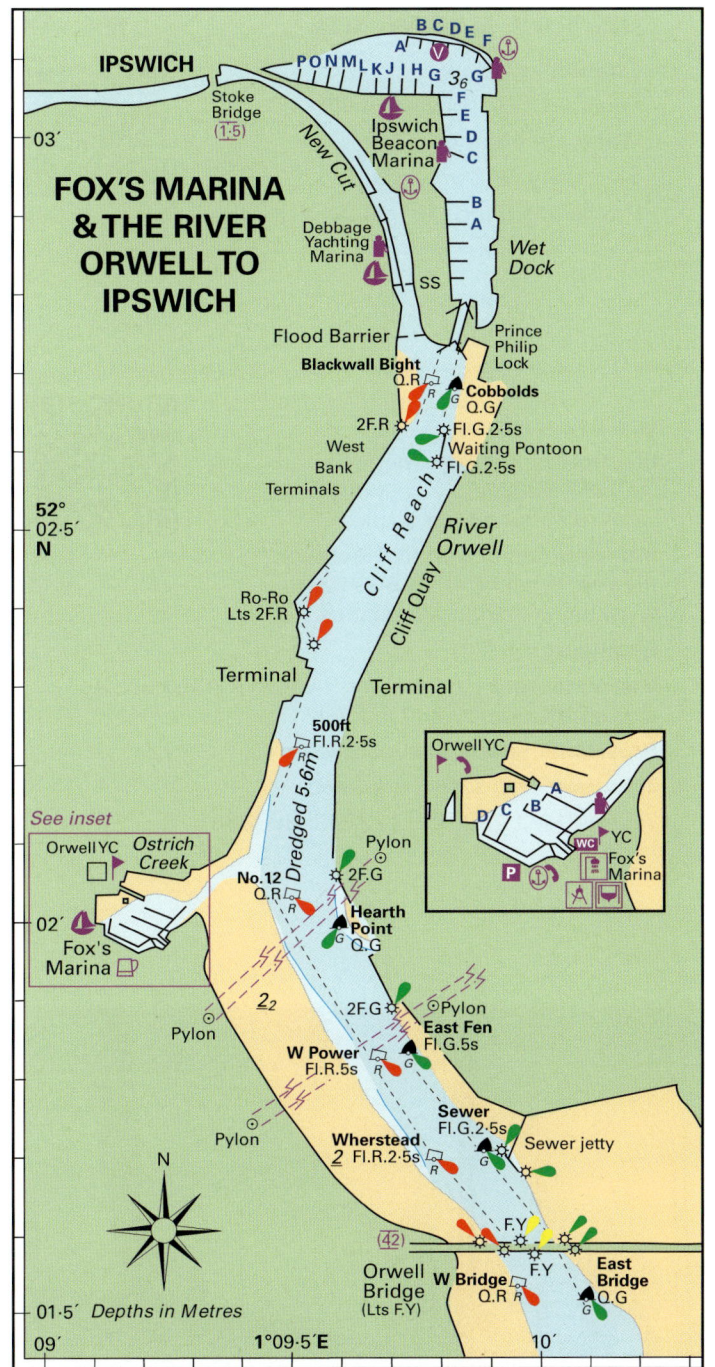

Approaching the Prince Philip Lock

East Coast Pilot • 71

7. RIVER ORWELL

hundred yards further on at K pontoon. Both marina sites offer the usual facilities and are equidistant from the town centre shops, a 10 minute walk away in the town itself. Beacon Marina has its own bar and restaurant, while the N dockside is steadily being redeveloped with bars and restaurants; it is a pleasant walk round the dock to the lock. Ipswich itself boasts restaurants, pubs, cinemas, a large park, and a highly regarded theatre.

NEPTUNE MARINA SITE IP4 1AX
Contact as below
Facilities WC, showers, WiFi
Water On pontoons
Electricity On pontoons
Provisions Shops 10 minute walk

IPSWICH BEACON MARINA IP3 0EA
Contact
VHF Ch 80
Callsign *Ipswich Beacon Marina*
Harbourmaster ☎01473 236644
ipswichbeacon@abports.co.uk
www.beaconmarinas.co.uk/our-marinas/ipswich-beacon-marina/
Facilities WC, showers, laundry, WiFi
Water On pontoons
Electricity On pontoons
Boat size Max 20m
Boat repairs Crane, 75-T boat hoist
Fuel Diesel from fuel berth pontoon C
Gas Ask at office
Electronics Rainbow Marine
☎07757 529686,
www.rainbowmarine.co.uk
Refrigeration Haven Refrigeration, Paul Meecham ☎07968 378231, www.havenrefrigeration.co.uk
Engineers On site
Bar/restaurant Last Anchor ☎01473 214763 on site, and others nearby and in town
Provisions Shops 10 minute walk
Transport Trains (15 mins walk)
Taxi ☎01473 222222, 222248, 888888

Inside the lock going into the Wet Dock complex

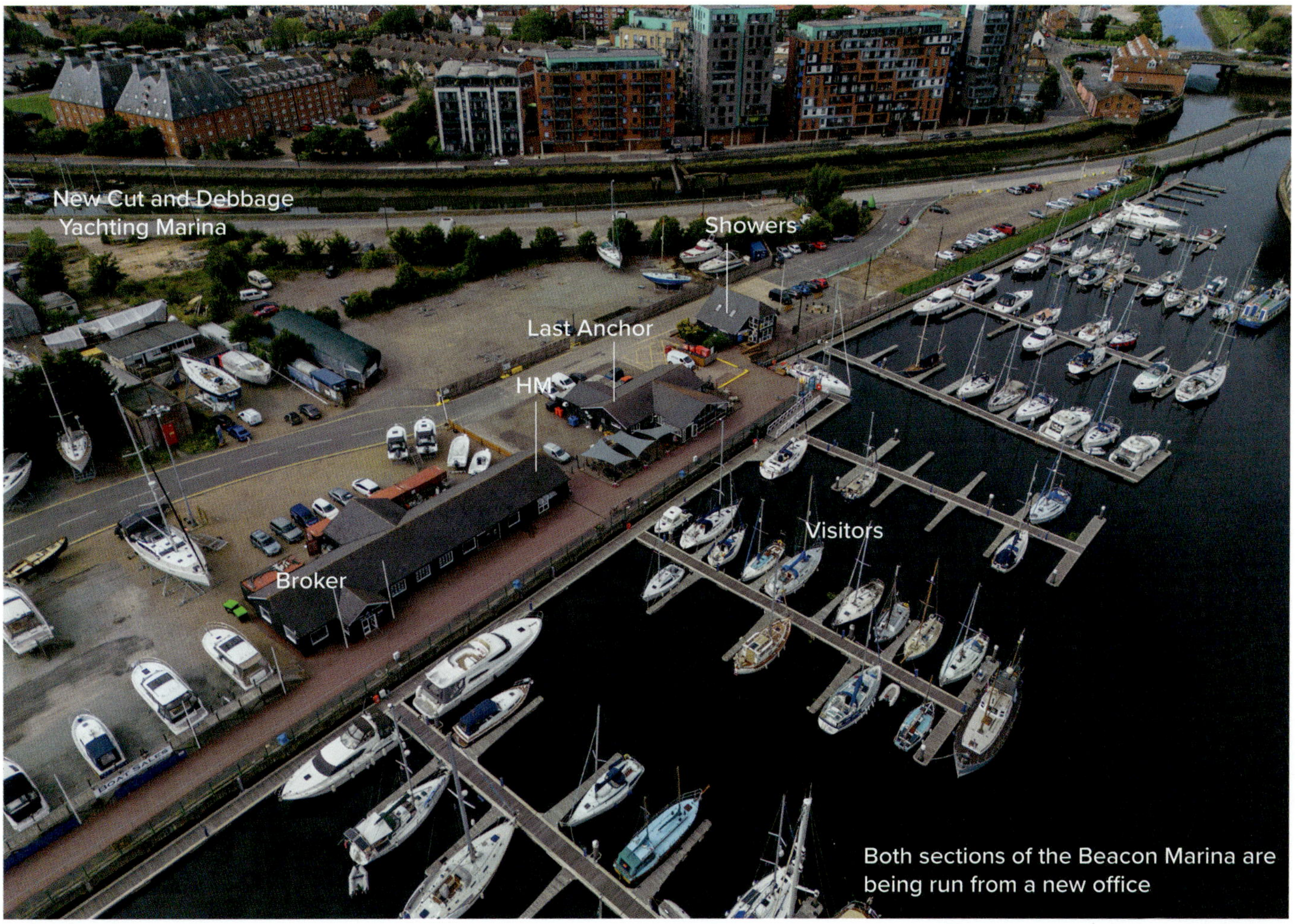

Both sections of the Beacon Marina are being run from a new office

The New Cut

To port of the entrance to the Wet Dock is a stretch of water called The New Cut. It is the point at which the river Gipping (from which Ipswich got its original name of Gyppeswick) joins the Orwell. Here Debbage Yachting has a yard and small marina situated about halfway between the entrance and the Wherstead Road Bridge, above which navigation is by dinghy only. Boats lie alongside pontoons and dry out. You can obtain fuel and water.

Debbage Yachting ☏01437 601169 / 07774 694226
office@debyacht.co.uk

A flood relief gate crosses the entrance to the New Cut; it normally lies on the riverbed, but when required it is raised to close the Cut. There are large warning signs and three vertical red traffic lights indicate when it is raised and that access to boats is denied.

Ipswich Wet Dock and the Beacon Marina. Plans are to remove the berths on the left and amalgamate them with the berth complex on the right

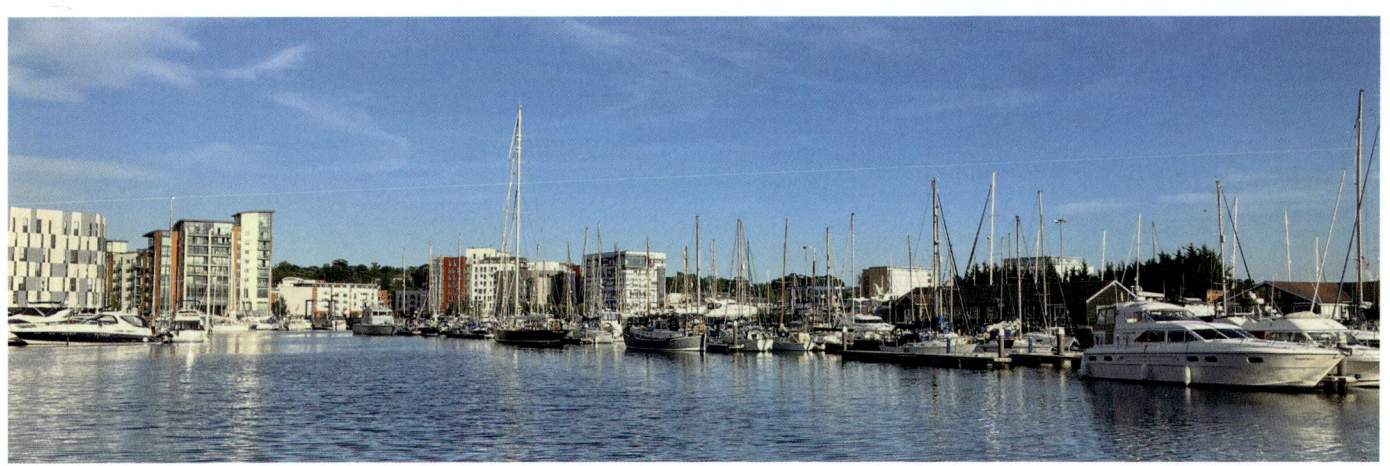

8. RIVER STOUR

Erwarton Bay • Shotley gate • Shotley Point Marina • Harwich & Dovercourt SC • Trinity House Quay • Harwich Town

Harwich has a long seafaring tradition

8. RIVER STOUR

⊕ **Landfall waypoint**

51°55'·20N 001°18'·50E SW of Landguard NCB on recommended yacht track

Charts

Imray 2000, C28

Admiralty SC5607, 1491, 1594, 2693

Tides

Walton HW

Mistley Quay HW Walton +0025

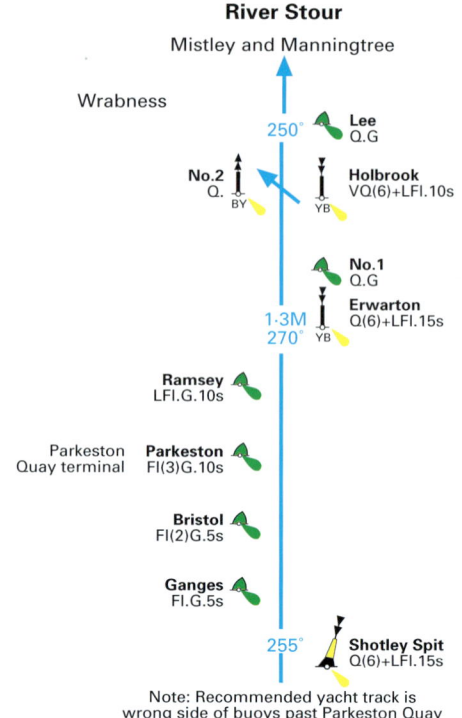

Introduction

The Stour forms the boundary between Suffolk and Essex and is one of the most attractive waterways on the East Coast, arguably running a close second to the River Deben. Less populated than the latter it is nevertheless an integral part of the 20-odd square miles of sheltered water within the Harwich Haven area. When winds blow hard from E or W you take to the Orwell, but if it's blowing from N or S, the Stour comes into its own, offering sheltered anchorages and good holding for most of its length.

Landmarks and approach

After crossing to the N side of the main shipping channel at the Guard PHB (Fl.R.5s Bell), turn W at Shotley Spit SCB (Q(6)+L.Fl.15s). Pass Shotley Marina control and workshop buildings to starboard (the roof of the workshop is marked MARINA in big black letters), below the Ganges Cliff, on top of which is a conspicuous pale green water tower and the newly refurbished mainmast (it is a Grade II listed monument) – the site is being developed for housing.

Beyond Shotley Spit you can often find a couple of Trinity House light vessels awaiting refit. The next landmark to starboard is the old *Ganges* jetty with a white radar tower on the seaward end.

Around the *Ganges* and Shotley jetties are several yacht moorings that extend up river into Erwarton Bay. Over on the S side of the river is the Harwich

Ramsey is the start of the Stour

International Port (Parkeston Quay), the seaward end accommodates wind farm tower erection vessels, while at about halfway along is the ro-ro berth for the

Crossing Harwich Harbour and passing Shotley Point

76 • East Coast Pilot

River Stour

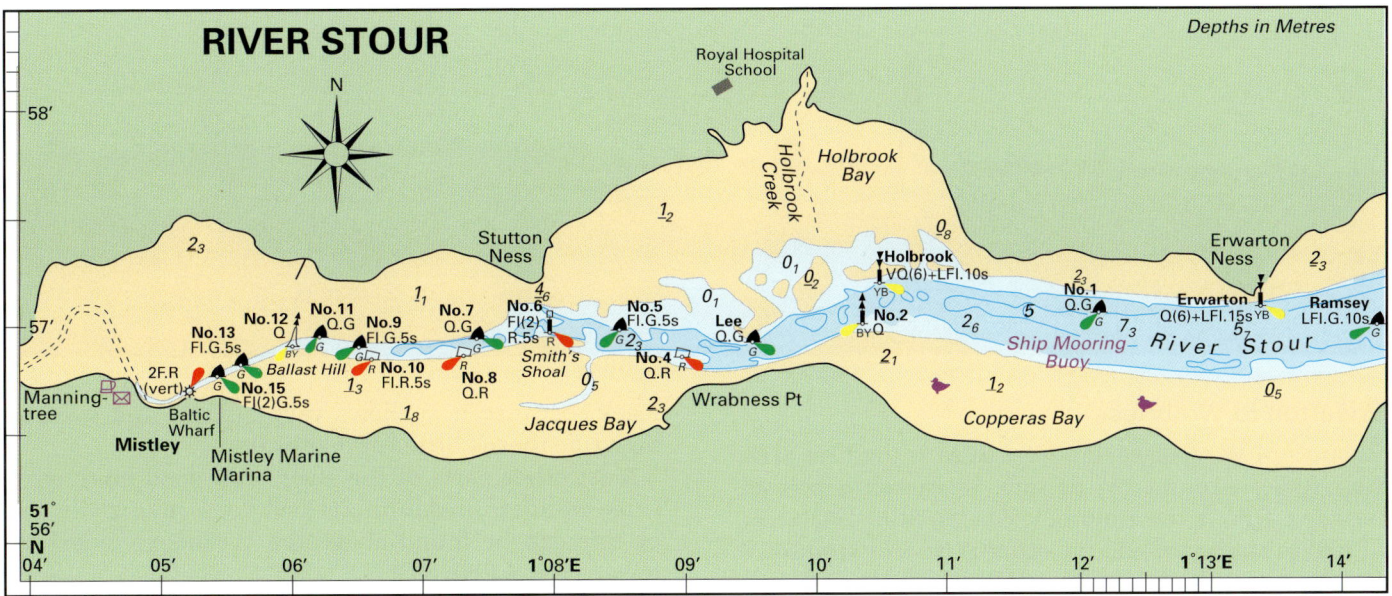

North Sea ferries. At the upriver end is an oil berth with a major fuel storage depot behind it.

There are two green buoys, Bristol (Fl(2)G.5s) and Parkeston (Fl(3)G10s) opposite the quays and yachts should keep the wrong side of these to leave room for ships turning and berthing or leaving. A third green, Ramsey (LFl.G.10s) marks the change from Harwich Harbour to the River Stour proper. There is an 8kn speed limit over the whole river.

River Stour to Erwarton Ness

The river is at its widest here where it opens out into Erwarton Bay on the N side. At the W end of Erwarton Bay is Erwarton Ness with a SCM (Q(6)+L.Fl.15s). Erwarton is a popular anchorage, although it lacks shelter in either E or W winds. There's good holding up river from the beacon but take care down river where there can be patches of kelp. There's good clean landing on a sand and shingle beach at HW ±1½hr and a muddy landing can be made at other times using an old barge hard that extends out from the shore to the base of the Ness Bn, almost to LW. There are several footpaths along the foreshore, one of which goes N across the fields to the village of Erwarton.

In S winds, if the Erwarton anchorage becomes uncomfortable, it is possible to find shelter across on the S shore in Copperas Bay in 4-6m of water.

From Erwarton the river runs almost straight for a good two miles with the deepest water a little N of the centre line with only one particular hazard to watch out for – a large ships' mooring buoy on the S side of the channel, W of Erwarton Ness. Occasionally you may find the most oddest of things moored here, such as 1,000m long pipes for feeding wind farm cables under the river Deben!

Just above Erwarton Ness is a popular anchorage in good holding mud

8. RIVER STOUR

Royal Hospital School, Holbrook, dominates the N shore

Erwarton to Wrabness

About ¾M W of Erwarton Ness SCM is the first SHB, No.1 (Q.G). Around 1M further W there's a pair of beacons. One is the Holbrook Beacon SCM (VQ(6)+L. Fl.10s) to starboard and the other is No.2 Beacon NCM (Q) to port. The pair act as a gateway to Wrabness.

The Holbrook Beacon also marks the entrance to the drying Holbrook Creek. This little waterway meanders N across Holbrook Bay towards the palatial buildings and prominent clock tower of the Royal Hospital School standing on the N shore. The NE corner of the bay is a popular wind- and kite-surfing area and has moorings for local boats.

There are two or three moorings laid in the lower reaches of the Creek. Anchoring positions are best found below half tide and by careful depth sounding.

WRABNESS

There are many moorings at Wrabness, which is marked by a plethora of beach huts under a low cliff on the wooded S bank; landing, except in emergency, is strongly discouraged as the beach is private. It is usually possible to pick up an empty mooring for a short stay but anchoring in the main channel is not recommended, because the holding is poor and it's used by small coasters bound to or from the Baltic Wharf at Mistley.

On the N side of the channel, opposite the cliffs, lies No.3 SHB (Q.G.), designated Lee. Do not stray N of this mark, because it shallows very quickly and even at high tide there's little depth of water.

Most other parts of the river offer good holding in some wonderfully glutinous East Coast mud and some of this can be found above the Wrabness moorings towards No.4 PHB (Q.R).

Wrabness to Mistley and Manningtree

The river is well marked all the way to Mistley, largely to assist the coasters that use the waterway, and it is essential to avoid sailing too far away from the buoyed channel, because the whole area dries extensively. This is another East Coast area where visitors are advised to set off up river before the mud banks are covered and to be aware that buoys can be blown across the banks they are marking.

Leaving Wrabness and carrying the tide with you, pass No.5 SHB (Fl.G.5s) to starboard and aim for the No.6 beacon (Fl(2)R.5s) about ¾M above the Wrabness moorings. It marks the N edge of the Smith Shoal, which moves the channel and best water well over towards the N side of the river at Stutton Ness. There's a good anchorage opposite No.6 under Stutton Ness, which has a sandy beach that can be reached by dinghy and is popular for picnics.

Leaving No.6, the channel is well buoyed and fairly straight with the buoys all well within sight of each other. Deeper draught boats should keep pretty well to the channel, although it's often tempting to follow a small bilge keel or centreplate cruiser gaily tramping across wide expanses of open water between Smith Shoal and Ballast Hill. Unless you have good local knowledge or are sure of your depth sounder and have an adventurous spirit, don't try it. You could find yourself stuck on some really sticky mud or some very hard gravely ground from which the aptly named Ballast Hill gets its name. In days of yore barges would settle on the hill and load shingle ballast.

After passing the unlit No. 12 NCB at Ballast Hill, the channel dives SW towards Mistley Quay. Head for Nos.13 (Fl.G.5s) and 15 (Fl(2)G.5s) SHBs and the Quay lies straight ahead. Keep close to the quay, because the whole area to starboard dries at low water.

Yachts used to lie alongside Mistley Quay at HW ±1½hr, depending on draught, the bottom being fairly level soft mud, but landing is now strictly forbidden and made impossible by a 6ft high steel mesh fence

Wrabness can be uncomfortable in E or W winds against the tide

Wrabness to Mistley and Manningtree

No.6 PHM

No.12 NCB

installed along the outer edge of quay. Unfortunately, the bollards are within this fence, so finding a ring or projection to secure to and rest before heading back down river is now not possible.

Mistley Marine runs a small drying marina on the S bank just down river from the Baltic Wharf (where small coasters unload building materials and general cargoes). Mistley Marine also runs a small boatyard and marine engineering works and operates a dredging barge. River moorings and quayside moorings dry out. There are no toilet or shower facilities.

MISTLEY MARINE
VHF Ch 71
☎01206 392127, 07850 208918

With care and a shallow draught, it's possible to reach ½M beyond Mistley to Manningtree at HW. Approach Manningtree by following the channel buoys carefully and remember that the whole area dries soon after HW. Boats with a draught greater than 1·5m need to avoid a nasty sand bank some 50m in front of the Stour SC clubhouse and quay. The advice is to skirt along the line of moorings.

Facilities have been greatly improved with a new pontoon standing off the quay wall adjacent to the club's secure compound, which has power and water laid on. In addition, there are three visitor's moorings, all drying. Best to call the Club's mooring master to ensure you get one, though. The club manages a total of 130 moorings in the upper reaches of the Stour. You must also be able to take the ground comfortably if you plan a stay. Visitors are few, but increasing, as people get to know about this attractive little town that has all a crew needs close to hand, including pubs, restaurants, shops, banks and a train service to London. You'll get a warm welcome at the Stour SC with its waterfront clubhouse, with showers and loos by arrangement, small hard jetty and slipway.

STOUR SC   CO11 1AU
☎01206 393924
Mooring master ☎01206 399006
www.stoursailingclub.co.uk

Manningtree is the head of navigation on the Stour and is the gateway to Dedham Vale and Constable country

East Coast Pilot • 79

9. WALTON BACKWATERS

⊕ **Landfall waypoint**
51°55'·1N 001°17'·9E Close N of Pye End buoy

Charts
Imray 2000, Y16
Admiralty 5607, 2695

Tides
HW Walton

ECP Honorary Port Pilot
Alec Moss ☏ 01255 850266
walton@eastcoastpilot.com

Main hazards

The Walton Backwaters lie S of Harwich, well protected by the Pye Sand and Sunken Pye on the seaward side of the narrow Pye Channel approach. This sand is unyieldingly hard and grounding should be avoided, particularly in onshore winds or when a swell is running. In fact, it would be unwise to attempt entry to the Backwaters at all in strong NE winds when big seas are breaking on the shallows and running up the Pye Ch itself.

Approaches

The two main landmarks when approaching the Harwich area from seaward are the cranes of Felixstowe container terminal and the Naze Tower standing on the cliffs just N of Walton-on-the-Naze. Either or both can be seen from several miles away in clear conditions.

Ideally you should locate the Pye End SWB (L.Fl.10s) before approaching the Backwaters. Finding the buoy especially in dirty or gloomy weather or at dusk with a setting sun in your eyes, can be difficult. Binoculars and GPS are a great help. At night the light can be hard to identify against the background of Felixstowe dock lights if approaching from SE.

Pye End SWB with Felixstowe container port in background

From N Approaching the Backwaters from Harwich, follow the charted yacht track to stay W of the deep water channel until near Cliff Foot (Fl.R.5s) before turning SW towards the Pye End Buoy. This course avoids the Cliff Foot Rocks and the shallow waters over the Halliday Flats off Dovercourt.

From NE Following the coast S from the Deben or Ore, cross the Harwich deep water channel by way of the charted yacht track to arrive at Inner Ridge PHB (Q.R) on the S side, then alter course W for the Pye End buoy.

From E Arriving from the continent see *North Sea Passage Pilot* (Imray) for passages to the Harwich area and follow local routes.

From S When arriving from the Blackwater, Colne or Crouch via the Wallet and the Medusa Channel in clear weather, the Naze Tower and the cranes of Felixstowe docks will be sighted while still S of Walton Pier.

Pass the Medusa SHB (Fl.G.5s), which is positioned 2¼M seaward of Walton Pier, and Stone Banks PHB (Fl.R.5s), while aiming for the Felixstowe cranes. This course should keep you E of the Pye End buoy but bring you close enough to spot it and identify it.

Once N of Walton Pier, all the way to Pye End, keep a sharp lookout for pot markers and fishing floats. You will also encounter several yellow racing marks in the area.

Entry

Entering the Pye Channel pass close to starboard of the Pye End SWB. From the buoy, shape a course of about 240° for just under 1M to reach the PHB No.2 (Fl(2)R.5s). Take care especially in murky conditions or with the late afternoon sun in your eyes as the buoys are quite small.

At this stage a look ahead will show no sign of a break in the coast; the Backwaters do not reveal themselves until much closer in. Not for nothing did Arthur Ransome name his famous book *Secret Water*.

The next buoy to make for is Crab Knoll No.3 SHB (Fl.G.5s), distant ⅓M, followed closely by an unlit SHB No.5, Heather J.

The lit PHB High Hill No.4 (Fl.R.10s) marks the N end of a deeper section of the channel towards the unlit No.4A and then the lit SHB No.7 (Fl.G.10s) and unlit PHB No.6. From there pass No.8 PHB and head directly for PHB No.10 (Q.R) and look for the small Island Point NCB (Q), which is not always easy to find and often appears to be out of position to the W.

First time visitors should keep a close eye on the depth and not stray outside the marks; the sand is as hard as concrete!

It is common to enter the Backwaters in the afternoon and the sun's glare on the water at that time can mean a very hard time spotting and identifying

Walton Backwaters

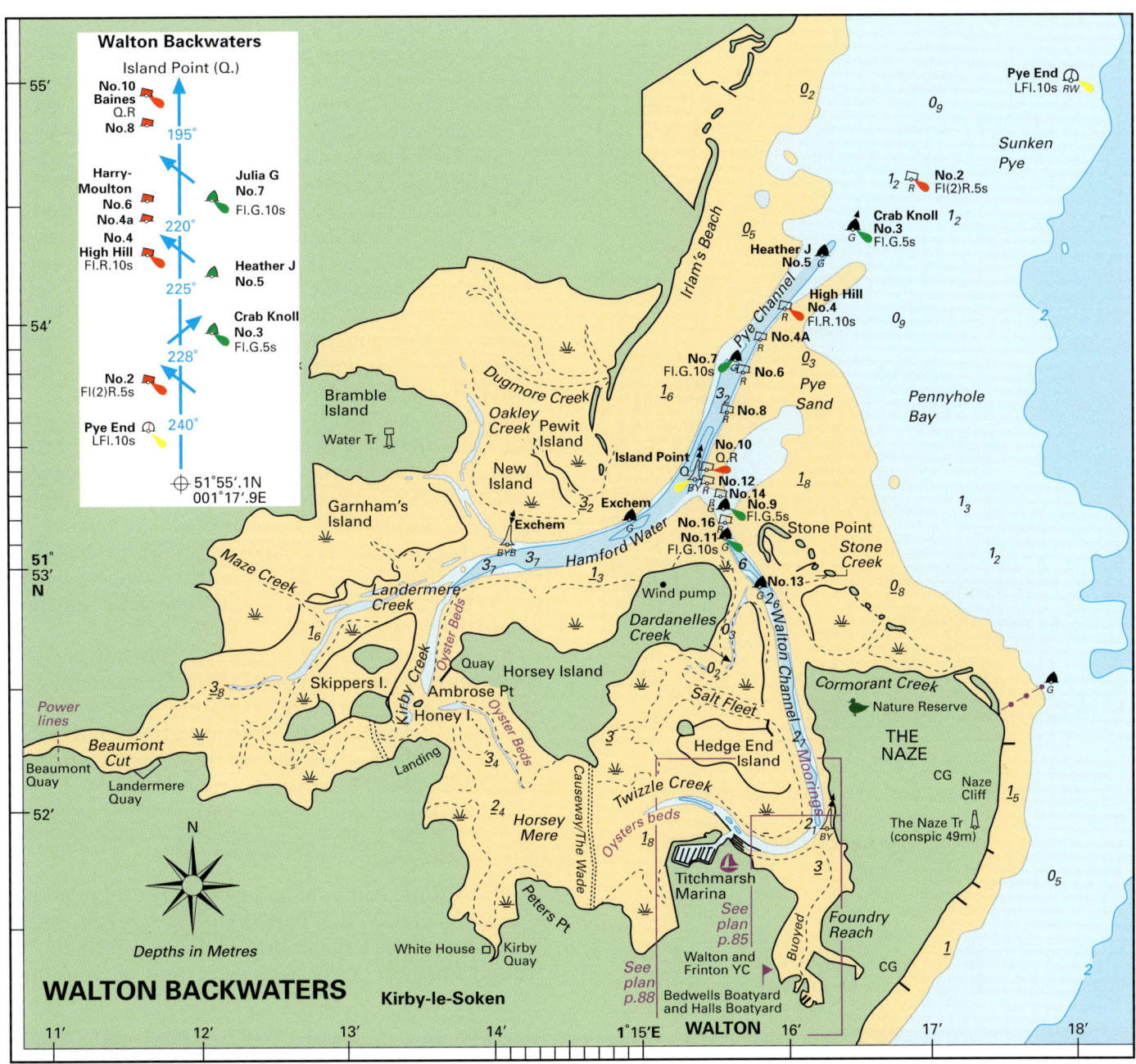

buoys until almost upon them. Polarising sunglasses may help and binoculars always do.

Because the Pye Channel is so narrow, running between banks of hard sand, the tide funnels through it and can easily reach speeds of more than 2kn, particularly on the early ebb.

Departing the Backwaters at night can also be an interesting experience, because the buoys that are lit tend to be hidden among the background lights of the docks at Felixstowe, while the unlit ones simply disappear in the darkness. It's essential to work out rough courses to steer. An up-to-date chart plotter can be of real benefit.

Speed limits

There is an 8kn speed limit in the approaches and within Hamford Water and this reduces to 6kn in creeks and channels leading off Hamford Water and to 4kn in congested areas.

Stone Point

Major changes have taken place at Stone Point, the junction of the Pye Channel with Hamford Water and the Walton Channel. Massive sand shifts meant the twisting channel around Stone Point had to be dredged and re-buoyed, luckily it seems to have stabilised (2023). The channel is narrow and steep sided and ebb tides at springs can run to a fierce 6kn at peak flow (in the second hour). At LWS there is around 0·6m over chart datum, but the bottom is uneven with ridges left from plough dredging operations. A useful up to date chartlet of the area can be found on the downloads page at www.eastcoastpilot.com, and on the WFYC website.

When bound up the Walton Channel towards Titchmarsh Marina or Walton town, leave the Island Point NCB (Q) to starboard and bear round SE to follow the line of unlit red PHBs. These and the No.9

9. WALTON BACKWATERS

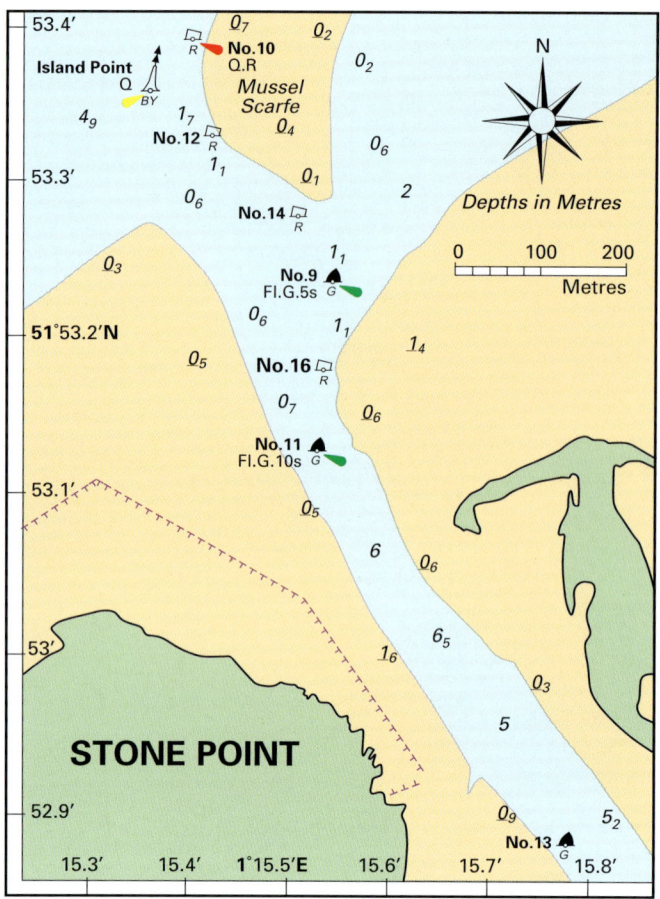

A check in late 2023 showed no change on this 2021 chartlet (original credit John Hale/W&FSC and available to download and print from www.eastcoastpilot.com)

SHB (Fl.G.5s) mark the way past Mussel Scarfe where the channel is narrow and at LW the buoys are often blown well out of position and lie over the banks or in the channel. Careful consideration must be given to tide and wind direction before deciding how close to pass these buoys and a sharp eye should be kept on the depth, which varies considerably.

The channel runs very close in to the beach around Stone Point where that side is steep to and forms a popular anchorage off the sandy beach. The water is relatively deep and tides run fast (3–6kn on a spring ebb), so care must be taken when setting an anchor. On occasion this may be tricky and more than one attempt may be needed to ensure a good grip. Nonetheless, it's a popular anchorage.

Small boats should be wary of a swirl or mini whirlpool that forms on the upriver side of Stone Point on the flood and again on the down-river side on the ebb. Both are strong enough to cause a sudden change of direction if not expected. The channel is narrowest opposite No.16 PHB and care must be taken when passing a vessel going the other way, especially on the ebb, which runs strongly. Take your time and follow the buoys carefully.

Landing is possible at all states of the tide and the beach upriver from the Point is good for swimming or having a picnic, but there is a nature reserve nearby and care must be taken not to disturb birds or damage plant life. Indeed, since the whole of the Backwaters is a Site of Special Scientific Interest (SSSI), such care must be taken throughout the area.

Walton Channel

W of the Stone Point anchorage is a SHB No.13 where a shallow creek, The Dardanelles, branches off to starboard around the E end of Horsey Island. The Walton Channel starts here with lines of moorings

Looking SE across Twizzle Creek towards Walton

84 • East Coast Pilot

Foundry Reach

The Spit NCB marks a long narrow spit jutting out into the junction between the Walton and Foundry Chs

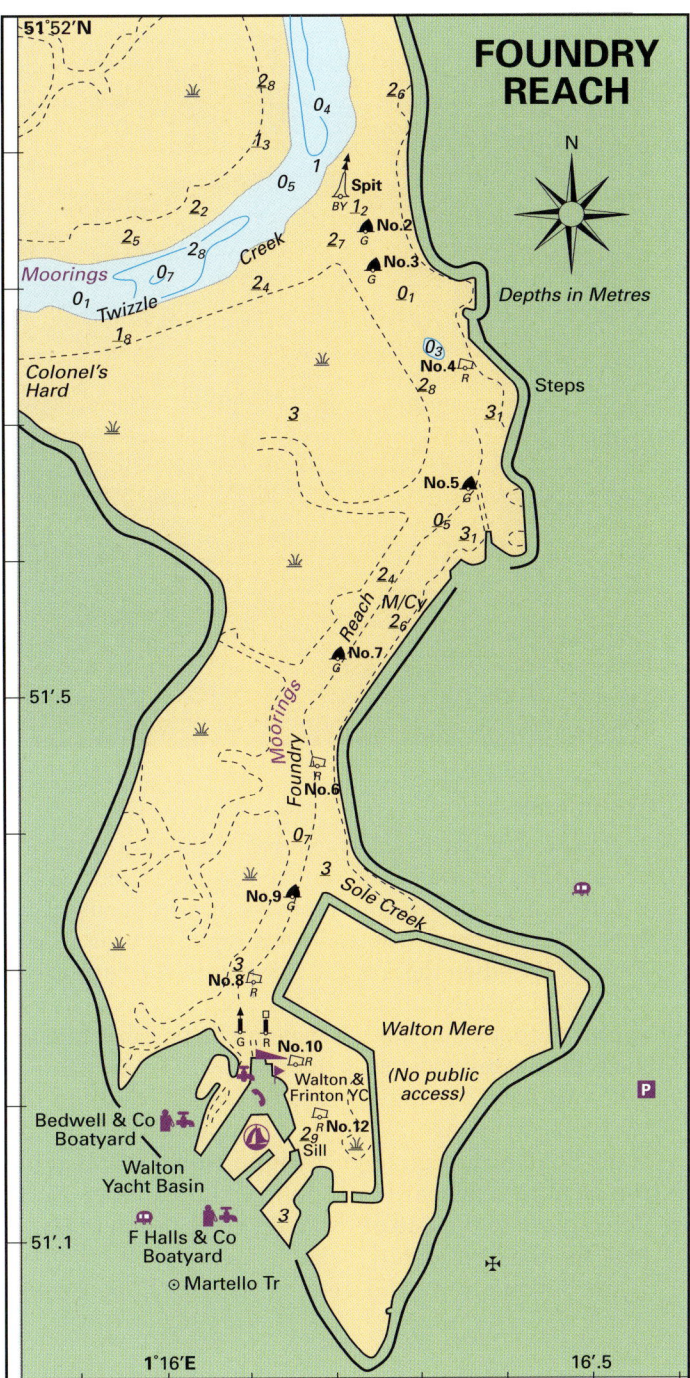

either side of the channel and extending S for almost 1M to the Spit NCB. This NCB marks the end of a spit between the Walton Channel, which runs on S past the buoy as Foundry Reach, and The Twizzle, which turns W towards Titchmarsh Marina and Horsey Mere. The spit is extending so if turning from The Twizzle into Foundry Reach stand well out round the mark. Equally, if coming upstream and turning into the Twizzle near LW, stay close to the moorings on your stbd side for the best water.

Walton & Frinton YC

The W&FYC has buoyed and marked the drying channel right up to its clubhouse, but the channel is tortuous, occasionally shallow and some of the buoys can be hidden by nearby moored boats, revealing themselves only at the last moment.

It is wise to wait until above half flood before heading up Foundry Reach, but then enter it by leaving the Spit NCB to starboard and heading straight through the 'gate' formed by No.2 PHB and No.3 SHB. Ahead you'll see a landing place on the E bank at No.5 SHB, but this is not for public use and does not offer access to the town.

Follow the port and starboard hand buoys in careful sequence. You will see the W&FYC clubhouse ahead from around No.7 SHB but continue to follow the channel buoys as far as No.8 PHB. At that buoy, if you intend to lie alongside the W&FYC quay on the W side of the clubhouse or to visit Bedwell's boatyard, turn

Approaching the W&FYC on the rising tide

to starboard between a green topped SHM post and a small flat topped buoy painted black over yellow with 'N cardinal' written on it. Be sure to leave this NCB to port (i.e. stay N of it). Then leave a red-topped post PHM to port and make for the quay ahead to port or turn to starboard, keeping close around boats in mud berths, and head on for Bedwell's quay.

The W&FYC quay is accessible at or near HW and there is a two-hour time limit on boats lying alongside it. There is a good hard and concrete ramp for dinghies right under the front of the clubhouse (its N side) where the end of the concrete landing is marked by a red topped PHM post, which must be left to port if going alongside the club quay. In days of yore W&FYC was a wind driven corn mill and barges used to lie alongside in the drying creek to load and unload.

9. WALTON BACKWATERS

The newly refurbished Walton Yacht Basin

Walton Basin

The Walton Yacht Basin is entered through a 5m wide break in the sea wall from the creek on the E side of the W&FYC. A retaining gate (opened by arrangement) is lowered to the creek bed to allow entry or exit for a short time at HW when there is 2-2·5m over it. A tide gauge is positioned beside the gate. Contact Bedwell & Co, as you approach (details in box). It may not be possible to open the basin's gate on low neap tides.

If you have arranged with Bedwell's to enter the yacht basin or are planning to approach the Frank Halls boatyard, turn to port round No.8 PHB, leaving the NCB to starboard, and follow the PHBs to No.12 (keep close to the end of the W&FYC pontoon at No.10 PHB for the best water).

Just beyond No.12 and a conical GRN/Y buoy turn to stbd and aim for the centre of the narrow entrance to the gated basin, initially, at a slight angle straightening up close to the entrance.

If you see a triangle on top of a pole in the centre of the entrance to the basin, do not attempt entry – this mark stands on top of the raised gate. Only enter when the gate and its mark have been lowered beneath the water and sufficient depth is shown on the tide gauge beside the gate. A green flag is shown at the entrance when the gate is open.

There are 60 berths with water and electricity on the pontoons. The entrance has been widened to enable larger boats to use the basin, maximum width 5m, the basin is accessible to yachts up to 2m draught and 12m LOA

Walton Yacht Basin gate open

Walton Yacht Basin gate closed

Titchmarsh Marina

WALTON ON THE NAZE   CO14 8PF

Contact
Walton & Frinton YC ☎01255 678161
office@wfyc.co.uk/ barandc@wfyc.co.uk
www.wfyc.co.uk
Access HW ±2hr
Facilities WC, showers
Slipway (contact club)
Water At W&FYC and in basin
Electricity On pontoons in basin
Provisions In town

Telephone At W&FYC
Post Office In town
Boat repairs Frank Halls ☎01255 675596
Bedwell & Co ☎01255 675873 or 07957 848031
Both located close to W&FYC with cranes/slips
Yacht Basin Bedwell and Co (out of hours)
John ☎07738 279642 or Petra ☎07798 731336
bedwellsboatyard@btinternet.com
www.waltonyachtbasin.co.uk
Pub/Restaurant W&FYC (☎01255 675526) and many in town
Taxi ☎01255 675910, 676887, 833441

The Twizzle

The Twizzle (or Twizzle Creek) runs W and NW from the Spit NCB, in the Walton Channel, along the S shore of Hedge End Island and W into Horsey Mere. Titchmarsh Marina is cut into land on the SW side of the channel.

From the Spit NCB, moorings continue along both sides of the creek and, just over a cable in, there are pontoons on the SW side (just as the creek turns NW) where boats berth alongside. Watch your depth passing the start of these pontoons, as boats lying alongside take the ground at low water and there are shoal patches in the channel.

Titchmarsh Marina

The entrance to Titchmarsh Marina is between the NW end of the pontoons and the SE end of a second line further up the creek, also on the SW side. A tide gauge on the SE end of the further pontoons shows the depth in the marina's entrance channel.

Turn in as soon as the entrance opens. There's a slipway to port with the fuelling pontoon beside it (at the head of 'A' pontoon) and the marina offices are in the buildingabove. Once past the fuelling berth the channel turns hard to starboard past the ends of each pontoon. 'A' is nearest to the marina office, 'H' the furthest away. Most pontoons have hoops rather than cleats.

The Twizzle (Twizzle Creek) — Walton Ch — Twizzle Creek — Entrance to Titchmarsh Marina

9. WALTON BACKWATERS

Titchmarsh Marina with Horsey Mere beyond

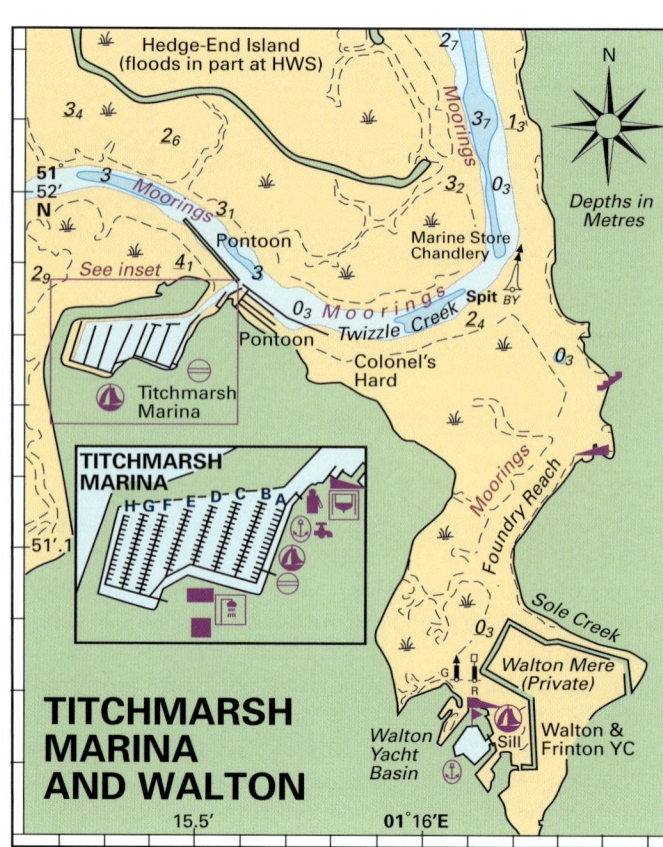

Note that it's about 1½M into Walton itself, so you may wish to get those bikes out to get there or to Frinton. Walton town centre is busy and there are grand views south across the Thames Estuary. At the time of writing the Harbour Lights restaurant was undergoing a major refit and was expected to re-open by Easter 2024 as a predominantly fish restaurant.

TITCHMARSH MARINA   CO14 8SL

Contact
VHF Ch 80 (0800–1800 in season)
Callsign *Titchmarsh Marina*
Marina Office ☎01255 67218
info@titchmarshmarina.co.uk
www.titchmarshmarina.co.uk

Access HW±5hr (1m - 1·3m in entrance at LWS)
Fuel Diesel (self-service) at berth in entrance
Facilities WC, showers, WiFi
Water Taps on pontoons (no hoses but can be borrowed from office). Also, on fuelling berth where hoses are provided
Electricity On pontoons, by card purchased from office
Gas Ask at office
Chandler Titchmarsh Chandlery ☎01255 676411, on site

Slipway Contact marina office
Brokerage David Morris ☎01255 781516 (Matt 07473 3493489)
www.davidmorrisboats.co.uk
Engineers French Marine Motors ☎01255 850303
Electronics Willmyboatfloat Ltd ☎01255 762505
Provisions In town plus some basics at chandler on site, including fresh bread to order
Post Office In town
Boat repairs 2 x 35-T travel-lifts, 25-T mobile crane, engineers and electronics on site
Scrubbing berth Against wall near fuel berth
Pub/Restaurant on site
Taxi ☎01255 675910, 676887, 833441

Horsey Mere

Above Titchmarsh the Twizzle continues to wind its way NW and then W out into the open area of Horsey Mere. It is navigable to the W end of Hedge End Island by shoal draught boats at most states of the tide, but care must be taken to avoid grounding on oyster layings marked by withies.

At HW the Mere is a large expanse of shallow sailing water, but at LW it is just a sea of mud. A causeway, The Wade, crosses the middle of the Mere from the mainland to Horsey Island. Boats with a draught of not much more than 1m can cross it, but it must be close to HW, preferably on spring tides. There is no obvious point at which to cross the Wade or where you can expect the greatest depth of water; it's a case of watching the depth sounder and taking it gently while being prepared to retreat.

At HW springs, if heading westward across the Mere, take care on the approach to Kirby Creek where it's hard to spot the submerged, marshy extremity of Horsey Island. Stand well off the island until you're sure you're into the deeper waters of Kirby Creek.

On the W side of the Wade, Kirby Creek (see page 89) leads away NW and runs round the W end of Horsey Island to join Hamford Water. An even less well-defined arm of the creek heads off S towards Kirby Quay. Readers of Arthur Ransome's book set in the Backwaters, *Secret Water*, will recognise Kirby

Quay as Witch's Quay and Horsey Mere as the Red Sea with Hamford Water as the *Secret Water* of the title. Unfortunately, Kirby Creek, where it winds S to Kirby Quay, is not so well marked as in the book, but it still provides a wonderful area to explore by dinghy.

Hamford Water

Hamford Water – sometimes known locally as the West Water – runs SW from the Island Point NCB (Q) at the S end of the Pye Channel (the entry channel to the Backwaters). Leave the Island Point buoy to port and Hamford Water opens ahead.

Depths are good up past the SHB marked Exchem, where the channel bends more to the W, and on as far as the ECB, also named Exchem, at the entrance to Oakley Creek. This is a popular reach in which to anchor, but can be uncomfortable if the wind picks up from NE or E. An anchor ball or riding light is strongly advised.

Oakley Creek

The Exchem ECB, which carries a radar reflector, marks the end of a spit out from Garnham's Island on the W side of the entrance to Oakley Creek. Leave the buoy close to port to avoid the mud on the E side when entering Oakley. Silting has created a bar across the entrance, but it's not enough to prevent entry after half flood (earlier with shallow draught). Seals often bask on the exposed mud inside the entrance.

Oakley creek runs N between Bramble Island and Pewit Island with a branch, Bramble Creek, turning off W along the S side of Bramble Island. Posts topped with red squares or green triangles mark the winding channel in from the entrance and must be followed carefully.

At the top of Oakley Creek is the Great Oakley Dock, which serves an explosives factory at the head of the creek. Small coasters call in, usually at weekends and this, combined with the narrowness and lack of water above Bramble Creek makes Oakley a place where you shouldn't anchor. However, if you enjoy exploring creeks and gutways on the tide with a good chance of seeing plenty of seals, it's worth visiting as the tide rises, even if only by dinghy.

Back in Hamford Water, the short stretch between Oakley Creek and the entrance to Kirby Creek is a popular anchorage with good depths.

Kirby Creek

Running S from Hamford Water, between Horsey Island and Skipper's Island, Kirby Creek turns SE around the corner of Horsey out into the Mere.

When approaching the entrance to Kirby Creek, keep a close eye on the depth, but it is best to enter from E along the Horsey Island shore to avoid the long spit out from the NE corner of Skipper's Island, which is unmarked and is a magnet for yacht keels.

There is an amateurish and dilapidated sign warning against anchoring because of oyster layings on the port hand side going in from Hamford Water

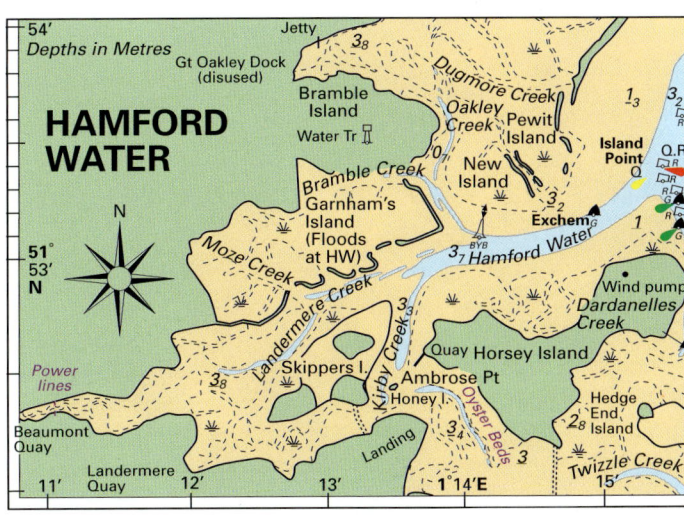

and there are no withies marking the beds and no indication of oyster beds when entering from Horsey Mere.

It is possible to anchor where Kirby Creek divides around Honey Island, best water is in the stbd arm where there are several moorings, before heading E into Horsey Mere. It is possible to land by dinghy on the mainland shore opposite the SE corner of Skipper's Island. From there it's a sea wall walk of about 1½M to Kirby-le-Soken for shops and a pub.

Landermere Creek

Immediately W of the entrance to Kirby Creek there is a mud bar where the spit from Skipper's Island has broadened across the main channel. Depending on draught, it may be necessary to wait until above half tide to cross this bar into Landermere Creek itself. Once over it, there is a ½M reach in which to find depth enough to anchor before the creek turns sharply SW around the corner of Skipper's Island towards Landermere Quay.

In the reach along the W side of Skipper's Island there are a couple of moorings, but plenty of room to anchor N of them. Immediately S of the moorings the creek divides with one arm rounding the SW corner of Skipper's Island and returning E to join Kirby Creek, and the other continuing W towards Landermere Quay.

For going ashore at Landermere Quay it is best to anchor or borrow one of the moorings then go in by dinghy, because the approach is not clear and is unmarked.

Towards HW it is also possible to explore by dinghy above Landermere Quay, even reaching Beaumont Quay, the most W'ly point of the Backwaters by way of Beaumont Cut, a straight, dug channel that is crossed by low power cables, preventing anything much larger than a dinghy with a mast from reaching the quay. Guy's Hospital, London, built the quay in 1832 using stone from the old London Bridge, which was demolished in that year. There's a preserved lime kiln at the eastern end.

10. RIVER COLNE

10. RIVER COLNE

⊕ **Landfall waypoint**
51°44'·0N 001°05'·4E Immediately NE of Knoll NCB
Charts
Imray 2000, Y17
Admiralty SC5607 and 3741 for Colne N of Brightlingsea
Tides
HW Walton +0025
Contact
Harbourmaster
VHF Ch 68
Callsign *Brightlingsea Harbour*
☏ 01206 302200 ☏ 07952 734814

Main hazards

The main hazards to be avoided when approaching the Colne are the long NE–SW stretch of the Gunfleet Sands and Buxey Sand, followed by the shoals of the Knoll, Eagle, Priory Spit, Colne Bar, Bench Head and Mersea Flats.

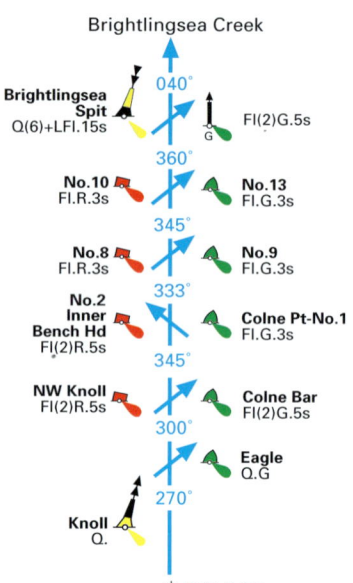

N Eagle NCB, target for vessels coming down the Wallet

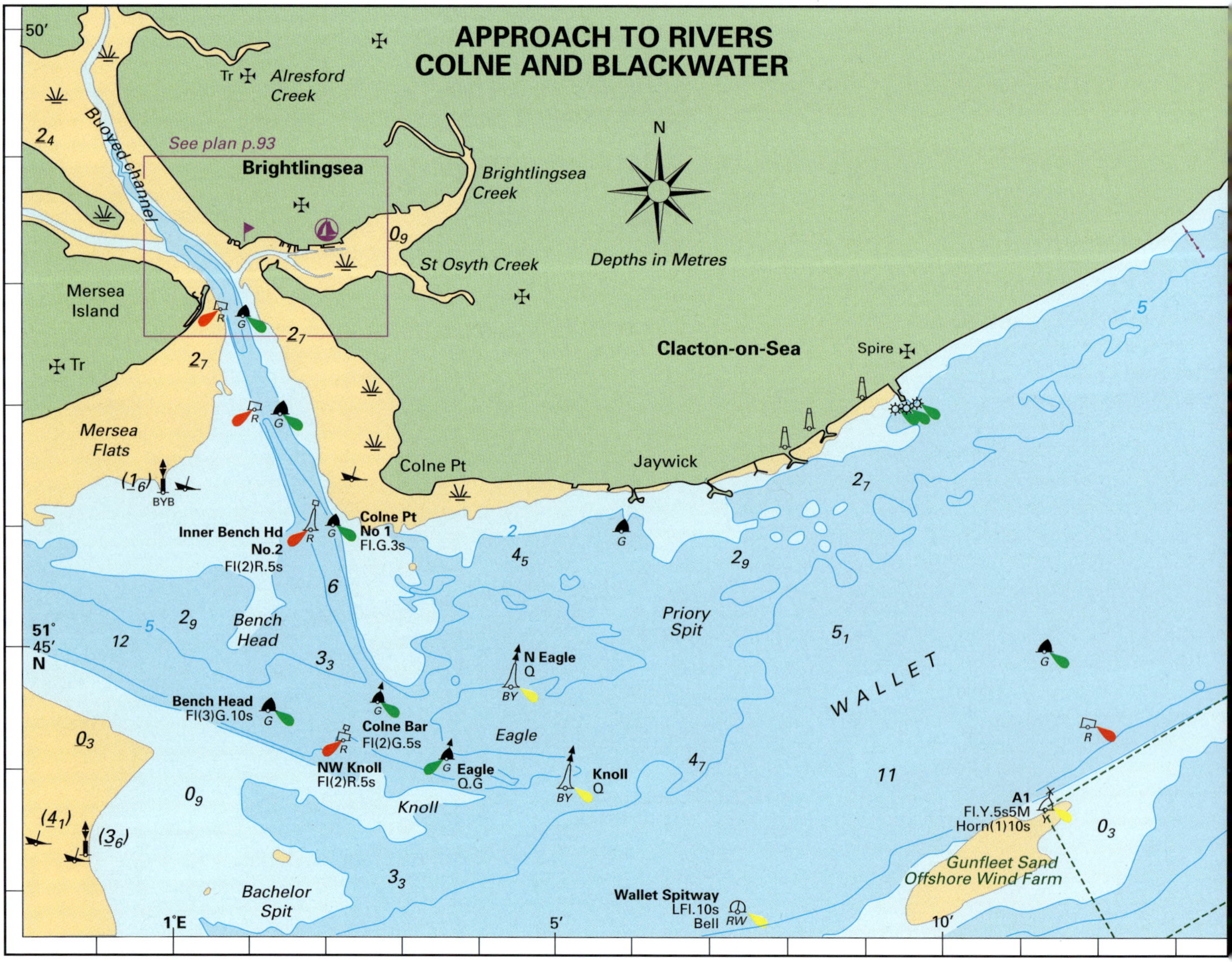

92 • East Coast Pilot

River Colne

Channels through or around these hazards are well buoyed, but navigators must identify each buoy carefully and ensure that progress is made from one to the next in the correct sequence. It may be tempting to cut corners, but it's rarely worthwhile. It may appear that you are in clear water with good depth but wander off course and that can change with little warning.

Buoyage moves and changes as banks and shoals shift, so keep your charts up to date.

Approaches

You can approach the Colne from the NE (Harwich and rivers to the N), the SE or S (across the Thames Estuary or from the Crouch and Thames), and from the W (River Blackwater). For routes from the Continent see *North Sea Passage Pilot* (Imray). It can be entered night or day.

From the NE, SE or S All routes from seaward converge on the Knoll NCB (Q), which should be left

East Coast Pilot • 93

10. RIVER COLNE

to port. From there, shape a course to leave first the Eagle (Q.G) and then the Colne Bar buoy (Fl(2)G.5s) to starboard with the NW Knoll (Fl(2)R.5s) to port.

When sailing round from Harwich, a course close to the coast enables vessels to pass N (inshore) of the N Eagle NCB (Q) and from there to make for the Colne Bar buoy.

Above half flood a course direct from the N Eagle to the Inner Bench Head buoy may be considered, but this means crossing the Colne Bar, which can be rough in stronger winds and should be avoided on the ebb. Be aware too that the tide sets strongly to the W here on the flood (and E on the ebb).

From the Bar buoy a course of about 345° will take you to Colne Pt No.1 SHB (Fl.G.3s) and the Inner Bench Head No.2 PHB (Fl(2)R.5s).

The Inner Bench Head marks the beginning of the deepwater Colne channel. Few buoys are now used to mark the channel and the next buoys are a mile distant. These are the No.8 (Fl.R.3s) PHB and the No.9 (Fl.G.3s) SHB.

The Colne Bar buoy marks the seaward end of Colne Bar

Inner Bench Head, the real start of the Colne

From W When approaching from the W (the River Blackwater), sea state, tide and draught will dictate how far off the Mersea Flats you need to stand. With a deep draught and rough seas at low water (last of the ebb out of the Blackwater, first of the flood up the Colne) you may need to sail out round the Bench Head SHB (Fl(3)G.10s), towards the Colne Bar buoy and then N towards the Inner Bench Head to avoid the very extensive Bench Head Shoal.

With less draught or more water and better sea conditions a course across the shoal directly to the Inner Bench Head is possible. If taking this approach, beware the large unlit 'Fishery' yellow spherical buoy positioned about a cable W of the Inner Bench Head buoy.

Finally, with shallow draught or towards HW with calm water, an inshore course can be set to skirt the Mersea Flats, keeping S of the Molliette ECM wreck beacon on the Cocum Hills. From there a course of about NE will lead to the No.8 PHB (Fl.R.3s) and the deep water Colne channel.

The Mersea Flats, inside the Molliette ECM, are indeed flat, but only cross them above half tide and with shallow draught in calm conditions. It does shorten the passage to the Colne, but by surprisingly little.

When approaching the Colne from the Blackwater at night, it's best to do so via the Bench Head and Colne Bar buoys. It might be a longer route than you would take in daylight, but it follows the deep water and you have the benefit of lit buoys. Similarly, from other directions, finding the Knoll then approaching from there means a lit approach in deep water all the way. It's certainly a good plan in rough weather at the bottom of the tide.

Entry

Once into the Colne deep water channel, it is marked with pairs of port and starboard lit buoys. The sides are steep to (more so on the W side), so if tacking, keep an eye on the depth and it will be quite apparent when you leave the channel across the line of buoys.

Once past No.8 PHB and No.9 SHB, the shingle bank of East Mersea Stone appears ahead to port, probably with a few craft at anchor, and the town of Brightlingsea ahead to starboard with its prominent block of waterfront flats making a clear landmark.

From No.10 PHB (Fl.R.3s) and No.13 SHB (Fl.G.3s) onwards, the river can be quite busy, particularly if there are dinghies out racing, so a sharp lookout is needed to avoid other craft as well as to pick out the necessary navigation marks. Note also that there is plenty of commercial traffic in and out of Brightlingsea.

The main place for mooring and re-supplying on the Colne is Brightlingsea, while a popular anchorage is across on the W side in the Pyefleet.

BRIGHTLINGSEA

From No.13 SHB, Bateman's Tower (Fl(3)20s), a pale coloured structure with a dark conical roof can be seen ahead on the shore beyond the Brightlingsea Spit SCB on Westmarsh Point. Entrance to Brightlingsea Creek and harbour is to stbd between the Brightlingsea Spit SCB (Q(6)+L.Fl.15s) and the green SHM Beacon (Fl(2)G.5s) off the Point Clear shore.

Leave the Brightlingsea Spit SCB close to port and the SHM beacon, which has a gauge on it showing depth in metres over the bar, to starboard. The channel has been dredged to +1m below CD right up to Oliver's the commercial wharf. Refer to the depth on the gauge as you enter.

Make good a course of about 041°T from close to the PHM to keep the two leading marks on the shore in transit. These are vertically striped white/red/

Brightlingsea entrance is marked by a post with tide gauge on stbd side

The leading lights can be difficult to spot against the clutter of houses and roofs

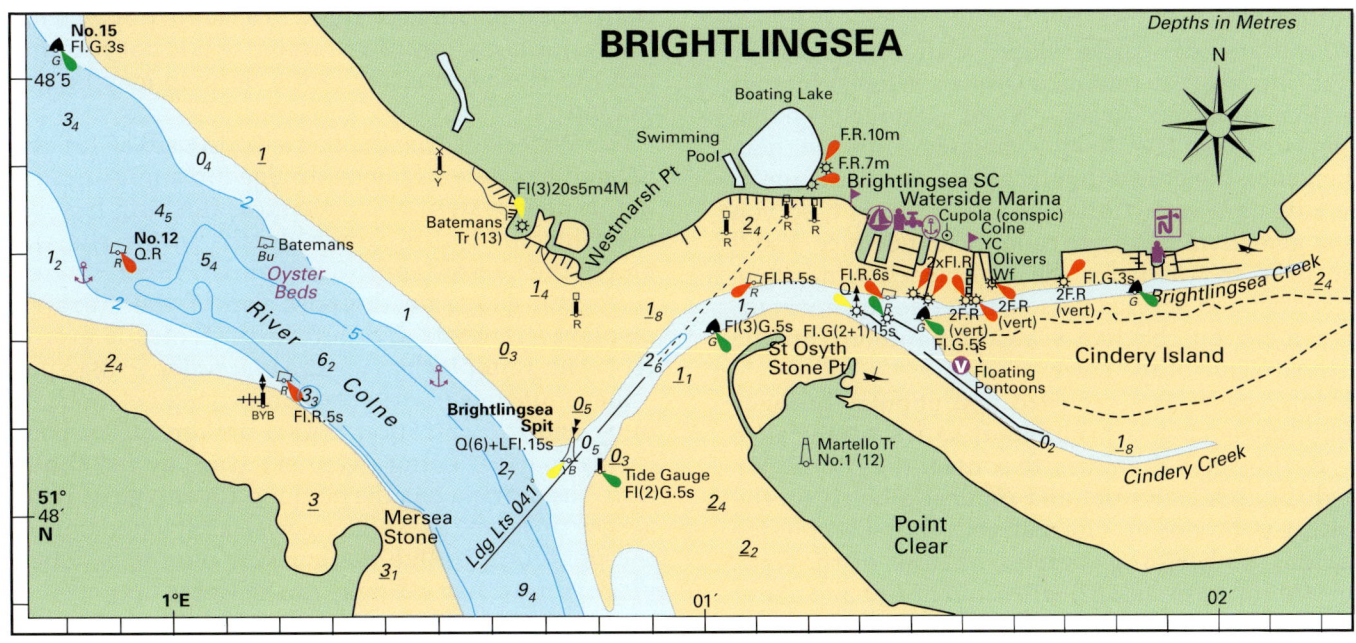

10. RIVER COLNE

The channel into the marina is marked by a red can on the downriver side of the entrance channel. The HM will guide you in and take your lines

Brightlingsea is a busy harbour and you need to keep a sharp lookout

white panels on white posts W of Brightlingsea SC's white clubhouse and are lit at night with 2 F.R. lights. (They are known locally as the 'cricket stumps' and can look white/black/white if the light is poor or the sun behind them.) They can be hard to see from a distance but look for a tall spire that stands up behind them, but not quite in line.

Follow the lead line until abeam the green buoy (Fl(3)G.5s) and turning to stbd pass about 50m S of the PHB (FlR.5s), ie in mid-stream. When the red buoy is abeam turn further to stbd and pass 10m N of the NCM (Q.Fl) at the seaward end of the first pontoon. There's a welcome sign on the beacon. There's a PHB (FL R.6s) on the N side of the creek that marks the entrance channel into the Waterside Marina, which has a sill that dries 1m above CD.

At night you may have trouble sorting out all the lights. There's the block of flats to port, the Waterside PHB (Fl.R.6s), and lights beyond on the end of the long town jetty (2 F.R) and pairs of fixed red vertical lights on the Colne YC hammerhead, as well as the wharf just upstream, while ahead to starboard you will see the pontoon NCM (Q), and the second pontoon Fl.G(2+1) 15s.

A variety of cargo ships visit the Port of Brightlingsea (the renamed Oliver's Wharf) further up Brightlingsea Creek, N of Cindery Island, especially near HW. Keep a sharp lookout for them when entering or leaving the creek, because some of the ships are constrained by their draught, so you must give them adequate room to manoeuvre. You'll also need to watch for the high-speed wind farm personnel and service vessels that use the harbour. They moor on the two seaward pontoons on the starboard side of the river.

Brightlingsea is a crowded and popular harbour where anchoring is prohibited, so it's essential to try, during daylight hours, to contact the HM (Ch 68 Brightlingsea Harbour) and request a berth on the floating pontoons or, alternatively, in the Waterside Marina, the berthing complex in front of the flats. The HM (or an assistant) will often be out and about on the water to help, advise and guide visitors to a harbour pontoon berth and will probably come out to meet you just to seaward of the pontoon NCM, in a harbour launch with 'Harbourmaster' written on the topsides during working hours.

You may also need to avoid the Brightlingsea/Point Clear/East Mersea Stone ferry, which plies to and fro across the harbour. The speed limit within the harbour is 4kn.

To the SE of the first two pontoons, there are a further two in parallel, which are very long indeed. If you arrive out of harbour office hours, leave the first pontoons to starboard and berth in a visitor's berth at the seaward end of the northern of the two longer pontoons about 150m beyond the NCM.

At LW there is limited depth on the inshore side of the pontoons, so be careful when turning. Tides run swiftly in the creek (up to 2kn) and must be considered when berthing alongside or departing.

A water taxi service (also on Ch 68) makes trips ashore from the pontoons easy and it's much safer than crossing from the shore in a laden dinghy when the water is choppy. If the water taxi is not running, call the Harbourmaster on Ch 68 who may be able to help.

The Waterside Marina has a drying sill at 1m over CD and has recently been dredged to a minimum of 2m, a new system of mechanical flushing has also been installed to maintain depths inside the wall and in the narrow approach channel. There is a clear sill depth gauge on the port arm of the entrance, displayed inwards and outwards. Access is around HW±3hr. Enter by leaving the Waterside PHB to port – there may also be a port hand withy between the buoy and the entrance; it gets broken off by boats trying to enter being swept sideways by the ebbing tide. The marina has the obvious advantage of ready access to shore, as well as power and water taps on the pontoons, unlike the harbour pontoons, where visitors must use a dinghy or the water taxi.

Brightlingsea

BRIGHTLINGSEA CO7 0AX

Harbour pontoon moorings

Contact
VHF Ch 68 Callsign *Brightlingsea Harbour*
Harbour office ☎01206 302200
www.brightlingseaharbour.org
mail@brightlingseaharbour.org

Access All Tide

Water taxi VHF Ch 68 01206 302200

Waterside Marina
For berthing contact HM. Water and electricity on pontoons. Meter card from HM

Weather and Tidal Height Details on Hbr App and the website at www.brightlingseaharbour.org/live-data

Scrubbing posts and slipway (Town Hard) call harbour office

Fuel Diesel by arrangement with harbour office, sited by Pioneer Sailing Trust shed

Facilities New uni-sex facilities with showers and laundry at flats complex (code from HM)

Pump-out By diesel berth, as above, by arrangement with harbour office – Free

Water CYC hammerhead. Activated by a coin in slot on box on E end wall of CYC or Marina

Foot ferry and Wivenhoe ferry details from HM's office

Gas from chandlers

Chandler Two nearby

Provisions In town

Post Office In town

Boat repairs At nearby yards

Engineer French Marine Motors ☎01206 302133
www.frenchmarine.com
D B Marine ☎01206 304391 www.dbmarineeng.co.uk

Sailmakers In town, Ratsey & Lapthorn
☎01206 302863
Advantage Sails Tel 01206 618244
advantagesails.co.uk
Andrew Watson Tel 07519 816944

Clubs
Colne YC CO7 0AX ☎01206 302594
waterside@colneyachtclub.org.uk
www.colneyachtclub.org.uk
Brightlingsea SC CO7 0DY ☎01206 303275
(commodore ☎07894 507812)
commodore@sailbrightlingsea.com
www.sailbrightlingsea.com

Pub/Restaurant Several nearby, in town and at Colne YC (weekends and some weekdays)

Taxi ☎01206 302491

Cindery Creek moorings and St Osyth Creek

10. RIVER COLNE

Brightlingsea has an attractive waterfront with the Colne YC and a lovely timbered building, now converted to flats, with a cupola on the roof prominent at the top of the busy hard. The older part of the town, between the hard and the shopping centre, has retained its nautical air with various marine companies dotted about and boats appearing over garden walls. It is the home of James Lawrence Sailmakers, now Ratsey and Lapthorn (largely for traditional craft), the Colne Smack Preservation Society (next to the CYC pontoon) where several smacks are berthed, and the Pioneer Sailing Trust. Sadly, the old shipyards have gone now, but boatyards remain busy.

The Hard is a popular launching place for all sorts of craft but is also the location of some of the busiest scrubbing posts on the East Coast. To use them, talk to the Harbour Office (01206 302200) or make enquiries at the white hut at the top of the Hard. The same applies for launching on the hard if you wish to launch a trailer-sailer.

The town jetty, just upstream from the block of flats and marina, has a 24m-long hammerhead. A Thames barge often picks up and discharges passengers from the berth, but yachts may lie there for up to 15mins to load or unload, although it's best to check first with the HM. Tenders and small craft can be secured inside the hammerhead or on the access walkway for up to 2hr but beware the inside may be dry at LW. The jetty is the terminus for the water taxi and the Point Clear foot ferry and is very popular with children for crabbing.

The small 12-passenger foot ferry operates from the jetty to Point Clear (St Osyth) and East Mersea Stone from Easter to the end of October. For details of service times see www.brightlingseaharbour.org/boat-trips-foot-ferry or 07981 450169.

A second route operates a new electric boat between the jetty and Wivenhoe and Rowhedge, but must be booked with the Harbour Office by 1300 on the day of travel.

St Osyth

St Osyth Creek runs SE from where the two arms of Brightlingsea Creek and Cindery Creek reconnect at the E end of Cindery Island (see photo on page 97). It's a narrow, twisting and attractive creek with best water at the entrance between the little Pincushion Island and the S bank of the creek.

The creek is unmarked but is well worth a visit in the dinghy on the rising tide, when it's possible you might see seals lolling in the shallows along with a wide variety of bird life on the way up to the St Osyth Boatyard beside the road bridge at St Osyth. The village is known to have been a port as far back as 1215 and the bay beside the road bridge is full of houseboats and some barges in for repair. There is a line of mud berths at stagings along the waterfront below the boatyard.

Boats of up to 1·5m draught can reach the quay at HW but must either seek a berth alongside and dry out or return down the creek in good time, because it dries at LW. For a berth contact St Osyth Boatyard.

ST OSYTH — CO16 8EW
Access HW±1½hr
Facilities WC
Water At boatyard
Provisions In village – ¼M
Post Office In village
Boat repairs St Osyth Boatyard, CO16 8EW
07547 539567
www.stosythboatyard.co.uk
Slipway At boatyard
Pub/Restaurant Several in village

East Mersea Stone

Sometimes known as East Mersea Head, the point has a steep shingle beach with clean landing and the attraction of the Dog and Pheasant pub about a mile inland 01206 383206. The foot ferry from and to Brightlingsea also lands and picks passengers up from here. It is a convenient way to go shopping for stores in Brightlingsea while lying at anchor off the Stone.

The shore is steep to and if the anchorage is busy it may be necessary to anchor in relatively deep water or just around the point, but the holding is good and an evening stroll ashore pleasant. It is occasionally useful too as a waiting anchorage if catching a tide early in the morning but do keep as close to the Point as possible and show a riding light, because plenty of yachts come and go at night.

A tide rip forms off Mersea Stone on the ebb. Beyond is the entrance to Pyefleet Creek curving away W

Pyefleet to Arlesford

Looking down Pyefleet to Brightlingsea in the distance

The Pyefleet

Pyefleet Creek or The Pyefleet, which runs along the N side of Mersea Island, eventually reaching the Strood (the causeway to the island), is the main anchorage on the River Colne and is a favourite amongst East Coast yachtsmen, which means it can become very crowded during summer weekends.

The entrance lies about 2 cables N of the PHB (Fl.R.5s) and the unlit ECB (a post) marking the wreck of the SS *Lowlands* on the W side of the river above Mersea Stone. Sailing barges often anchor in the mouth of the Pyefleet and several smacks have moorings there. Indeed, there are now a lot of moorings in the Pyefleet off the Colchester Oyster Fishery's landing, including several more large red-buoyed visitor moorings belonging to the fishery. There is a fee payable for using these – in 2023 this was £15 a night collected by trot boat early in the morning. There is room, however, to anchor above these moorings between the Mersea shore and Pewit Island, but much beyond that and you come into an area of oyster layings, where you must not anchor or ground. The creek also shallows rapidly, W of Pewit Island, making it hard to find a hole to lie afloat clear of the layings.

Holding in the Pyefleet is generally good, though in places the mud is very soft, and boats do drag their anchors unexpectedly. In fact, Pyefleet mud seems to have a character of its own and delights in sticking firmly and in great quantities to both anchor and chain, making recovery a messy business. It is common to see boats motoring seaward as their crews expend much energy dipping buckets and scrubbing the mud off ground tackle, decks, topsides and selves.

The Pyefleet has great charm and a place in the heart of most East Coast sailors, but it can also prove a particularly uncomfortable berth in the wrong conditions. Should the wind come either from the E or W and blow hard against the tide, the whole creek cuts up rough with boats pitching and tossing all over the place. It occasionally becomes so bad that a boat will dip her head under at times.

A further attraction for a lot of visitors to the Pyefleet is the presence of the Colchester Oyster Fishery's sheds on the S shore from where it is possible to buy oysters and cooked crabs and lobsters.

Colchester Oyster Fishery ☎01206 384141
orders@colchesteroysterfishery.com
www.colchesteroysterfishery.com

Pyefleet to Alresford

Leave the No.12 PHB (Q.R) to port when leaving the Pyefleet to head seawards or to cross to Brightlingsea or to continue up the Colne.

Half a mile up the Colne, the N and S Geedon Channels open on the W side to surround Rat Island. These channels lead in towards the Fingringhoe firing ranges, where activity is indicated by numerous red flags on the seawall, and cannot be used much, but there is a small hole that local craft sometimes anchor in, just inside the mouth of the S channel.

After passing No.17 SHB (Fl.G.3s) follow the line of red PHBs from No.16 at North Geedon up to No.24 (Fl.R). Pass close to each (as river traffic allows), because they lie along the W edge of the channel while the E side, which shelves gradually, is unmarked until No.19 (SHM), N of Aldboro Point. Keep a close watch on depths when tacking in this area and beware the dogleg in the channel around No.18.

SHB No.19 (Fl.G) off Aldboro Point is at the apex of a long right hand bend extending from N of No.18 PHB round to No.21 SHB. In the middle of the bend on the W bank, at Fingringhoe Nature Reserve, there's a jetty inshore from No.22 PHB, marked 'no landing'.

10. RIVER COLNE

Alresford Creek dries

The next landmark is the gravel works and remains of a jetty in Alresford Creek on the E side of the river.

Alresford Creek

Alresford Creek is entered from immediately upstream of No.21 SHB (Q.G) with a line of small port hand pillar buoys and starboard hand conical ones showing the line of the narrow channel.

Laid and maintained by a group of local yachtsmen who have moorings in the creek, these marks are clear and easy to use, but the creek dries out completely and there is little space for visiting craft to lie.

Within the creek there is a disused jetty on the N side from which ballast was loaded for many years (the ballast is now taken out by road) and a hard landing at a ford. From the landing it is about a mile to Alresford where there's a pub, the Pointer ☎01206 824378, a Post Office and a train station.

Alresford to Wivenhoe

Above Alresford, the Colne continues between wooded banks with Alresford Grange nestling among the trees on the E bank just where the channel runs closest to that shore before sweeping W towards the disused Fingringhoe ballast quay.

There is a line of fore and aft small craft moorings along the E edge of the channel opposite the quay, making this a busy area. It is within sight of the Wivenhoe tidal barrier and Wivenhoe itself.

Immediately below the barrier, on the E bank, is the Wivenhoe SC which has a slipway and floating pontoons where vessels of under 2m draught can lie alongside at about HW ±2hr before drying out in soft mud. Visitors are welcomed but only on the inner side of the pontoon and stays are limited to 48 hours.

WIVENHOE SC CO7 9WS
☎01206 822132
Email via the website contact page
www.wivenhoesailingclub.org.uk

WIVENHOE

Just above the ballast quay to port and the club to starboard, the river is spanned by the massive structure of the Wivenhoe tidal barrier. It's an unattractive edifice, but the central section is normally open for vessels to pass through unimpeded.

Approach from No.29 SHB with the open section directly ahead. There's a pair of port and starboard hand buoys (Nos 38 and 31), followed by a substantial pair of port and starboard hand beacons (Q.R/Q.G) to guide boats into the passageway through. The barrier is marked on each side by 2F.R/F.G (vert) lights. (These signals are also shown on the upstream side for passage down through the barrier.)

Traffic warning signals on the N pier show 3F.R.(vert) lights, directed both downstream and up, to indicate that the barrier is closed or that a large vessel is in transit. In either case, do not try to pass through.

The opening in the barrier is 30m wide, so two-way traffic is practical, but be careful to pass port to port and at less than 5kn.

Behind the ugly barrier lies the attractive water front of Wivenhoe, with its iconic mud berths

Once through the barrier, Wivenhoe waterfront opens to starboard with boats berthed bows on in mud berths with all activity watched by visitors to the popular Rose and Crown pub. Unfortunately, there is limited scope for getting ashore. Immediately beyond the barrier, to starboard, there is a modern pontoon jetty but it is private. Another more substantial modern jetty projects from the starboard bank a few yards further on but, like the long quay higher up, it has railings along its edge making it unwelcoming to any visiting boats. Just beyond it is the newer town slipway where you can at least land from a dinghy There is a line of small craft fore and aft moorings to port with some more a little higher up, off the quayside where new houses and blocks of flats overlook the river. Boats can berth briefly on the tide at this quay, but again the railings are right on the edge of the quay, making landing difficult.

There are shops and a Post Office in Wivenhoe, plus pubs and restaurants, doctors, dentists and a chemist.

Sadly, in such an attractive spot, finding a mud berth along the quay is a matter of chance and even then an empty berth may not prove comfortable, once the tide has gone, if your boat's hull does not match the hole made by the resident vessel. It is better to moor at the Wivenhoe SC below the tide barrier.

FINGRINGHOE

There is no buoyage beyond the Wivenhoe barrier, so for best water use charts and/or generally follow the outside of bends. As the river bends away from Wivenhoe, another creek opens on the S shore, just before an extensive new housing development. This is Fingringhoe Creek, commonly known as the Roman River. It mainly dries and should only be explored by shallow draught vessels near HW, when it is an attractive waterway leading up to Fingringhoe, a once thriving port. A low slung power line blocks the passage for vessels with tall masts.

ROWHEDGE

Above the mouth of the Roman River, the Colne takes a turn to the N past a development of modern apartments on the old quay and Rowhedge appears on the W bank. Once a busy centre for boat building, plus having a large fishing fleet, the Rowhedge waterfront is now quiet with few obvious signs of its commercial maritime past.

It's still possible to moor along the pretty quayside at Rowhedge, close outside the waterfront pubs, but timing is dependent upon draught and it's likely that you will only have from perhaps HW -2 to HW +1½hr unless planning to dry out there.

The village, which is right by the river, offers several pubs, including Ye Olde Albion and The Anchor on the quay, as well as a Post Office and shops.

There is a floating pontoon upriver of the pubs at which yachts can berth for a visit to the village, but they share it with the ferry from Wivenhoe, although that usually berths on the inside. Boats with a draught of up to 5ft can get alongside at HW ±2½hr, but the pontoon dries completely at LW. Boats are welcome to moor temporarily but are normally requested to move onto the quay at HW if they wish to stay overnight. However, if the owner is happy to dry out, they may stay by arrangement with the water bailiff, Jo Brennan, ☎01206 728764.

10. RIVER COLNE

The attractive waterfrontage of Rowhedge

Rowhedge to Colchester

The Colne runs a further two miles from Rowhedge to Colchester and frankly we question the wisdom of this part of the trip. Almost as soon as you clear Rowhedge the countryside takes on an abandoned look and closer to the Hythe, you pass through rundown industrial wharves and warehouses until you reach King Edward Quay on your port side, at the end of which is a low-level road bridge. The river bottom for this latter part of the trip is littered with old wrecks (seen with side band sonar) so be careful.

Near to HW there is enough water for a boat of over 2m draught to creep right up to the road bridge, but this would be within an hour of HW and time must be allowed to return down river to deeper water. It is possible to dry out at the King Edward Quay, in gaps you may find between a variety of permanently moored craft, but it should be undertaken with caution – as you might expect, there is debris around, and you should test the depth each side before committing yourself.

There is also a 42-metre visitor pontoon by the quay (filled with local craft at the time of our visit), not far below the conspicuous lightship (home to various activities including local Sea Cadets), and shoal draught boats up to 9m in length should dry out reasonably level in mud beside this pontoon. Stays are limited to 48 hours. There is electricity and water but no other facilities. Rafting out may be

The upper reaches of the Colne are littered with abandoned craft. The chartlet shows the position of the mid-channel wreck in the picture revealed by side-band radar

Credit Roger Gaspar

Rowhedge to Colchester

Sadly, there seems to be little will among Colchester's burghers to improve the water front and make it into somewhere worth visiting. Indeed, on our visit late summer 2023 we found that part of the river wall had collapsed into the mainstream and that raw sewage was "escaping" onto a flood tide. The general environment was of run-down buildings covered in graffiti to stbd and rows of abandoned boats and liveaboards to port.

Collapsed river wall is a physical hazard while sewerage was pouring out of the culvert on the rising tide

uncomfortable for the outside boats where the mud slopes more steeply.

The section of quay close to the bridge has been renovated and provided with bench seats and lighting, making it tidier than it once was. The town centre is about a mile away while supermarkets and restaurants are closer. A lot of student accommodation is built nearby. Colchester Borough Council, responsible for the area, can be contacted on ☏01206 282222.

There is a winding hole to starboard below the pontoon. It was originally intended for turning coasters, but beware – the main area has silted up very badly.

The head of Colne doesn't inspire visitors

East Coast Pilot • 103

Downs Boatyard and Marina

11. RIVER BLACKWATER

The point of furthest navigation on the Blackwater/Chelmer river is Maldon

11. RIVER BLACKWATER

⊕ Landfall waypoint

51°44'·0N 001°05'·4E Immediately NE of Knoll NCB

Charts

Imray 2000, Y17

Admiralty 5607, 3741

Tides

Bradwell HW Walton +0030
Osea HW Walton +0050
Maldon HW Walton +0100

Blackwater River Bailiff

Nigel Harmer ☏ 07818 013723

nigel.harmer@maldon.gov.uk

ECP Honorary Port Pilot

Nigel Harmer as above

blackwater@eastcoastpilot.com

Main hazards

The River Blackwater shares its entrance with the River Colne. The dual entrance is NW from the Knoll NCB (Q), with the rivers diverging at the Colne Bar SHB (Fl(2)G.5s). The Knoll lies at the SW end of the Wallet channel and is N of the Buxey Sand and W of the Gunfleet Sand. Approaching the buoy is straightforward if arriving from the NE through the Wallet, but from S, either from the Crouch or Thames, it means crossing sandbanks. As with everywhere in the Thames Estuary, these banks are hazards to navigation and must be treated cautiously.

From the S, the best approach to the Knoll is via the Spitway between the Swin and Wallet channels, which saves a long haul NE to round the NE Gunfleet and return SW through the Wallet.

From the Crouch, shallow draught craft can cut through the Rays'n, but even they then take a NE

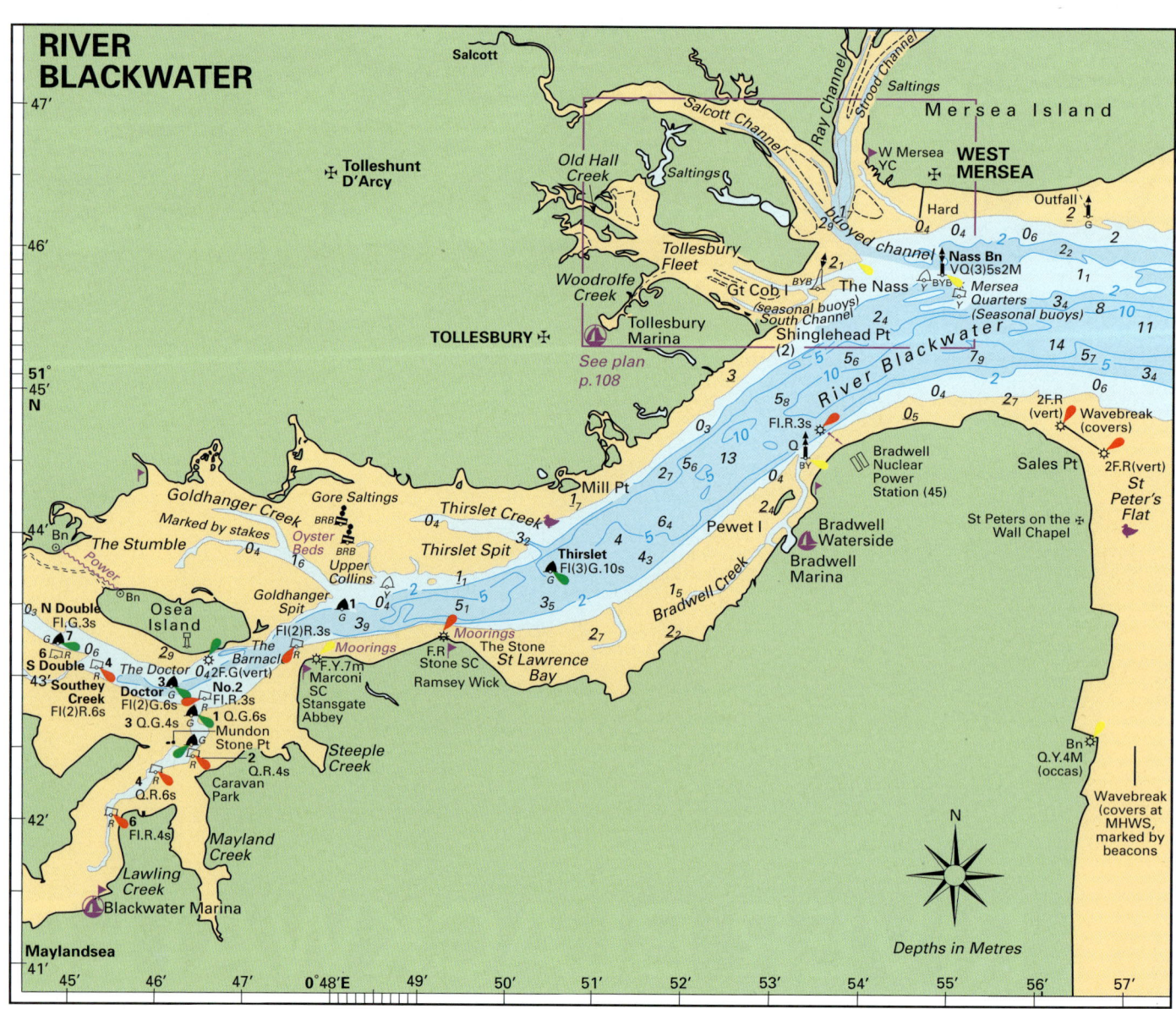

River Blackwater

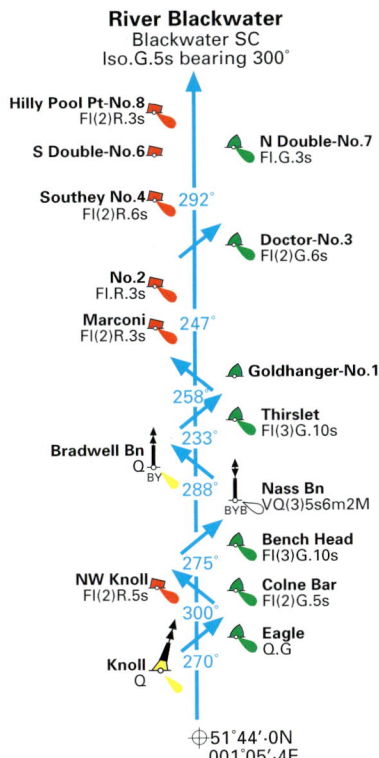

North Eagle NCM

Colne Bar Buoy

course to cross the Swire Hole to avoid drying patches on the Batchelor Spit, before heading for the Knoll on a transit with Wallet Spitway (RW.LFl 10s bell).

Once the Knoll is reached, from any direction, navigation becomes less hazardous although compass courses will be needed in poor visibility.

Approaches

From the Knoll NCB (Q) shape a course to leave the Eagle SHB (Q.G.) close to starboard, then pass between the NW Knoll PHB (Fl(2)R.5s) and the Colne Bar SHB (Fl(2)G.5s). From there, steer to leave the Bench Head SHB (Fl(3)G.10s) to starboard. The Bench Head buoy is generally thought of as the beginning of the Blackwater proper.

Craft approaching the estuary from the NE by way of the Wallet may, if tide and weather conditions permit, shorten their passage slightly after passing Clacton by ignoring the Knoll NCB and leaving the North Eagle NCB (Q) on their port side before making for the Colne Bar SHB, then aim for the Bench Head buoy.

When crossing from the River Colne to the Blackwater, sea conditions, draught and state of tide will dictate your course. At low tide on a rough day, it will pay you to go right out to the Bench Head but a more likely route is out round the Inner Bench Head, then on a course of about 250° into the deep water channel with the Bench Head buoy bearing about 110°. Shallow draught boats can leave the Colne S of No.8 PHB and make good a course of about 220° to stay S of the ECM (1M distant) marking the wreck of the Molliette on the Cocum Hills. From there

Molliette Beacon on Cocum Hills

11. RIVER BLACKWATER

they can turn onto about 250° with Bradwell Power Station fine on the port bow until again finding the deep water of the Blackwater itself.

Entry

Once past the Bench Head it's often difficult to identify any marks other than the two massive lumps of Bradwell Power Station on the S shore and a general view of 'that's W Mersea' on the starboard bow. Although the power station is decommissioned, the landmark sarcophagi will remain for many years.

From the Bench Head, steer a course of about 290° towards the Nass Beacon ECM (VQ(3)5s6m2M) four miles ahead marking the entrance to Mersea Quarters and Tollesbury, with the option of leaving it to the N and going on up the Blackwater.

WEST MERSEA

First port of call on the Blackwater is West Mersea. Enter the Quarters from close E of the Nass Bn ECM (VQ(3)5s 6m2M), following the line of mainly unlit port and starboard buoys towards the mass of moorings. Do not venture into the area close SW of the beacon where there is a dangerous obstruction. A course of about 280° for half a mile will take you from the Nass Bn to the Quarters Spit buoy ECB (Q(3)10s), which must be left to port. Further in, to starboard, you will see No.7 SHB (Fl(2)G.5s). From No.7 inwards you must rely on the lines of moorings to show where the best water is.

Quarters Spit ECB

There are boats moored well out in Mersea Quarters, but there is still room to anchor, although it can be rather exposed at HW with a heavy swell if the wind is from E or SE.

Once you're among the moorings there's no room to anchor safely and you must pick up a mooring. For this it's best to call the West Mersea YC launch, call sign YC1 on VHF Ch 37 (M), from close to the Nass Bn. The launchman will do his best to find you a mooring and can take you to and from the shore, for which journeys there is a charge, as there is for short term and overnight mooring. (The launch charge may be refunded if you eat or drink in the WMYC.) As an alternative to a swinging mooring, YC1 may ask you to moor fore and aft on either the row of piles or on

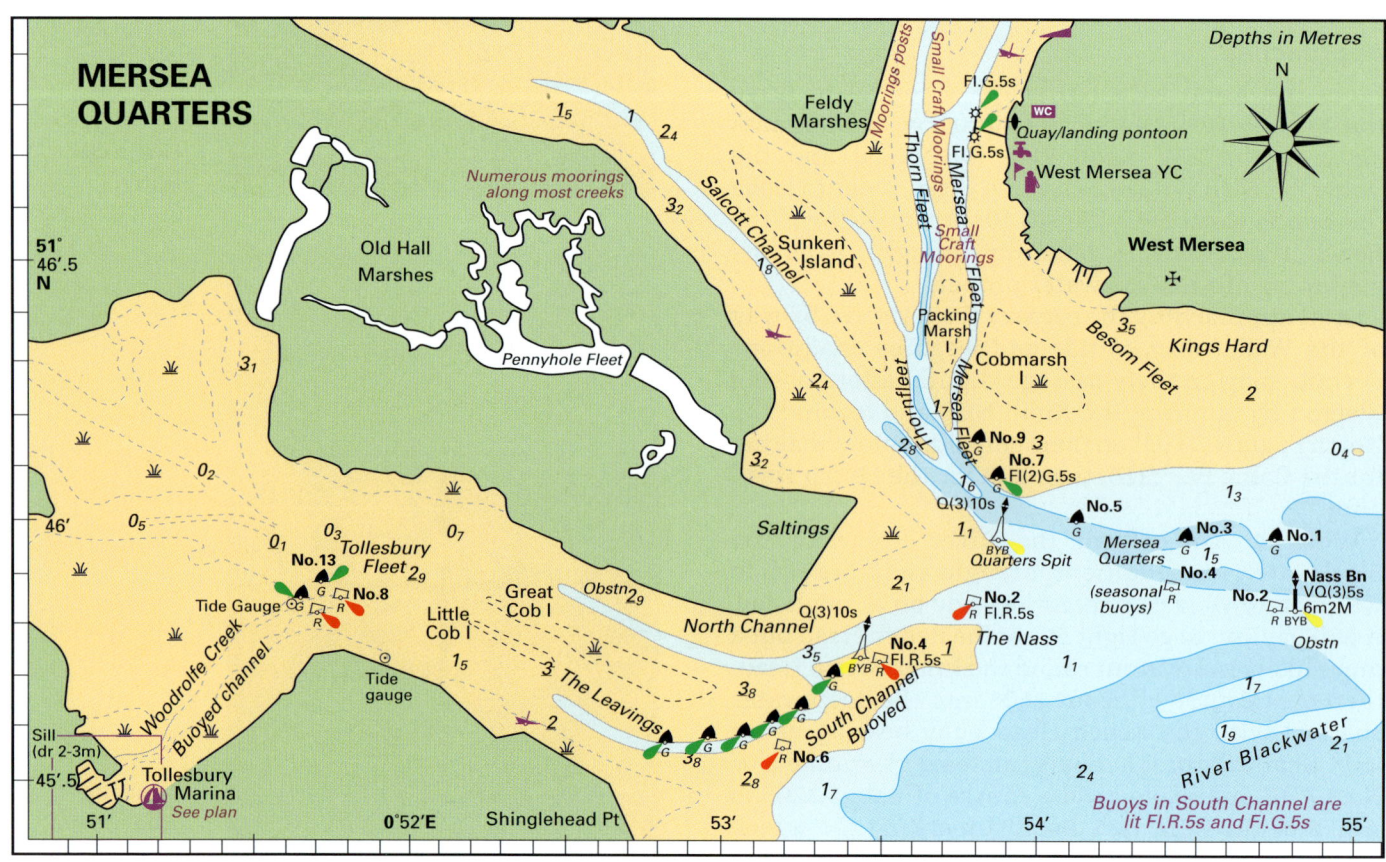

108 • East Coast Pilot

West Mersea

West Mersea is a popular East Coast yachting centre *Credit John Fielding/Flickr*

several pontoons that hang between some of them in the Ray Channel.

Beyond the Quarters, the channel divides into several separate arms. Each of these generally has a clear lane of best water to follow between the lines of moorings, but at slack water boats may lie athwart the channel, making it hard to pick out.

Steering about NW from a position between the Quarters Spit ECB and No.7 SHB will take you up the Salcott Channel to the W of Sunken Island. Heading a little to starboard, the middle line of moorings leads into Thorn Fleet on the W side of Packing Marsh Island with its distinctive oyster shed. (Following Thorn Fleet will take you to the pile moorings in the Ray Channel.) On the E side of Packing Marsh Island is the shallower Mersea Fleet and the third line of moorings, while way over to the E of Cobmarsh Island is Besom Fleet, which runs right along the West Mersea foreshore.

A narrow channel, The Gut, cuts through from the Thorn Fleet and Ray Channel to Mersea Fleet and the Strood Channel opposite the hard and landing pontoon. The Strood Channel runs on N from the RNLI lifeboat station and Dabchicks SC to turn NE round the back of Mersea Island towards the Strood itself, which is the causeway between Mersea and the mainland. (Beyond this causeway is the head of the Pyefleet, which runs E into the Colne.)

All the Mersea channels are thick with moorings and their headwaters are really only suitable for exploration by dinghy. Best water is generally found between paired lines of moorings in each fleet or channel. Whatever you do, don't cut across from one

The Old Packing Shed sits on its island in the middle of the Mersea channels

WMYC runs a regular trot boat service

11. RIVER BLACKWATER

Approaching the landing pontoon on the West Mersea front

fleet to another, the water is shallow and the mud hugs keels. Withies generally mark oyster layings, not good water.

WEST MERSEA — CO5 8PB

Contact
Moorings: WMYC launch
VHF Ch 37(M) Callsign *YC1*
☏ 07752 309435 (seasonal, daily but hours vary, check club website for details)
Additional Water taxi VHF Ch 72
Callsign *Lady Grace* ☏ 07791 859624
0800-1800 (and evenings by prior arrangement).
Access 24hr
Clubs West Mersea YC CO5 8PB
☏ 01206 382947
Email info@wmyc.org.uk
www.wmyc.org.uk
Dabchicks SC ☏ 01206 383786
www.dabchicks.org
Fuel Garage in town
Water On pontoon hammerhead
Gas Ask at chandlers
Chandlers Marinestore Wyatts Chandlery ☏ 01206 384745
Scrubbing posts Contact WMYC
Boatyards and repairs Peter Clarke's Boatyard (incl. slipway) ☏ 01206 385905
West Mersea Marine ☏ 01206 382244
Sailmakers Gowen Ocean ☏ 01206 384412
Shipwright David Mills ☏ 01206 382161
Engineers A B Clarke ☏ 01206 382706; OHM Engineering ☏ 07905 243414
Provisions In town
Post Office In town
Pub/Restaurant Many along front and in town, including WMYC (☏ 01206 384463 to book)
Transport Buses to Colchester
Taxi ☏ 01206 384666, 731257

TOLLESBURY

Tollesbury shares a common entrance with Mersea from the Nass Bn ECM (VQ(3)5s 6m2M), its creeks running W from Mersea Quarters. To enter, follow the line of PHBs from the Nass Beacon for about 2 cables NNW and turn W leaving the Quarters Spit ECB (Q(3)10s) to starboard, before following the charted channel W and WSW for several hundred yards to find a small PHB No.2 (Fl.R.5s).

A word of warning is needed here. In common with many East Coast ports, when entering Tollesbury in the late afternoon, the sun will be low and directly ahead. This makes spotting buoys and/or identifying them extremely difficult, so proceed with caution. New visitors are also advised to follow the buoyed channel and not be distracted by local boats whose draught and local knowledge enable them to cross the Nass at the right state of the tide.

The No.2 PHB is the first of three PHBs placed along the N edge of the Nass sand bank. Depending on wind and tide conditions, at anything less than HW, these buoys can drift over the bank, so watch the depth and be prepared to stand off them a little. The second PHB, No.4 (Fl.R.5s), is paired with an ECB 'Indigo' (Q(3)10s) at the seaward end of a long spit out from Great Cob Island, forming a 'gate' into the buoyed South Channel. The South Channel, which is the main Tollesbury channel, carries on SW leaving the Indigo ECB on your starboard side. (You might also see local boats make their way to Tollesbury by leaving the ECB to port, entering the North Channel and then on to Tollesbury via the W end of Great Cob Island.)

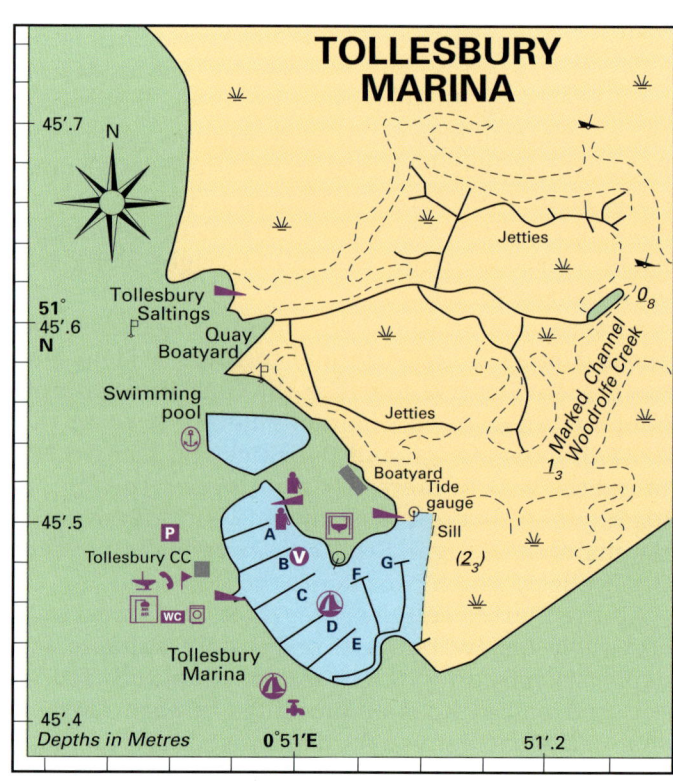

Tollesbury

Entrance to Tollesbury is via twisting, drying Woodrolfe creek

Once through the 'gate' into the Tollesbury South Channel, you should find it buoyed along its N side with about five SHBs (the number varies), each showing a flashing light, but there is also the third of the PHBs, No.6 ('Mouse'), to take note of on the edge of the Nass about 200 yards up the channel. No.6 marks a hard, drying sandy knoll on the Nass but, although the buoy itself can dry out, once the tide is flooding there is usually deeper water close to it, so tend to pass close to this buoy, remembering that the wind can blow it over the shallows.

At the last SHB, No.11, the channel turns sharply to starboard in a NW direction into a reach known as The Leavings, which used to be an anchorage for local fishing smacks, but now sees the beginning of the Tollesbury moorings. Follow the line of these moorings, and Woodrolfe Creek will open to port. You will see the landmark white blocks of flats over the saltings, together with the masts in the marina and a red light vessel, which is HQ for the Fellowship Afloat Charitable Trust.

There is a landing place half way up the Leavings on the S side, which gives access to a walk along the seawall into Tollesbury. It can be used at most states of tide. Off the mouth of Woodrolfe Creek are some white conical mooring buoys, for use when there is not enough water to get into the marina.

There is a tide gauge, marked in feet, on the N bank of Woodrolfe Creek entrance, showing the depth over the marina sill.

The creek dries and has a narrow, winding channel, but further up it is marked with a few port and starboard buoys, mostly lit Fl.R.5s or Fl.G.5s. The line of moorings also gives guidance as to the best water.

As you pass the light vessel to starboard and approach Tollesbury Marina the entrance is clearly seen to the left of an old black weatherboard granary shed beside the Woodrolfe Boatyard slipway. An arm of water also turns sharply to starboard along Tollesbury waterfront, but it should not be followed without current advice unless previously inspected at LW. It gives access to the self-styled 'natural marina' run by Tollesbury Saltings, where mud berths for visitors may be available on request, accessible close to HW.

Tollesbury Saltings ☎07521 318155
www.tsl-online.co.uk

The small buoys marking the Tollesbury approach get heavily weeded and virtually sink

Yachts moored in the Leavings

11. RIVER BLACKWATER

The sill at the entrance to the marina is marked with a green post with the depth in feet painted on it

Right: Tollesbury Marina and its approach via Woodrolfe Creek

A final tide gauge is painted on a hefty green starboard hand post sited on top of the sill, immediately outside Tollesbury Marina, to show the depth in feet over it, which is about 2m at HWS and 1·5m on neaps. The sill is hard, uneven concrete.

On entering the marina, the fuel berth is hard round to starboard towards the boatyard crane. The first pontoon you pass on entering is G, with A down the far end. Visitors are allocated empty slots on any pontoon.

The marina has been plagued with silting and a programme of dredging is underway

TOLLESBURY MARINA   CM9 8SE

Contact
VHF Ch 80 Callsign *Tollesbury Marina*
Harbourmaster ☎ 01621 869202/868471
Email hm@tollesburymarina.com
www.tollesburymarina.com
Access HW-1½hr to HW+1
Fuel Diesel at berth below crane
Facilities WC, showers, laundry, WiFi, swimming pool, tennis courts
Water On pontoons
Electricity On pontoons (chargeable)
Gas Ask at chandlery
Chandler On site
Provisions In town (Fred's Stores 10 minute walk)
Pharmacy and doctor In town
Post Office In town

Boat repairs 20-T boat lift and cranes, three slipways up to 20T.
Slipway Contact marina office
Engineers Volspec nearby
Telephone At Harbour View restaurant
Pub/Restaurant Harbour View on site, pub in town
Clubs Tollesbury Cruising Club ☎ 01621 869202
Transport Buses to Maldon, Colchester, or Witham
Taxi ☎ 07788 480542
Other Tollesbury facilities:
Tollesbury Saltings ☎ 07521 318155
www.tsl-online.co.uk
8T travel hoist at Tollesbury Saltings
Tollesbury SC ☎ 01621 869406
principal@tollesburysc.com
www.tollesburysc.com

BRADWELL

The outstanding landmark when entering the Blackwater is Bradwell Power Station on the S shore, close to which lie Bradwell Creek and Bradwell Marina. The distance diagonally across the Blackwater deep water channel from the Nass Bn to the isolated power station breakwater, which has 2FR(vert) lights at each end and can often look like a ship from a distance, is a shade under 1½M.

A cable beyond the W end of the breakwater there's a NCM beacon (Q), the Bradwell Beacon, which carries a depth gauge indicating depths in feet at the marina entrance (at the time of writing this was missing and plans to replace it were vague). To enter Bradwell Creek and the marina, leave the beacon to starboard and head in between the red buoys to port and withies to starboard. Shoal patches have been noted near the beacon and close to the third red buoy, so be very careful if entering at LW±1½hr. The tide can run strongly across the approach channel with the buoys being pushed across the bank or into the channel, making it narrower than ever. The depth will vary frequently until well into the marked channel and it is best approached on a rising tide (especially at springs).

In recent years, greater depth of water has been found outside (E of) the buoyed channel, so if you need to enter or leave near to LW this may be worth a

The giant sarcophagi of the decommissioned Bradwell Nuclear power station are both a landmark for entry to the Blackwater but also to Bradwell Creek and Marina

try but check our website for up to date information and watch the echo sounder. (We were warned that the bottom E of the channel is littered with old mooring chains and detritus).

At the last PHB bear hard to port and head for a green conical SHB. The line to this buoy is shown by a pair of leading marks on the seawall – two small red

The Beacon off Bradwell Creek entrance

Turn hard-a-port at the last red and hard-a-stbd at the next green

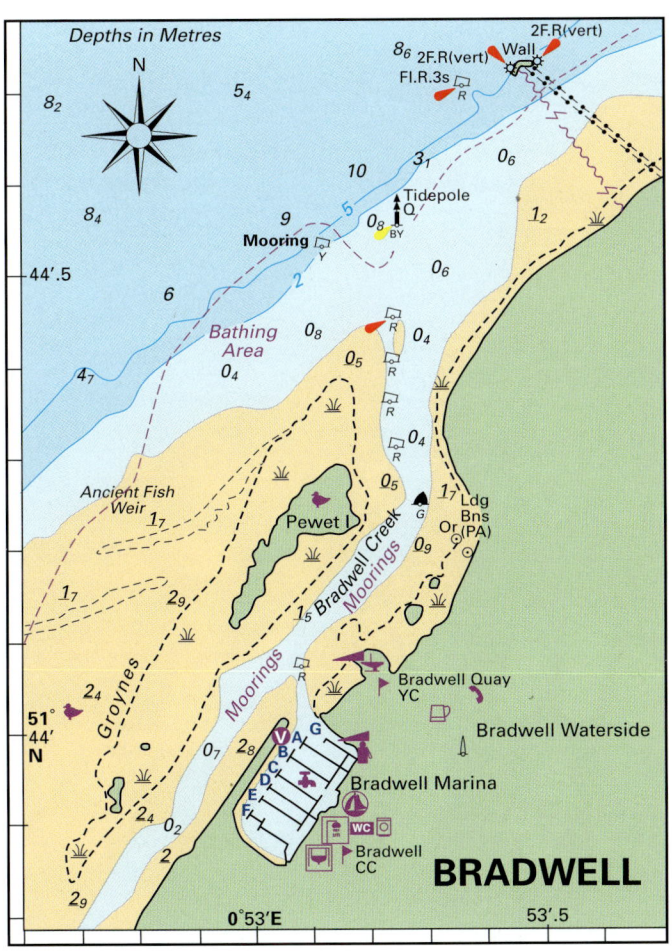

11. RIVER BLACKWATER

Left: Approaching the SHB the leading marks are out of alignment

Right: Bradwell Quay YC

triangles against a white painted patch on the wall. These marks are adjusted for a change in the channel and are not always easy to make out; binoculars will help. (On our last visit, late summer 2023 they were of no practical use). Leaving the SHB very close to starboard, turn hard to starboard and follow the lines of moorings into Bradwell Creek. Best water is between the innermost line of small boat (drying) moorings and the S line of bigger boat moorings. Here the tide runs very strongly through the creek.

To port will be seen the remains of Bradwell Quay and some scrubbing posts (belonging to the nearby Bradwell Quay YC) beside a public slipway. Off the end of it is a large red beacon that must be left on your port side. Shortly beyond is a single red PHB. Turn to port around this and the marina entrance is ahead between red and green piles, the tide sets swiftly across the approach.

Bradwell Creek and Marina

Bradwell Marina

Turn on the PHB and aim between the piles. 'A' pontoon is dead ahead

Pass between the piles and, unless directed elsewhere, the main visitors' berth is on the hammerhead berth dead ahead (row A) with a secondary berth on the hammerhead next to it to starboard (row B). The fuelling berth is ahead on the starboard side of the high jetty beneath the blue and white marina tower.

The marina's entrance channel can be navigated by shallow draught vessels at all states of neap tides, but at springs all craft must take care and time their entry for 90 minutes or so after LW. The marina itself is generally dredged to 1·8–2·4m.

The marina is in the hamlet of Bradwell Waterside, which has one pub and no shops. There is a useful community-run shop and PO in the village of Bradwell-on-Sea, a 20-minute walk away.

If holidaying and staying at Bradwell, it is worth the walk, either by way of the sea wall or through the village, to visit St Peter's on the Wall www.bradwellchapel.org. Established by St Cedd in 654AD, it is an extremely simple but calm place of worship, perhaps the oldest surviving church building in England.

The power station outfall, the Ross Revenge and Thirslet Spit SHM all align, requiring a dog leg up the river

BRADWELL MARINA — CM0 7RB

Contact VHF Ch 80
Callsign *Bradwell Marina*
Harbourmaster ①01621 776235/776391
arthur@bradwellmarina.com
www.bradwellmarina.com
Access HW ±4½hr
Fuel Diesel and petrol berth at base of tower (0830–1700). Tight turning space
Facilities WC, WiFi, showers, laundry, chemical toilet emptying point
Water Taps on pontoons (supply your own hoses)
Electricity On pontoons
Gas Ask in office
Provisions Bradwell Community Shop and PO (①01621 776274, www.bradwellshop.co.uk)
Boat repairs 45-T boat lift, self-launch slipway (contact marina)
Engineers Althorne Marine Services – Steve Rook ①07904 329236 John Rook 07939 100822
Pub/Restaurant Marina bar-restaurant on site
Munchies Café on site
Green Man ①01621 776226, at Waterside
King's Head ①01621 776224, in village
Clubs Bradwell CC www.bradwellcruisingclub.co.uk
Bradwell Quay YC honsec.bqyc@btinternet.com www.bradwellquayyc.org (HQ near the Green Man)
Transport Weekday buses to Burnham-on-Crouch
Taxi ①01621 713421, 835111

Bradwell to Thirslet

When departing Bradwell Creek, leave the beacon at the end of the creek to port, before turning up river. Due W an unlit SCB guards the end of the remains of Tollesbury Pier on N bank. It is then tempting to make directly towards Osea Island, which appears dead ahead, but between Bradwell and the island lies Thirslet Spit on the N side of the main channel. It is

11. RIVER BLACKWATER

marked by the Thirslet SHB (Fl(3)G.10s) (wrongly spelt Thirstlet on the buoy itself), which, is obscured by the Radio Caroline pirate ship the *Ross Revenge* lying at anchor on the transit.

Thirslet Spit is extremely hard sand and is steep-to on its river side. Many vessels have grounded on it as they make their way straight up or down the Blackwater. A dog-leg around it is essential, so steer for the moorings at Stone rather than directly towards Osea. (When returning down river, from Osea, keep the old Bradwell power station buildings fine on your port bow, after passing close outside the Stone moorings, until past Thirslet.)

Thirslet Creek runs NW from the spit buoy and can provide a sheltered anchorage when the sand banks are uncovered. However, once the banks are awash it becomes rather exposed.

Opposite Thirslet, on the S shore, St Lawrence Bay is an area popular with PWCs and water-skiers.

STONE

On the S shore ½M above Thirslet is Stone with a long shingle beach, many moorings and several large, highly active fleets of racing dinghies that criss-cross the entire river from Stone Sailing Club.

SHB 1 marks the end of Goldhanger Spit and the entrance to Goldhanger Creek

approximately 5 cables N of Goldhanger No.1 SHB, marking two wrecks.

A charted causeway runs from Decoy Point on the mainland to West Point on Osea Island and can be crossed by most craft about an hour either side of HW springs. A suitable deeper gap on the causeway is usually indicated between two withies.

There are oyster layings in Goldhanger Creek making it difficult to find an anchorage. Like Thirslet, it only offers shelter once the banks are dry. Several small craft do lie at the head of the creek where there is also the Goldhanger SC www.goldhangersailingclub.org.uk. If your boat can take the ground comfortably then there is a landing and Goldhanger village with its pubs, The Chequers Inn and The Cricketers, a reasonable walk away.

Across on the S shore at Stansgate there are more moorings and the Marconi SC. There is a free visitor mooring, 'A0', the western-most mooring on the outer row, if you wish to visit the club. The outer three rows of moorings are all-tide.

> **STONE SAILING CLUB**   **CM0 7NF**
> ☎ 01621 779344 when open
> www.stonesc.org.uk

Tides run fast through the moorings and it's best to pass outside them all. With wind over tide the area is quite rough with boats bouncing and rolling around.

Stone to Osea

A further ¾M up river, across on the N side, the small No.1 SHB marks the end of Goldhanger Spit and the entrance to Goldhanger Creek. The spit extends from the E end of Osea Island and the Creek cuts NW towards the village of Goldhanger with an arm breaking away to run behind Osea Island towards The Stumble, eventually rejoining the main river and making Osea an island. If you choose to sail this area, look out for the isolated danger buoy,

Stone SC is an active club with large fleets of racing dinghies and cruising yachts

> **MARCONI SC**   **CM0 7NU**
> ☎ 01621 772164 when open
> info@marconi-sc.org.uk
> www.marconi-sc.org.uk

NW of Stansgate, at the W end of the Marconi SC moorings, there is the Marconi PHB (Fl(2)R.3s), which doesn't always stand out too well. It is placed in good water, but at a point where the river channel narrows and it should be left to port for safety. The area between Stone and the anchorage E of Osea pier, particularly around the Marconi buoy, is frequently choppy and can be disturbingly rough with wind against tide.

Lawling Creek

There is a safe anchorage offering shelter from NW to NE winds down river of Osea jetty

Osea

The remains of the pier at Osea still carries 2F.G(vert) lights that act as a useful guide. There's good depth and holding E of the pier, off which are a couple of sizeable moorings, with the shell beach of Osea a popular place for walking and picnicking. Note however that the island is privately owned and you may not be welcomed above the HW mark. At LW, deep draught boats must beware The Barnacle shoal patch a cable E from the pier.

There's good holding if you set the anchor properly and shelter from N winds, in addition to offering a pleasant place to stretch your legs ashore or swim off the beach – and children can paddle about the anchorage in dinghies, practising their boat handling skills.

Lawling Creek

South from Osea is the No.2 Mayland Spit PHB (Fl.R.3s), which marks the S side of the main river channel, but also the W side of the entrance to Lawling Creek. This creek runs SW to Maylandsea and the Blackwater Marina (see plan on page 118).

Enter Lawling Creek by leaving the Mayland Spit buoy to starboard (it is a PHB for the river only). All the creek buoys that follow are now unlit, although they do have red or green reflective tape. Steer to leave the SHB Lawling Creek No.1 SHB to starboard. From there, leave No.3 Mundon Point SHB to starboard and No.2 PHB to port, altering course to about SW towards No.4 Mayland Creek PHB off the entrance to Mayland Creek. Continue to No.6 PHB from where the Harlow (Blackwater) SC lies ahead and the moorings provide a guide to the channel up to the Blackwater Marina.

There is a sheltered anchorage with good holding on the S side of Mundon Stone Point but be careful, the mud bank inside the headland is extensive. The small knoll of sand that forms the headland is often used for barbeques by visiting club cruises and is also a frequent perch for herons and cormorants.

Opposite Mundon Pt is the entrance to the drying Mayland Creek, which has several moorings in it.

About a mile in from the entrance, on the E bank, where there are more moorings, stands the Harlow (Blackwater) SC.

HARLOW (BLACKWATER) SC   CM3 6AG
☏ 07929 734684
Email via website, or HBSCcommittee@gmail.com
www.harlow-blackwater-sailing-club.com

The club has 25 swinging moorings – the boats float at HW ±2hr – and a launching ramp that has water at similar times.

From HBSC you can see the Blackwater Marina on the port hand, but you must approach by continuing to follow the winding line of moorings carefully, keeping them close on your starboard hand, until you reach the final few moorings from where the

Just inside the entrance to Lawling Creek, Mundon Stone Point offers a sheltered anchorage with good holding and colonies of cormorants, herons and seals

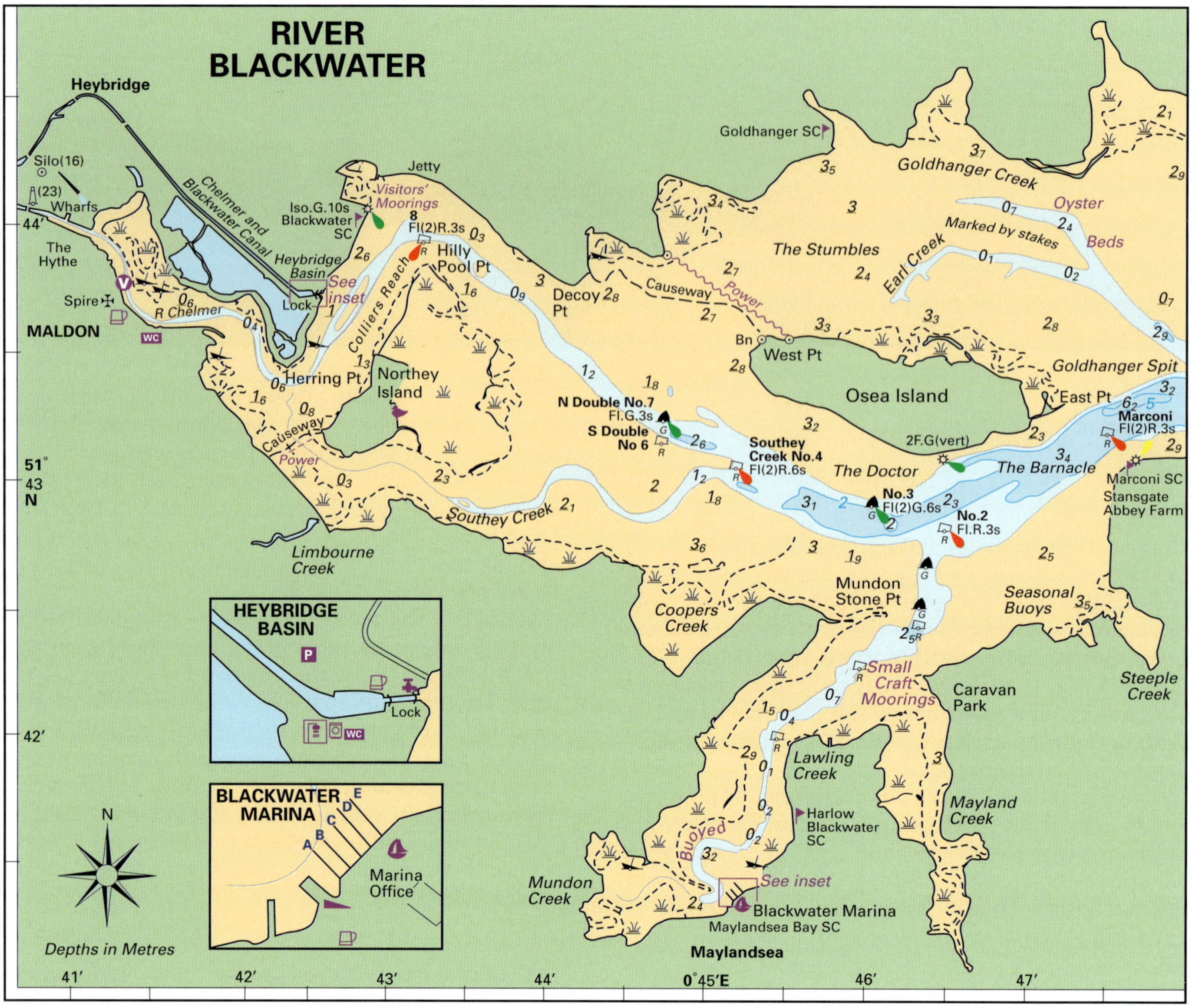

11. RIVER BLACKWATER

pontoons are clearly visible ahead. (You may see large brown box buoys; these are race marks and can be disregarded).

At these final moorings the channel sweeps around to starboard and is marked by small red and green buoys as it curves back again to port until it heads straight for the southern-most pontoons in the marina. 'A' pontoon is beside the slipway; 'E' is at the seaward end.

These are all drying pontoons, but there are also 100 marina owned all-tide moorings laid about half way down the creek.

Just short of 'A' pontoon the creek swings southwest again and narrows rapidly and eventually dries completely, but there is an active club, Maylandsea Bay SC, just upriver from the marina. The club manages a few drying moorings (owned by Maldon DC) for its group of cruising members.

MAYLANDSEA BAY SC   CM3 6AL
☎ 01621 740470 when open
Email via website
www.maylandseabay-sc.org.uk

Entering or leaving the marina means taking a wide sweep away

Lawling Creek to Heybridge

Blackwater Marina

BLACKWATER MARINA   CM3 6AL

HW Walton +40

Contact
Harbourmaster ☎01621 740264
Duty phone 07572 228641
(Office not manned on Sundays)
info@blackwater-marina.co.uk
www.blackwater-marina.co.uk

Access HW-2½ to HW+1½
Fuel None
Facilities WC, showers
Water Taps and hoses on pontoons
Electricity On pontoons
Boat repairs Slipway, 18-T travel hoist, 15-T crane. Dry dock, engineers, rigging
Slipway Contact marina
Gas Gaz (must be pre-ordered)
Provisions In village, five minute walk
Post Office In village (in Nisa store)
Pub/Restaurant Blackwater Bistro on site ☎01621 928110) and takeaways in village
Taxi ☎01621 741621

Lawling Creek to Heybridge

From Osea, leave No.2 PHB (Fl.R.3s) to port and No.3 the Doctor SHB (Fl(2)G.6s) to starboard. The water along the Osea Island shore looks inviting, but beware the Doctor flats, which have caught the keel of many a yacht trying to take a short cut inside the buoy.

At the Doctor SHB the river turns NW and the next buoy is the No.4 PHB (Fl(2)R.6s) marking the entrance to Southey Creek. This creek winds away W behind Northey Island and rejoins the main Blackwater River opposite Herring Point. It is a broad expanse of water at HW, but quickly narrows and dries as the tide ebbs. You can sail behind Northey on a good tide but beware the hard causeway between the island and the mainland at the SW corner.

Just above Southey Creek a pair of buoys, the Doubles, mark a distinct narrowing of the fairway, which shoals to less than 1m at LWS. The SHB, No.7 North Double is lit (Fl.G.3s) and marks the junction of the arm of Goldhanger Creek that has gone around the N side of Osea Island, with the main river.

The river now runs up to Heybridge between the NE shore of Northey Island to port (site of the Battle of Maldon in 991 AD) and Mill Beach, which stretches from Decoy Point, at the mainland end

11. RIVER BLACKWATER

of the causeway across to Osea Island, up river to Heybridge. The channel off Mill Beach is narrow and there's little water at LW, although at HW on a big spring tide Northey Island now largely floods.

There are moorings all along the Mill Beach foreshore, but the main marks to look for ahead are the towers of the old granary, with the tiny Salcote SC on the shore beneath, and the Blackwater SC (a long white building with a black roof set behind the seawall), which shows an Iso.G.10s light at night.

The club has several drying moorings, a concrete launching ramp and a floating wooden pontoon that cruisers can go alongside at HW.

BLACKWATER SC   CM9 4SD
01621 853923 Contact via website
secretary@blackwatersailingclub.org.uk
www.blackwatersailingclub.org.uk

Off the Blackwater SC the channel turns SW around the No.8 PHB (Fl(2)R.3s) Hilly Pool Point off the N tip of Northey Island. As its name implies, the river bed here is uneven, and the best water is found towards the mainland (W) shore.

Heybridge Basin

Half way along Colliers Reach, so-called from the days when colliers brought up here, lies Heybridge Basin, the seaward end of the Blackwater & Chelmer Navigation, a canal running inland to Chelmsford. The basin is a traditional wintering berth for yachts but has also become a popular summer stopover. Its popularity means that prior booking is essential.

Drying moorings extend along the foreshore between the Blackwater SC and the Basin lock, but not much further. The entrance to the lock is readily identifiable by a large clump of trees and white buildings with a space (the lock) between them. It is usually difficult to tell whether the lock gates are open or shut until directly in line with them as a red traffic light on the left hand side isn't used anymore. Having contacted the HM on arrival you will be called to enter the lock in order.

The approach channel begins at the small Lock Reach SHB and is marked by a curving line of withies to be left close on your port side. There are depth gauges on either side of the lock entrance (shown in metres on the left, in feet on the right) and the lock is worked for about two hours before HW. There's plenty of knowledgeable help with mooring lines once in the lock. Visitors should berth in the basin as directed. The Lock Master's cottage and office are on the port side of the lock.

Once berthed in the Basin it is a pleasant dinghy trip up the canal (which has a 4kn speed limit) to land at a pontoon behind Tesco supermarket in Maldon to re-provision. There's also a group of useful shops at Heybridge, reached by walking or cycling about 1M up the towpath and turning right along the road that crosses the canal. These include smaller supermarkets, a pharmacy, PO and small restaurant/takeaways.

As an alternative to locking into the Basin, CRS Marine has drying pontoon moorings just outside the lock on the N side of the entrance, albeit with similar access times to the Basin, and some swinging moorings in the river.

Heybridge Basin

Low tide reveals the gutway leading to Hebridge Basin lock

Follow the curving line of red painted withies to enter the lock

HEYBRIDGE BASIN — CM9 4RX

Contact
VHF Ch 80
Callsign *Heybridge Lock*
Lock Master Paul Hindley
☏ 07712 079764
paul.hindley@waterways.org.uk
www.essexwaterways.org.uk

Access HWS -2hr, HWN -1hr;
0600-2000 May-Sept, 0800-1700 Oct-April, as tides demand

Facilities WC, showers, laundry
Water Taps, Use own hoses
Pump-out and chemical toilet disposal
Electricity At shore points – tokens from Lock Office
Boat repairs Stebbens Boatyard ☏ 07974 530269
CRS Marine ☏ 01621 854684 / 07850 543873
Cranes 16-T at basin, 7-T at CRS Marine
Pub/Restaurant The Old Ship ☏ 01621 854150
The Jolly Sailor ☏ 01621 854210
The Tiptree Tea Room on seawall ☏ 01621 854466
Provisions Basics from small shop at rear of the Jolly Sailor, open in pub hours ☏ 01621 854210
Transport Bus to Maldon (infrequent)
Taxi ☏ 01621 855111, 850850

Heybridge to Maldon

From Heybridge Basin, Colliers Reach continues SW to Herring Point, where the Blackwater becomes the River Chelmer, and turns NW once more, then W, and winds up to Maldon. A few smacks may be anchored opposite Herring Point in the bight off the end of the mole, but they dry out soon after HW.

Leave Herring Point No.9 SHB to starboard and keep following the red and green buoys as the channel first twists to the N, close to the E shore, then back W past the end of the Promenade (mole). **Maldon YC** www.maldonyc.org.uk stands on the W shore just S of the Promenade. A large yellow/black post with a yellow X topmark stands a short way along the promenade marking the inner end of a concrete launching ramp.

Lines of drying moorings outside the channel on both the Prom foreshore and the opposite bank, together with the channel buoys, give a good indication of the deep water. A sharp turn to starboard at the No.19 final SHB brings you onto a course parallel and close to the beginning of Hythe Quay. Beware Thames barges motoring to and from the Quay around tide time, because they need the full width of the deep water to manoeuvre, particularly if they are turning to berth at the quay with their heads downstream.

Visitors should lie alongside the floating pontoon set parallel to the N end of the Quay and be prepared to dry out unless their visit is to be a swift one at HW. There is no charge for the occasional overnight stay alongside this pontoon, though a charge may be made for longer stays. It has perhaps 2·5m at HWS and 1·0m at HWN.

Above Hythe Quay, there is a small drying marina, run by Shipways Boatyard, followed by boatyards and mud berths lining the W bank right up to the road bridge at Fullbridge, but there are likely to be few available berths. A drying berth may be available on the upstream side of the first pontoons belonging to Shipways Boatyard (see box), which is immediately above the Queen's Head pub and has Marinestore Chandlers on site. It's advisable to call first and enquire.

Maldon town climbs the hillside with the spire of St Mary's church standing clear above the masts of barges lying in their permanent berths at the Hythe, while further upstream and to the right are the grey buildings of the old timber yards and flour mills. This was once a thriving port with smacks lining the foreshore along the prom, barges being repaired at

11. RIVER BLACKWATER

Walter Cook's yard (where the blocks are still used by barges), and barges and coasters coming and going to the mills, plus several busy boatbuilding yards above the town and a sailmaker in between. Today the barges at the Hythe are used for corporate and private charters, and yachts and motor boats fill the mud berths that line the bank from the Hythe right up to the Fullbridge. However, the commercial traffic and smacks have gone, although several yards are still busy with yachts.

Maldon Little Ship Club stands behind the Quay and the Jolly Sailor and Queen's Head pubs serve the needs of thirsty sailors. The River Bailiff no longer has an office on the quayside. The whole Quay has been 'sanitised', but there is still an East Coast air that thickens as you move up river through the various boatyards, where the charm of mud and old wooden boats persists.

MALDON — CM9 5HN

Contact
River Bailiff ☎ 07818 013723
rivers@maldon.gov.uk
www.visitmaldon.co.uk

Access MHWS ±1hr to visitors' pontoon at Hythe Quay

Water Tap use own hoses

Chandler Marinestore, North St ☎ 01621 854280

Gas ask at Marinestore Chandlers

Provisions In town

Post Office In town

Pharmacy and doctor In town

Boat repairs Various yards along North St and Downs Road including Shipways Boatyard ☎ 01621 854280 15-T crane, slipway, 20-T winch; Hedgecock's ☎ 07836 715685, 15-T crane; Downs Road Boatyard ☎ 01621 859373

Rigger TS Rigging ☎ 01621 874861
www.tsrigging.co.uk

Pub/Restaurant Queen's Head ☎ 01621 854112
Jolly Sailor ☎ 01621 853463
Many others in town

Club Maldon Little Ship Club ☎ 01621 854139 (Open weekends, Weds/Fri evenings)
www.mlsc.org.uk

Maldon YC
info@maldonyc.org.uk
www.maldonyc.org.uk

Taxi ☎ 01621 850850, 855111

Barges rounding Herring Point, where the Blackwater becomes the Chelmer and heading for the Hythe Quay

Maldon

Final approach to Maldon, with iconic EC barges moored at The Hythe

Once a major trading port Maldon is now a popular yachting centre

North Fambridge Yacht Club

North Fambridge Yacht Station and moorings, looking down river

12. RIVER CROUCH

⊕ **Landfall waypoint**
51°41'·8N 001°08'·3E
Just S of Swin Spitway SWB

Charts
Imray 2000 series, Y17
Admiralty 5607, 3750

Tides
Burnham-on-Crouch HW Walton +0042
Fambridge HW Walton +0100

Crouch Harbour Authority
Harbourmaster ☎01621 783602
Harbour Office VHF (occasional watch only) Ch 16
Crouch Harbour' working Ch 11.
info@crouchharbour.org.uk
www.crouchharbour.uk

Harbour dues are payable on vessels kept afloat on the Crouch (and Roach), while visiting vessels are free of any charge for up to 14 days. Beyond that, 'Short Visit' dues may be payable.

Main hazards

The Whitaker Channel, leading in towards the River Crouch, runs roughly NE-SW between Foulness Sand (on the S side) and the Buxey and Ray Sands (on the N side). All of these sandbanks are extremely hard and present a serious hazard to any vessel grounding in rough weather. The buoyage in the channel is excellent with marks at frequent intervals – and all of them lit.

There is shoal water across the whole of the Crouch entrance between the Swin Spitway and the Whitaker Beacon, across the eastern tails of the Swallowtail bank and Whitaker Spit.

Tides are strong, but follow the courses of the channels without too much set across the sands.

Watchkeepers must keep a lookout for both inbound and outbound ships using the main channel along the S side of the River Crouch.

There are speed limits on different stretches of the Crouch and these are clearly indicated by marked buoys.

Approaches

From NW, N & NE From the Rivers Colne and Blackwater, and the Wallet, the normal route will be through the Spitway, which is the shallow channel running between the Wallet and the Swin. Identify and pass comfortably close to both the Wallet Spitway (L.Fl.10s Bell) and Swin Spitway (Iso.10s Bell) SWBs before turning WSW towards the Swallowtail route, or heading S for the Whitaker Channel.

As an alternative to the longer haul out to the Spitway, shoal draught boats coming from the Colne or Blackwater may slip through the shallow inshore Ray Sand (Rays'n) Channel. This runs between the Buxey Sand and the Dengie Flats. It is a passage recommended only on a rising tide, above about half tide, and with a close watch kept on the depth sounder. Recent information may be found at www.crossingthethamesestuary.com.

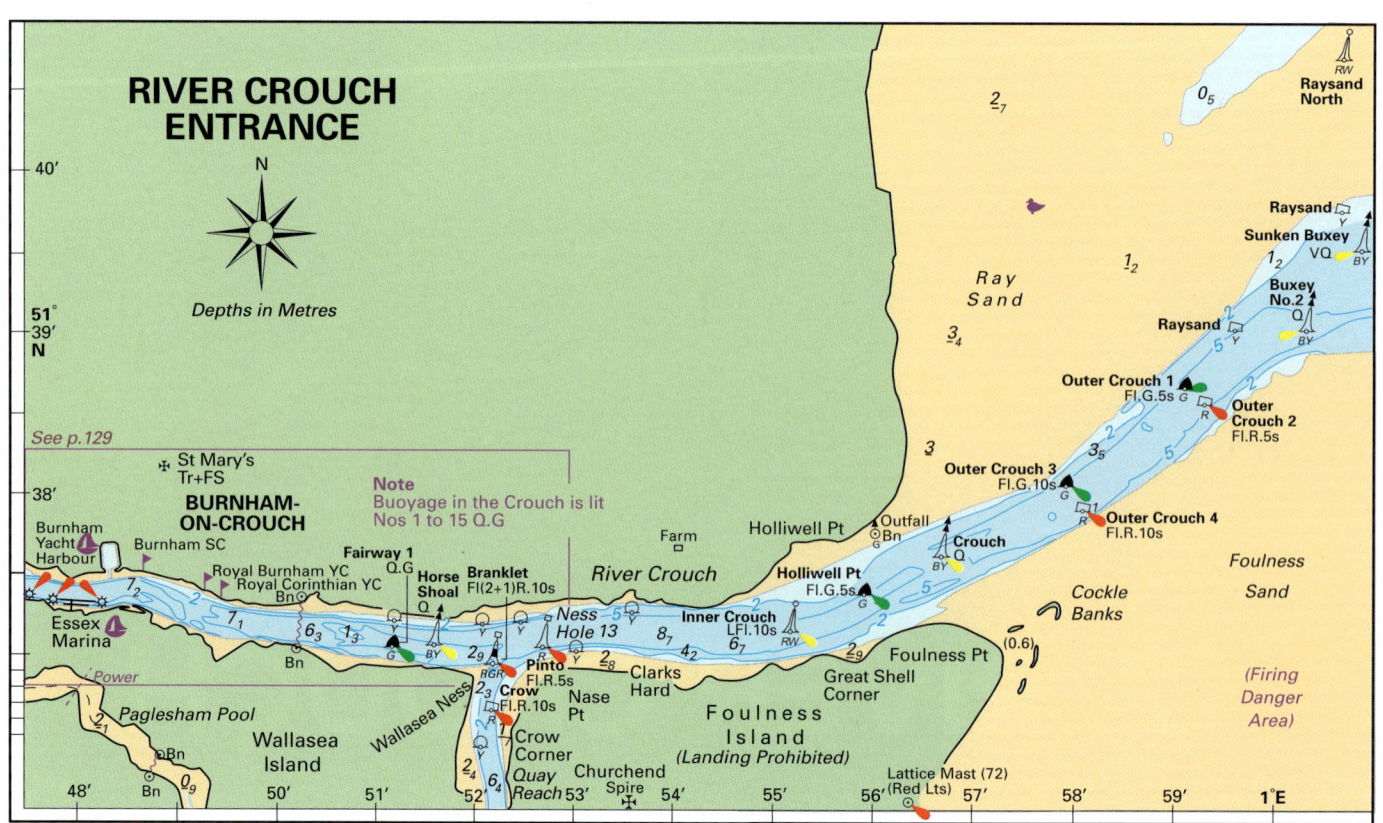

River Crouch

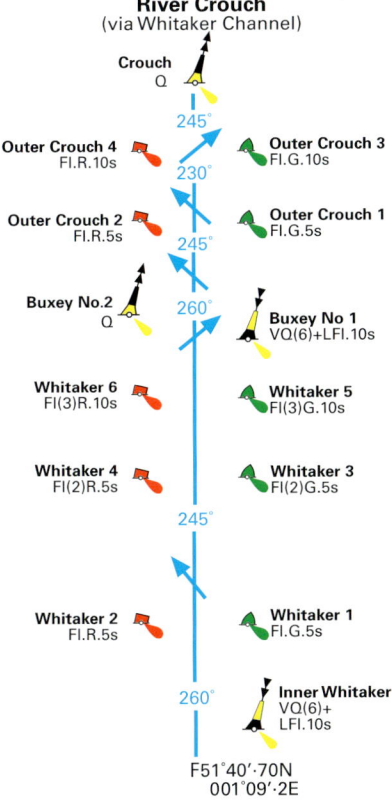

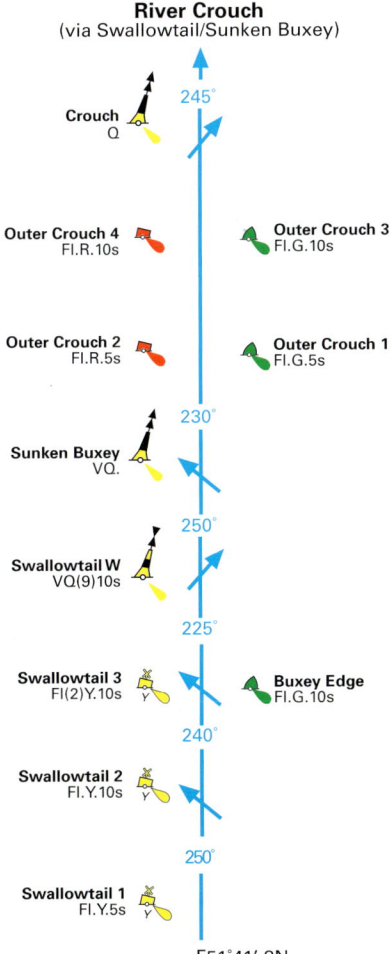

Starting from the Knoll NCB, reach the Swire Hole with its rapidly changing depths, then head WSW until the Buxey Bn bears S. Then alter course to about SSW, leaving the Buxey Beacon ½M or so to port and look for the unlit Raysand North yellow pillar mark (the 'Ron Pipe') which in 2023 was moved to a new position just E of the 1°E meridian. Then turn S to find the unlit spherical yellow 'Ray Sand' buoy which lies on the northern edge of the Crouch (there is no longer a 'Raysand Middle' buoy). Once in the deeper water, head SSW towards the Outer Crouch No.1 and No.2 buoys.

From E, S & SE Coming in from the E means navigating through the off-lying sand banks towards the Inner Whitaker SCB (VQ(6)+LFl.10s) before heading SW into the Whitaker Channel.

From the River Thames or the North Kent coast, the navigator will again have to work through the sands before carefully crossing the NE end of the Whitaker Spit, which in recent years has been slowly growing to the NE.

Note that the NE extent of the Shoeburyness Outer Firing Danger Area covers almost the entire drying area of the Foulness Sand.

Entry via Whitaker Channel

From the Inner Whitaker SCB, the Whitaker Channel runs SW for almost 9M to the Crouch NCB (Q) at Shore Ends. The deeper buoyed channel lies along the edge of the Foulness Sand with good water all the way, although care must be taken in the region of the Sunken Buxey where there is a kink in the channel between Buxey No.1 SCB (VQ(6)+L.Fl.10s) and Buxey No.2 NCB (Q). From there head to the twin Outer Crouch 1 and 2 buoys.

Some competition on the long haul in from the Whitaker

East Coast Pilot

12. RIVER CROUCH

Entry via Swallowtail

The alternative route into the Crouch is along the Buxey side, although it does have one area of shallows. From the yellow Swallowtail No.1 (Fl.Y.5s), pass the Swallowtail No.2 (Fl.Y.10s), then through a gate formed by the Swallowtail No.3 (Fl(2)Y.10s) and the Buxey Edge SHB (Fl.G.10s); cross shallows to pass the Swallowtail W WCB (VQ(9)10s) and the Sunken Buxey NCB (VQ), joining the main channel at the twin Outer Crouch 1 and 2 buoys.

Beyond the Outer Crouch 3 and 4 buoys, the Crouch NCB (Q) marks the start of the River Crouch itself. There is often a sizeable seal colony hauled out on the Foulness Sand shortly before Shore Ends, or sometimes on the shallows opposite on the north side of the river, which makes a fine sight.

Shore Ends to Burnham

From the Crouch NCB the river runs westwards past the Holliwell Point SHB (Fl.G.5s) which guards shallows close inshore of it, and the Inner Crouch SWB (LFl.10s) in the middle of the deep channel, for about 2¾M to the mouth of the River Roach, which opens to the S. A further PHB (Fl.R.5s), Pinto, lies over a wreck just E of the Roach entrance. On the W side of the Roach entrance is the red/green/red Branklet 'preferred channel' buoy (Fl(2+1)R.10s), which marks the mud spit reaching out from Wallasea Ness and must be left to port when heading for Burnham, or to starboard if heading into the Roach.

From the Branklet buoy a slight dog-leg around the Horse Shoal NCB (Q) should keep you in a dredged section up to the Fairway No.1 SHB (Q.G), perhaps an unnecessary diversion for small craft unless near LW.

BURNHAM–ON–CROUCH

From Fairway No.1 (marked 'F1') the marked deep-water channel runs onwards along the S shore of the Crouch, past Burnham town to just beyond the marinas. However, once the lines of moorings are reached there is good water anywhere across the river – but be aware of the tide, it can easily run at up to 3kn. Be careful also, when beating up river, not to stray into the breaks in the Wallasea Island sea wall opposite the whole Burnham waterfront. These breaches, made to create a wetland nature reserve on the island, have submerged obstacles in them to prevent navigation and the ebb pours out strongly through the gaps.

Approaching Burnham-on-Crouch, the first of the long lines of swinging moorings on the N side of the river starts at the Rice & Coles boatyard, identified by a crane on the seawall and a landing pontoon. Note the charted crossing point for high voltage power cables and make no attempt to anchor nearby. Anchoring is also prohibited anywhere in the Fairway and is to be avoided anywhere within the moorings.

Outside Burnham Week (usually the last week of August) there are many moorings available up and down the river. These are looked after by the various boatyards and yacht clubs, which also have their own landing pontoons.

The first landmark for Burnham is the big white building of the Royal Corinthian YC. This club welcomes paying visitors on its all-tide pontoon which has power and water. They may also use facilities overnight. If you would like to use the pontoon or one of the club's several visitor moorings (launch service available), call the club secretary (open for food Weds and Fri for lunch/bistro, all day Sat, Sun for breakfast/lunch/dinner).

Horse Shoal NCB, head for the Fairway no.1 SHB here

ROYAL CORINTHIAN YC
www.royalcorinthian.co.uk
info@royalcorinthian.co.uk ☎01621 782105

The Royal Corinthian YC

Fairway no.1 buoy

Burnham-on-Crouch

Burnham waterfront

Royal Burnham YC

ROYAL BURNHAM YC
www.rbyc.uk
info@rbyc.org.uk, ☏01621 782044

A short distance westwards from the RCYC, the Royal Burnham YC also offers their pontoon hammerhead for visitors using the club, if there's space, with a small charge made for overnight stays. *Note* that this club takes card payments only.

On westwards, prominent buildings include the Anchor, The White Harte, Prior's boatyard, and finally the Burnham SC before reaching Burnham Yacht Harbour. It's an interesting waterfront steeped in history, but is steadily changing as older sites are taken up with modern housing. A ferry service currently runs from Burnham Yacht Harbour across the river to Wallasea at Essex Marina in summer, pending long-outstanding restoration of the Burnham town pontoon which was their previous base (for current ferry details see information panels).

A further dinghy club, Creeksea Sailing Club, is on the N bank beyond the marina.

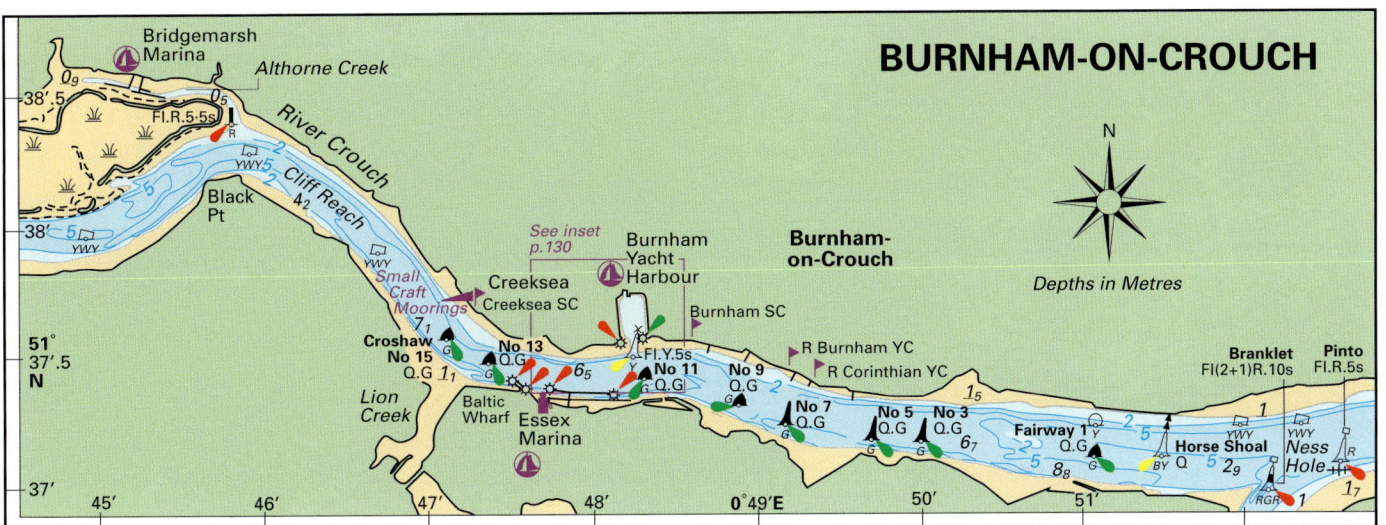

East Coast Pilot • 129

12. RIVER CROUCH

Burnham Yacht Harbour

The harbour is cut into the N shore of the Crouch, just up river from Burnham town, the entrance marked by a yellow pillar offing buoy with an X topmark (Fl.Y.5s). It is important to pass close to this buoy, because it lines you up for the entrance channel which is dredged through the shoreside mud bank.

From this offing buoy, head straight into the marina, passing between the pair of large metal posts, red (Fl.R.10s) to port and green (Fl.G.10s) to starboard.

There is no designated visitors' berthing, so call ahead and, if expecting to arrive outside office hours, request codes for the gate to the pontoons and the door to the ablutions block.

From the entrance, turn to starboard for pontoon row A and to port for row H. Berth numbers are on ends of fingers with low numbers close to the shore and high numbers near the river. Some fingers, particularly in row A, are shorter than the boats occupying them, which can make spotting the numbers difficult.

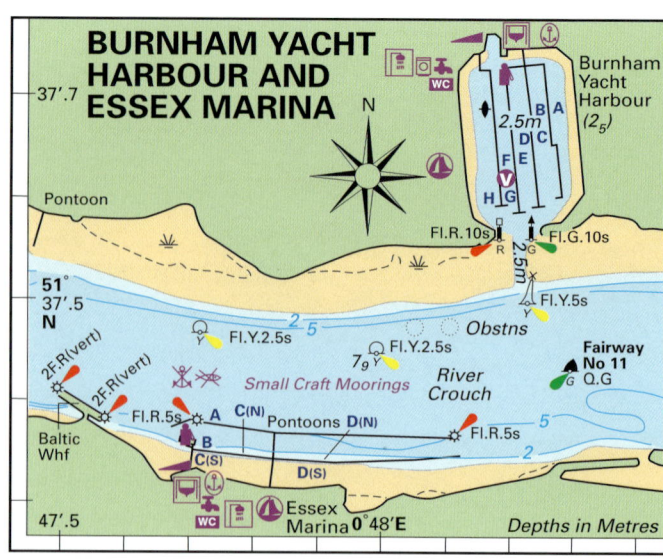

In 2023, short stays, e.g. over lunchtime, were being offered free if crews ate in the Swallowtail Restaurant at the marina.

Burnham Yacht Harbour

Essex Marina

Sunset over Burnham YH

Essex Marina

BURNHAM YACHT HARBOUR　　CM0 8BL

Contact
VHF Ch 80
Callsign *Burnham Yacht Harbour*
Harbourmaster ☎01621 786832, office ☎01621 782150
admin@burnhamyachtharbour.co.uk
www.burnhamyachtharbour.co.uk

Access 24hr
Fuel Diesel berth on row 'F', landward end close to boat lift. Tight turning space
Facilities WC, showers, laundry, WiFi (free)
Water Taps and hoses on pontoons
Electricity On pontoons.
Gas ask in HM's office
Chandler In town, WetWorks 01621 786413
www.thewetworks.co.uk
Boatyard Boat repairs, 35-T travelift, 100-T slipway, all services
Sailmakers Lonton & Gray ☎01621 786200
www.lontonandgray.com
Provisions At Co-op (Fiveways), about 10 minutes walk up road from marina, or in town, about 15 minutes walk.
Post Office and Pharmacy At Fiveways (near Co-op, see above)
Pub/Restaurant Swallowtail on site (check hours ☎01621 785505), several more in town
Pharmacy At Fiveways near Co-op
Ferry Crossings to Essex Marina Apr-Sept ☎07704 060482 www.burnhamferry.co.uk
Trains Direct to London
Taxi ☎07496 609697 (Dengie Taxis), 01621 786963 (Gemini)

Essex Marina and Wallasea

On the S shore of the Crouch, slightly upstream from the Burnham Yacht Harbour, is Wallasea Bay and the Essex Marina, whose pontoons run parallel to the river. Warning buoys mid-river ask for wash to be kept down.

Approaching Essex Marina is more a case of not passing it by. Outer and inner pontoons run parallel to the river with entrances at both ends and a linking walkway between them to the shore in the middle. Riverside berths (along N side of arm 'A') are alongside the main pontoon, while all others are on fingers, every berth having a finger on both sides. Contact the marina office for berthing instructions and ask whether to enter from downstream (east) or upstream (west) end.

ESSEX MARINA　　SS4 2HF

Contact
VHF Ch 80
Callsign *Essex Marina*
Harbourmaster ☎01702 258531
info@essexmarina.co.uk
www.essexmarina.co.uk

Access 24hr
Fuel Diesel and petrol from barge at W end beside boat lift
Facilities WC, showers, WiFi, laundry
Water On pontoons
Electricity On pontoons
Gas Ask in office
Boat repairs 70-T travel-lift, slipway
Pub/Restaurant restaurant/bar, open to all, Weds-Sun.
Ferry Crossings to Burnham Yacht Harbour, Apr-Sept ☎07704 060482 www.burnhamferry.co.uk
Trains Rochford (4M away) for London
Taxi ☎01702 217430

12. RIVER CROUCH

Ada Point beacon and Althorne Creek entrance

At the W end of Wallasea Bay, just beyond the marina, is Baltic Wharf which is a busy shipping facility, and watchkeepers must keep a sharp eye out for vessels manoeuvring in the main channel.

Wallasea to Althorne Creek (Bridgemarsh)

Above Wallasea and the Baltic Wharf the river turns NW through Cliff Reach with shallows along the N shore, so it's wise to leave Fairway buoys 13 and 15 Croshaw, both Q.G, to starboard. Here the marked Fairway ends, off Creeksea SC, and the river scenery becomes more rural and interesting when compared to the reaches below Burnham.

The NW section to Althorne Creek and Bridgemarsh Marina, known as Cliff Reach because of the 40-50ft cliffs along the N shore, offers one of the few places in the Crouch with any shelter from NE winds. Anchorage can be found under the cliffs, but there are some foul patches along the low water line. If the wind goes into the W it can be very uncomfortable here and a move to anchor under the opposite shore may be worthwhile.

Throughout Cliff Reach and indeed most of the reaches beyond, the best water lies about midway between the banks, but keep towards the outsides of bends as there are often spits and shoals off points and headlands.

To port at the top of Cliff Reach is Black Point where the main river bends back SW and Althorne Creek runs off to the N behind Bridgemarsh Island (where no landing is allowed). Althorne Creek is the location of Bridgemarsh Marina.

Bridgemarsh Marina

A large red beacon (Fl.R.5·5s) labelled Ada Point, off the E tip of Bridgemarsh Island, is the first sign of Althorne Creek. If entering the creek, leave this beacon to port and, as the entrance opens up, follow the line of red can buoys leading in around the bend W to the marina hidden behind the island. (In 2023 these were not obviously red as the paint

First sight of Bridgemarsh Marina from the entrance

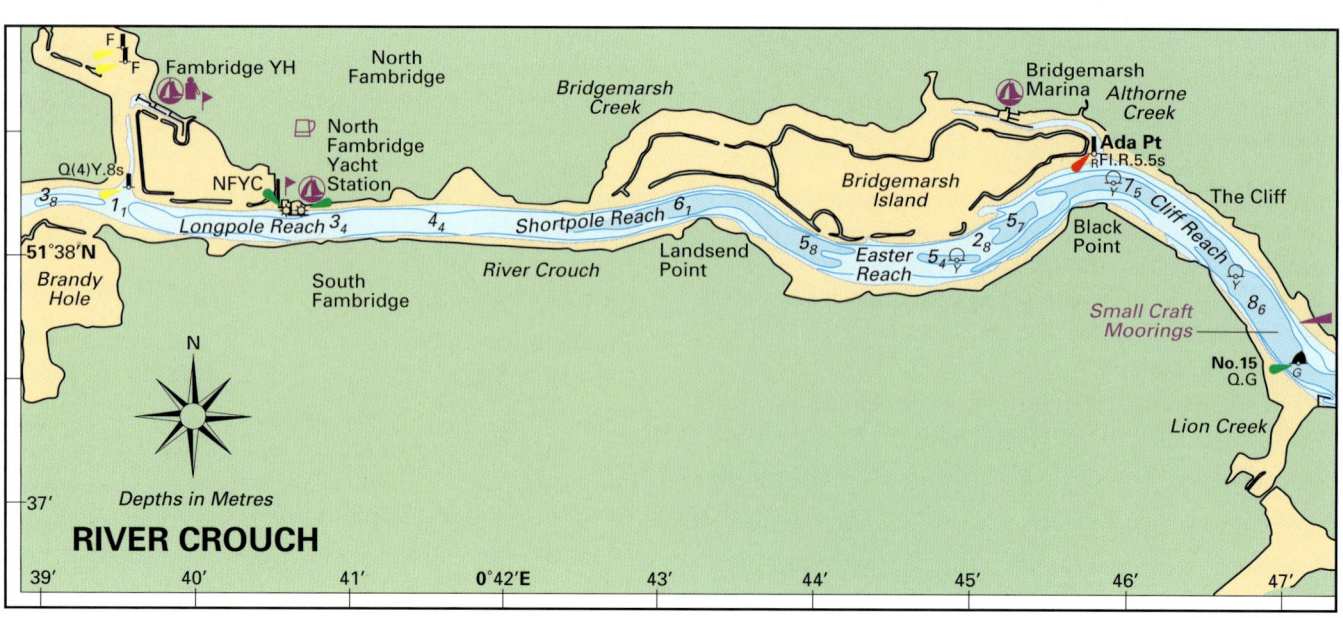

Althorne to Fambridge

Bridgemarsh Marina, the entrance at the far end

was peeling off – but they are all port hand buoys). Once round through the entrance, the end of the main pontoon comes into view directly ahead, with a shorter parallel pontoon to starboard of it. A sign indicates that the fairway continues to port along the S side of the main pontoon. A separate, second pontoon stands beyond the first, on the far (W) side of the yard's slipway.

All pontoons and access walkways in this marina have recently been renewed, with a total capacity of 195 berths.

Any intending visitors should call first, stating their boat's draught - spaces are limited and the depth at LW varies. The bottom is soft mud.

Bridgemarsh Marina, looking east

BRIDGEMARSH MARINA   CM3 6DQ

Contact
HM 07859 957719, Office
☎01621 786503 (closed on Sundays)
info@bridgemarshmarina.co.uk
www.bridgemarshmarina.co.uk

Access HW ±4hr

Facilities WC, showers

Fuel None in 2023 but may be reinstated - ask

Water On pontoons

Electricity On pontoons

Gas Ask in office

Boatyard Minor repairs, slipway, 9T crane, boat storage, scrubbing posts.

Transport Railway station - trains to London and Burnham.

Taxi ☎01621 783007, 784878

Althorne to Fambridge

From Ada Point the main river takes a dive SW past the yellow Canewdon racing mark (summer), then W along the S shore of Bridgemarsh Island, which floods on spring tides, through Easter Reach and NW through Raypits Reach before returning to a W'ly course with Shortpole Reach passing the W end of Bridgemarsh Island. Circumnavigating Bridgemarsh Island by way of Althorne and Bridgemarsh Creeks is possible near HWS with a fair wind and a very shallow draught boat or dinghy, but there's an old ford to cross and the channel is tortuous, so it's quite an adventure.

12. RIVER CROUCH

Fambridge Yacht Station, berthing on both sides

North Fambridge Yacht Station

A little over 1M above Bridgemarsh Creek (the W end of Bridgemarsh Island) there are lines of moorings at Fambridge, with the North Fambridge YC and North Fambridge Yacht Station on the N shore. The Yacht Station is a 120m long floating pontoon outside the North Fambridge YC clubhouse for visiting boats to lie alongside. This and the moorings are operated by the Yacht Haven (see below). Posts at each end of the pontoon are lit Fl(3)G.4s. Anchoring is only advisable above or below the moorings, but there is good depth. Astonishingly, the North Fambridge YC clubhouse, at the top of the ramp up from the pontoon, was designed by Brunel for use as a field hospital in the Crimean War!

As you approach Fambridge from downstream (E), you only see the end of the pontoon and may not appreciate its length until you are much closer. Berthing is available along both sides (1·2m least depth), as directed, but it can be crowded, and is not bookable. Rafting is permitted. If you have found a berth, you can pay the berthing fees either via smartphone and QR code at the locked gate (which then allows access to and fro), or by phone to the Yacht Haven office.

If manoeuvring upstream of the pontoon, be aware that depths shallow rapidly inside the first line of moorings.

NORTH FAMBRIDGE YACHT STATION   CM3 6LR

Contact
VHF Ch 80
Callsign *Fambridge Yacht Haven*
☎01621 740370
fambridge@yachthavens.com
www.yachthavens.com/fambridge

Access 24hr to moorings/pontoon
Fuel Diesel in cans from Yacht Haven
Facilities WC, showers, WiFi (free with code)
Water On pontoon
Electricity On pontoon
Gas Ask in Yacht Haven office
Boat repairs Slip and 25-T hoist
Club North Fambridge YC
www.northfambridgeyachtclub.co.uk
info@northfambridgeyachtclub.co.uk
Pub/Restaurant Ferry Boat Inn at top of yard
☎01621 740208
Transport Railway station 1M in village, trains to London or Burnham (complimentary pick-up / drop-off service may be available, ask in office)
Taxi ☎01621 850850, 855111, or ask in office

Note The North Fambridge Yacht Station and the Fambridge Yacht Haven are under joint management, hence the duplication of some contact and website details.

Leading marks on shoreline

Buoyed route up Stow Creek

Fambridge Yacht Haven

Fambridge Yacht Haven (Stow Creek)

A little over ½M upstream from Fambridge, Stow Creek branches off to the N with Fambridge Yacht Haven at the top. A lit yellow buoy lies in the river off the entrance. In the mouth of the creek there's a beacon, known as Stow Post (Q(4)Y.8s), showing a 4kn speed limit sign. This should be left to port when making for the marina, despite some charts still suggesting it should be left to starboard, and there is a small green buoy on the E side of the entrance.

The ¼M channel is dredged, straightforward and is marked with small red and green buoys, all with reflective tape. There is a pair of lit (2Ldg.F) leading mark posts at the N end. The creek has shoaled in recent years and safe access is now suggested between HW+/-4 hours. There is a substantial building on the skyline beyond that appears directly above the leading posts when on track. As soon as the marina opens up to starboard you can turn sharply in along the long pontoon, the fairway being on the S side. The fuel berth is just over halfway along.

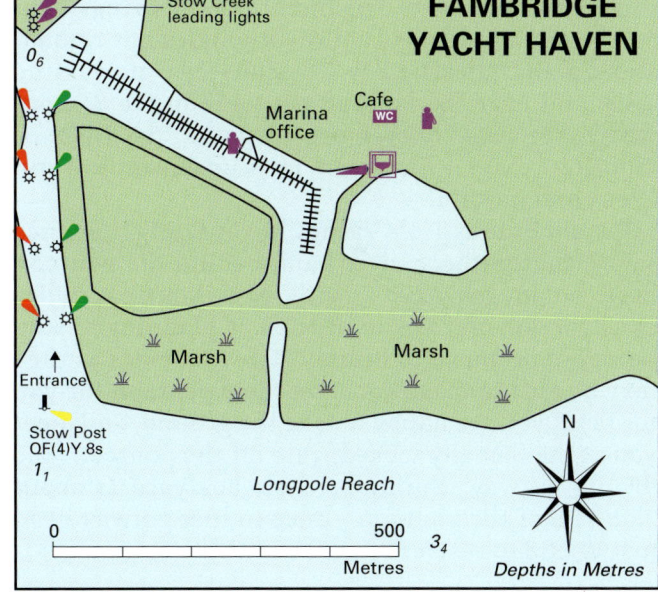

FAMBRIDGE YACHT HAVEN — CM3 6LU

Contact
VHF Ch 80
Callsign *Fambridge Yacht Haven*
Office ☎01621 740370
fambridge@yachthavens.com
www.yachthavens.com/fambridge
Access Approx HW+/-4
Fuel Diesel berth; petrol by jerry can or available for boats on trailers
Facilities WC, showers, laundry, WiFi (free with code), Childrens' playground, bike hire
Water On pontoons

Electricity On pontoons
Gas Ask in office
Chandler Small stock on site
Boat repairs Slip and 40T boat hoist, engineer, GRP repairs etc; also customer workshop facility
Pub/Restaurant 'River Breeze' café/bar on site ☎07443 871549
Ferry Boat Inn, N Fambridge (10-minute walk) ☎01621 740208;
Transport Railway station 1M in village (complimentary pick-up / drop-off service may be available, ask in office), trains to London or Burnham.
Taxi ☎01621 850850, 855111, or ask in office

12. RIVER CROUCH

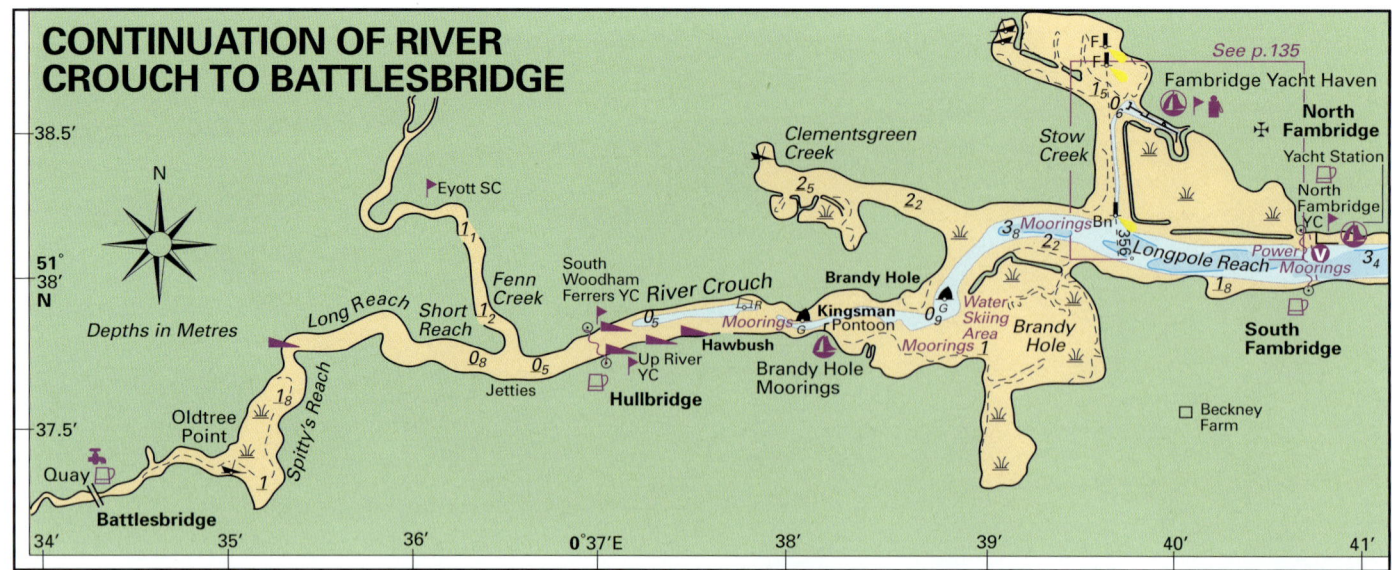

Stow Creek to Brandy Hole

Just W of Stow Creek the main river turns SW past a small red buoy, while an arm called Clementsgreen Creek carries on W, but is not navigable for cruisers. The SW stretch of the river, called Brandy Hole Reach, has a SHB 'Brandy Hole' halfway along, and sees the Crouch becoming much narrower and shallower. A notice warns against anchoring above this point because of shellfish beds. Moorings here and beyond mostly dry at LW, although some remain afloat in Brandy Hole Bay, a designated water-skiing area, and near the landing pontoon on the S shore where the river once more turns W. The lines of moorings extend for over a mile upstream to Fenn Creek and beyond.

The old Brandy Hole Yacht Club building that once sat on the southern river bank behind the pontoon here no longer exists, with new housing under construction on the site in 2023. If planning to stop here, phone ahead to Brandy Hole Moorings as they may be able to make room on their pontoon for you to stay if you are happy to take the ground, and meet you at the (usually locked) gate off the pontoon. The drying gutway leading to their boatyard is about 75m ESE of the pontoon – once in that gutway head just W of S to reach the yard slipway.

Arriving at Hullbridge and its two clubs

BRANDY HOLE MOORINGS   SS5 6QB

Contact
☏ 01702 231496 or 07788 470718
info@brandyholemoorings.co.uk
www.brandyholemoorings.co.uk

Access HW ±4hr

Facilities Moorings, slipway, boat repairs, canvas work

Landing At pontoon, but shoreside access gate may be locked; contact Brandy Hole Moorings

Provisions and Post Office Ferry Road, Hullbridge, 20–30 minutes walk

Pub/Food The Anchor, Hullbridge (walk up river along sea wall) ☏ 01702 230777

Brandy Hole to Battlesbridge

The channel meanders on upstream through moorings, the deeper route marked by two unlit buoys, the Kingsman SHB and beyond it, the Hawbush PHB. We are now so far up river that HW is half an hour after Burnham, yet there are two very active clubs here and large numbers of moorings. Reaching Hullbridge (on the south bank), the Up River YC has a private slipway and a clubhouse with bar, kitchen and changing rooms, plus moorings in the river. Both the dinghy and cruiser fleets are very active right through the season.

Hullbridge

The river and moorings at Hullbridge

UP RIVER YC   SS5 6PA
Contact via website
www.upriver.org.uk

The South Woodham Ferrers YC stands on the N bank near the ford just E of Fenn Creek and opposite the Up River YC. The club has cruiser moorings, workshops and a large concrete slipway. There are showers and toilets in the clubhouse.

SOUTH WOODHAM FERRERS YC   CM3 5WP
Contact via website
www.swfyc.com

Hullbridge is certainly an attractive possibility for a stop-over across HW and an excursion ashore by dinghy for refreshments, if you can borrow a mooring for a couple of hours.

From Fenn Creek the river runs west for a short distance, through moorings and past houses with shoreside moorings on the S bank. Occasional yellow buoys beyond the last mid-river moorings appear to suggest the best water, although the bottom seems fairly flat. From there, the river follows a winding, reasonably wide route until the final bend at Oldtree Point when the old mill buildings and antiques centre at Battlesbridge come into view. Here, the banks suddenly close in and space to manoeuvre becomes severely restricted.

Battlesbridge

A visit to Battlesbridge is certainly an adventure. In the absence of any dredging, sadly the reed-covered mudbanks are steadily encroaching on what was already a very narrow gutway for the final few hundred yards, and we suggest now that only a smaller boat with a lifting keel can reasonably arrive, perhaps for a swift drink in the local pub across HW, and then depart again. Do not linger when the tide turns, and think about how you are going to turn round as soon as you arrive.

If you are really interested in staying across a LW, there is a private small craft landing stage on the S bank just before the bridge, where a notice says that boats of up to 20ft can lie free of charge for a maximum period of 3 hours. The ground at this small craft landing is fairly flat, but the mud at the opposite N wall tends to slope outwards and lying there with bilge keels would mean leaning out at an alarming angle, while a single keel boat would need to be leant inwards rather carefully to avoid rigging and guardrail damage.

Beware also of a drying horse in midstream, which is ready to catch your keel as you turn the boat to head down river. With so little room to turn, only undertake the manoeuvre at or (better) just before HW.

Perhaps the best advice for any newcomer keen to try Battlesbridge is not to plan on staying over a tide, or perhaps even visit at all, unless you have first reconnoitred by road at LW and sized up the situation.

Battlesbridge at half tide, viewed from the road bridge

13. RIVER ROACH

Upstream view at Paglesham

13. RIVER ROACH

The Roach entrance and the Branklet buoy, to be left to stbd when entering the Roach

⊕ **Waypoint**
51°37'·0N 000°52'·3E Just E of Branklet buoy

Charts
Imray 2000, Y17
Admiralty SC5607, 3750

Tides
Paglesham HW Walton +0040
Rochford HW Walton +0050
Crouch Harbour Authority
Harbourmaster ☎01621 783602
info@crouchharbour.org.uk www.crouchharbour.uk
Roach Sailing Association
Contact details on website www.roachriver.org.uk/rsa

Main hazards

There are two ways of entering the Roach and the only notable hazard is the entry via the Havengore Bridge, which requires good weather and shallow draught, plus permission from the live firing range officials. Otherwise, there are no real hazards within the Roach, provided you follow the channels and avoid spits extending from offshoot creeks.

There are a lot of fishing boat movements in the river, so anchorages need to be chosen with care to avoid obstructing fairways.

There is an 8kn speed limit in the Roach, reducing to 4kn in the creeks and through the Paglesham moorings.

Approaches

The Roach can be entered either from its junction with the Crouch or directly from the sea across the Maplin Sands, then through the Havengore lifting bridge and the inside creeks.

Section 1 of this chapter deals with the approach and entry from the Crouch, and the details of the river as far as Paglesham.

Section 2 describes the approach and entry from the sea across the Maplin Sands through the Havengore Bridge, and then on northwards through the creeks to join the Roach near Paglesham.

Section 3 describes the upper reach of the Roach from Paglesham to Rochford.

1. FROM THE CROUCH TO PAGLESHAM

Approach from the Crouch

When approaching from the Crouch, make for the red/green/red Branklet 'preferred channel' buoy (Fl(2+1)R.10s) ½M E of the Horse Shoal NCB (Q), but remember to leave it on your starboard hand – the Branklet Spit is extensive.

Entry from the Crouch

Leave the Branklet preferred channel buoy close to starboard at the entrance in order to keep off the mud bank spreading out from Nase Point on the E shore. Then keep to the middle of the channel, favouring the outside of bends. There are racing buoys, but once past the Crow PHB (Fl.R.10s) there are no further channel marks until approaching Paglesham.

Branklet to Paglesham

Unlike the Crouch, there is shelter to be found within the Roach from all wind directions. The first useful spot is in Brankfleet at the N end of Quay Reach, just within the mouth of the river, under the W shore, where there is fair depth close in under the sea wall and good holding. Be sure to remain N of the yellow racing buoy Jubilee, because this is positioned off a bay that dries out.

A few boats are occasionally moored on the E side of Quay Reach near a landing on Foulness Island, charted as 'The Quay'. The landing is none too clean and somewhat slippery, but gives access to the

Do not anchor close inshore S of 'The Quay'

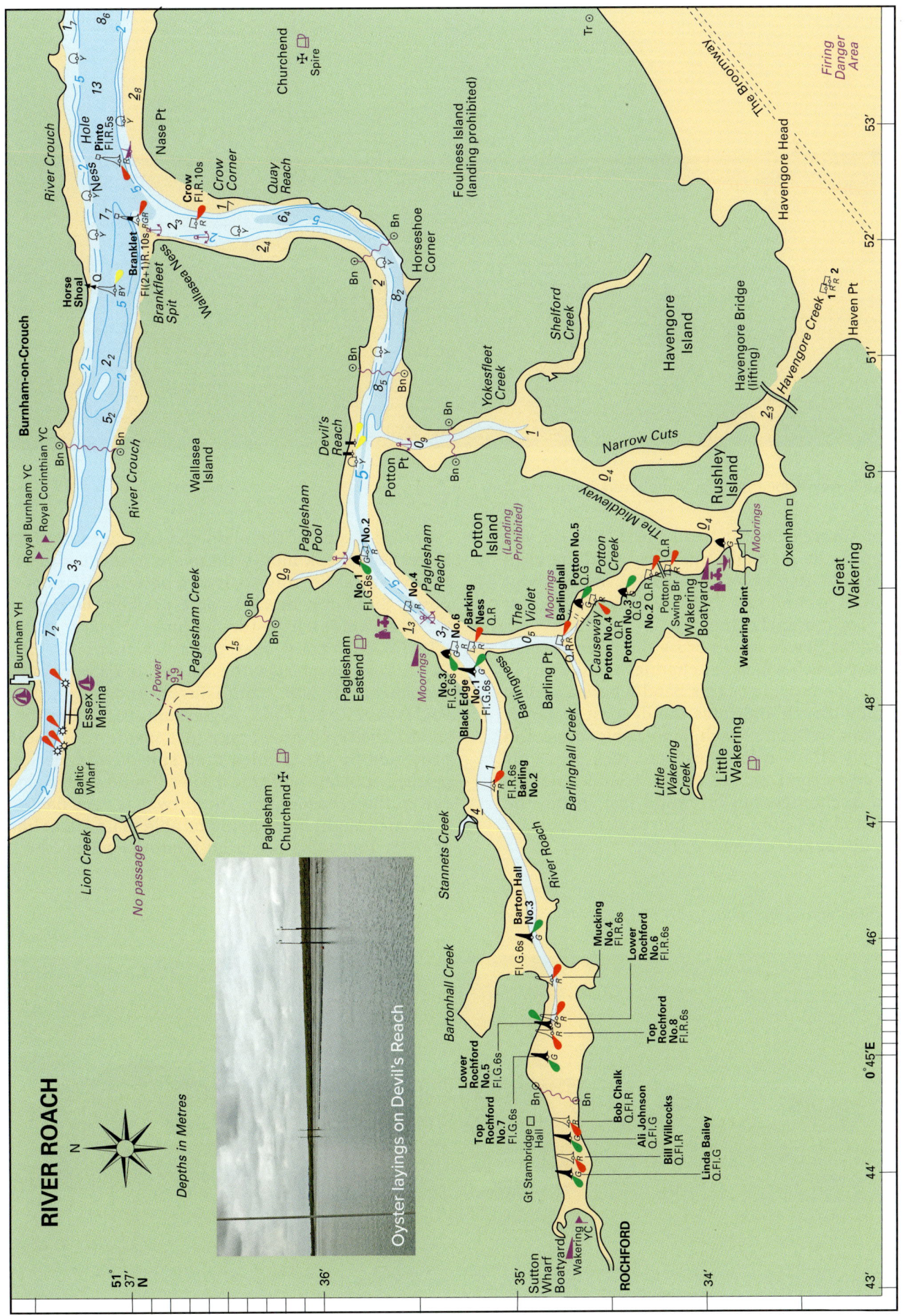

13. RIVER ROACH

Paglesham Creek/Pool entrance, a sheltered anchoring spot

hamlet of Church End. It is all MOD land, so you must keep to the footpath, then road, and the walk is about a mile. In view of a 2019 CHA notice about possible foul ground just S of the quay, we suggest you stay N of it if anchoring.

Underwater power cables cross the river at the S end of Quay Reach where the channel bends sharply W. Keep to the outside of this bend where a yellow racing buoy 'Roach' indicates the deepest water. A short way on, in Devil's Reach, more cables cross and immediately afterwards Yokesfleet Creek opens off S to run down the E side of Potton Island. Another sheltered anchorage can be found just inside the entrance under Potton Point, but beware the mud banks on either side of the entrance.

On the N side of the main channel close W of the Yokesfleet Creek mouth there are oyster layings on a substantial floating structure between pairs of lit posts. Similarly, beware some possible layings on the Potton side a little further on.

It's at this point that the river turns SW into Paglesham Reach. On the corner, a narrow creek branches off NW, confusingly known as both Paglesham Creek and Paglesham Pool. There's a small, sheltered anchorage just inside the mouth, protected by the withied mud spit off the western point, but below half tide it's best found with a close eye on the echosounder. The gutway is very narrow. A shoal draught boat should be able to lie afloat here at LWS. There is a potential landing spot on the W

Landing ramp across the mud

Through Havengore Bridge to Paglesham

Close-up of the clean landing west of the yard

side about 200m above the pillbox on the point, an old timber walkway laid directly on the saltings.

Also on the corner are fairway buoys No.1 (Fl.G.6s) and No.2, which start the buoyed channel through the Paglesham moorings. This fairway is used by fishing vessels going to and from their moorings up the river, and anchoring is prohibited. Boats wishing to anchor must do so either above or below the lines of moorings and set a riding light. The Roach Sailing Association (see RSA contact details at start of this chapter) manages most of the moorings downstream from the hard, and visitors are welcome to use any vacant ones.

The pontoon landing and hard of what for years was Shuttlewood's yard will be seen on the N side, together with probably several massive old steel barges under conversion to house boats, the current business of the yard. Landing on the pontoon (which has seen better days) is not encouraged and mooring on it is not allowed though it's unlikely you will face objections if using it to get ashore by dinghy; you may choose instead to use the concrete slipway immediately beyond the pontoon.

There is an alternative landing point upstream of this congested area - the RSA also manages a short stretch of shoreline immediately upstream of the old yard, including a landing ramp across the mud,

and you are welcome to land there by dinghy near HW if you wish.

It is under the mud of the Paglesham foreshore that the remains of HMS *Beagle* are believed to have been found. Darwin's famous ship was pensioned off after her third voyage, a survey of Australia, and used for some years as a Customs watch vessel in the Roach. Then she was sold for scrap in 1870 and what are believed to be her remains were discovered in the Paglesham mud downstream of the yard, together with possible parts incorporated in the structure of Shuttlewood's black shed. Sadly, the shed (shown in the 2023 aerial photo at the start of this chapter) was badly damaged in storms in January 2024 as we went to print, and has probably now been demolished.

From any of the Paglesham landing points described above, it is possible to walk to the Plough and Sail pub at the top of the un-made lane above the boatyard. If planning to eat there, it is very popular and booking ahead is advised.

Plough and Sail ☎01702 258242
www.theploughandsail.co.uk

2. THROUGH HAVENGORE BRIDGE TO PAGLESHAM

Approaches across the Maplin Sands to Havengore Creek and onwards to the Roach

The main barrier to entering via the Havengore Bridge is the depth on the Maplins, particularly over the Broomway, which is an ancient raised track that dries about 4m, so has only about 2m over it at HWS (on a big tide) and often as little as 0·5m at neaps. On an average spring tide, boats with as little as 1–1·5m draught may still touch as they cross the Broomway and, sensibly, should only attempt it in smooth sea conditions. A local saying has it that when there's 5m height of tide at Southend, there's 5ft over the Broomway. It seems to be a reasonable equation, but monitor the PLA's broadcasts detailing actual tidal heights, which include Southend, on VHF Ch 69 at H+15 and H+45, to discover any significant variation from the predicted height.

Huge houseboats under construction at Paglesham between the pontoon and the slipway

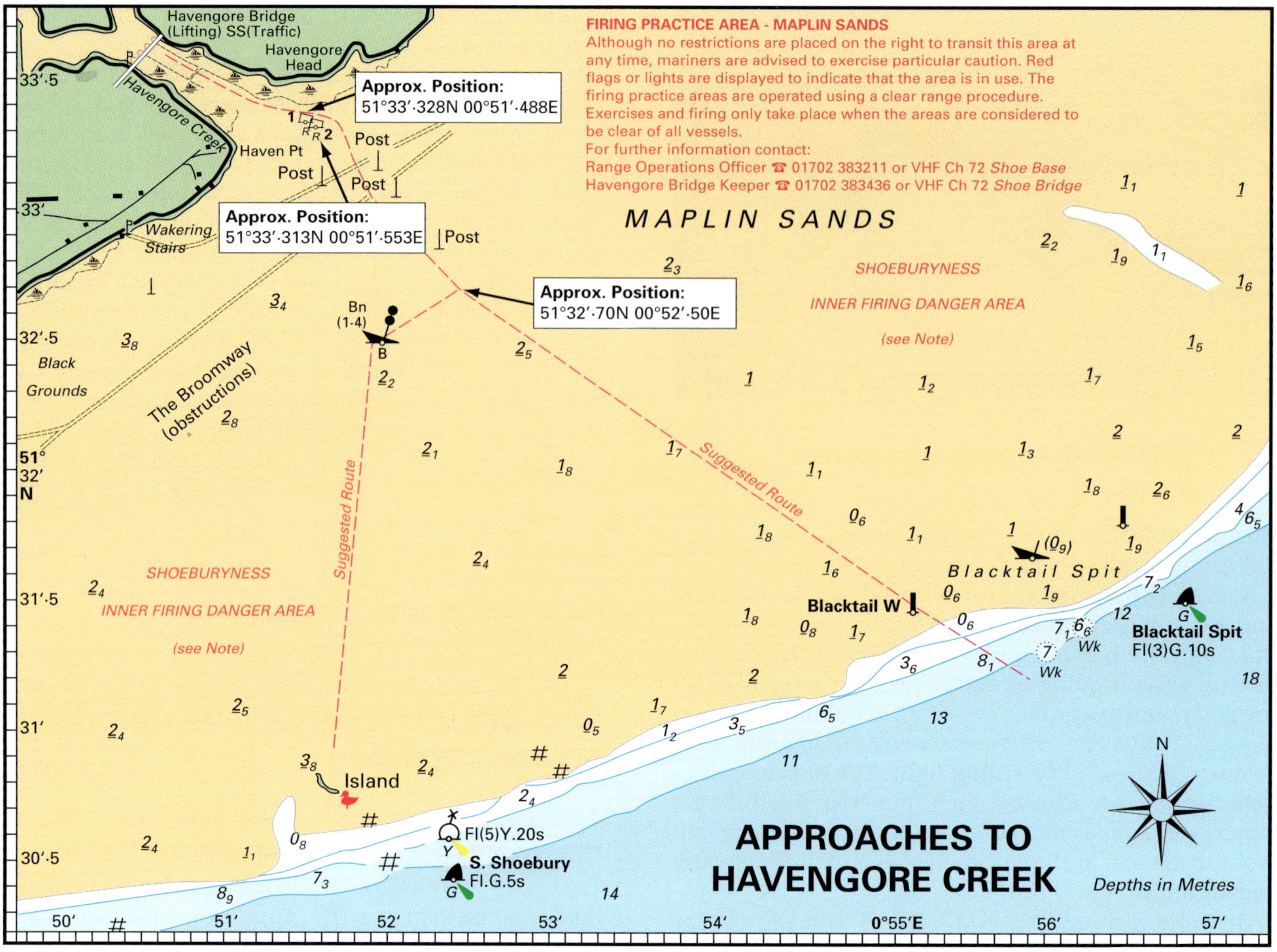

13. RIVER ROACH

APPROACHES TO HAVENGORE CREEK

Red flags are flown along the shoreline SW from Havengore Creek when the range is active but are barely visible from the southern edge of the sands. The approach across the sands requires good weather and a suitably high tide, plus permission from the Shoeburyness Firing Range Officer VHF Ch 72 *Shoe Radar* or ☎01702 383211 before setting off across the sands towards the Havengore Bridge. Maximum recommended draught for using this 'overland' approach (or exit) is 1·5m, even at HWS. The Shoebury ranges are used on most weekdays from 0600-1630 (1230 on Fridays), and on some pre-announced weekends, although permission to cross them even when in use may be granted if circumstances permit, with 24hr notice to the Range Officer. The bridge is manned every day HW±2hr (daylight hours only) and may be lifted on request. It has bars hanging beneath it and there is no room nor indeed permission for any craft to pass without the bridge being lifted. Contact the Bridge Keeper VHF Ch 72 *Shoe Bridge* or ☎01702 383436 to confirm opening – but be warned, it has been prone to periods of breakdown in recent years. The ECP website usually carries news of any long outages in its News section, and warnings may also be included in the regular MSI broadcasts from Dover CG.

There are two suggested routes for the first part of the passage towards the bridge across the Maplin Sands shown on the chartlet above. Start either route no earlier than HW-1½hr. Watch the depth constantly and keep your boat speed down, because uncharted obstructions do exist on the sands although these routes are used frequently by leisure craft. Contact the Bridge Keeper when about 1½M away.

The first route, for boats approaching from E, starts close to the Blacktail West beacon and requires a course made good NW for 2·8M to reach the vicinity of the SE end of a line of three large steel posts. These

Blacktail West beacon, the start of one suggested route to the Havengore. The bridge can seen beyond, 3½ miles away

144 • East Coast Pilot

River Roach

Havengore Creek PHB and the bridge beyond

posts are not usually charted, the area to head for is at approximately 51°32'·70N 000°52'·50E, again shown on the chartlet on page 141.

The second route begins close to the S Shoebury SHB (Fl.G.5s). If early, and the weather is quiet, the 'artificial island' close NW provides a waiting anchorage in a gully on its W and N sides. Recent charts may show that this island (an experiment in land reclamation) does not cover, but it appears to be eroding quickly. From the island, a course of 006° made good for 1·7M will bring you to a charted wreck shown on the chart as an unlit IDM. Leaving this mark a good 25m to port, turn onto a course of about 065° for 0·45M towards the area mentioned above at 51°32'·70N 000°52'·50E.

From that point, looking NW you should see (in 2023) three large steel posts in a generally straight line leading 320°, and the bridge will be seen some 1·5M distant, bearing 305°. Leave each post to starboard. The third and final post reached differs from the other two in that it has cross-pieces attached all the way up, and is close to the Broomway, where the shallowest water may be expected. We should add that these posts are unmaintained and may well eventually collapse.

Havengore Creek entry

After this final post, look approximately NW close to the eastern side of Havengore Creek entrance where you should see two small unlit PHBs, red cans, laid in late 2023. Be aware there is an unmarked submerged wreck 50m to stbd of the rhumb line from the post to the first can. Reaching the first can (marked '2'), continue to the second (marked '1') about 100m further into the creek. If the cans are missing, note that the 2023 position of no.2 is shown on the chartlet (see page 144) to enable you to set it as a waypoint for entry into the creek.

From here, head along Havengore Creek towards the bridge. You will probably find slightly deeper water slightly east of centre of the creek although generally the firm mud sea bed is quite flat. Ignore a group of poles seen across the channel to port, on the S side near Haven Point.

Caution Be aware also that any withies in this whole area, as in similar places, do come and go over time as they collapse or are knocked down, and eventually replaced. That any withies and buoys are there at all is due solely to the voluntary work of Roach Sailing Association members.

Havengore Bridge

The bridge is much larger than might be expected and is used by MoD traffic as well as leisure craft, but the Keeper will do his best to accommodate yachts wishing to pass through. Traffic lights show clearly when to proceed through the open bridge. If the tide is still flooding, you may find it running hard beneath the bridge. Yachts in particular should keep to the E side passing through the single-bascule bridge to ensure enough air draught.

Close-up of the bridge, inside near LW, its barrier beneath

13. RIVER ROACH

Once through the bridge, Rushley Island lies immediately ahead. Boats heading for the Crouch and Paglesham will generally take the right fork, Narrow Cuts, and that is the recommended route N for those not thoroughly familiar with these waters. The left fork leads to the S ends of both the Middleway and Potton Creek.

HAVENGORE

Contact
Havengore Bridge ☎01702 383436
Range Officer and Marine Control
☎01702 383211
VHF Ch 72
Callsigns *Shoe Radar* (Range Officer);
Shoe Bridge (Havengore Bridge keeper)
Range activity information is often included in MSI broadcasts

Range Information
https://qinetiq.com/en/shoeburyness/public-safety/information-for-mariners

---

You may find it helpful to view online aerial photography of the area (e.g on Google Earth) as this can give a good idea of the route to take for the best water. These are all creeks for exploration on the last of a rising tide with plenty of time to retreat before being stranded, but they do have an air of muddy secrecy that can be appealing.

1. ROUTE INBOUND FROM THE BRIDGE VIA NARROW CUTS

Though drying, Narrow Cuts, as its name implies, is a narrow, dug channel that gives the best route between the Havengore Bridge and the Middleway and Yokesfleet Creek beyond, and onwards to the Roach. It is marked with withies, but they are infrequent so do follow them carefully - at HWS the expanse of water seems wide because the saltings each side are covered all the way to both sea walls. In particular, note that nearing the N end of Narrow Cuts the best water is very close to the eastern sea wall, from a point where a red beacon stands on the wall with railings and steps down.

Reaching the junction with the Middleway, be aware of the extensive mud spit that stretches out from the western corner, and turn NNE. Shortly after joining the Middleway, two other creeks branch off SE. The first is the dammed New England Creek; the second is the narrow and drying Shelford Creek which is a dead end.

Yokesfleet Creek

The Middleway becomes Yokesfleet Creek, swinging NNW and on to its junction with the Roach. A good anchorage can be found in the last half-mile or so, and also close under Potton Point, with shelter from all but N or S winds.

Reaching the Roach, be aware of the long spit of mud extending from Potton Point as you turn into the river. Turn west here, upstream, to reach Paglesham after about a mile, or east towards the Crouch.

2. ROUTES INBOUND FROM THE BRIDGE VIA THE MIDDLEWAY AND POTTON CREEK

Taking the left fork westwards after passing inbound through Havengore Bridge, you should find occasional withies leading you past the west side of Rushley Island, the best water generally following the outside of the bends. After about half a mile you will see pontoon moorings ahead at the S end of Potton Creek, where the Middleway also begins - if following the shallow Middleway, turn north with the better water favouring the west side to meet the junction with Narrow Cuts described above.

To enter Potton Creek instead, do not cut the corner, only turn into it just S of a white withy close to the southern tip of Potton Island. Potton Creek can be used by boats with as much as 2m draught, but only near HW on a good tide. The bottom along this stretch is fairly flat with no defined gutway, reaching the pontoons, cranes and slipway of Wakering Boatyard at Bullman's Wharf on your port side.

There is good water up to the yard, over 3m at HWS. Great Wakering village is a good mile's walk from the yard.

WAKERING BOATYARD   **SS3 0DA**

Contact
☎01702 219422
wakeringboatyard@outlook.com
www.wakeringboatyard.co.uk
Access HW±2hr
Facilities WC
Electricity On pontoons (limited)
Water
Slipway
Services Boatyard storage with water and electricity available, tradesmen, 7·5T-hoist, 10T-crane, salvage

---

Continuing N'wards beyond the yard, Potton Bridge comes into view. This swing bridge will operate on demand, HW±2hr, call **VHF Ch 72 Potton Bridge**, ☎**01702 219491**. The deepest water from hereabouts follows a gutway, well-marked by withies and buoys. Pass through the bridge on its east (Potton Island) side to reach a port-hand withy soon after. Continuing

146 • East Coast Pilot

Wakering Boatyard

Upstream in Potton Creek, passing Wakering Boatyard

N along the marked channel which generally tends towards the outside of bends, Potton Creek crosses a ford, which is very hard and raised about 2ft above the river bed. It should be approached with caution, and above half tide.

Soon after the ford, after a narrow gate between a PHB and a withy, a branch off to the SW is reached, Barlinghall Creek which meanders narrowly and muddily up towards Little Wakering. Continuing N instead, along The Violet, another half mile brings you to the Roach, heeding the No.6 PHB which marks a long spit reaching out from Barling Ness. Paglesham is then in view to starboard, close downstream. Although you have Potton Bridge to negotiate, this route from the Havengore to Paglesham is more than a mile shorter than using the Narrow Cuts / Yokesfleet route.

Potton swing-bridge, best water on its E side

13. RIVER ROACH

Pass between yellow cable marker buoys

3: FROM PAGLESHAM TO ROCHFORD
Paglesham to Rochford

The final stretch of the Roach up to Rochford begins a short way above the last of the Paglesham moorings, at fairway buoys No.3 (Fl.G.6s) and No.6, N of Barling Ness. The main channel of the Roach continues W above Barling Ness. There is good water with up to 1·5m at LW as far as the old Barling Quay on the S shore, but then it shallows considerably and, sensibly, can only be explored close to HW. That said, boats of up to 1·5m draught do make it up the next 1½M towards Rochford on the top of the tide. Pilotage in this section was made easier in recent years with the laying of new lit buoyage for much of the route.

The buoys encountered first on the way upriver are brightly coloured plastic pillar buoys about a metre high, each lit Fl.6s in their respective colours. The first of these, Blackedge, is a SHB just beyond the entrance to the Violet. The channel is wide and reasonably deep here and the second buoy, the

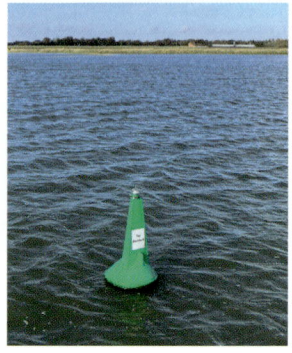

Typical SHB used above Paglesham

Barling PHB, is ¾M further on, as the river bends to the SSW just before the old Barling Quay. The Bartonhall SHB is a further ¾M upstream, opposite Bartonhall Creek. The Mucking PHB closely follows, then a few hundred yards beyond and round the next river bend to W and then WNW, there are two 'gates' of buoys, closer to the N shore, the Lower Rochford PHB and SHB, then Top Rochford PHB and SHB. Between the two gates, you may see 8kn speed limit reminder buoys with lollipop topmarks.

The channel swings to port after passing between the Top Rochford pair, passing between two yellow flat buoys at the charted cable crossing, and from here the best water is marked by a succession of

Approaching Sutton Wharf, the Wakering YC pontoon on your port side. Note the metal withy in the foreground, leave to stbd

Sutton Wharf

Sutton Wharf Boatyard, looking E at about half tide; Wakering YC pontoon on far left

Final turn on arrival

port- and stbd-hand buoys, all lit QR or QG. These are laid and maintained by local organisations. You may also see a few withies, and the RSA advises that any you find should be stbd-hand withies. These withies are metal; also beware a couple of old algae-covered pot markers in this last stretch.

The river makes its final bend to starboard (towards the old Stambridge Mills) at the last of the SHBs, Sutton Wharf No.1 QG.

Opposite, to port, you will see the Wakering YC pontoons which are lit 2R(vert) on their ends. The club has drying berths alongside the walk-ashore pontoons with water (and possibly electricity if pre-booked) and space for visiting shoal-draught boats, call 07703 774686 in advance for visitor berth availability.

Following the river to starboard, round the SHB, the large Sutton Wharf Boatyard lies to port. The yard has drying pontoon and quay berths, and other services.

SUTTON WHARF   SS4 1JU

Contact
01702 546147
suttonwharf@outlook.com
www.suttonwharfboatyard.com

Slipway 50T/80ft limit

Crane 35T-hoist

Berthing Pontoons, alongside and swinging (all drying)

Electricity

Water

Repairs Including upholstery

Yacht Club Wakering YC 01702 542545
https://wakeringyachtclub.org.uk
Email via the website
Open Fri evenings and Sunday lunch times, bar only

Fixed road bridge and flood barrier

Benfleet Motorboat & YC

14. CANVEY & LEIGH

Looking W at the head of Benfleet Creek

14. CANVEY & LEIGH

Charts Imray 2100, C1, C2
Admiralty 5606
Honorary Port Pilot Rob Scriven ☎07860 828048
canvey@eastcoastpilot.com

This chapter is in two sections – the first describes the north and east aspects of Canvey Island, and nearby Leigh-on-Sea, while the second describes Holehaven on the west side of the island.

Note There is no water-side marine fuel available anywhere in this whole area.

1. LEIGH, EAST CANVEY AND BENFLEET

⊕ **Landfall waypoint**
51°30'·95N 000°42'·90E Close S of Leigh SHB
Tides HW Sheerness

Hazards
Apart from Ray Gut itself and parts of Hadleigh Ray, this entire area, including many moorings, dries soon after half ebb. Potentially extremely uncomfortable in strong E winds unless in the creeks. Only attempt entry on a rising tide and only in a shoal draught boat.

Entry
The unlit Leigh SHB marks the entrance to Ray Gut, which gives access to Benfleet, Smallgains and Leigh Creeks, and lies ½M 290° from the end of Southend Pier (2F.G.13m8M).

Apart from the pierhead, there are no lit marks at all in this area.

It is unlikely that you will find enough water to pass the Leigh buoy much earlier than HW-4. Benfleet YC's members' rule of thumb for getting right up Benfleet Creek from here is that the nearby Marsh End Sand should already be covered and the tide rising.

From the Leigh buoy, head NW and for the best water (at end-2023) pass 75m to the east of a curving line of three PHBs, through to a pair of R and G buoys during the first ½M, the channel curving slightly to port. Then turn onto about 290° as you head for the large fishing boat moorings in deeper water in Hadleigh Ray. About 0·9M further on, small buoys, some lit, leading off generally NW show the entrance to Leigh Creek.

LEIGH-ON-SEA

Clubs
Leigh SC www.leighsailingclub.org
Essex YC ☎01702 478404 www.essexyachtclub.co.uk
mail@essexyachtclub.co.uk
Leigh MBC ☎01702 714858
www.leighmotorboatclub.com

Boatyard Mike's Boatyard Ltd SS9 2EN
Wharfage, repairs, 8-T crane
☎01702 713151 mikesby@talk21.com
https://mikesboatyard.wordpress.com

Pub/Restaurant Several in town
Transport Bus station, trains to London
Taxi ☎01702 334455, 861998

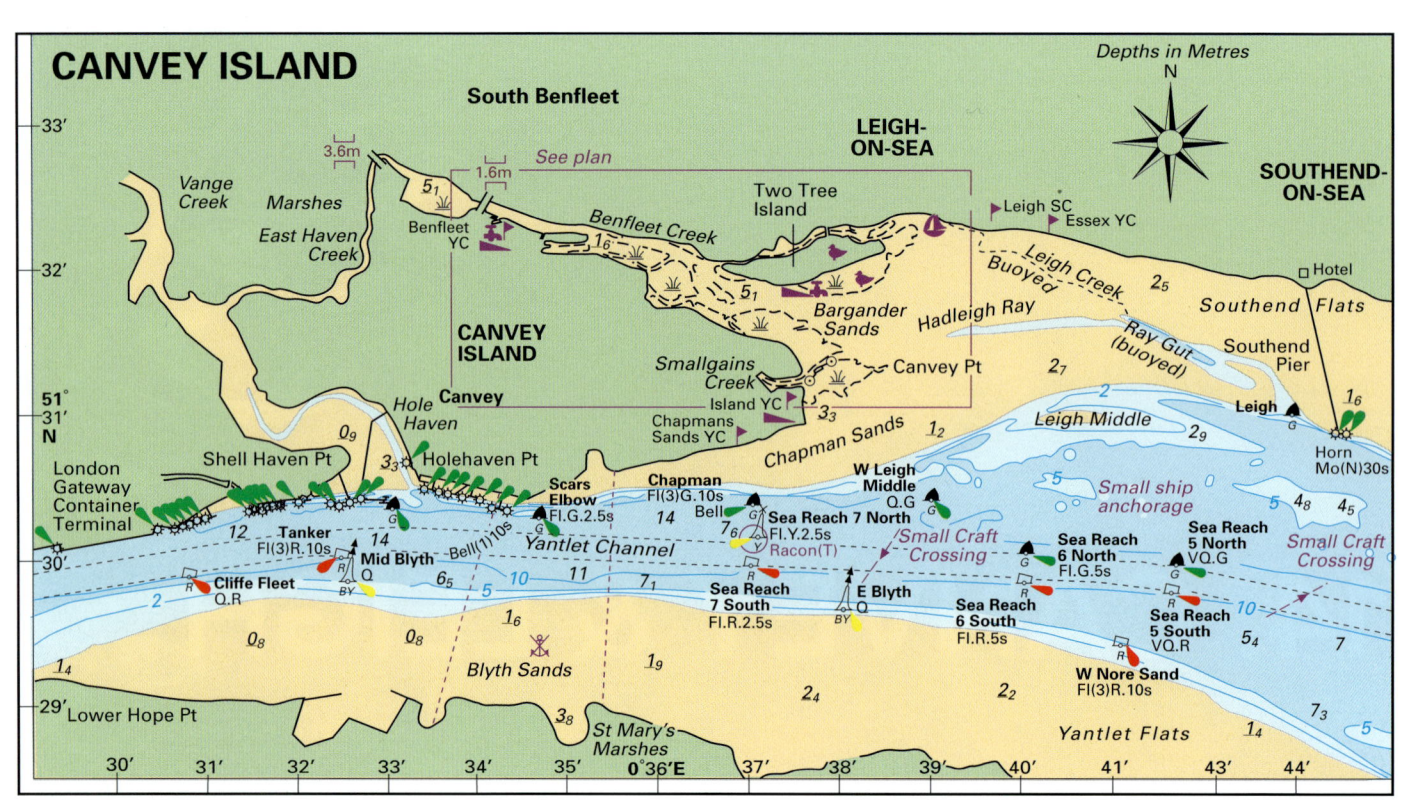

Leigh on Sea at LW

Leigh Creek is marked with lit buoys, the lights on some being unreliable; there is a port/stbd pair at its start at the side of the Ray, then port-hand buoys only. It has an exaggerated S-bend, first to right then left, as it passes outside the large cluster of yacht moorings, and is quite narrow. For a trip ashore to the interesting Old Leigh or beyond, you could consider staying afloat in Hadleigh Ray and taking the dinghy into the creek.

You may find room to dry out alongside Bell Wharf (W side has flat mud) or against the E side of Victoria Wharf, although both can be busy with fishing boat movements. Alternatively, it may be better to request a spare mooring from one of the two clubs in the town. Leigh SC is based in the old railway station behind Bell Wharf, and the Essex YC is based in the old minehunter *Wilton* 200 yards to the E, where there is also a drying pontoon on the ship's E side with fresh water available.

The two clubs' moorings are mostly on firm flat mud where a bilge-keeler should stand upright, but do ask the club(s) for local advice, especially if you choose to anchor instead, as there are occasional holes and gullies. It is not advisable to try to walk ashore at LW.

Leigh Marina has a growing set of drying pontoon moorings at the far W end of the waterfront, reached by following the narrow gutway past the town (see aerial photo above).

The drying gap between Bell and Victoria wharves

Essex YC in the old minesweeper *Wilton*, a pontoon on her far side

14. CANVEY & LEIGH

Entry into Leigh Marina to the right of the lighter

LEIGH MARINA
SS9 2ES

Contact
☎ 01702 479009
www.leighmarina.co.uk
Facilities WC, showers
Electricity On pontoon
Water On pontoon
Boatyard Slipway, 20-T crane, 13-T travel hoist, engineer, repairs.

Leigh Creek meanders on behind Two Tree Island to its road bridge, where you will find Leigh Motor Boat Club based in an old barge.

Smallgains Creek

The Island YC stands on the very eastern point of Canvey, looking out SE across the Estuary, close by an old Roman dock and pottery on the S shore of the drying Smallgains Creek. The creek has a forest of wooden staging club moorings along its S shore with some more on the N side near the entrance.

To reach the club, continue W along Hadleigh Ray past the entrance to Leigh Creek, following the large fishing boat moorings along the S side in the deeper water. Monitor the depth constantly. Pass the club's yellow waiting buoy (dries at LWS), then follow the channel WSW between lit PHBs and SHBs and posts to the entrance to Smallgains Creek, and enter between the wooden piers, the eastern ends of which are lit 2FR (vert) and 2FG (vert). The club advises that if you enter at HW-1 with 4' draught you should be OK. Just inside the entrance there is a

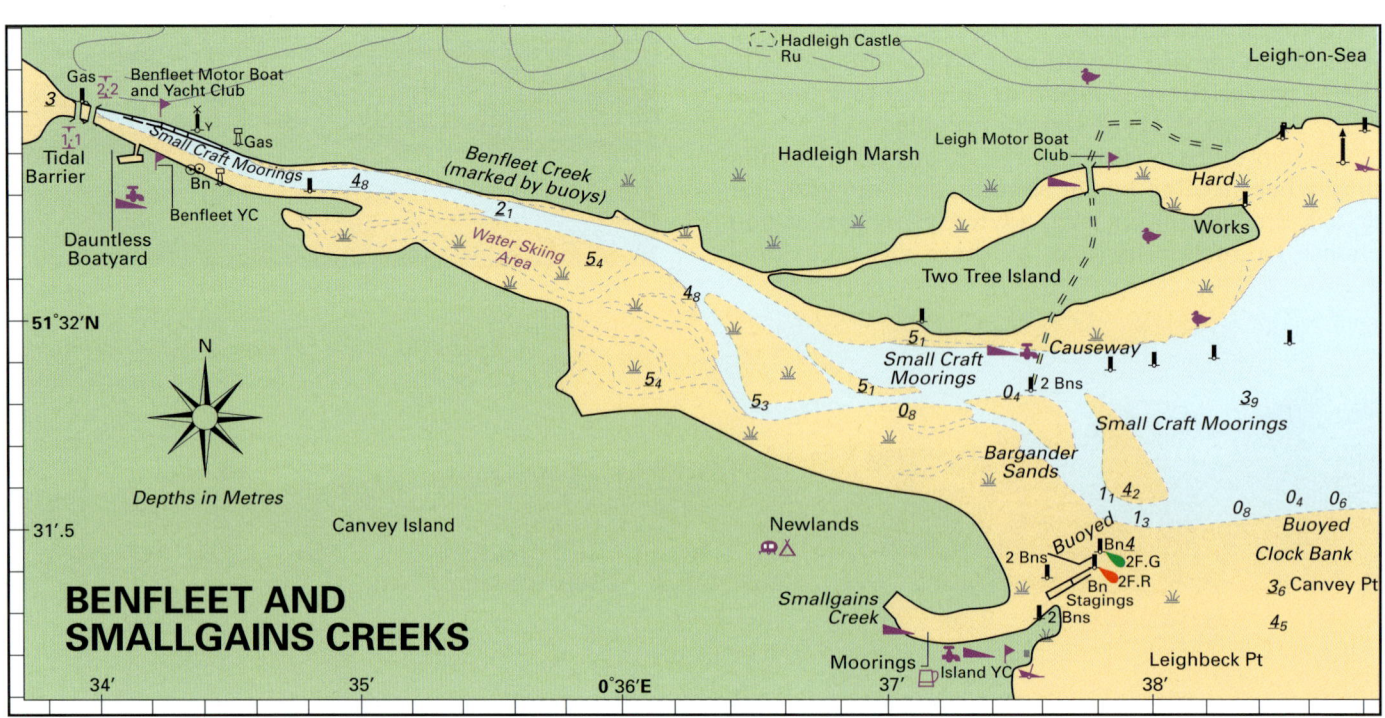

Smallgains Creek

Approaching the entrance to Smallgains Creek and the IYC moorings

short, steep slipway up onto the S staging, which is suitable for tenders.

The deeper water follows the N shore once inside, past two green buoys, then crosses to the S after the creek bends to port – two green posts in the water and a pair of leading mark posts on the S bank show the crossover route. From there, follow the S shore one boat's length off the sterns of moored craft.

There's a broad club-owned slipway on the S shore and immediately before it is the club's visitors' pontoon, alongside Brinkman's Wharf, which is the quayside area where IYC stores boats and gear. Some visitors choose to pick up a mooring out in the Ray – anchoring there is not advised because of clutter on the bottom – and land by dinghy. However, the club says that visitors will always be found a space in the creek.

There is a National Coastwatch Institution watch station by the E end of the club's boatyard.

Just upstream from the IYC slipway is the start of AW Marine's extensive staging and pontoon moorings, all drying, very crowded on our last visit

Island YC visitor pontoon and slipway

Smallgains Creek, westwards from above its entrance with Island YC's moorings lining its S shore as far as the slipway

14. CANVEY & LEIGH

but where you may be able to find a visitor berth if you ask well in advance. Half way along the S shore is their main slip, opposite which, on the N side, is another slip serving boats on that side of the creek.

ISLAND YACHT CLUB   SS8 7TX
Contact
☎ 01268 510360
admin@islandyachtclub.org.uk
www.islandyachtclub.org.uk
Access HW±1hr
Facilities WC, showers, visitors' pontoon, slipway
NCI station VHF Ch 65, National Coastwatch Canvey, or phone 07393 658946
Taxi ☎ 01268 681999

AW MARINE 'The Marina'   SS8 7TJ
Contact
awmarine66@gmail.com
Access HW ±1hr
Facilities WC, showers
Slipway 40-T cradle
Boat repairs Shipwright on site
Services Electrical, electronic, engineering, rigging services to order
Café On site, Shell's Marina Tearoom ☎ 07703 624206
Taxi ☎ 01268 681999

IYC's mooring stagings line the S side of Smallgains Creek

Benfleet Creek

At the W end of Hadleigh Ray, close to the entrance to Smallgains Creek, a narrow buoyed channel heads off NW towards Two Tree Island and becomes Benfleet Creek. Just over two miles up Benfleet Creek, Benfleet YC stands on the N shore of Canvey Island, E of the tidal barrier across Benfleet Creek, and has moorings in the creek. The creek and its approaches dry, so if you are unfamiliar with the creek and are trying to reach the club, a rising tide is essential, as is shoal draught. If planning to visit the club, it is essential to call well ahead so that a suitable berth can be found for you, either a bankside mooring or a spot where your boat can stand on the creek bed. A bilge keeler may be able to stand across tides on the wide club slipway. Do refer to the excellent comprehensive guidance notes and diagrams on Benfleet YC's website.

Passage from Hadleigh Ray to Smallgains Creek and Benfleet Creek shown clearly at LW

Credit Patrick Roach

Benfleet Creek

The twin stbd beacons on the end of the causeway at Two Tree Island

At No. 16 buoy, take the dogleg across to the S side of the creek

Next stbd-hand buoy

The buoyed route from the Hadleigh Ray, known locally as 'The Hole', curves around roughly NW, with the shallows of the Bargander Sand along its N edge. Beyond the initial buoys, follow the line of moorings, which includes two waiting buoys belonging to BYC, towards a pair of starboard hand posts with conical tops.

These starboard hand posts mark the end of a wide concrete causeway/slipway extending S from Two Tree Island, where there is water available. The island is a nature reserve and is 20 mins walk from Leigh Station.

Leaving the posts at the end of the causeway close to starboard, turn WSW and leave more moorings close to starboard, aiming for a large yellow mooring buoy in the distance close to the S side of the creek, before reaching the first Benfleet YC large green buoy just beyond it. Then follow the R and G buoys (all these club race buoys are numbered and coloured port and starboard hand, but be aware there are also a few yellow or white buoys too, which do not mark the channel) as the channel meanders from one side of the creek to the other, eventually guiding you close to the N bank where you pass the start of the club's stagings on your port side. Just beyond, at the no16 buoy, take particular care to follow the buoyed dogleg from the N bank to the S bank – there is a submerged cliff of mud to catch you if you carry straight on. The channel on this dogleg is quite narrow. After crossing over, continue upstream along the S side until the clubhouse and slipway show on the port bow.

Drying pontoon moorings lie parallel to the shore just beyond the club slipway, but will not be suitable for all craft as the mud shelves steeply away from the pontoon.

On the N shore, opposite BYC, are the moorings of Benfleet Motor Boat and YC ☎01268 753311, actually a

Benfleet Yacht Club lies on the S side of the creek, its slipway just before it and its pontoon beyond

14. CANVEY & LEIGH

Benfleet Yacht Club's pontoon, beside the clubhouse. See text regarding suitability of this pontoon

pub, which may also be able to help out with a berth although in generally even shallower water.

Note that even the locals will not leave Benfleet Creek once the tide is ebbing – always leave with some flood left. The ebb runs so fast that if you touch, you will almost certainly not get off.

BENFLEET YACHT CLUB SS8 0QT
Contact
① 01268 792278
secretary@benfleetyachtclub.org
www.benfleetyachtclub.org
Open every day
Tides HW Sheerness +0010
Club Benfleet YC
Facilities WC, showers, slipway
Water From club and on pontoon
Catering Refer to club website
Chandler (close outside club gate):
Dauntless Yacht Centre ① 07771 944288
www.dauntlessyachtcentre.co.uk
info@dauntlestachtcentre.co.uk
Boatyard Dauntless Boatyard ① 01268 793782
www.dauntlessboatyard.com
info@dauntlessboatyard.com
Toilets, slipway, travel hoist 20T/46ft, crane 18T, boat repairs and engines
Engineer and GRP work Essex Marine (inside Dauntless Boatyard) ① 01268 795554
Gas from Camping & General (20 minute walk)
① 01268 692141
Pub/Restaurant In south Benfleet, 10 minute walk
Taxi ① 01268 556666

2. HOLEHAVEN CREEK

⊕ **Landfall waypoint**
51°30'·50N 000°33'·19E (close S of creek entrance)
Tides HW Sheerness +0010

Holehaven is a possible venue to wait for the tide when on passage up or down the Thames. Its shallow entrance may limit its usefulness on upstream passages. These days it is a less hospitable place, perhaps suitable only for true shoal-draught and lift-keel craft. A dinghy trip ashore is possible.

Hazards and approach

There is little depth in the entrance at LWS, and indeed little depth in the creek generally as reported recently. Heavy commercial traffic passes the entrance and has to be crossed on arrival and departure because all small craft in this part of the Thames must use the south side of the river, whether bound up or down stream.

Final approach to Holehaven Creek entrance will need to be made from a point on the opposite shore when traffic permits.

Entry

The entrance, close downstream from the London Gateway Container Port, is not obvious until close to and the access channel is narrow with little water at LWS. There are large mooring buoys on the E side, large ships may be lying moored to the E of these. Enter close to these buoys. The line of moored fishing boats is on the W edge of the best water. The gutway appears to be very narrow in places.

Holehaven

HOLEHAVEN SS8 0NR
Contact
PLA Duty Officer, 01474 562215 (use only if problems)
Fuel Petrol station 1M
Pub/Restaurant See text

Anchor toward the S end (not amongst moorings) or you may be able to borrow a mooring – all are private, and there are no visitors' moorings. Beware of stone groynes on the E side.

Two cables in, there is a slipway to starboard (with a starboard hand post at its outer end), which is steep at its inshore end where dinghies can land. Behind the wall is the Lobster Smack pub (☎01268 514297) with its popular restaurant; the pub is mentioned by Charles Dickens in *Great Expectations*.

The creek runs on for another ½M before reaching the disused Chainrock Jetty, which has 11m air draught clearance. If access N is required by boats that can't pass beneath the jetty, follow the drying gutway that starts just W of the jetty to join the deeper water again behind Coryton.

The channel meanders on inland, marked by lit PHBs, to a junction where the drying East Haven Creek wanders away NE towards Benfleet beneath a tidal barrier (2·8m) and a fixed road bridge (3·1m). Alternatively, the equally shallow Vange Creek can be followed NW beneath another tidal barrier (8·8m) then through small boat moorings to Wat Tyler Country Park.

The shallowing Holehaven Creek, from above its entrance

15. RIVER THAMES

Credit St.Katharine Docks Marina

15. RIVER THAMES

⊕ **Landfall waypoint**
51°29'·56N 000°52'·61E Close N of Sea Reach No.1 North

Charts
Imray 2100, C1, C2
Admiralty SC5606 1185, 1186, 2151, 2484

Tides
HW Sheerness; HW London Bridge

Port of London Authority (PLA)
☎ 01474 562200
www.pla.co.uk/boating
London VTS See text

Thames Barrier Control
VHF Ch 14 Callsign *London VTS* ☎ 020 8855 0315

HM Coastguard
London Coastguard (Shell Haven to Teddington) – VHF Ch 16 Callsign *UK Coastguard* ☎ 020 8312 7380

Main hazards

Large ships, floating debris, shallows on the bends, fast river buses upstream from Woolwich, and broken water above Greenwich. As on any river, substantial floating debris can be encountered and a good lookout should be kept, even though the Thames is much cleaner than it used to be. There are many large mooring buoys, some now lit with a fixed blue light, but others unlit.

Approaches

The pair of Sea Reach No 1 buoys marks the seaward end of the dredged channel into the River Thames and is the gateway to the centre of the deep water shipping channel.

Small craft should stay outside this main channel and make their approach to the Thames following the edges of the drying shallows, staying well out of the way of commercial shipping to comply with the PLA's General Direction 39, which states: *'The Master of a sailing vessel or vessel less than 20m in Length Overall shall ensure that the vessel keeps out of the way and does not obstruct or impede the operation or safety of any vessel approaching, leaving or manoeuvring on or off any berth or ship facility on the Thames'*.

Sea Reach to Tower Bridge: General information

A first trip up the Thames from out in the Estuary may seem daunting, but it's straightforward and should be an interesting experience to be enjoyed and remembered.

The Port of London Authority (PLA) is responsible for navigational safety and related matters on the tidal Thames and publishes a useful River Thames Recreational Users Guide, available as a booklet or downloadable from the recreational area of its website, www.pla.co.uk/boating, where there is much other useful information.

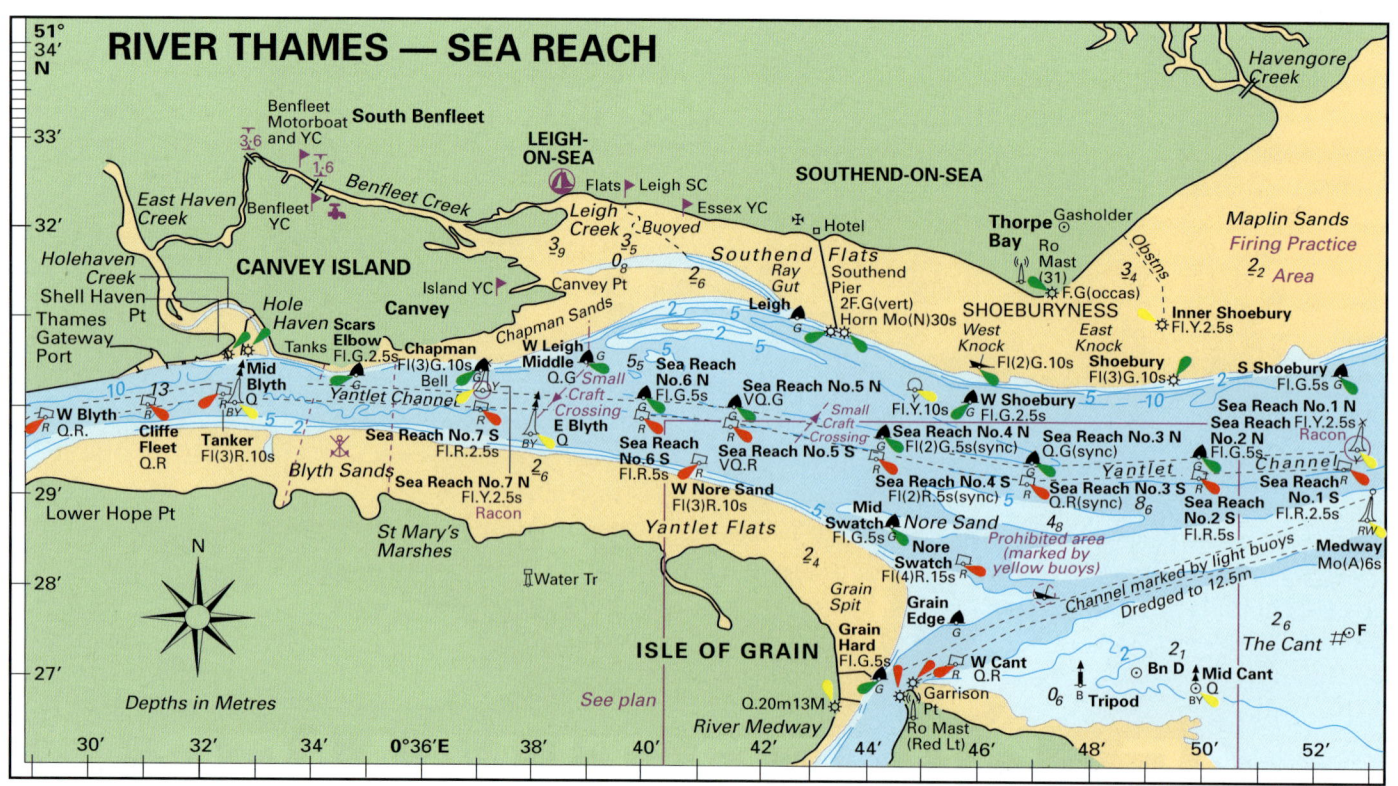

River Thames

> **VHF Communications**
>
> The entire route, from Sea Reach to Tower Bridge, is effectively a single port controlled by London VTS and we regard it as essential that all skippers should monitor the relevant VTS VHF channel.
>
> **LONDON VTS**
>
> Callsign *London VTS*
> VHF Ch 69 (PLA seaward limit to Sea Reach No.4)
> Ch 68 (Sea Reach No.4 to Crayfordness)
> Ch 14 above Crayfordness including the Thames Barrier Control Zone

The river passage begins at the two Sea Reach No.1 buoys, although the PLA's Lower River Sector actually starts at the pair of Sea Reach No.4 buoys Fl(2)5s(sync) R and G respectively, N of the Medway entrance.

The river is heavily used by commercial traffic, large and small, hence a constant radio watch on the appropriate London VTS channel is sensible. Like any port controllers, the harbourmasters who man the VTS communications are primarily there for commercial shipping, but will always help leisure sailors with advice and guidance in a professional manner. If in doubt, ask, and remember that good and succinct radio procedure will smooth the way if you do talk to them.

Information is broadcast by London VTS on Ch 14 and 69 at H+15 and H+45, and on Ch 68 at H and H+30.

If you transmit AIS on passage, it is doubly important to monitor VTS because they can specifically identify you and may wish to contact you.

Finally, a point about distress calls on the river – because virtually everyone is monitoring the correct London VTS frequency, a distress call made on that frequency rather than the conventional Ch 16 would be instantly heard on many craft. The PLA Harbourmasters and London Coastguard, who sit in the same room at the Thames Barrier Control Centre, tell us that this is now common practice. So if you are short of channel capacity on your VHF, listen to VTS rather than 16.

Passage planning

When planning your passage there are five particular areas of importance:

1. Will you have enough time?

The tides run strongly in the river, reaching 4kn in places at springs, and if you want to run the whole way to St Katharine's in one 'hit', the 40M can be readily achieved with a boat speed of 5kn – HW London Bridge is about 1hr later than at Sheerness.

Conversely, the trip down river gives only about 5hr of fair tide. However, the combination of the tide plus 5kn of boat speed should still see you off the Medway by LW if you set off downstream from Tower Bridge at HW-1 (London Bridge).

With the need to depart upstream at LW, the Queenborough moorings and Stangate Creek anchorage are ideal spots to wait for the tide. A good time to leave Queenborough is 1-1½hr before LW Sheerness.

A possible alternative point of departure is Holehaven (see 'Canvey and Leigh' chapter) on the western edge of Canvey Island. It's 8M up river from the Nore Swatch and that allows a later start – however we understand the creek is silting badly, with little depth at LW, so perhaps this option is suitable now only for true shoal-draught boats.

You could also break the journey using moorings at several locations, described in this chapter.

2. Will the Thames Barrier be open?

The Thames Barrier is closed regularly for testing, as well as in times of flood risk. If you are planning the river passage after periods of heavy rain, the Barrier Duty Officer should be contacted to ensure closure is not planned for the day of your trip. Test closure dates are published in advance by the PLA and can be accessed via the 'Downloads' page at www.eastcoastpilot.com. When the Barrier is closed, other flood gates are closed too, for instance sealing off Embankment Marina (Gravesend). Most tests are done across LW, but at least two each year are for longer periods and would affect your journey.

3. Which side of the river should you use?

It is a PLA requirement that the first part of your upstream journey has to be made along the S shore to stay clear of the commercial installations at Canvey, Coryton and the London Gateway Container Terminal, and well south of the buoyed Yantlet Channel and outbound Yantlet Secondary Channel. Note that you may encounter ships coming downstream in this Secondary Channel, which means they will be S of the buoyed main channel and close to your route!

Despite this widely known requirement, the authors have frequently seen skippers of leisure craft not complying with it. Skirt the shallows on the south side, stay out of trouble and stay safe.

If leaving from Holehaven, cross immediately to the S side when safe to do so. If inbound from NE, cross to the S side of the estuary from W Leigh Middle SHB (Q.G) heading SW towards E Blyth NCB (Q), this crossing point is shown on charts.

Further up, in Lower Hope Reach, resume the

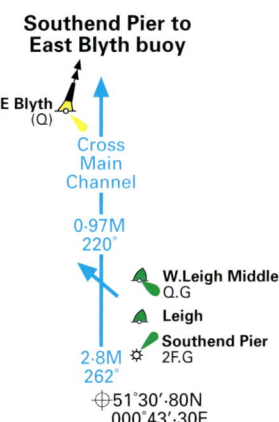

Southend Pier to East Blyth buoy

15. RIVER THAMES

starboard side of the river (again as shown on charts) and stay to starboard for the rest of your journey upstream.

Outbound, it is again a PLA requirement to stay on the S shore throughout, crossing NE, if necessary, only between the pairs of Sea Reach Nos.4 and 5 buoys. This crossing point is also clearly charted.

4. Have you got enough fuel?

It should be noted that there is only one location on the Thames between the Estuary and Tower Bridge where you can readily take on fuel alongside through a hose, and that is at the fuel barge just downstream from St Katharine Docks. There is no fuel available at Queenborough or around Canvey. The nearest in the Medway is at Gillingham.

5. Have you booked a berth?

Note that visitors are generally only accepted at the four London marinas – West India, South Dock, Limehouse, and St Katharine's – if they have booked a berth in advance, so you should regard this as essential. The marinas are usually busy and often full, especially in high season. You may be asked to show proof of third party insurance on arrival. Incidentally, you may well be visited by the police making routine security checks at any London marina, or even on the river itself during your passage.

Medway to Gravesend

For the passage to London, leave Queenborough at LW-1 to 1½hr and route by way of Grain Hard SHB (Fl.G.5s) and Grain Edge SHB (unlit) to the Nore Swatch PHB (Fl(4)R.15s). Shoal draught craft will cut this corner with care across Grain Spit shallows.

From Nore Swatch, make good about 295° through the Swatchway S of Nore Sand, past the Mid Swatch SHB (Fl.G.5s) and 290° to the W Nore Sand PHB (Fl(3)R.10s). Just W is a wandering gutway marked with a conical beacon that leads into Yantlet Creek, a possible stopover for shoal draught boats able to take the ground.

Continuing past the Yantlet Flats, towards the E Blyth NCB (Q), the small town and holiday area of Allhallows is prominent on Grain. From there the N and S shores close in, and it starts to feel more like a river than an estuary.

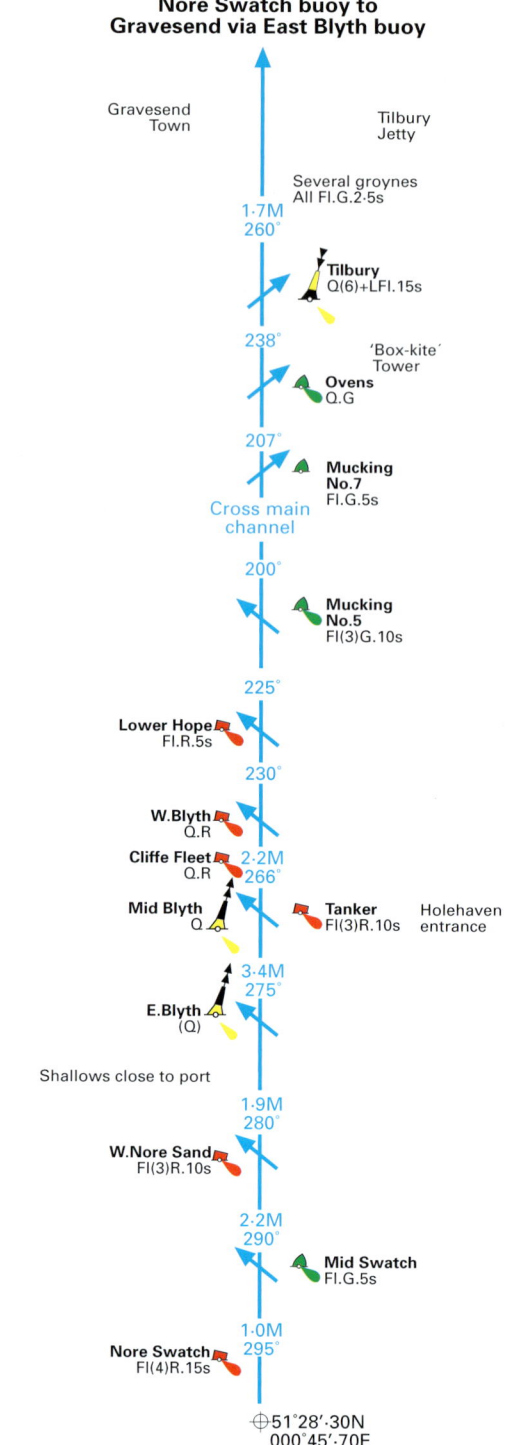

Passing Holehaven Creek in a brisk NE'ly

London Gateway container port – stay well clear!

Medway to Gravesend

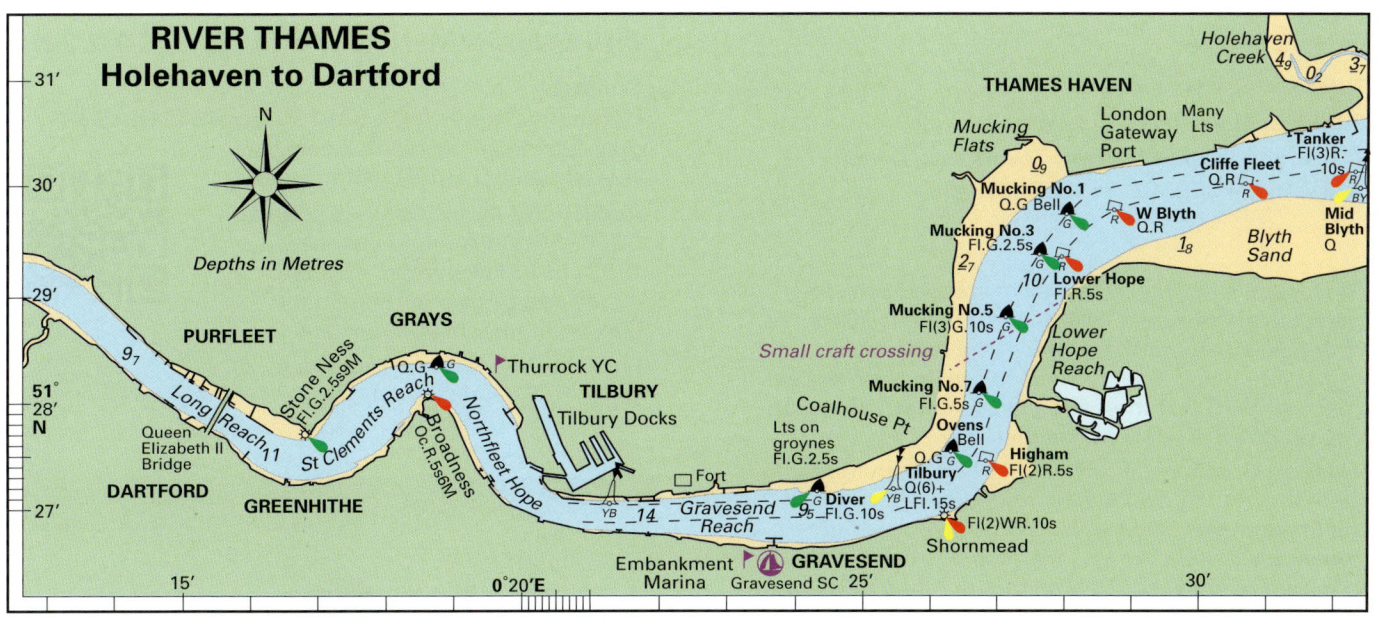

Coalhouse Point looking downstream – stay outside the beacon and the line of buoys!

Take care with the depth along this stretch all the way to the Cliffe Fleet buoy – the shallows on the S shore push further to the N. The huge London Gateway container port stretches along the N shore beyond Holehaven.

The entrance to Holehaven Creek (see page 156) opens on the N shore about ¾ mile before you reach the Mid Blyth NCB (Q). The creek can be hard to make out from afar, but the entrance is just W of the four commercial jetties on Canvey. Enormous container ships call at the container port beyond, and are turned in the river on arrival to berth facing downstream.

About 3M further on, once past the Cliffe Fleet (Q.R) and Lower Hope (Fl.R.5s) PHBs, the river turns S into Lower Hope Reach (The Lower Hope). The shore to port is flatter and shallower around the bend, so do not cut the corner.

The deep water channel here is much narrower and it's time to change sides of the river. Look for a gap in the traffic, particularly watching astern for small, deep-laden coasters typically using the same inshore course, and plan to reach the W side beyond Mucking No.5 SHB (Fl(3)G.10s).

The river now bends to starboard round Coalhouse Point, with its curious tower that looks exactly like a giant box-kite, into Gravesend Reach. Rounding the bend just inside the Ovens SHB (Q.G Bell), a line of yellow buoys stretches from the shore out to the S end of the first of six groynes, all marked with posts and lit Fl.G.2·5s. It is essential to leave them all to starboard. Pass close N of Tilbury SCB (Q(6)+LFl.15s) to keep clear.

Once in Gravesend Reach, Gravesend town is in sight ahead on the S shore.

Approaching Gravesend, the Embankment Marina location shown

East Coast Pilot • 165

15. RIVER THAMES

GRAVESEND

Tides HW Sheerness +0025
Pub/Restaurant Many in town
Transport Trains to Medway Towns and London.
Taxi ☎01474 369369, 353535, 535455

Gravesend is an interesting town steeped in history with pleasant riverside walks. Sadly there is still an air of dereliction about the land E of the marina gate, in contrast to the splendid esplanade to its west, but we heard in 2023 that there are plans afoot to redevelop the run-down area for residential use.

If visiting Gravesend from downstream, then returning, there are several options for moorings including the Embankment Marina. However, if you plan to continue upriver, then you will probably be wanting to depart near LW so the marina is not then a useful option because it can only be accessed close to HW. In those circumstances you may be better off on the 'Gravesend Pontoon' or a GSC or PLA mooring.

Large tugs moor along the S shore downstream of the Embankment Marina and the Gravesend SC, both of which can be hard to spot. The GSC clubhouse is about 500 yards before the town proper and is a low building with a white flagpole. There is a long apartment block behind to the SW. The gated entrance to the marina faces NW and is immediately adjacent to the E side of the clubhouse behind a swing-bridge and, like several locations on the tidal Thames, also has a floodgate.

The Embankment Marina is in the old basin of the Thames and Medway Canal, built early in the 19th century to carry munitions from the Thames to the naval dockyards at Chatham. The canal was never successful and it was soon superseded by the railway (which actually uses the canal tunnel near Strood), and much of it has been filled in. The marina, dredged to 1·5m over soft mud, is basic but it is a potentially useful stop, although limited by access – only the inner lock gate survives and so it

The entrance to Embankment Marina can be hard to make out

Entry gutway runs NW-SE
Marina lock gate

THE EMBANKMENT MARINA DA12 2RN

Contact
Harbourmaster ☎01474 535700, or 07549 394531
gravesendmarina@outlook.com
www.theembankmentmarina.co.uk
Access HW-1hr to HW via lock gate,
0800–2000 1 April–31 October;
1000–1600 1 November–31 March
All locking by prior arrangement
Max length/beam 27m/6m/2m
Facilities WC, shower, pump-out
Water, Electricity On quayside

Inside the marina, the single pair of lock gates

is only opened near HW on free flow. The approach to the entrance is along a gutway which runs NW-SE from the deep water, and through the swing-bridge. Phone in advance to arrange a visit.

Please note, if arriving by road, the postcode shown is unreliable on a car sat-nav! Instead use the directions on Gravesend Sailing Club website's 'Contact' page.

Gravesend Sailing Club has no designated visitor moorings but will always try to allocate you a vacant club mooring if you ask – maximum length 36ft. The club has a useful but drying pontoon attached to the frontage and parallel to the marina gutway (this alignment is helpful on your approach), which affords brief access to dry land without ladders at around HW. The club also may be able to help with launching craft up to 20' and one ton. Contact the GSC well in advance to make any arrangements.

The Port of London Authority (PLA) has a number of local moorings, large yellow cans laid off and just up river from GSC, which may be available for a small charge ☎01474 562421, VisitorMoorings@pla.co.uk. A PLA launch (the PLA offices are just up river) may

GRAVESEND SC
☎07506 367699

secretary@gravesendsc.co.uk
www.gravesendsc.co.uk

Gravesend

Embankment Marina, a handy stop but limited by tide

call to collect mooring fees and give advice. There is also a sturdy wooden all-tide ramp at the W end of the promenade (300 yards W of GSC) where you can land from a dinghy.

Prominent buildings beyond the club and the esplanade include the downstream London VTS base, and an RNLI station on the first pier.

Gravesend's other potential place for a visiting boat, but again only if booked in advance, is to moor on the large pontoon joined to the downstream end of the public Town Pier (this is the second pier you come to upstream from the marina and GSC – there is a prominent old lightship against the river bank close by). It is a very substantial metal-sided pontoon, and can be subject to wash from passing ships – be sure to arrange adequate fendering even if you are berthed on the inside. Shoreside access is via the Town Pier, and it's regularly used by the small Tilbury ferry. A berth here is bookable with Gravesend Pontoon Ltd, which also manages three swinging moorings immediately downstream from the pontoon, another option for visitors.

GRAVESEND PONTOON — DA11 0BG

Contact
☎ 07949 750236 or 07798 885332
www.gravesendpontoon.co.uk
alan.kew@btinternet.com

Access 24H

Electricity, water On pontoon (water incurs a cost)

Gravesend Pontoon mooring, and three swinging moorings close downstream

Gravesend YC's pontoon at LW, and the gutway leading into the marina

15. RIVER THAMES

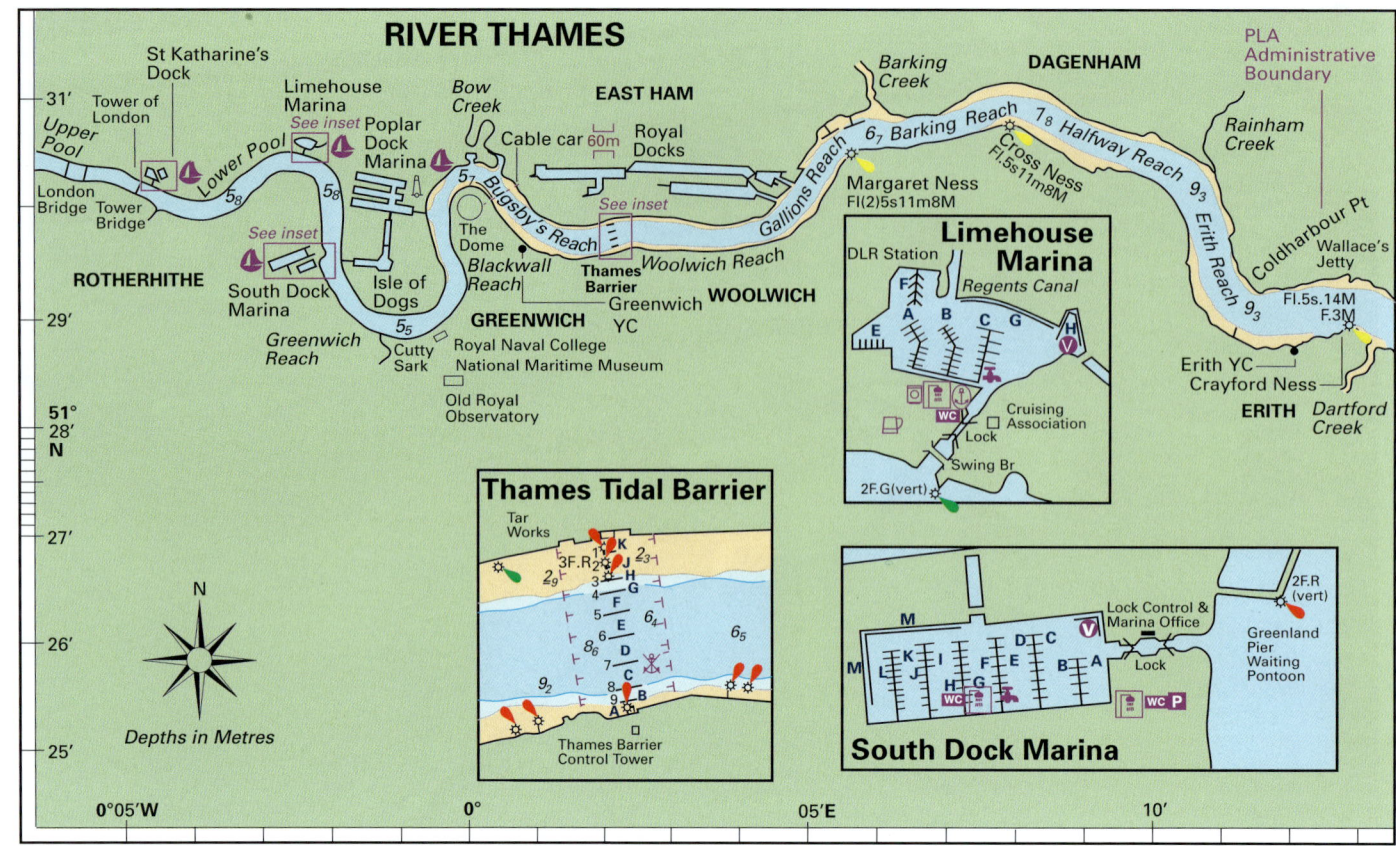

Gravesend to Erith

As you continue westwards passing the town of Gravesend, the Tilbury cruise ship and ferry terminals are seen on the N side. A small ferry runs across the river here from the Town Pier.

The shipping activity continues, especially on the N shore, as you leave Gravesend Reach and turn gently to starboard into Northfleet Hope. (Incidentally, a 'fleet' is an area of shallow water and 'hope' means a small bay and the anchorage off it.) Round this corner, facing W, is the lock entrance to Tilbury Docks, used by merchant ships – your listening watch on VTS Ch 68 will help with news of movements, and you will be asked to wait downstream if necessary. There is a container ship terminal to starboard just beyond the lock entrance, followed by a large grain terminal which can be an unpleasant source of dust in a N wind. Also this area can be choppy in strong winds as the currents swirl around the bend.

Up ahead to starboard, as development thins out on both shores, is Thurrock YC, identifiable by three large grey and white tower blocks close by and yachts moored in the river near the end of the club's landing stage. The club is now in a fine building ashore, but was once in the ancient Gull light vessel whose light mast stands at the head of the slipway.

Boats of up to 38' are welcome to use a spare mooring on the row of buoys closest to the centre of the channel. The western-most mooring is designated for visitors, but if occupied you can pick up any other spare mooring (i.e. without strops) on this row.

There is no charge for using the moorings, however a donation would always be welcome. If the clubhouse is open you are welcome to visit.

Please note that if the clubhouse is closed, the gates are also likely to be closed meaning that you cannot leave the club premises to go into Grays town centre. Opening hours are available on the club website.

Thurrock YC and its moorings

THURROCK YC RM17 6JF
☎ 01375 373720
VHF Ch M/37 if open.
Opening hours at www.thurrockyachtclub.org.uk

168 • East Coast Pilot

Erith Yacht Club

Greenhithe, a historic town with possible moorings

The QE2 Bridge, busy berths on the N shore

After Thurrock, the river turns SW for a mile or so in St Clement's or Fiddler's Reach and a modern housing development at Greenhithe covers the S bank with woods behind. Towards the W end of the modern housing development there are a few PLA-owned moorings close inshore, some occasionally unoccupied - as at Gravesend, a PLA launch may call to collect mooring fees. There is a charted sturdy wooden slipway S of the moorings where you can land by dinghy. The interesting historic part of Greenhithe (Sir John Franklin's ill-fated Arctic expedition departed from here in 1845) is all close to the top of this ramp, fronted by the old Pier Hotel, which dates to 1814; no longer a hotel, it does include a restaurant DA9 9NN, ①01322 382291. There is a corner shop and a large superstore, both about a 10-minute walk, and a railway station very close to the river with trains to London and the Medway Towns.

Continuing upriver, vast modern warehouses lie to port and the huge QE2 road bridge (53m) dominates the view ahead, as the river turns NW into Long Reach. Here the tide can run well in excess of 3kn under the bridge and you have 17M to go to Tower Bridge.

Beware of ships manoeuvring at busy berths on the N shore below and above the bridge. Beyond the bridge and to port is the prominent concrete blockhouse of the Dartford Creek Tidal Barrier, straddling the River Darent and protecting floodplain that extends into Dartford and Crayford. In the far distance, large wind turbines can be seen at Dagenham.

Rounding Crayford Ness to port, you must switch your London VTS listening watch from Ch 68 to Ch 14.

Erith Yacht Club

Once round Crayfordness, Erith YC, a large building with a sloping roof, is now conspicuous ahead on the S shore with many yacht moorings close by and downstream. The club welcomes visitors and offers a useful stop if you are running out of tide on passage between London and the Estuary; there is likely to be a vacant swinging mooring for monohulls up to 11m on request – contact the secretary using details

Approaching Erith YC and its many moorings, a very useful stop to wait for the tide

Erith YC and its drying pontoon and slipway

15. RIVER THAMES

ERITH YC DA8 2AD

Tides HW Sheerness +0030
Contact
VHF Ch 37A / M1
Callsign Erith Yacht Club
☎ 01322 332943, Hon Secretary
☎ 07946 068358
secretary@erithyachtclub.org.uk
www.erithyachtclub.org.uk
Open Sundays all year, Weds lunchtime, Fri evening (Apr-Sept)
Facilities WCs, showers
Max length on moorings 11m
Water/Electricity On tidal pontoon
Fuel 1M away at garage
Provisions See text
Transport Buses pass the end of the main road; trains from Erith and Slade Green stations.

Thames Barrier signal station on the N shore

below. Be aware that 2·1m below the surface there are bridles between adjacent moorings in each line. Larger boats can anchor just upstream, where holding is good in mud. You will be able to lie afloat for a short time alongside the pontoon in front of the clubhouse between about HW+/-2 – this has about 3·5m depth (max at its upstream end) and dries – but the club cannot accommodate overnight stays on it.

Immediately upstream of the clubhouse is a long concrete slipway, its end marked by a red post, on which you can land from a dinghy at all states of tide.

About ¾M further upstream (beyond the substantial commercial jetty and close to two tower blocks) is the charted town causeway, where you can also land by dinghy, with a large supermarket close by. There is a smaller supermarket a short walk from the club.

Erith to Thames Barrier

Continuing up river, the environment once again becomes industrial with an enormous landfill site on the N shore at Rainham Marshes and the Ford motor works at Dagenham beyond, around Jenningtree Point.

Rounding Cross Ness point into Barking Reach and passing the modern sprawl of Thamesmead to port, a huge illuminated sign board stands on the N shore in front of stacks of shipping containers. This is the downstream signal station for the Thames Barrier. It displays the London VTS VHF Channel and phone number, and the CEVNI symbol for 'Stop as required by regulations'.

The sign is 3M from the Barrier; after another ¾M as you round Margaret Ness, you are required to call 'London VTS' at the Thames Barrier Navigation Centre (TBNC) on VHF Ch 14, and announce your position and intentions. Keep it brief – wait for a pause in the constant radio traffic then, having established initial contact, say for instance: "London VTS, yacht 'XXXX', Margaret Ness, upstream, permission to pass through the Barrier please." You will usually be given the all clear and told which span to pass through, or you may be asked to call again when you have the Barrier in sight.

Once past the north bank location of the now-closed Gallions Point Marina, the river sweeps past Gallions Point itself, with Woolwich and its old Arsenal buildings to port, you turn W into Woolwich Reach. Just ahead are the Woolwich Ferry terminals, large rectangular buildings standing on each shore. The two ferries (if both are operating – outside rush hour there may be only one working) cross the river frequently, but they will use Ch 14 to give warning if needed, and will respond to a VHF call.

The Thames Barrier

The Thames Barrier, less than a mile beyond the Woolwich Ferry, displays clear lights on each bascule to indicate which span (gap) to use: the lights form a green arrow pointing in from each side of the span in use, and a red 'X' either side of spans that are closed. Make that call again to London VTS

Approaching the Woolwich Ferry and its two white terminal buildings

170 • East Coast Pilot

Greenwich Yacht Club

Approaching the Barrier, unusually two spans have green lights but you must use whichever one you were told to use

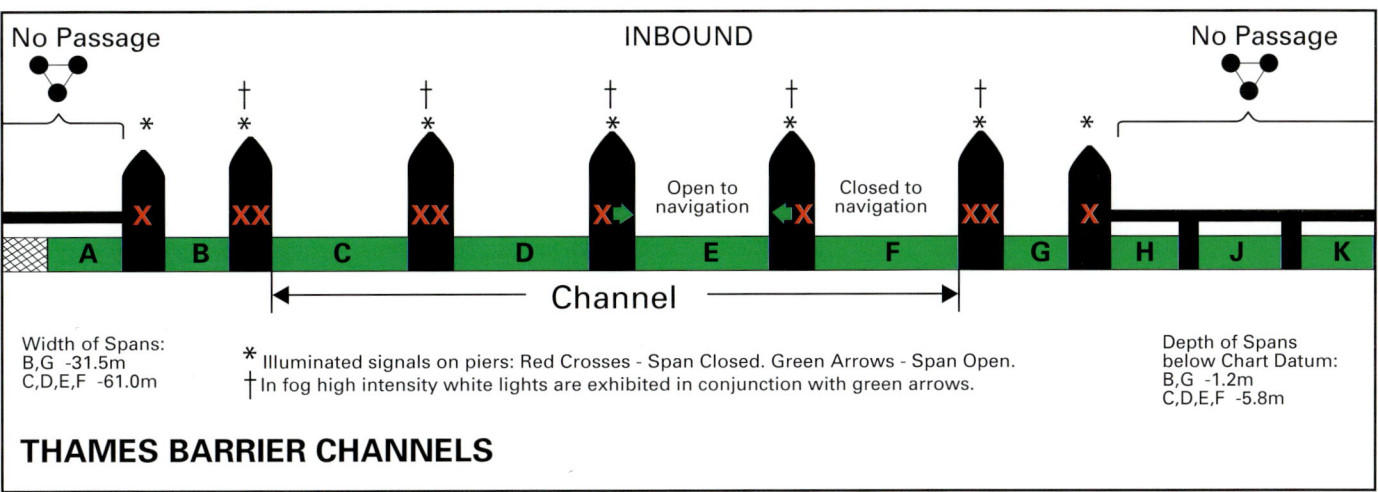

THAMES BARRIER CHANNELS

(Ch 14) if that was requested when you called earlier at Margaret Ness.

Charts show the designation of the spans (B to G with C, D, E and F most frequently used), also see the diagram above. When you are told which span to use, London VTS will use the letter, e.g 'Foxtrot Span'. These letters are not marked on the barrier itself.

Provided you are on the starboard side of the river, the green arrows will be obvious – they have a narrow beam and would not be visible to anyone travelling up stream on the incorrect side of the river (as we understand sometimes happens). Do not approach within ¼M of the Barrier unless you are on passage through it and, if you have a working engine, you are required to use it, not sail through. If in any doubt, do not hesitate to contact the TBNC, where your query will be handled with courtesy.

Thames Barrier Navigation Centre (TBNC)
Contact
VHF Ch 14
Callsign *London VTS*
0203 260 7711

Thames Barrier to Greenwich

Greenwich Yacht Club

About 1M above the Barrier, the grey building of Greenwich YC stands on stilts against the S bank. The club welcomes visitors and is open on Tuesday evenings and at weekends. A call ahead to the Harbourmaster may result in permission for an overnight stop or short stay on one of their 90 fore-and-aft trot moorings upstream of the club, or possibly against the all-tide pontoon in front of the clubhouse if you are less than 13m LOA. The pontoon has water and electricity and least depth about 1·5m. At night, the pontoon is lit 2F.R.(vert). The pontoon can be badly affected by wash from passing barges and the tide runs strongly, so fender up well and ensure lines are strongly secured.

The club has a slipway and travel hoist, and there is a beach just W of the slip usable by boats able to take the ground.

Good transport links make GYC an ideal spot for crew changes.

Greenwich YC and its pontoon

15. RIVER THAMES

GREENWICH YACHT CLUB   SE10 0BW

Tides HW London Bridge -0010

Contact
Enquiries ☎020 8396 0321 ext 0
Harbourmaster ☎as above ext 31,
or 07415 682823
harbourmaster@greenwichyachtclub.co.uk
www.greenwichyachtclub.co.uk
Open weekends and Tues evenings

Facilities WC, showers in the boatyard

Water On pontoon

Electricity On pontoon

Fuel Garage 10min walk

Slipway Yes, with 10T hoist (call the Yardmaster, ext 51)

Provisions supermarkets within 15 minute walk

Clubhouse and bar Open weekends & Tuesday evening. Bar snacks on Saturday, full menu Sunday and Tuesday.

Transport Thames Clippers, Underground (N Greenwich), buses, and Cable Car (20min walk)

Trinity Buoy Wharf and the entrance to Bow Creek

Just beyond the elegant white towers that carry a cable car system across the river, modern apartment blocks and the huge white dome of the O2 now dominate the scene, virtually filling the Greenwich Peninsula at the end of Bugsby's Reach.

Beside the O2, on Blackwall Point, is the upstream-facing signal station for the Thames Barrier, identical to the one downstream at Barking and serving the same function – from here you will call 'London VTS' again on your return journey.

A point of interest to starboard is London's only lighthouse, on Trinity Buoy Wharf, once used for testing and training at this former maintenance site for Trinity House.

West India Dock

Once past the Dome and into Blackwall Reach, the Greenwich Meridian is crossed and the massive office blocks of Canary Wharf stand out to starboard. Over on the W side of Blackwall Reach, through an impressive blue-painted lifting bridge, lies the West India and Millwall Docks complex; this includes marinas in Poplar Dock and Blackwall Basin, as well as extensive quayside moorings in West India Dock.

Access to Blackwall Basin and Poplar Dock involves an air draught limit of 5·2m, passage through a lock and five more bridges after the Blue Bridge and is not normally possible at all during business hours. Furthermore, we understand that neither generally offers visitor moorings.

However, West India Dock, which covers a huge area behind the lock, normally has moorings available for visiting leisure craft, but only for pre-booked groups of six or more boats. In the recent past it has

The cross-river cable car and the O2, upstream from Greenwich YC

West India Dock

The 'Blue Bridge', entrance to the West India docks complex

The huge lock behind the Blue Bridge

been popular for club visits, and it also regularly accommodates superyachts, Naval visits and tall ships. But, while the current published charges for mooring are not unreasonable for London, the charges for operation of the lifting bridge and the lock are very considerable (in 2023) and quite possibly impractical for average owners of small leisure craft, unless they can be shared amongst a large fleet. Current charges can be found in Annex A of the Harbour Regulations and Guidelines (see the information box below).

West India Docks complex from above
Image courtesy of Canary Wharf Group
Photographer Peter Matthews

15. RIVER THAMES

On approach to West India, having booked at least 5 days in advance, contact West India Marine Control on Ch 13 when about 10 minutes away.

The lock is immense, hence the preference for fleets rather than single leisure boats. Berthing beyond is usually against the S wall, which has a low timber 'rubbing strake' that may be awkward for any less able crew members on boats under 30ft with low freeboard. The dockside has water, power and toilets, but is in a public area without the security normally offered by a marina. You may be asked to show proof of insurance including 3rd-party cover up to £4M.

The nearby Museum of Docklands E14 4AL, ☎020 7001 9844 is well worth a visit.

WEST INDIA AND MILLWALL DOCKS

Tides HW London Bridge -0010

We recommend that you read the 'West India and Millwall Docks Harbour Regulations and Guidelines' at www.canalrivertrust.org.uk, a lengthy and changing document which does give all details and charges.

Fendered up before the wash gets too rough

WEST INDIA DOCK   E14 9ST
(Canal & River Trust)

Contact
VHF Ch 13
Callsign *West India Marine Control*
HM's office (weekdays 9-5)
☎020 7517 5557/5559/5555
HM email: WIDharbourmaster@canalrivertrust.org.uk
General enquiries ☎0303 0404040
enquiries.londonsoutheast@canalrivertrust.org.uk
www.canalrivertrust.org.uk

Visitor moorings Fleets of about six or more only; pre-booking essential

Access The Marine Control Room is manned 0700-1900 weekdays, 0800-1600 weekends. Locking is possible 0830-1600 weekdays, 0900-1500 weekends. Minimum height of tide 2m for locking in/out.

Facilities WC, showers (Key available from office)

Water Quayside

Electricity Quayside

Gas available nearby

Pub/restaurant Many in area

Provisions Shops at Canary Wharf

Transport South Quay (Docklands Light Railway), Canary Wharf (Tube), Buses

BLACKWALL BASIN   E14 9SF
(Canal & River Trust)

Visitor moorings not generally available

Contact for entrance See West India details above
www.canalrivertrust.org.uk

POPLAR DOCK MARINA   E14 5SH
(Aquavista Marinas)

Visitor moorings not generally available

Contact for entrance See West India details above

Contact for office ☎0207 308 9930 / 07484 521 353
https://www.aquavista.com/find-a-marina/poplar-waterside-marina

Upriver from the entrance to West India, beware of shallows on the inside of the bend as the river swings to starboard round Saunders Ness to reveal the glorious buildings of the Royal Naval College at Greenwich and the National Maritime Museum, together with the legendary tea clipper *Cutty Sark* in an old dry dock.

From here onwards, the river is usually made uncomfortably choppy by the wash from barges and coasters, as well as the many pleasure boats and very fast river buses that ply the waterway. Great care should be taken when working on deck – prudent skippers should now consider preparing fenders and shorelines, wherever is their destination.

The Royal Naval College, housing the National Maritime Museum; and the 'Cutty Sark' beyond

South Dock Marina

South Dock entrance just to the left of the ramp down to Greenland Pier

Greenwich to Tower Bridge

After Greenwich the river turns N into Limehouse Reach and, half way up on the W side, is London's largest marina, the 200-berth South Dock Marina at Rotherhithe.

South Dock Marina

Inbound to the marina, call the lock office when passing *Cutty Sark*. Advance booking is required. The entrance is just downstream from Greenland Pier, a large pontoon with a white painted and roofed ramp to the shore.

This pier is a frequent stop for the fast river bus services and the area is often very choppy, especially in a breeze. It is possible to wait on the inside of the Greenland Pier pontoon – there's enough length for a 34-footer N of the ramp – but it can be very rough indeed there and boats must be very well fendered and not left unattended. Alternatively, there are several large mooring buoys just downstream of the entrance and you may be able to hang off one of these. The authors would choose instead to wait on idling engine just downstream of the lock.

On the marina office beside the lock, there are digital displays showing the depth over the cill, one facing the river and the other into the lock itself. Traffic lights indicate when it is safe to enter or depart.

Beware of strong cross currents when entering the lock. Inside, there are permanent looped lines hanging down on each side of the lock and, if you can moor starboard side-to, the lock keeper may also be able to pass lines.

This marina is unique among the London destinations in that it is on the S bank of the river; many Thames visitors seem to pass it by, but its public transport connections are very good indeed, it is particularly close to the attractions of Greenwich and there is good local shopping.

There is a sailing centre with a slipway in the adjacent huge Greenland Dock, once busy with the whaling trade.

Greenland Pier, and the South Dock lock gates beyond to the left

South Dock lock, looking N towards the river. Useful chains hang down each side

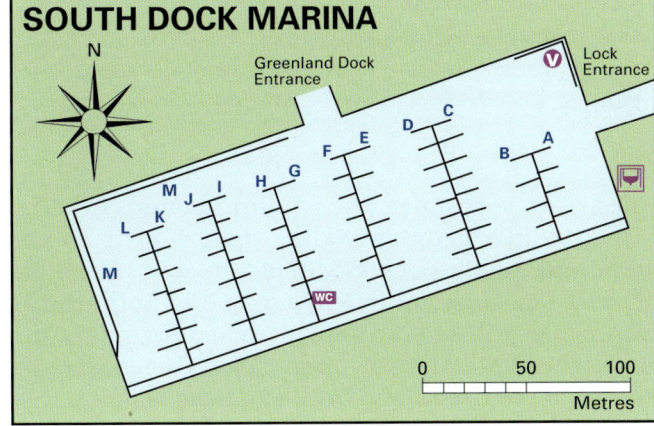

East Coast Pilot • 175

15. RIVER THAMES

South Dock Marina, on the S shore of the river

SOUTH DOCK MARINA — SE16 7SZ

Pre-booking essential for visitors
Tides HW London Bridge -0010
Contact
VHF Ch 37, 80
Callsign *South Dock Marina*
Lock office ☏020 7252 2244
Emergency out of hours ☏07950 805509
southdockmarina@southwark.gov.uk
www.southwark.gov.uk/leisure-and-sport/south-dock-marina
Access From 0700-1900 (0800-1700 Sundays and Bank Holidays) when tide allows: nominal 2.85m over the cill, locking between approx. HW+/-2
Max length/beam 25m/6m
Facilities WC, showers, pump-out, WiFi near office, laundry

Water On pontoons (use own hose)
Electricity On pontoons
Gas Ask in office
Slipway At adjacent Surrey Docks Water Sports Centre
☏0844 893 3888
Crane 18T (20T if spreader bars not used)
Boatyard For boat owners' use 0800–1800 weekdays, 0900–1400 weekends (but no noise on Sundays). Many boatyard trades available locally: ask at the office.
Pub/restaurant Several close by
Provisions Small supermarket 150m from SW corner; many shops at Surrey Quays Retail Centre (10min walk)
Transport Buses; Rotherhithe, Surrey Quays and Canada Water Tube stations (15 minute walk). River bus.

The area is very quiet, and wildlife abounds here.

If you like country walks, then a visit to the park and Russia Dock Woodland created in the old Surrey Docks, running N-S across the Rotherhithe peninsula, will be both a surprise to newcomers and a delight to all. Find the road called Onega Gate on the N side of Greenland Dock and head N.

From South Dock Marina, the river runs ½M N before another turn to port. On the N side of the bend is another possible destination for cruising yachtsmen, Limehouse Marina.

Limehouse Marina entrance is just beyond the tall block with the small turret

The lock into Limehouse Marina lies behind a swinging road bridge. Waiting pontoons are on the right in the entrance

Limehouse Marina

The entrance actually faces SW and can be hard to identify from downstream. It comes after a tall apartment block that towers above others along this stretch and has a small painted turret on its roof. There is a white flagpole by the pub just W of the entrance. Strong cross tides at the entrance can make it very choppy in a breeze. Access is through a swinging road bridge and then a lock.

If you do get a berth, insurance details may be requested. Traffic lights apply – Red, Red/Green (stand by) or Green. If your boat is canal-capable, you must hold a CRT licence to enter.

There are two waiting pontoons accessible HW±1½hr (both of which dry), one before and one behind the road bridge, both with shore access, but beware that you cannot return to the outer one after

Note: Advance visitor booking at Limehouse, readily available in the past, was being refused in early 2023 unless at very short notice and it seemed difficult generally for any visitors to be able to use this marina. However, Aquavista, which runs Limehouse Marina, confirmed later that year that visitor spaces are still usually available, with limitations. You should contact the marina office well before arrival and on VHF Ch 80 when you reach Limehouse. Visitors will normally be directed to pontoon H, almost underneath the DLR track and with a maximum 2m depth, or on the eastern wall where there is no power or water, or (best of all) perhaps a vacant resident berth if one is available. If planning to visit, by all means check the current policy, first of all looking for any updates on the ECP website.

Waiting pontoons – not easy to use, see text

15. RIVER THAMES

Limehouse, an attractive place but perhaps not so easy to visit these days

going ashore. Particularly in a SW wind, waves can funnel into the entrance and cause the pontoons to heave around quite violently. Fenders must be set very low if using them. Once through the bridge and on the inner pontoon, a vessel is effectively trapped, so it may be better to wait out in the river until able to enter.

The lock has some mooring lines hanging vertically against the walls around which you can loop your own lines; the office is in the building to port by the basin entrance. To starboard is the headquarters of the Cruising Association, where visitors, even if non-members, may use the bar and restaurant in the evenings. There are also several good restaurants close by in Narrow Street, including the Bread Street Kitchen on the River (☏020 7592 7950), a bar and restaurant owned by Gordon Ramsay, and there are plenty of other eating opportunities a few minutes' walk away in Commercial Road.

Limehouse Marina is another convenient and quiet base for visiting London with good facilities and supplies available nearby, plus good transport links. The Rotherhithe road tunnel entrance is close by.

When returning to the river from the marina, you should make a long sound signal because you cannot see approaching traffic heading upstream from your left.

Beyond Cuckolds Point, opposite Limehouse, the river turns SW into the Lower Pool, passing the famous Prospect of Whitby pub to starboard. The next bend to starboard has the headquarters of the River Police on the N shore and brings Tower Bridge into sight ahead in the Upper Pool with The Shard (306m high) dominating the scene beyond.

LIMEHOUSE MARINA E14 8EG

Pre-booking essential for visitors, but see note see note on previous page.

Contact
VHF Ch 80
Callsign *Limehouse Marina*
Lock office and bookings ☏020 7308 9930; Lock Keeper 07766 774726
limehouse@aquavista.com
www.aquavista.com/find-a-marina/limehouse-waterside-marina

Access HW±4hr, 0800–1800 April–September, 0800–1600 October–March. Other times between 0500-2200 may be possible on request with 24hr advance notice

Max length/beam 28m/7·5m

Facilities WC, showers, launderette, pump-out

Water On pontoons, use own hose
Electricity On pontoons
Gas Ask in office
Repairs Ask in lock office
Provisions Shops nearby and in Commercial Road, 5 mins walk
Pubs/restaurants In Narrow Street nearby and Commercial Road, 5 mins walk
Club Cruising Association ☏020 7537 2828 www.theca.org.uk
Transport Docklands Light Railway from Limehouse Station, just NW of the marina; Buses on Commercial Road

Journey's end for yachts

Approaching Hermitage Moorings, the visitor spaces are on the outside pontoon

Hermitage Community Moorings

Three cables W of the Police HQ, there is a substantial set of pontoon moorings joined to the N shore by a walkway. This is Hermitage Community Moorings, a not-for-profit location established mainly for large traditional river barges, many of which are residential. There are two visitor berths on the downstream end of the outermost pontoon, one inside the pontoon, one on the outside. Minimum depth on the inside berth is approximately 1·0m LAT (beam and tide dependant, see details below) and the bottom is hard – there is more water on the outside berth, but it could be very uncomfortable in a small modern lightweight boat especially during day time, even though the pontoons are very substantial and deaden some of the chop. The usual facilities are provided.

The moorings are a very short walk from St Katharine's and have the obvious benefit of being in

Hermitage Community Moorings

15. RIVER THAMES

Visitor berths at LW, little depth on the inside berth

the river itself and not behind a lock gate. Advance booking is advised. Initial contact is best made by phone. Special rates apply for historic vessels. There is paperwork available at the visitor berths in an 'honesty box' for weekend use when the place is unmanned, when members of the 'co-op' can help out if needed. If arriving at night, the visitor berths are either side of the downstream post which carries 2F.G lights.

> **HERMITAGE COMMUNITY MOORINGS**
> **E1W 1NG**
>
> Pre-booking advised for visitors
>
> **Tides** HW London Bridge
>
> **Contact**
> ☎020 7481 2122 (weekdays only 1000-1700)
> www.hcmoorings.org
> manager@hcmoorings.org
>
> **Access** Outer berth: all-tide, least depth 2·1m. Inner berth: restricted near LW, least depth 1·0m at point 5m inshore from pontoon
>
> **Facilities** WC, showers, pump-out
>
> **Water** On pontoon
>
> **Electricity** On pontoon
>
> **Fuel** As St Kats
>
> **Provisions** As St Kats
>
> **Pubs/Restaurants** As St Kats
>
> **Transport** As St Kats

Just upstream of Hermitage Moorings, also on the N side, is the large fuel barge *Heiko*. Be aware that the advertised operating times are approximate and the barge does not operate at all at weekends. If you require fuel, contact is preferred by phone (see St Katharine Docks details, page 181) and follow directions – you may be asked to tie up on the N side of the barge to shelter from the chop.

On upstream from the fuel barge, the entrance to St Katharine Docks (widely known as St Kats) is on the N shore just short of Tower Bridge.

St Katharine Docks Marina

This marina enjoys a splendid position, almost in Central London and within walking distance of many attractions, and its looks and ambience make it a tourist attraction in itself. Its prices do reflect this, although the period rates can be much better value than daily rates. It is very popular and often completely full, especially when one of the frequent large events is being hosted in the Central Basin. Advance booking (at least a week ahead in mid-season) is essential; nonetheless it may be worth calling the day before if you decide to try at short notice.

Access is through a large lock from about HW-2hr to about HW+1½hr, although this depends on the height of tide. Locking times are published on the St Kats website. Report in by VHF when you are 5 minutes or so away.

The lock into St. Kats. Both lock gates fold down. The Central Basin is beyond

St Katharine Docks

There are waiting buoys SE of the entrance. These are rather close together and the inshore row has only 1·2m least depth. Furthermore they are not easy to use as the PLA has not allowed the marina to fit pickup lines. The waiting pontoon shown on some older charts is no longer available. If you want an overnight waiting berth on the river, call ahead and ask about possibly using St Katharine's Pier just upstream of the entrance, or perhaps think of using Hermitage Moorings (see pages 177-178).

At busy times, waiting outside for the lock can be hard work for helmsmen as they cope with stemming the strong current, avoiding other boats waiting to enter and frequent large and noisy river ferries using the neighbouring pier. You will normally be called in individually, but sometimes there can be an unseemly rush into the inviting lock by the waiting skippers as soon as the traffic lights on the pierheads change to green. Inside the lock, the starboard side is preferred, where there is a floating timber pontoon with cleats at deck height. To port is the old stone wall with bollards and hanging chains. There is often quite a surge felt in the lock until the outer gate closes, and skippers may find it easier on arrival to secure a stern line first.

From the lock, you pass through a lifting road bridge into the Central Basin where suddenly all is still. There are two more basins, East Dock and West Dock, leading off from it through lifting footbridges.

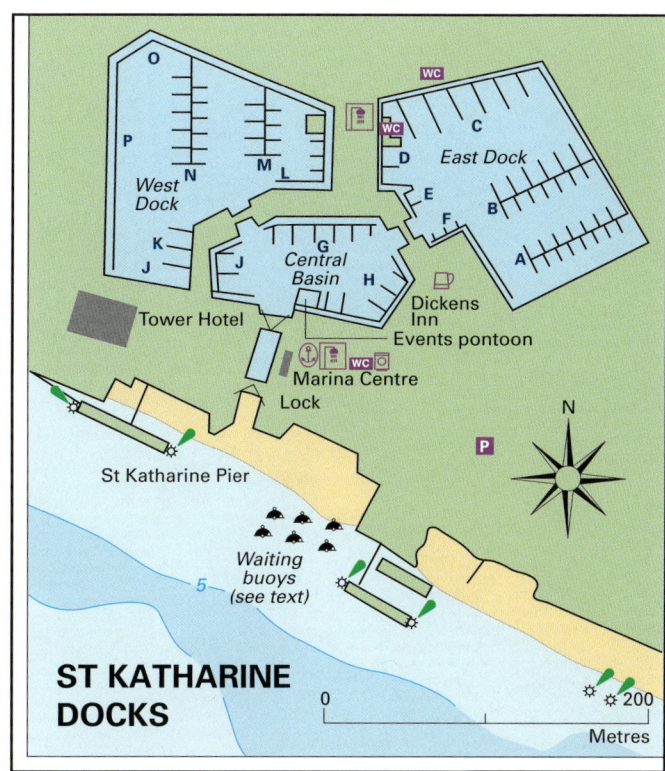

All berths are behind smart-card security gates. The whole area is usually beautifully kept and the marina is surrounded by trees, flower beds and

The bascule bridge lifted to allow access into the marina

15. RIVER THAMES

The three basins at St Kats

hanging baskets. Although it's busy – there are many shops, cafes and restaurants, and plenty of people walk through the docks on their way to and from work – it can at times be uncannily quiet, although aircraft noise can intrude when the wind is in the east. The East Dock is certainly the quietest of the three. Visitors are provided with a useful discount card which can be used in many of the businesses around the marina.

You may be asked to show proof of insurance. Locking out on departure must be booked in advance.

Craft of all sizes visit St Kats

St Katharine Docks

ST KATHARINE DOCKS **E1W 1LA**

Pre-booking essential for visitors

Tides HW London Bridge

Contact
VHF Ch 80 (during locking times)
Callsign *St Katharine's*
Office ☎020 7264 5312 (0900-1700)
marina.reception@skdocks.co.uk
www.skdocks.co.uk/marina

Access Approx HW-2hr to HW+1½hr, Apr-Oct 0600-2030, Nov-Mar 0800-1800, but see marina website for exact daily times

Facilities WC, showers, launderette, pump-out (accessible from most berths)

Water On pontoons

Electricity On pontoons, separate metered charge

Gas Ask in office

Fuel Thames Marine Services, on barge Heiko in river. Call TMS office on ☎020 3935 4814 or 07827 816004 or the barge direct on VHF Ch 14, call sign Heiko. Also a 24H petrol station on The Highway, 15-minute walk.

Doctor Close nearby in Thomas More Street, ☎020 7488 3653

Pub/restaurant Many inside marina, more nearby outside.

Provisions Small Tesco supermarket outside to W, large Waitrose store outside to E

Fuel barge *Heiko*, just downstream of St Kats entrance

A rally of 'Dunkirk Little Ships', and one of the many eating opportunities beyond

Looking down over the West Basin. Beyond, the Central Basin is crammed with a special event

East Coast Pilot • 183

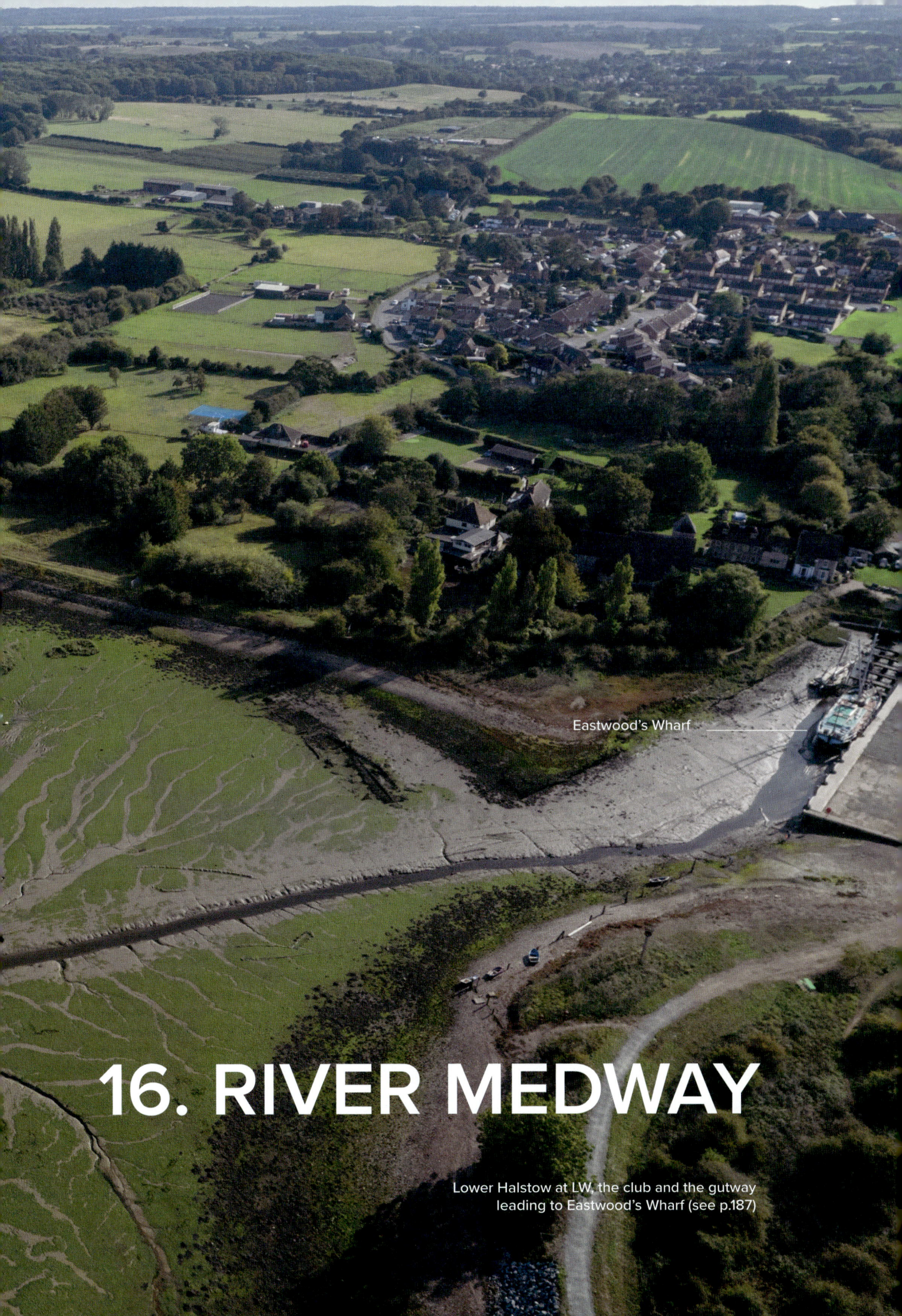

16. RIVER MEDWAY

Lower Halstow at LW, the club and the gutway leading to Eastwood's Wharf (see p.187)

Eastwood's Wharf

16. RIVER MEDWAY

⊕ **Landfall waypoints**
From E 51°27'·20N 000°45'·60E
Close E of West Cant PHB (Q.R)
From W (Thames) and N:
51°28'·36N 000°45'·55E
Close N of Nore Swatch PHB (Fl(4)R.15s)
Charts
Admiralty 5606, 1834
Imray 2100, Y18
Tides
Entrance HW Sheerness
Chatham HW Sheerness +0009
Allington Lock HW Sheerness +0035 to +0055
Harbour Authority (Peel Ports London Medway)
Contact
VHF Ch 74
Callsign *Medway VTS*
Harbour office Sheerness ☎01795 596596
Medway VTS Office ☎0151 949 6650/6418

For any additional leisure boating information, including a useful 'visitor chart', contact the Medway & Swale Boating Association, www.msba.org.uk

> **THE MEDWAY**
>
> This chapter describes pilotage in the tidal Medway from the sea inland 25M to Allington Lock, although for most yachts the head of navigation will be the fixed bridge at Rochester, 13M upstream from Sheerness.
>
> As a tourist destination the Medway Towns have much to offer with the Historic Dockyard Museum, modern shopping centres, Royal Engineers' Museum, Rochester Cathedral, castles and Dickensian festivals. Away from it all in the lower reaches of the river, there is fine sailing as well as interesting and peaceful creeks and inlets. The upper reaches beyond Rochester Bridge pass through an interesting mix of rural scenery, quiet villages and industrial history.

Main hazards

The lower part of the Medway carries commercial traffic, some of it large, and close attention should be paid to shipping movements. Listen to Medway VTS on Ch 74. Note that the VTS personnel are not based locally and have no direct view of the river, only through CCTV.

This traffic uses Sheerness Docks, close to the mouth of the river, Thamesport container terminal and a natural gas (LNG) terminal, both in Saltpan Reach, while other ships travel right up river almost to the fixed bridge at Rochester. The very large LNG tankers (often brightly coloured) have strict exclusion zone rules (see below); again listen to Medway VTS.

There is a dangerous wreck (the *Richard Montgomery*) immediately N of the approach channel, 2M NE of Sheerness, in a total exclusion zone marked by yellow light buoys.

There can be overfalls by Garrison Point on the first of the ebb and there are many drying areas on both shores along the river, with some shore features completely covered at HWS.

Approaches

From E Approach across the Cant shallows from the Spile buoy or along the S edge of the main shipping channel. Note that there is a 'secondary' shipping channel along the S edge of the main channel, marked on its S edge by yellow buoys, all Fl(2)Y.5s. Stay S of both channels, but avoid the shallows S of the West Cant buoy (Q.R) and an outfall marked by a small NCB (Q).

From N, NE or the Thames The Nore Swatch (Fl(4) R.15s) marks a convenient point from which to head S to the unlit Grain Edge buoy on the N side of the main channel opposite the West Cant, taking care to skirt around the shallows of Grain Spit.

SHEERNESS

Contact
VHF Ch 74
Callsign *Medway VTS*
VTS office ☎0151 949 6650/6418

Sheerness is a commercial port and does not accommodate leisure craft. However, one small part of the original Royal Naval Dockyard remains, a small dock called the Camber, just S of the old fort and Port Office at Garrison Point. This dock is used

Few features define the Medway entrance from the N

River Medway

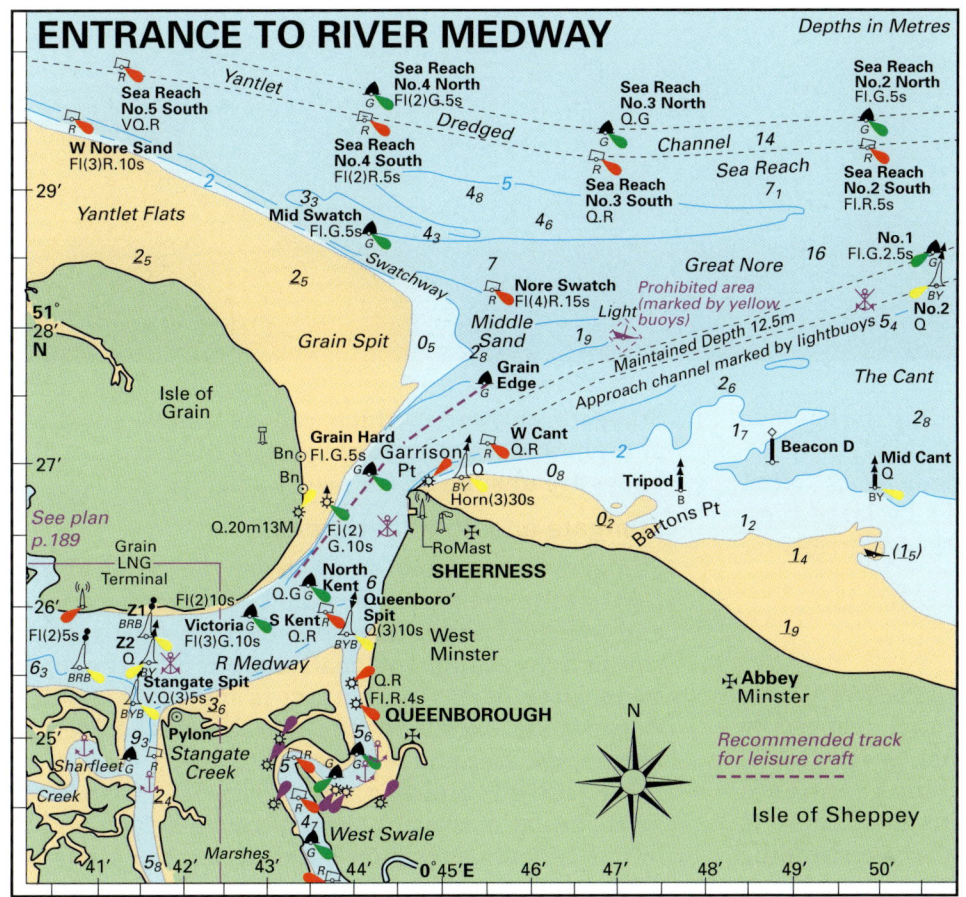
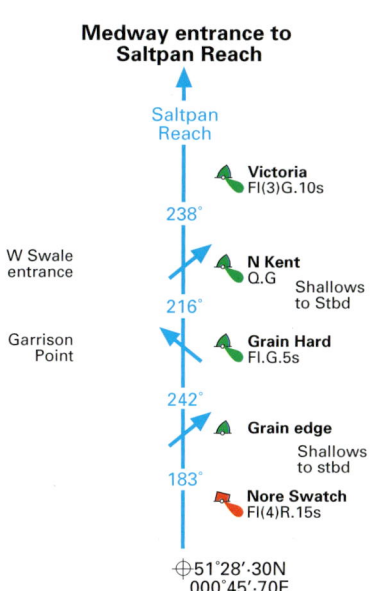

by fast pilot boats and Sheerness RNLI lifeboats, but could be a place of refuge in an emergency with the consent of Medway VTS.

Entry to River Medway

Beware a ferry terminal jetty protruding N from Garrison Point – the ebb sets quickly E beneath it. From time to time large car/truck ferry services do use this jetty, although not at the time of writing in 2023.

The Port Control building stands on top of the large fort on Garrison Point and displays a bright light (Fl.7s) warning of movements of large ships (over 130m). The light is directed upstream if traffic is inbound and to seaward if traffic is outbound.

Unless certain that there is no traffic, use the charted recommended leisure craft track on the W shore, from the No.11 SHB (Fl(3)G.10s) to Grain Hard SHB (Fl.G.5s). The ebb is also weaker on this side. Heading on towards the N Kent SHB (Q.G), take care not to stray onto the steeply shelving bank to starboard, especially W of Grain Hard buoy where

Possible emergency refuge in the Camber dock

Garrison Point, looking NE

East Coast Pilot • 187

16. RIVER MEDWAY

Stangate Creek entrance lies to the west of the electricity pylons

there are charted obstructions including the obvious Grain Tower Fort.

Heavy shipping leaving the Medway is often escorted in this section of the river by large tugs, whose skippers can be unsympathetic to leisure craft close to the main channel.

Medway Entrance to Stangate

From the N Kent SHB, the entrance to the West Swale can be seen on the S side of the channel, marked by the Queenborough Spit ECB (Q(3)10s). See page 225.

Once through the relative narrows of the entrance and into Saltpan Reach, which runs E-W, there is more scope for using the width of the river, shipping permitting. Off to starboard, on Horseshoe Point, the LNG terminal receives very large ships and further W stand the cranes at Thamesport container terminal. You must stay at least 150m clear of the LNG terminal, 250m clear if there is a ship berthed there (these limits are rigorously enforced and if you transgress you may well be prosecuted), and beware of very large ships turning opposite either terminal. We stress that it's sensible to monitor the VTS channel, 74.

During WW1, Saltpan Reach saw the second of two major tragedies on the Medway, when the liner *Princess Irene*, requisitioned as a minelayer, exploded in May 1915 with the loss of 352 lives.

Bearing about 240° from the Victoria SHB (Fl(3) G.10s), the Stangate Spit ECB (VQ(3)5s) marks the W side of the entrance to Stangate Creek, the first anchorage in the Medway. A line of electricity pylons from the SE, ending immediately E of the entrance, is prominent. There are heavy mooring buoys along the S side of the main channel, E of Stangate entrance, which can be almost invisible at night and are often occupied by huge barges. The buoys are unsuitable for use by small craft.

Stangate and Sharfleet Creeks

Stangate Creek runs due S from the Medway for 1·6M from the Spit buoy and is a very popular and peaceful anchorage, but be sure to display a riding light at night as boats are often on the move there after dark. The bottom is mud and holding is generally excellent. The marshes each side are nature reserves and teem with birdlife.

The ruined building on Burntwick Island (to starboard at entrance) once housed a steam engine to pull a defensive chain boom across the Medway. Evidence of much older settlements includes fragments of Roman pottery still found there.

Half-a-mile into Stangate Creek, after passing an unlit SHB with a wreck very close W of it, Sharfleet Creek turns off to the W and then NW into a horseshoe curve. This creek too is popular, although you need to choose your spot so as not to take the ground at LW and to avoid blocking the channel. There are no marks or withies.

Parts of Sharfleet, once the best oyster grounds in the Medway, are very deep, and most of it has more than 2m at LWS. Many head for the deeper water on the W side of the 'horseshoe'. In a N'ly breeze, we have noticed that machinery noise can carry across from Thamesport, but otherwise this is a peaceful place. With shoal draught and a rising tide, the adventurous skipper can take a shortcut W across the Ham Ooze from Sharfleet to Half Acre Creek or to the Medway in Kethole Reach.

Stangate Creek continues S from its junction with Sharfleet Creek with good holding everywhere.

A strictly enforced exclusion zone exists around gas tanker ships

The engine house for an old chain barrier across the river

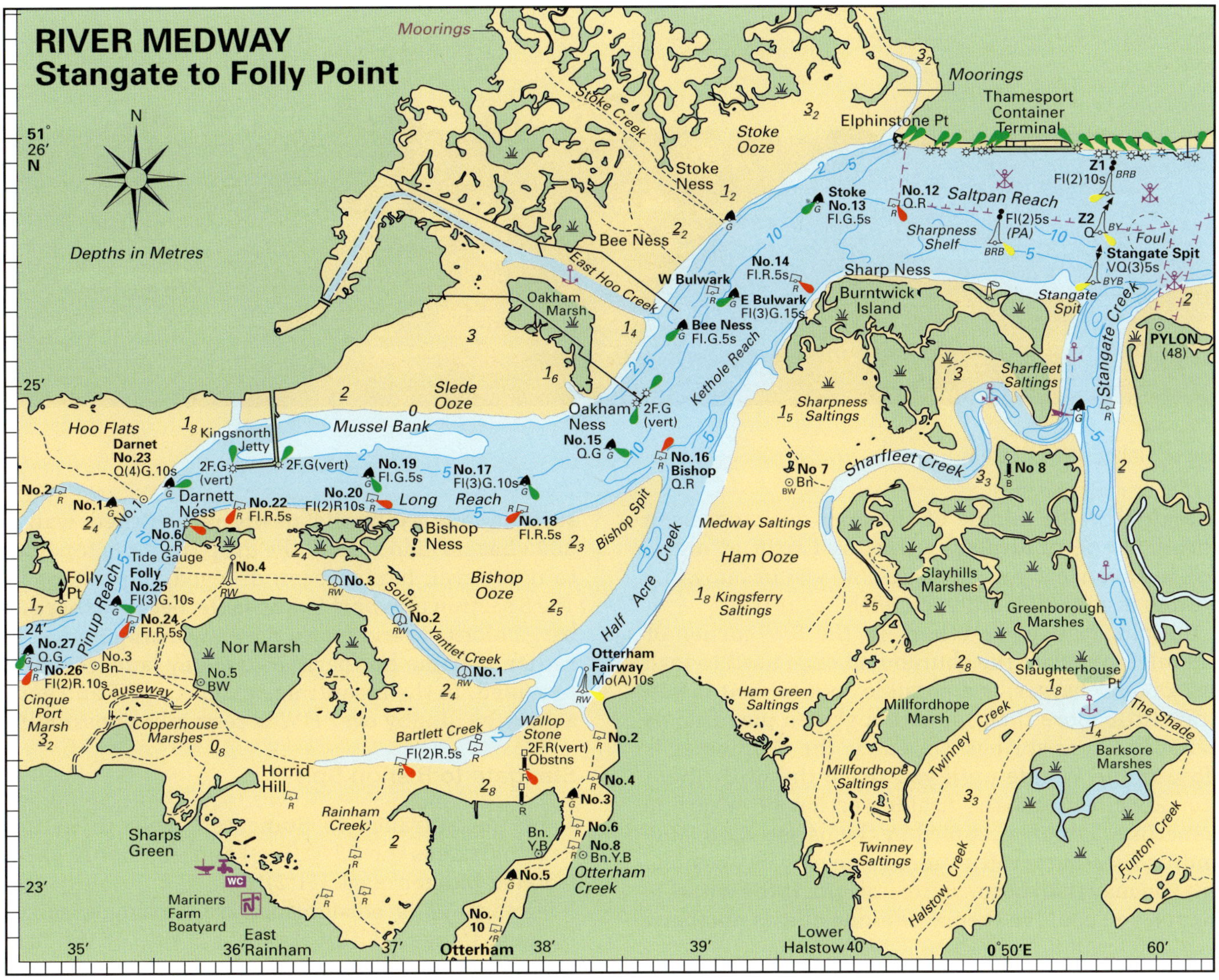

Visitors generally anchor on the windward side of the creek, although the surrounding countryside is marsh and does not give much shelter from strong winds near HW. The creek divides at its S end with the Shade to port offering another possible anchorage. Beyond the Shade, Funton Reach soon peters out into the drying areas of Funton Creek and Bedlams Bottom, graveyard of the famous racing Thames barges *Sirdar* and *Veronica*.

To starboard at the S end of Stangate Creek, immediately S of Slaughterhouse Point, there is a pool affording better shelter in a N wind. Some charts show this pool, and an area near the N end of Stangate, as 'explosives anchorages', but there now seems to be no reason for these to be charted, a leftover perhaps from the Medway's naval dockyards.

SW from this pool, Halstow Creek will take shoal draught boats right up to Lower Halstow on the tide, but note that the whole area dries.

LOWER HALSTOW

Lower Halstow is a peaceful village with an ancient church, a pub, a village shop and an old quay. In the SE corner of the inlet is **Lower Halstow YC**, www.lhyc.org.uk, access HW+/-1½, with its many drying moorings, a short jetty and a slipway. To reach the club from Stangate Creek, head SW midway between between the E shore and the small islet

The N end of the old wharf with a dinghy landing spot

16. RIVER MEDWAY

Lower Halstow Yacht Club

and aim for the middle of the club moorings seen ahead. The jetty displays a fixed red light at night. Ask in advance if you can use a club visitor buoy. The bottom is generally quite flat with 2m at HW.

The old Eastwood's Wharf in the SW corner of the inlet, opposite the church and once used to load bricks onto barges, is a possible spot to visit if you draw little more than 1m, although you may find as much as 2m at springs. On entry, the best water is close to the W side until you reach the wall. There are no toilets and the usable section of wharf is sometimes largely occupied by the barges *Edith May* and/or *Tollesbury*; rafting alongside may be possible, but you may then not sit quite upright. If the wharf is empty, you could in theory lie alongside its northern section, but sadly the newly-refurbished wall in 2023 has no ladders and the drop from the top down to mud level, having been dredged, is perhaps 15'. The S section of wharf is unusable, because there are barge blocks there, marked by a warning notice. All rather a shame but perhaps one day ladders will be provided. In the meantime, anchoring off and going ashore by dinghy over HW is certainly a possibility.

Stangate to Bishop Spit

N of the entrance to Stangate Creek, in Saltpan Reach, there is the Z2 NCB(Q) and, further N, the Z1 Isolated Danger mark (Fl(2)10s).

Pilotage W is straightforward, noting a second Isolated Danger (Fl(2)5s) on the S side of the main channel opposite Thamesport. Large ships turn in this area of Saltpan Reach.

Passing the No.12 PHB (Q.R), the river turns SW into Kethole Reach. Over to starboard, the drying Stoke Saltings was one of the areas in the Medway used by 19th century gangs of 'muddies', who, between two tides, could fully load a Thames barge with the blue clay used in cement making. An unlit SHB on the edge of the flats marks the start of Stoke Creek, another drying inlet with a small boatyard and moorings at its head.

Half way along Kethole Reach, the E Bulwark SHB (Fl(3)G.15s) and unlit W Bulwark PHB mark the extremities of the wreck of the 15,000-ton battleship HMS *Bulwark*, which exploded in November 1914 with the loss of over 700 lives. The disintegrating Bee Ness disused jetty juts out nearby from the NW shore and on its SW side is the entrance to East Hoo Creek, a narrow anchorage running NW and carrying over 2·5m almost to its head in Damhead Creek.

If you venture into East Hoo Creek, another wartime relic can be visited by dinghy near LW – the hulk of a German U-boat lies north of Bee Ness jetty at about 51°25'·8N 000°37'·9E, abandoned there after she surrendered at the end of WW1.

Barge blocks at the S end of Eastwood's Wharf

SW of the No.14 PHB (Fl.R.5s), charts show a line of heavy mooring buoys along the SE shore – these are virtually invisible at night, although in 2023 only one was in place, no.23. Just past this area is the entrance to Half Acre Creek, marked on its W side by the No.16 Bishop PHB (Q.R), behind which lies the extensive and drying Bishop Spit.

Half Acre Creek

Running SW, Half Acre Creek provides a wide, deep water passage for a mile beyond the entrance. Keeping industrial buildings on Motney Hill on the bow, watch for cross-tides. The large tripod of the No.7 beacon is across the flats to port, in the area where a shortcut is possible to or from Sharfleet Creek near HW. Further on SW, some charts show a barge on the E side of the channel, but this has not been seen in modern times. At the Otterham Fairway SWB (Mo(A)10s), Half Acre Creek divides into three, as follows:

South Yantlet Creek runs off to starboard, curving NW following a string of unlit SWBs, numbered 1 to 3. Beyond the third of these is a drying area N of Nor Marsh island, which may be crossed with 2m after HW-3 towards the fourth and final red and white No.4 SWB pillar buoy. Best water is just S of this buoy. Continuing W for 2 more cables across mud that dries about 2·5m in places, the channel rejoins the Medway in Pinup Reach.

Otterham Creek runs S from the Otterham Fairway buoy for about 1·5M and is a buoyed but drying route to the boatyard at Otterham Quay, which is to port at the end, opposite a commercial wharf. Most tides will allow a 2m draught boat to reach the quay, a destination for (mainly commercial) boat repairs, stainless steel work or winter storage, but with no provision at all for casual visitors.

Bartlett Creek is the third, middle branch from the Otterham Fairway buoy and heads WSW past a prominent wreck to an unlit PHB, then W towards the Rainham Fairway PHB (Fl(2)R.5s) at the N end of the gutway of Rainham Creek.

Continue W from the Rainham Fairway PHB for a short distance with the distant apartment blocks at Gillingham on the bow, then a gutway marked by occasional withies leads SW towards the unlit Mariners PHB off Horrid Hill.

The Mariners buoy is laid by Mariners Farm Boatyard, a nearby boat storage venue popular for winter lay-up, but unfortunately not geared up at all for visiting boats.

With shoal draught and a rising tide, an alternative route from up river to Bartlett Creek runs SE from further up the River Medway opposite Folly Point, passing between a post and a red can to cross the causeway off the SW corner of Nor Marsh, then on SE past Horrid Hill to meet Bartlett Creek. This remote and interesting area south of the main Medway channel is nationally and internationally important for many species of birds and is full of life in winter and summer, and exploring it quietly in a gentle breeze and a shoal-draught boat can be a real delight.

Bishop Spit to Darnet Ness

Continuing up stream on the Medway past the entrance to Half Acre Creek, the main river runs W in Long Reach. It is safe to stay out of the main channel by skirting along its N edge, past SHBs No.15 (Q.G), No.17 (Fl(3)G.10s) and No.19 (Fl.G.5s). Beyond No.19, on the N shore, the long coal jetty of the now-demolished Kingsnorth Power Station was still standing in 2023 with its impressive array of machinery. It remains unclear whether this will remain or be demolished too. Opposite, the S shore of Long Reach shelves steeply, mostly covers at HWS, and frequently catches out the unwary on a falling tide.

OTTERHAM CREEK   ME8 7XE

Access HW±1hr

Boat repairs Otterham Creek Boatyard ☎01634 260250 or 07882 655497; 9-T crane and dry docks (max. length 80ft)

Engineers On site

Darnet Fort, on Darnet Ness opposite the Kingsnorth jetty

16. RIVER MEDWAY

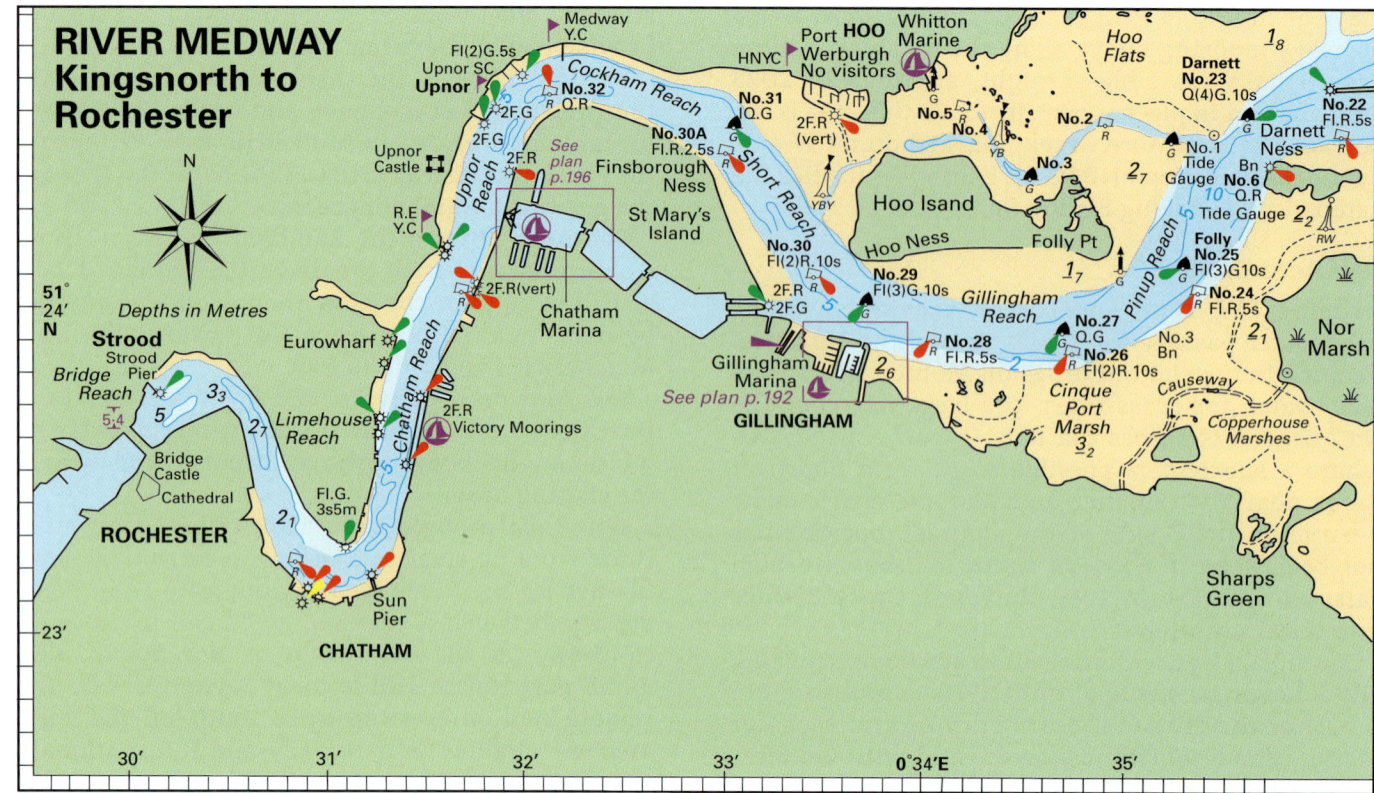

The final PHB in Long Reach, No.22 (Fl.R.5s), stands close to the N edge of Darnet Ness, a small island on the S side of the river where it turns SW into Pinup Reach with R beacon No.6 (Q.R) on its corner. A Palmerston Fort stands on Darnet Ness, built in the 1860s and once housing heavy muzzle-loading rifled guns for defence of the Naval dockyards at Chatham.

Middle Creek

At this bend, the adventurous shoal-draught skipper may choose to take the twisting Middle Creek that heads WNW by the No.1 Beacon, either to visit the boatyard at Whitton Marine, reach Hoo Ness YC's slipway or simply to circumnavigate Hoo Island, at suitable states of the tide. The channel is buoyed, but the buoys are not shown on all charts. Starting with a SHB No.1, follow WNW to a PHB marked No.2, rounding this and turning SW to find No.3 SHB. The channel then roughly follows the shape of Hoo Island about 50m off, turning NW towards No.4, an SCB in line with a distant church steeple.

At this point, with enough tide, you could carry on NW past No.5 PHB towards the Hundred of Hoo SC and Whitton Marine, which offers services including marine engineering and may find room for visitors alongside drying pontoons.

Otherwise, continue W through some moorings towards the R and G posts close to the Hoo Island shore, which indicate a gap in the causeway between Hoo Island and the mainland.

From the R and G markers, head SW (initially staying close to Hoo Island shore – this stretch is the shallowest of the route) and join the Orinoco Channel, which leads either NNW to Port Werburgh, or SSE back to Short Reach in the Medway beside an unlit WCB (see page 194 for further notes about the Orinoco).

Darnet Ness to Gillingham Marina

If not entering Middle Creek but continuing up the Medway, head SW through Pinup Reach, where the shortcut through to South Yantlet Creek (see above) may be seen to port, before passing the No.25 Folly SHB (Fl(3)G.10s) and No.24 PHB (Fl.R.5s) off Folly Point. The channel is narrow here so take particular care with large traffic, and heavy lighters are often moored here. An unlit G post stands on the SE corner of Folly Point to starboard and the shallows extend

WHITTON MARINE — ME3 9LB

Contact
☎ 01634 250593
www.whittonmarine.co.uk
Access HW+/-1.5
Facilities WC, showers
Water, electricity On pontoon
Boat repairs Slipways, engineering
Club Hundred of Hoo SC
www.hundredofhoosailingclub.org
hundredofhoosailingclub@gmail.com
Pub, provisions In Hoo St.Werburgh, short walk.
Taxi ☎ 01634 251234

Marina Lock gates

Once round Darnet Ness, Gillingham Marina can be seen about a mile ahead

a long way S of Hoo Island – this island is home to a Palmerston Fort matching that on Darnet Ness. Gillingham is now in clear view ahead with a group of tower blocks standing just beyond Gillingham Marina.

Note The speed limit upstream from here reduces to 6kn.

At SHB No.27 (Q.G) and PHB No.26 (Fl(2)R.10s), the channel turns just N of W into Gillingham Reach and yacht moorings line both shores. Those on the N shore are close to shallows.

Medway Cruising Club and Segas SC are on the south bank, just beyond the next PHB, No.28 (Fl.R.5s), the Segas club having its own drying basin. Both clubs are usually open at weekends. The Commodore's Hard public slipway stretches into the river between these two clubs and can be used to launch or recover dinghies and small craft.

Approaching Gillingham Marina

MEDWAY CRUISING CLUB ME7 2SE
www.medwaycruisingclub.org.uk
medwaycruisingclub@gmail.com

SEGAS SC ME7 1TT
①01304 362842
www.segassailingclub.co.uk

Gillingham Marina

Immediately west of Segas SC's drying basin is the high E wall of Gillingham Marina, which has two basins, one behind a lock, the other tidal. Viewed from the river, the lock gate is towards the downstream end of the N wall, to the left of the large pale-coloured building (a restaurant and leisure centre) and the tidal basin is upstream, round behind the wall at the right hand end. The tidal basin dries to soft mud.

Berths should be booked in advance if possible. Berths in the locked basin are mostly alongside

16. RIVER MEDWAY

Gillingham entrance, lock gate open, fuel berth outside to stbd

finger pontoons, while a minority are box berths, stern-to a pontoon and bow secured between piles. .

The marina office is in the large building at the S end of the wall between the two basins.

Locking is not 24hr (see marina details) but there is a row of waiting buoys in deep water in front of the marina wall. The lock has traffic lights. Vertical cables are set in the lock walls to put lines around, if you cannot reach the bollards at the top, and there are floating fenders on each side. Lock keepers here are generally extremely helpful with assistance in securing lines. Free flow is sometimes used near to HWS.

Boats wishing to depart outside lock operating hours, e.g at night, can be offered berths in the tidal basin where most are box berths.

There is a refuelling pontoon on the river just upstream of the lock gate. It is angled out into the stream, which can make departure from it a little awkward on the ebb.

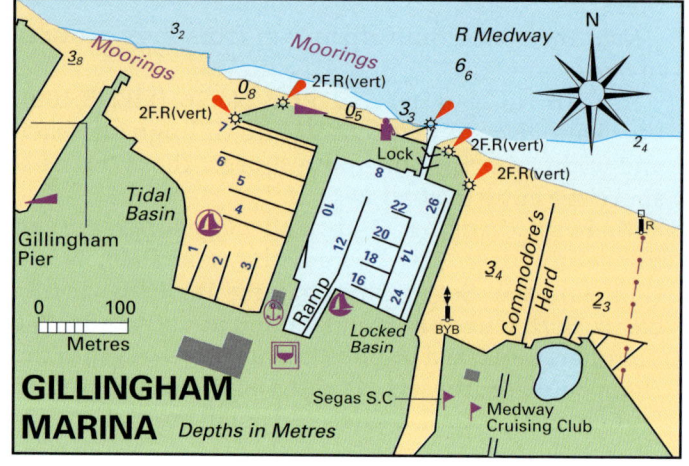

Gillingham Marina tidal basin at LW

Gillingham Marina

Photo labels: Tidal basin; Marina office; Waterfront bar and restaurant; Waiting buoys; Fuel berth; Lock entrance; Gillingham Marina

GILLINGHAM MARINA ME7 1UB

Contact
☎ 01634 280022
www.gillingham-marina.co.uk
berthing@gillingham-marina.co.uk
VHF Ch 80
Callsign *Gillingham Marina Lock*

Access Locked basin HW ±4½hr approx, 0600–2200 (summer) and daylight hours (winter)
Tidal basin HW ±2½hr approx
Max length/beam 16m/5·5m
Facilities WC, showers, launderette, pump-out, WiFi
Water On pontoons
Electricity On pontoons
Fuel Diesel and petrol from pontoon outside lock
Gas Ask in office
Boat repairs Full service boatyard, 65-T and 20-T boat hoists

Engineer On site
Rigger Medway Sling
☎ 01634 726400;
Pier Rigging ☎ 01634 8933
Sailmaker Dolphin Sails, Wilkinson Sails
Chandler Collection centre for Pirate's Cave Chandlery, in the marina office building. Order online for next-day delivery, or phone ☎ 01634 295233 for urgent same-day delivery. customerservices@piratescave.co.uk
Provisions Supermarket, turn right outside marina, 2 min walk
Pub/restaurant The Waterfront marina bar/restaurant on site, hours vary. Pubs close by – directions from office.
Transport Buses outside. Trains to London, Ramsgate and Dover
Taxi ☎ 01634 222222

16. RIVER MEDWAY

Gillingham Pier viewed from the river – slipway in the centre, pontoon berths to the left

Gillingham Pier

Immediately upstream from Gillingham Marina is a rectangular inlet known as Gillingham Pier ME7 1AF, where there is a high wharf on the W side, plus a wide Victorian stone slipway in the centre and a long mooring pontoon on the E side. The slipway has piles leaning inwards along both sides. The area is operated by Medway Council and anyone wishing to use the slipway or pontoon should contact the Piermaster first, on ☎07887 781407, Gillinghampier@btinternet.com. The Piermaster's office is in the base of the building inshore of the mooring pontoon. The slipway has a gentle gradient and could well be used for below-waterline maintenance as well as launch/recovery.

The 1924 paddle steamer *Medway Queen* (with a new hull, but many original components within) is moored here permanently against the western wharf.

Gillingham and Hoo to Rochester Bridge

At No.29 SHB (Fl(3)G.10s), which stands opposite Gillingham Marina, the river turns sharply NW round Hoo Ness into Short Reach. Watch out for shipping entering and leaving Chatham Docks through the locks on the W side of this bend.

The dock area called Gillingham Pier

The broad stone slipway at Gillingham Pier, the pontoon berths to the right

Halfway along Short Reach, there is a small unlit WCB on the edge of the shallows to starboard. This marks the W end of the route behind Hoo Island (see section on Middle Creek above); the Orinoco Channel leads NNE from the WCB, branching to port to the Port Werburgh entrance, and starboard to join Middle Creek. The Orinoco is withied, but some are metal and all are covered at HW, when it would be safer to cross the surrounding flats where you should find 1·5m.

Port Werburgh, the collection of residential barges and lightships seen on the N shore, has absorbed the old Hoo Marina, and does not accept any visiting craft. However, Hoo Ness YC remains on the shore there, with its drying jetty and slipway accessed through Port Werburgh's entrance, and can host club visits by prior arrangement using its swinging moorings in the river.

HOO NESS YC	ME3 9LB
☎01634 250052	
www.hooness.org.uk	

Continuing NW along Short Reach, Cockham Woods are ahead on the N bank and, to port, lies St Mary's Island. St Mary's was once part of the Chatham Naval Dockyard and is now a major waterside housing development, the shore lined with modern houses. Numerous yacht club moorings line the S side of the channel, spreading to the N shore once past the

Upnor Sailing Club

Medway Yacht Club and its all-tide pontoon

No.30A (Fl.R.2·5s) and No.31 (IQ.G) buoys. Beyond No.31, the dinghy sailors' Wilsonian SC stands on the shore, followed, as Cockham Reach bends to port, by Medway YC's headquarters beneath the woods on the N bank at the apex of the bend.

Medway Yacht Club

Medway YC can often provide a mooring for visitors on request, at a small fee. Visitors are welcomed and may use the clubhouse and facilities, including the bar and restaurant. There is an all-tide pontoon jetty for landing by dinghy, also a trot boat service, although you may be allowed to moor overnight on the hammerhead, where there is a fresh water tap.

MEDWAY YACHT CLUB   ME2 4XB

Contact
①01634 718399, 0900–1630 Monday–Friday, 1000-1400 Saturday
www.medwayyachtclub.com
office@medwayyachtclub.com

Trot Boat Callsign *Invicta* on VHF Ch 37, operates during season 0900–1800 (weekends), plus weekdays 0930 (out to moorings), 1330, and 1630 (collection from moorings).

Galley Restaurant Summer: Weds and Friday 1800-2100, Saturday 0900-2000, Sunday 0900-1600; Winter (subject to demand, check in advance): Weds 1800-2100, weekends 1000-1600.

Upnor Sailing Club

Upstream from Medway YC is the all-tide landing for Upnor SC where, as at Medway YC, it may be possible to borrow a mooring on request. Its clubhouse is set in a row of cottages behind the sea wall and close by are two large pub/restaurants, the Pier and the Ship, both popular with yachtsmen.

UPNOR SC   ME2 4UY

①0800 8321317
www.upnorsailingclub.co.uk
commodore.usc@gmail.com
Pub/Restaurant The Pier ①01634 717317; The Ship ①01634 290553

The river continues SW in Upnor Reach, where Upnor Castle sits on the W bank. In 1667, cannon fire from here failed to stop the Dutch raiders under Admiral de Ruyter, who sank 16 ships of the Royal Navy.

On your port side, across the river from Upnor Castle, you will find the lock gate entrance to Chatham Maritime Marina, built in the old No.1 Basin of the Naval Dockyard.

Upnor Sailing Club, its moorings and neighbouring pubs

East Coast Pilot • 197

16. RIVER MEDWAY

Upnor Castle

Chatham Maritime Marina

The tide runs hard directly across the entrance, which is fairly narrow – the lock widens once inside. Always seek permission before entering. Care needs to be taken not to end up going sideways into the lock. Check the tidal flow and apparent strength before entering and leaving. Inside the lock there are floating pontoons on each side with cleats at deck level. There are traffic light controls and sometimes the lock runs free-flow near to HW with the inner road bridge raised.

Heading into the lock, keeping well behind the yacht in front, watch for the strong cross-tide

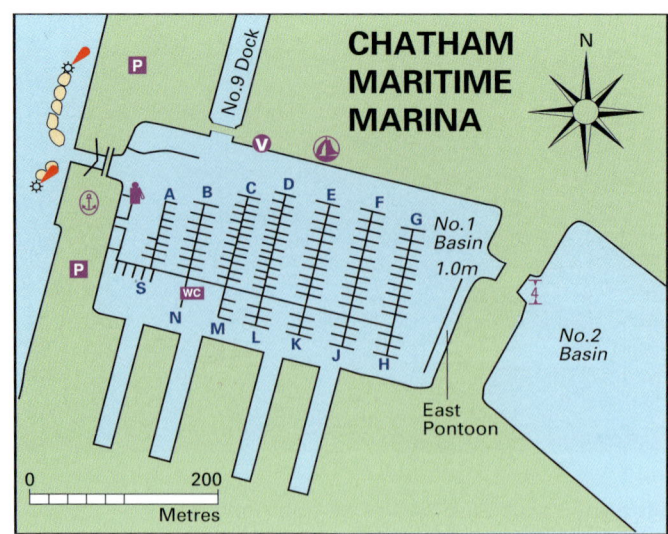

This 412-berth marina has the usual facilities – it is popular and often full at peak times. If you book in advance, MDL tend to ask for full payment ahead of arrival. The lock can be very busy indeed during summer weekends, and at the end of a visit you should book a locking-out time before you leave your berth.

Its surroundings have undergone major regeneration from dockyard days with housing and businesses springing up. It can be an attractive venue for those cruising with children on board - on its doorstep there is a growing number of family restaurants plus an outlet shopping mall, a multi-screen cinema, and even a gin distillery.

The town centre is several miles away, but there are bus stops on the SW side of the marina with regular services until late evening.

Close the W shore of the river and opposite the marina lock, swinging moorings that extend upstream belong to the Royal Engineer Yacht Club. The REYC are happy to let visitors use any spares, although any dinghy trip ashore has to be upriver to the old Dockyard mast slip, or downriver to Upnor. Contact ☎07486 875298 or 07870 433039.

The view inside the marina from beside the lock; the fuel berth is in the foreground to the right

198 • East Coast Pilot

Chatham Maritime Marina

Chatham Marina – wave-breaks each side of the entrance were missing at the time of the photo

Just up river from the marina, enormous sheds stand on the E shore. These are relics of the old naval dockyard, covered slipways where ships were once built and maintained, but now part of a vast museum, the magnificent Historic Dockyard (☎01634 823800 www.thedockyard.co.uk) for opening times, which is rated as one of Britain's major tourist attractions. If you are visiting Chatham Marina, ask in the office for details of any special offers on entrance to the museum, which is a 15-minute walk away.

Rope making is one of the many fascinating items to be seen, still being done in the traditional way on a ¼ mile long 'rope walk'.

CHATHAM MARITIME MARINA   ME4 4LP

Contact
VHF Ch 80
Callsign *Chatham Marina*
☎01634 899200
www.mdlmarinas.co.uk/mdl-chatham-maritime-marina
chatham@mdlmarinas.co.uk
Access 24hr (1·5m over cill at LWS). Occasionally limited access at top of HWS
Facilities WC, showers, launderette, WiFi
Water On pontoons
Electricity On pontoons (charged separately)
Fuel Diesel and petrol inside immediately to starboard once inside
Gas Ask in office
Rigger As Gillingham Marina, above

Boat repairs 16.5T crane in yard
Engineer Mike West ☎07769 677835
Sailmaker see Gillingham Marina details
Upholsterer Sewing Bee
☎01634 322 709
info@upholsterybee.co.uk
Chandler Pirate's Cave ☎01634 295233 (across river at Frindsbury, requires transport; Volvo Penta agent), and a small outlet at Gillingham Marina for collecting orders (30-min walk)
Pub/Restaurant Several nearby
Provisions Supermarket nearby
Transport Bus into town; Trains - Chatham or Rochester stations, services to London, Ramsgate and Dover
Taxi ☎01634 582582

16. RIVER MEDWAY

The covered slipways at Chatham Historic Dockyard

Historic ships in dry dock

Naval ships were built here from the late 1500s (including HMS *Victory*) and continued right up to the days of modern submarines, the last of which, HMS *Ocelot*, is one of the ships on display in a dry dock.

Chatham to Rochester

Upstream of the marina on Chatham Reach, on the E shore beyond the dockyard's dry docks, is a long floating pontoon, Thunderbolt Pier, running parallel

Victory Moorings on Thunderbolt Pier pontoon, upstream of the Dockyard Museum

to the river and connected to the shore at its N end. There, Victory Moorings runs as a berth holders' facility but may have room for visitors, although only if pre-booked. These are the only all-tide pontoon moorings in the Medway Towns downriver from Rochester bridge.

VICTORY MOORINGS

Antony Moss ☏07785 971797
asm-victory@hotmail.co.uk

Continuing along Chatham Reach beyond Victory Moorings, you will see in the distance the blue-painted Sun Pier on the S side as the river turns sharply round to NNW at Chatham Ness. There are no longer any moorings in Rats Bay, the area just below Sun Pier.

Brief landings for shopping or crew changes at Sun Pier (ME4 4HF) should be possible, if there is space on its 70ft steel landing pontoon, which has electricity and water and at least 2·5m on its outside at LWS (queries to Medway Council ☏01634 338122). Set your fenders high if you stop here. There is a token system for access to and from the shore.

Unless you are intending to pass beneath Rochester Bridge, the final stretches before you reach it have little to offer the visitor other than perhaps an interesting sail or motor.

Sun Pier, usually available for short stops

Rochester to the M2 Bridge

Rochester road and rail fixed bridges

Note the shallows of the Chatham Ness Shoal – the deeper water in Limehouse Reach is towards the W side for the first half of its length.

Much of the W bank of this reach has new walls, the old industries above having been cleared away as the extensive Medway Towns regeneration scheme gets underway.

Nearly a mile further on, having run up Limehouse Reach and turned SW again into Bridge Reach, Strood Pier on the NW shore is also, unfortunately, semi-derelict and unusable. A very large Russian-built Foxtrot-class submarine has lain rusting at anchor on the river here for a long time, but in recent years has been undergoing some restoration – it's quite a sight.

Just upstream, the fixed Rochester Bridge carries road and railway across the river with an air draught of 5·4m at HWS. Best water is on the starboard side, but there is negligible water under and immediately beyond the bridge at LW and easy passage is only feasible for motor cruisers or shoal draught yachts that can drop their rigs. You are unlikely to meet any large commercial craft under the bridge, but monitor Medway VTS on Ch 74 to be sure.

Rochester to Allington – general notes

Navigation beyond Rochester Bridge is best done on the flood from about half tide onwards and is very largely confined to motorboats with only a handful of small yachts to be seen. A journey along the full 12M to Allington Lock needs careful timing in relation to your boat's draught and overall height, not only to ensure adequate depth as you progress, but also to arrive at Aylesford Bridge while there is still enough air draught to pass beneath it (minimum 2.2m) and then to arrive at the lock during operating hours. Departure from Rochester at about HW-3½hr (Allington) can work well. HW time at Allington Lock varies based on HW Sheerness, about 35-55 minutes after Sheerness.

Although the river banks have a busy industrial past – and there is certainly clutter on the bottom in some stretches – you are unlikely to encounter any small cargo ships of the type that once ran up to the paper mill wharves.

The lock keeper at Allington (see details at end of this chapter) will be happy to help with advice on request.

Rochester to the M2 Bridge

Immediately above the bridge there are jetties and pontoons on both sides of the river. If on the move near LW, the W arch under the bridge has the best water, moving across to midstream 100m above the bridge.

Over on the port side beneath the towering ruin of Rochester Castle is Rochester Pier ME1 1QN, a council-run public pontoon that may be used for short daytime stops (requires a token, bought on

Council-run Rochester Pier, a short-stop pontoon

16. RIVER MEDWAY

the jetty, to return from shoreside – queries ☎ 01634 338122. Access is locked overnight from sunset to 0700. (In 2023 this pontoon was damaged and there was no shore access, with no published timescale to repair it).

Next, also on the Rochester shore, are the extensive pontoon moorings of Rochester Cruising Club. This club welcomes booked club visits and can also take individual visitors. It has diesel available for members, and visitors too provided they are staying overnight. The diesel berth is half way along the outer pontoon. The ancient Norman keep of Rochester Castle looms behind the club which is in a superb location as a base for local sightseeing, including not only the castle but also the quaint Dickensian main street and Rochester Cathedral.

ROCHESTER CRUISING CLUB — ME1 1QN
☎ 01634 841350
www.rochestercc.co.uk

Just beyond the RCC pontoons, and inshore, there is a marked wreck.

The first jetty to starboard after the bridge belongs to Strood Pelican Cruising Club, which doesn't normally accept casual visitors. Immediately beyond Rochester CC, beware of shallows midstream if near LW. The next club reached is to starboard - Strood YC, some of whose moorings are on an all-tide pontoon and some inshore on the drying saltings. Visiting boats can be accommodated, up to 40ft LOA – apply in advance using the form provided on their website.

STROOD YC — ME2 2AH
☎ 01634 718261
www.stroodyachtclub.uk
info@stroodyachtclub.uk

The river curves to the S and, ahead on the port side, in front of a mass of modern housing, are the remains of the slipways of the old Short Brothers seaplane factory, dating back to 1917 and now used as the base for the local rowing club.

Past Wickham Point (beware shallows on the inside of the bend), the river again turns SW towards the huge bridges of the Medway Crossing.

Just short of the Crossing, on the S shore, is the sprawling Medway Bridge Marina where advance booking is requested. There is a mix of all-tide, half-tide and mud berths, engineers, and chandler. Fuel

Rochester Cruising Club and its moorings on the East shore, Strood YC's moorings on the West side

Medway Bridge Marina

Approaching Medway Bridge Marina

MEDWAY BRIDGE MARINA   ME1 3HS

Contact
☎ 01634 843576
www.medwaybridgemarina.co.uk
info@medwaybridgemarina.co.uk

Fuel Diesel and petrol
Gas Ask in office
Facilities WC, showers, WiFi, slipway
Water On pontoons
Electricity On pontoons
Chandler On site
Shipwrights and Engineers At marina with 25-T hoist.
Boatyard Full boatyard services at Beacon Boatyard (ME1 3JN, outside marina gate). Dry dock, 7-T crane.
☎ 01634 841320 www.beaconboatyard.co.uk
Provisions Shops in nearby Borstal village
Transport Buses in Borstal village
Taxi ☎ 01634 363636

here is the last on the river before Allington Marina, beyond Allington Lock.

Beacon Boatyard is a separate moorings, dry dock and full-service boatyard business at the downstream edge of the marina.

Beyond Medway Bridge marina, the river runs beneath the Medway Crossing, which carries the M2 motorway and the Channel Tunnel Rail Link across the river. If moving near LW, beware unmarked shallows on the W side once through the bridge.

**RIVER MEDWAY
Rochester to Cuxton**

16. RIVER MEDWAY

The long pontoon berths at Port Medway, upstream of the Medway Crossing, and Cuxton Marina beyond

Medway Crossing to Aylesford

Still heading generally SW, two more marinas swiftly come up on the starboard side, the first of which is Port Medway with almost a kilometre of pontoon moorings, engineering and electrical facilities, plus two dry docks. There is a train station just outside the gate.

PORT MEDWAY MARINA   ME2 1AB
Contact
☎01634 720033
www.portmedwaymarina.co.uk
online@portmedway.co.uk
Access 24hr on outside pontoons
Facilities WC, showers, launderette
Water On pontoons
Electricity On pontoons
Gas Ask in office
Boat repairs 20-T hoist, dry docks (one roofed), slipway
Provisions In Cuxton, 10 minutes walk
Pub/Restaurant In Cuxton
Trains To Maidstone and Strood
Transport Trains to Maidstone and Strood; buses
Taxi ☎01634 515253.

Immediately upstream from Port Medway, with the same road access, is Cuxton Marina, with half-tide moorings, a slipway and hoist.

CUXTON MARINA   ME2 1AB
Contact
☎01634 721941
www.cuxtonmarina.com
Email enquiries@cuxtonmarina.co.uk
Access HW+/-4
Facilities WC, showers, launderette, slipway, 12-T hoist
Water On pontoons
Electricity On pontoons
Provisions, Transport As Port Medway, above.

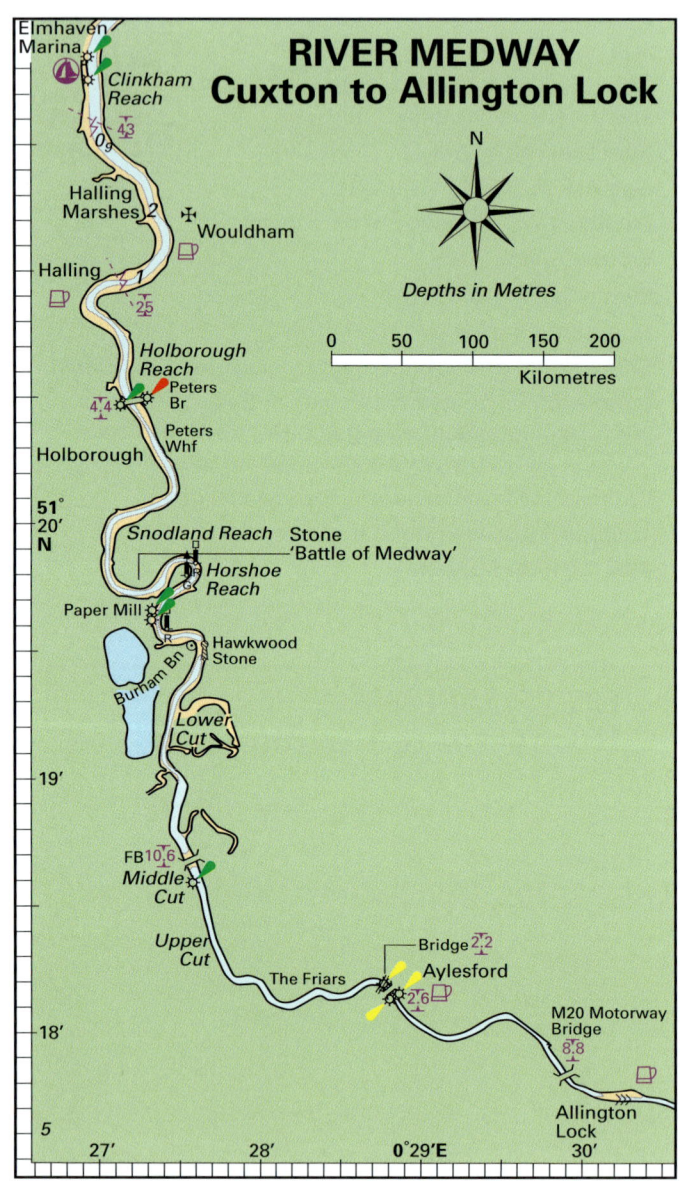

Above Cuxton there is a de-restricted stretch of the river used for waterskiing by the local club, whose clubhouse and short jetty are a few yards beyond the marina's pontoon. Connected with this there are many small buoys used for slalom on the east side of the river along this stretch.

The river runs on through open country with a chalk escarpment rising to starboard and, at Cuxton

Elmhaven Marina

Elmhaven Marina, approaching from downstream

Point, the river bends to port. Here to starboard is the peaceful and small Elmhaven Marina, last before Allington, close to the village of Halling and set at the foot of a chalk cliff. Visitors are advised to phone at least 24hr in advance.

ELMHAVEN MARINA — ME2 1AQ
Contact
① 01634 240489, 07951 418979
www.elmhaven-marina.co.uk
elmhaven@btconnect.com
Facilities WC, showers, slipway
Water On pontoons
Electricity On pontoons
Provisions Shops at Halling, 10 minutes
Taxi ① 01634 515253

Wouldham Church, resting place of a Trafalgar hero

Beyond Elmhaven, the village of Wouldham with its prominent church tower sits on the left bank; buried here is Walter Burke, who was purser on board HMS *Victory* at the Battle of Trafalgar and in whose arms Lord Nelson died. The river curves round sharply to starboard and modern housing in Halling stands on the river bank ahead with a short, modern promenade on the river's edge. In the centre of the wall beneath this promenade there is a small modern pontoon landing stage at the foot of a ladder set in the high walls and there are also stone steps at the upstream end of the wall. A short shopping stop in Halling village is therefore possible, although the promenade railing's low gates accessing the ladder and the steps are both usually kept locked. Unfortunately it seems there is nobody on hand to unlock them, but the reasonably nimble can climb over them if need be. There are sometimes anglers fishing here, so beware of their lines.

The river runs on through a contrast of rural scenery and the remains of the industries that once lined the banks. There are numerous old wharves, many rotting and overgrown, and although there are one or two more modern-looking docksides by the one remaining paper mill there is currently no traffic using them. Many of the reed covered bends have beacons on them, needed because in flood the edges of the main channel may be covered. Some charts may still show lights on wharves along sections of the river, but it seems these have now all gone.

In between the dereliction there are delightful stretches where one could be miles from anywhere, each bend bringing a surprise. Sometimes the banks are lined with very tall reeds, 8-10' high, and many wild birds are to be seen, especially grey herons.

Halling Pontoon, shore access not easy!

16. RIVER MEDWAY

Approaching Peter's Bridge

Beyond Halling in Holborough Reach, Peter's Bridge crosses the river (air draught 8m) connecting a large modern housing development called Peters Village on the E bank to the main road opposite. The bridge arch is lit 2FG(vert) and 2FR(vert).

Beyond the bridge the river snakes west, then east, and on the port-side river bank here, opposite Snodland Church, you may spot a large stone that commemorates the so-called Battle of the River Medway in 43AD - following the Roman invasion, the Catuvellauni tribes led by Togodumnus and Caratacus are said to have been defeated somewhere near here.

The depth steadily reduces and we stress the need to continue to match boat speed with the flood tide to ensure adequate depth but still sufficient clearance to get under the bridge at Aylesford and to reach the lock at Allington within locking hours.

A result of the plentiful reed beds is that there can be a fair amount of floating dead reed debris at some times of the year, worse after spring tides, debris which can wrap around and disguise more significant floating hazards like logs, and of course clog engine cooling inlet filters. The stuff generally follows the main current on the outside of bends, so much of it can be avoided. It does get cleared from time to time by the Port Authority.

Once past Snodland, the river snakes round a tight S-bend past Burham Marshes, reaching the Hawkwood Stone on your port side where the chart warns mariners to stay clear of the banks from here to Allington, because of piles and other obstructions. The Hawkwood Stone marks the southern limit of the Rochester Oyster Fishery, founded in 1728 and still ruling over fishing rights in the Medway between here and Garrison Point, Sheerness.

An inlet opens up to port a little further upstream, which the chart suggests was once the original course of the river, now drying up as an 'oxbow lake'. The shallowest patch you are likely to encounter on the passage is opposite this inlet.

Passing under a high (10·6m) disused footbridge, the river runs past New Hythe alongside a long wharf from more modern times. Beyond some untidy scrapyards, there is a recent housing development to starboard above a high stone wall before the river

The Hawkwood Stone

Reed and branch debris, a frequent problem after Spring tides

Aylesford

Aylesford Priory, now called 'The Friars'

The air draught gauge for Aylesford Bridge

swings to port and passes the beautiful Aylesford Priory, now known as 'The Friars', a religious house of the Order of Carmelites and founded in 1242, but rebuilt much more recently.

Around two more bends where great trees lean down to touch the water, the village of Aylesford comes into view on the left bank, a visual treat topped by its Norman church tower. More ancient history was made near here - in 455AD, Hengist and Horsa fought Vortigern in a defining battle between the Britons and the Saxon invaders, said to be centred around a ford where now stands the ancient stone road bridge with only 2·2m clearance at HWS.

A gauge on a wall on the port side about 50 yards below the bridge shows the air draught, unfortunately often overgrown down near water level, just where it needs to be read. There is a wharf on the starboard side just before you reach Aylesford where, if bound upstream on a falling tide, you could wait for sufficient clearance beneath the bridge. Do not dry out here, though, as the bottom is an unknown quantity. The 14th-century bridge stands on a blind right-hand bend, so approach with care and make a sound signal – normally the boat travelling against the tide should give way.

The village is a delight, but sadly (and very surprisingly) there is nowhere provided to welcome boating visitors.

Lovely Aylesford, but sadly nowhere to stop

16. RIVER MEDWAY

The ancient stone road bridge at Aylesford, a sound signal advised on approach

Aylesford to Allington Lock

A more modern road bridge follows soon after the old bridge at Aylesford. After two more tree-lined bends, traffic noise grows and the M20 motorway bridge is seen ahead. Take special care along here to stay in the middle of the stream as collapsed wharves jut out a long way beneath the surface.

Beyond the bridge and soon after passing Gabriels Wharf boatyard on the starboard bank, you will reach Allington Lock, the head of the tidal navigation.

The lock is on the starboard side of the river with a large weir beyond to port. The chances are that you will be locking near to HW, when the numerous bollards are within easy reach. Subject to space, short-term or overnight mooring may be possible within the lock cut – phone ahead to check with the helpful lock keeper. There are heated cabins for hire next to the lock keeper's office, and also a camping area. On the port side of the lock, the 'Little Old Toll House' is a popular café.

The lock is managed by the Environment Agency (EA), which requires any boat using the river beyond the lock to be registered. Registration can be on a daily, weekly or long-term basis and can be arranged with the lock keeper. Compliance with the BSS (Boat Safety Scheme) is compulsory beyond the lock.

Half a mile upstream from the lock, on your starboard hand just beyond Allington Castle, is the 100-berth Allington Marina, the first on the non-tidal navigation. A river bus runs between Allington and Maidstone.

See also the Medway River Users Association www.mrua.co.uk.

Allington Lock coming into view

208 • East Coast Pilot

Allington Lock

The view over the lock, looking downstream

ALLINGTON LOCK ME16 0LU

Contact
☎ 01622 752864
www.therivermedway.co.uk
Email via the website
Tides HW Sheerness +0100
Operating hours 0700–sunset (March–October) or 0700–1600 (November–February) and HW +/-2 Locking may be available outside these hours on enquiry and with 24hr notice.
Max beam 6m
Facilities WC, showers, pump-out, electricity (limited), water, chemical toilet disposal
Slipway Above lock
River licence See www.gov.uk/register-a-boat
Lock Café The Little Old Toll House Tel 07921 709902 Open 0800-1900 (summer), 1000-1400 (winter)
Pub/restaurant Malta Inn (just above lock on port side of river, at ME14 3AS) ☎ 01622 717251

Although our pilotage directions end at the lock, for completeness below are contact details for Allington Marina.

ALLINGTON MARINA ME16 0NH

Contact
☎ 01622 752057 (Closed on Tuesdays)
www.allingtonmarina.com
Email Via website
Facilities WC, showers
Boatyard Repairs, engineer, 35T crane
Chandler On site
Water On pontoons
Electricity On pontoons
Fuel Diesel
Gas Ask in office
Taxi ☎ 01622 750000

Kingsferry Bridge

17. THE SWALE

Queenborough and its moorings

17. THE SWALE

⚓ **Landfall waypoint**
51°24'·10N 001°01'·73E Immediately E of line between Whitstable Street PHB and Columbine SHB

Charts
Imray 2100
Admiralty 5606; 2571, 2572

Tides
Tides HW Sheerness

Harbour authority
Peel Ports Medway VHF Ch 74
Callsign *Medway VTS*

Honorary Port Pilot
Conyer and The Swale
Simon Smedley ☎01795 521562
conyer@eastcoastpilot.com

For any additional leisure boating information, contact the Medway & Swale Boating Association,
www.msba.org.uk

Main hazards

Tides

The Swale is not a river but a tidal waterway between the Isle of Sheppey and the mainland, and the tide floods and ebbs at both ends but not in a logical fashion. The stream runs E for much longer than it runs W, which can be put to good use on a passage E.

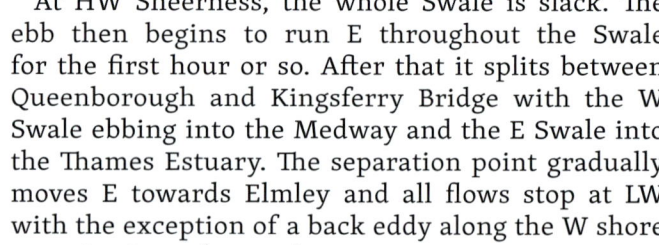

At HW Sheerness, the whole Swale is slack. The ebb then begins to run E throughout the Swale for the first hour or so. After that it splits between Queenborough and Kingsferry Bridge with the W Swale ebbing into the Medway and the E Swale into the Thames Estuary. The separation point gradually moves E towards Elmley and all flows stop at LW with the exception of a back eddy along the W shore opposite Queenborough.

When the flood starts, it comes in from both ends, the streams meeting at about Elmley. Later, the meeting point often moves E towards Fowley.

Although every day follows this general pattern, predicted tide timing and heights can be greatly affected by wind, weather and barometric pressure, especially in the E Swale.

Wind over tide in the popular anchorage at Harty, especially strong easterlies against the ebb, can raise a very steep chop. The central section of the Swale, between Elmley and Fowley, is very shallow at LW.

Shipping

Commercial shipping uses the W Swale, almost always entering and leaving via the Medway, to reach docks just E of the Kingsferry Bridge. On rare occasions, small coasters may use the E Swale as a short cut on a good tide.

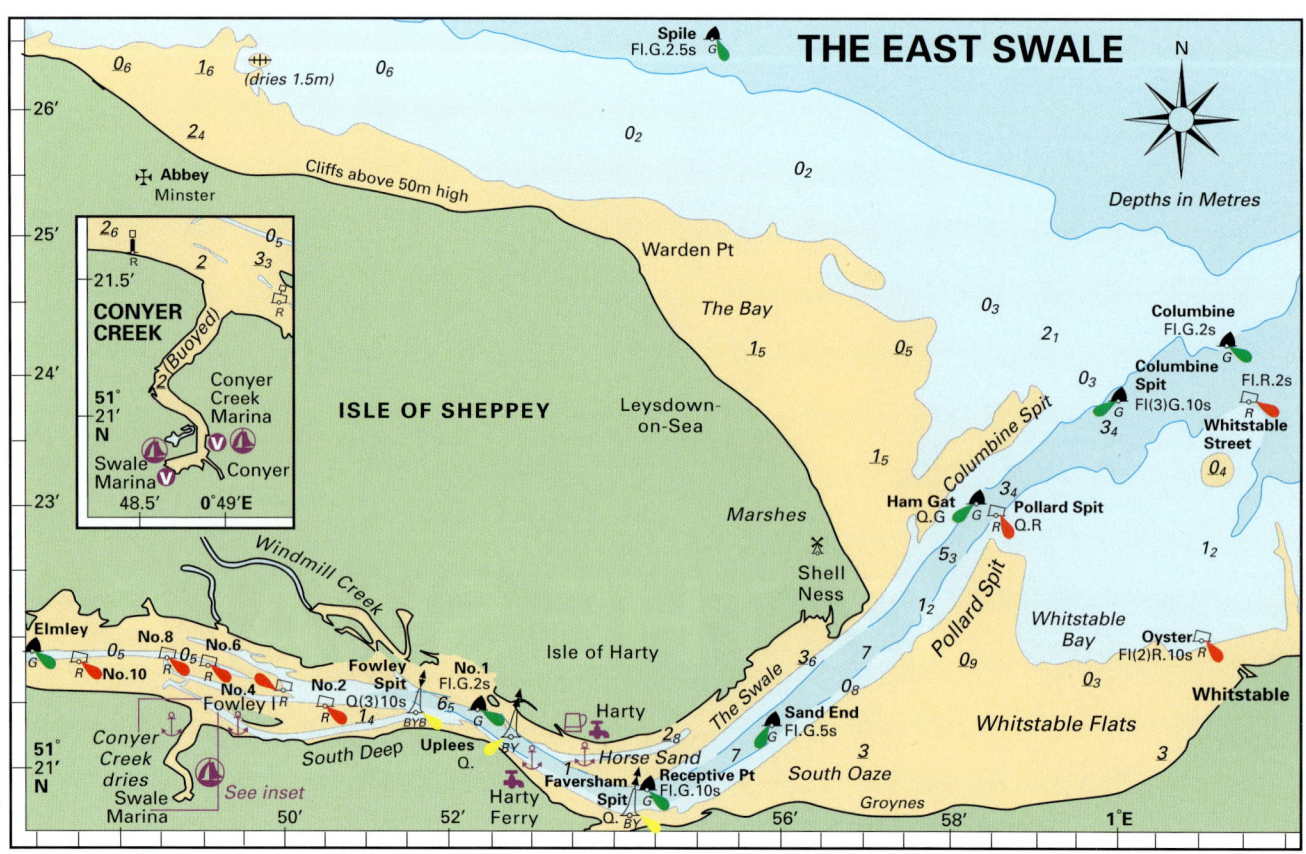

The Swale

THE SWALE

When it was wider and had greater depth, the Swale was a main route from the English Channel to London, but over the centuries the channel has narrowed and become shallower by silting and land reclamation to the point where the central section is barely navigable at LWS Sheerness.

With saltmarshes and mudflats on both sides, the Swale forms an area of international importance for breeding and wintering birds. Brent geese, widgeon, plover, oystercatcher and avocet and indeed all manner of wading birds are frequently seen, taking little heed of the hundreds of boats kept in the three main creeks – Faversham, Oare and Conyer – as well as at Queenborough.

At low water, the bones of many ships can be seen along the shores of these creeks and in the Swale itself, many of them relics of the hundreds of Thames barges that served the thriving local industries of brick, cement and gunpowder manufacturing, which are all now gone.

If you love the East Coast and the solitude it can offer, the Swale has considerable charm. It brings its own pilotage challenges, especially if you are on the move around low water, but if you run out of luck, the bottom is forgiving and there is plenty to look at while you wait for the water to return.

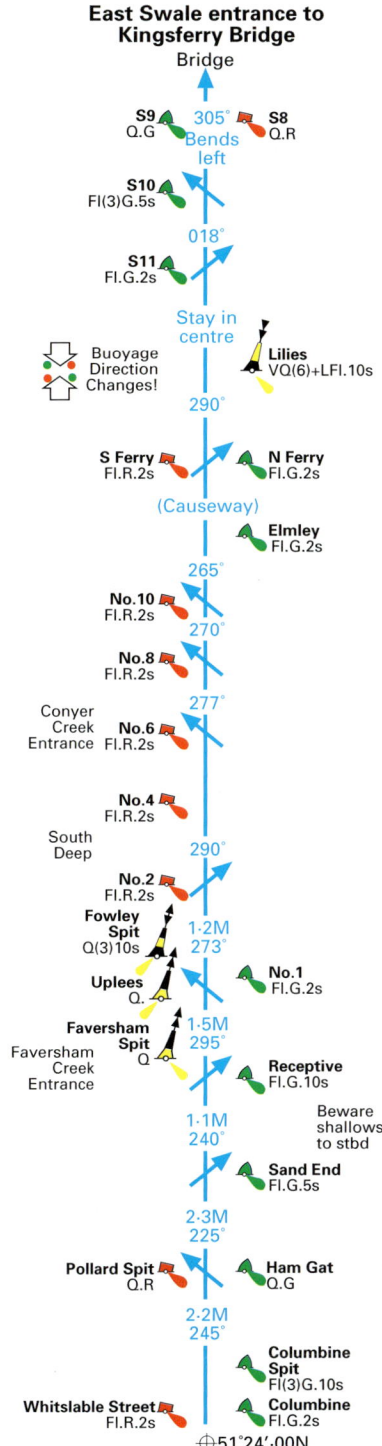

Approaches to East Swale

From the E, make along the coast to the Whitstable Street PHB (Fl.R.2s) as described in the North Kent Coast chapter.

From the W Take the Four Fathoms Channel from the Spile SHB (Fl.G.2·5s), making good about 105° to avoid isolated shoals to the S. If draught allows, and on a rising tide, alter course at the 001°E meridian to make 180° and join the E Swale approach at the Columbine Spit SHB Fl(3)G.10s. With deeper draught (or less water) continue E to Columbine SHB (Fl.G.2s) for more depth.

Note The lights on these buoys and those further into the Swale have sometimes been used by Trinity House in experiments with sequencing.

Watch www.eastcoastpilot.com for any changes.

From the N Again if draught permits, follow the 001°E meridian past the Red Sand Tower and the Middle Sand SWM. For more water, once S of the Middle Sand, turn SE to enter the Swale at the Columbine buoy. If your draught makes it impractical to cross any of these flats, then a SE course through the Kentish Flats wind farm, two rows of turbines in from its western side, will keep you in more water; once through, then 225° will take you to the vicinity of the Columbine SHB (Fl.G.2s). Skippers may of course prefer to approach the East Swale from the NE, leaving the entire wind farm to starboard.

Enter the channel by passing between the Whitstable Street PHB (Fl.R.2s) and the Columbine SHB (Fl.G.2s).

East Swale

With a strong SW'ly blowing against the flood tide there is often a nasty chop in this area, only smoothing out at the Ham Gat SHB (Q.G) and the Pollard Spit

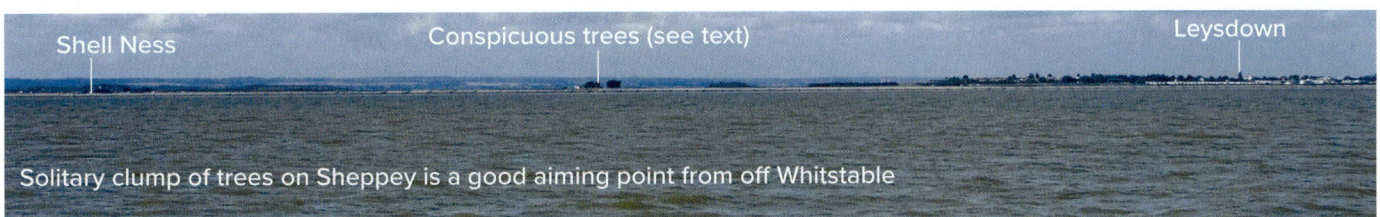

Solitary clump of trees on Sheppey is a good aiming point from off Whitstable

17. THE SWALE

The Ham Gat SHB, with Sheppey's Warden Point in the distance to the NW

PHB (Q.R). Indeed, any kind of W'ly seems to funnel straight out of the East Swale.

In daylight, from out by 'The Street' (Whitstable Street), the small Pollard Spit and Ham Gat buoys are difficult to locate against the bright sand of Shell Ness, but their bearing is about 240°, range 2·1M from midway between the Street PHB and Columbine SHB. Making good that course just scrapes the S side of the deep water in the channel. In some conditions a clump of trees around a farmhouse on Sheppey appears as a single prominent feature on the approximate bearing, as shown in the photo on previous page.

With the Pollard Spit PHB close to port, a course made good of 225° will take you on another 2·3M to the Sand End SHB (Fl.G.5s), which is again hard to see against the background clutter. In daylight, a good indication that you are heading in the right general direction is the pair of unusually tall electricity pylons each side of Faversham Creek, 4M from the Pollard.

Pollard Spit PHB

From Shell Ness westwards, most of the Swale has an 8kn speed limit enforced by the Port Authority.

Passing the prominent Shell Ness, with its bright beach (often covered with thousands of oystercatchers) and collection of remote houses, the W bank of the deep water channel is very steep to, while the E side remains a fairly gentle shelf. Avoid grounding on the charted shellfish beds in the area and, if tacking in, note there is a substantial mound on the E side of the channel, SSE of the Sand End SHB.

From the Sand End SHB there is a shallow route WSW passing N of the Horse Sand, otherwise follow the main channel SW to the Receptive SHB (Fl.G.10s), which also marks a wreck. Follow a slight curve to port of the rhumb line from the Sand End to the Receptive, to avoid the edge of the Horse Sand, where seals are often hauled out. On the S side of the channel is the Faversham Spit NCB (Q), at the entrance to Faversham Creek.

HARTY FERRY

From the Receptive SHB, the Swale turns NW, passing through the anchorage known as Harty or Harty Ferry. The Isle of Harty, no longer an island but part of the Isle of Sheppey, stands on the N side of the anchorage with an ancient Saxon church on the skyline and the white Ferry House Inn nestling on the S side of the hill.

Ferry House Inn ME12 4BQ ☎01795 510214
www.theferryhouseinn.co.uk

The pub is named for the ferry that once ran between here and the mainland, and which also gave the local

The S causeway at Harty Ferry, looking across the anchorage to the opposite shore and its pub

Harty Ferry

The Ferry House Inn looks out over the anchorage — Pub

area its name. A public causeway provides landing for visitors to the pub, which has accommodation and a restaurant. The landing is a little muddy, but the causeway is hard. It does not extend as far as LWS, but the mud beyond is quite firm. As visiting the pub by boat requires some effort, check opening hours beforehand as we have found that they can be 'variable'.

The S shore also has a hard causeway that extends right across the mudflats and is marked by substantial posts. A dark-roofed building owned by the Kent Wildlife Trust peers over the sea wall here and just across the road from it is a useful and much used fresh water spring, unusual on marshland, emerging from a cast iron hydrant that once supplied the long-gone widespread munitions factories that stretched westwards from here.

The village of Oare is a pleasant walk away, just over a mile along the lane from the mainland causeway, with two pubs but no shop. Or a dinghy trip can take you to the Shipwright's Arms at the junction of Faversham and Oare Creeks (see details for Oare Creek).

There are a few moorings on the N shore and many more to the S of the channel, most of them E of the causeway. These are a mixture of club and private moorings, where the usual rule applies that they may be used unless the owner or a club member appears; the private ones occasionally attract a charge levied by the local moorings manager. The club moorings are marked 'HCC' or 'CCC', and Club members obviously have priority. Anchoring clear of the moorings either side of the main channel generally finds good holding in soft mud.

The Harty anchorage is exposed to strong E winds, when it should be avoided if possible. With some N in the wind, you may find shelter under the N shore

Harty moorings

Useful freshwater spring behind the sea wall

about a ½M W of the causeway, although it is much shallower and you must avoid charted wrecks on the mudflats. Note the Uplees NCB (Q) a few hundred yards W of Harty, which marks a large wreck close to the surface.

Harty Ferry is a classic East Coast anchorage, but the tide can run hard here and this must be considered when going ashore by dinghy, especially with wind over tide. The area teems with bird life that may wake you early on a peaceful summer morning.

Faversham creek entrance at LW, and the Faversham Spit NCB. Note the PHB's in the creek high and dry on the mud

17. THE SWALE

FAVERSHAM

The Faversham area is served by two drying creeks: Faversham Creek which ends close to the town centre, and Oare Creek. Initial entry is into Faversham Creek, and Oare Creek branches off it to starboard at Hollowshore.

Faversham Creek initially runs SW from the Swale at the Faversham Spit NCB (Q). Speed limit in the creek is 6kn and careful progress on a rising tide is advisable. There is no commercial traffic, but quite large leisure vessels including Thames barges use Faversham Creek. If you are hoping for a berth at Faversham (see 'Iron Wharf to Town Quay', below), it would be best to phone ahead. Iron Wharf, the first berthing point in Faversham Creek, is about 2¼M away.

In Oare Creek there are several moorings operators, the creek ending at the village of Oare on the outskirts of Faversham itself.

Entry to Faversham Creek

Leave the NCB to starboard and follow the line of unlit PHBs, and a single SHB, until the creek bends to port opposite an SHM post marking a wreck. (The authors found this wreck to be a useful tide gauge – if its ribs are completely covered then there is sufficient depth in Oare Creek for a 1·5m draught boat to reach the head of the creek.) Give the PHBs room; in some wind and tide conditions they lie over the shallows (see aerial photo below).

Once past the final PHB, follow the centre of the channel S towards the buildings ahead at Hollowshore. Leave moored boats to starboard and be aware that sometimes there are ropes trailing in the water from laid-up derelict fishing boats. Overhead is a high tension electricity line with a charted safe air draught of 32m.

The first stretch of Faversham Creek, near LW

216 • East Coast Pilot

Faversham Creek, from Hollowshore to Iron Wharf

On reaching Hollowshore, Oare Creek feeds off to stbd, but turn to port to head for Faversham

The larger of the buildings at Hollowshore is a boatyard shed and the smaller white building is the Shipwright's Arms pub. These are at the junction of Faversham and Oare Creeks where Oare Creek splits off to starboard (for Oare Creek details, see below).

Faversham Creek, from Hollowshore to Iron Wharf

The general rule for going up Faversham Creek, unless you know it well, is to start at half flood or soon after, before the saltings are covered. The notes that follow are detailed, but in general the channel follows the outside of bends – quite extremely, in some cases, so don't be afraid to get close in to the bank. Don't just buoy hop – weave gently to stay with the best depth on your echosounder. The upper stretches of the creek have about 2·5m in the gutway at HW. The gutway shown on digital charts, although from old surveys, does still seem to match reality quite closely. Some of the buoys in the creek, detailed in the next paragraph, you may find missing from time to time. You can find a helpful chart diagram in the Faversham Navigation Guide, available from the Navigation section of www.msba.org.uk.

Approaching Iron Wharf Boatyard

Enter Faversham Creek proper with the pub to starboard and, passing PHBs 10 and 12, follow the line of the starboard bank until abeam the section of stone sea wall. Turn to port to bring the nearby pylon fine on the port bow to pass PHB 12A, getting close to the left bank N of SHB 3, before turning SE towards SHBs 5 and then 5A. Stay roughly mid-channel from here to pass SHB 7, then 7A, before crossing to starboard to pass PHB 14. From here, aim for two private pontoon moorings beyond some houses on the left bank (a boat may be moored there), opposite SHB 9, and then generally follow the outside of the right hand bend. SHB 11 follows, then a left hand bend around PHB 16.

Iron Wharf Boatyard and Chambers Wharf

17. THE SWALE

Reaching Standard Quay, home to several businesses and usually full

Keep in the middle of the stream until you reach PHB 18, when you'll see Iron Wharf ahead to port. Before you get there, keep clear of two red posts on your port side, marking a wreck.

Iron Wharf is a large friendly DIY boatyard with a chandlery. There are no pontoons, and any spare drying berths for visitors (on previous enquiry) will be in perhaps 2m (at HW) against the wall or possibly rafted out from it.

Iron Wharf to Town Quay

Immediately above Iron Wharf and also to port is Chambers Wharf, location of Alan Staley's boatbuilding and restoration yard. Just beyond, there is a tall brick building with an ancient sign saying 'United Fertiliser', followed by Standard Quay, opposite the start of some modern housing on the north bank. Standard Quay is usually packed with barges with no space to stop. The best water tends to be towards the starboard side of the creek in front of the housing, and ahead are some private pontoon moorings in a small inlet. Rounding a slight left-hand bend and resuming your passage in the centre of the creek, the Front Brents foreshore is on the starboard side a few hundred yards ahead, with a fixed road bridge beyond it. Boats moored off your port side are all on private moorings.

The Front Brents Jetty, owned and run by the Town Council, stands here on your stbd side parallel to the creek bank and provides drying moorings with security, power and water. Although visitors are not encouraged by the Town Council, if there is space and you want to stay for more than a brief stop, you can always ask: adrienne.begent@favershamtc.co.uk, ☏01795 503286.

Alternative alongside moorings lie slightly further up the creek, on the port side just before the fixed road bridge, at the small Town Quay, a length of wall that usually has room alongside for two 10m boats, plus perhaps one more rafted alongside. Fender boards are recommended. A drawback if boats are moored end to end is that the only ladder is at the centre of the wall. Without any recent dredging, depth here is barely more than 1·2m at HWN, and the area dries to soft mud and is quite flat. There is reported to be a narrow ledge low down on the wall, covered by mud, and bilge-keeler skippers should perhaps fender out away from the wall a little more than usual to avoid catching a keel on it.

A very high HWS can reach the top of the wall.

Front Brents Jetty

The tiny Town Quay at the current head of navigation

Iron Wharf to Town Quay

The top of Faversham Creek, up to the fixed bridge

There is no security, nor any facilities, so visiting boats will need to be self-sufficient. Town Quay is run by the borough council, which sets a maximum stay of two nights, and fees may be paid by phone ☎01795 417850, or at a local office – details are on a notice on the nearby wall.

There are plans for the road bridge to be rebuilt as a swing or lifting bridge and restore access to the basin beyond, but at the time of writing sufficient funding had not been raised.

Faversham is an interesting historic town to visit, with more than 475 listed buildings and what is said to be the country's best preserved mediaeval street, Abbey Street, which is a few steps away from the E side of the creek. Front Brents and the Town Quay are very close to the centre with its good mix of shops, pubs and facilities including restaurants. Shepherd Neame, the country's oldest and largest independent brewery, is across the road from the Town Quay.

FAVERSHAM

Tides Sheerness

Access HW-2hrs to HW+1½hr

Boatyard Iron Wharf Boatyard ME13 7BY ☎01795 536296 www.ironwharf.net manager@ironwharf.co.uk

Boat repairs 14-T crane, dry dock up to 90ft

Fuel Garage in town, ¾M

Gas Ask in chandlers

Facilities WC, showers, launderette

Chandler (at Iron Wharf) Faversham Chandlery ☎01795 531777, mark@favershamchandlery.co.uk www.favershamchandlery.co.uk Open Thurs-Mon.

Shipwright (Next to Iron Wharf) Alan Staley ☎01795 530668 www.alanstaleyboatbuilders.co.uk

Sailmaker (In town) Wilkinson Sails ☎01795 521503 www.wilkinsonsails.co.uk

Surveyor Toby Lester ☎07935 326656

Other moorings Front Brents Jetty, Town Quay adrienne.begent@favershamtc.co.uk, ☎01795 503286

Provisions, pub/restaurant Many in the town

Town information www.visitfaversham.org ☎01795 503286

Transport Buses; Trains to London, or to Ramsgate and Dover via Canterbury

Taxi ☎01795 536666, 591066

17. THE SWALE

HOLLOWSHORE

Hollowshore is the old name given to the small area, below sea level and behind the sea wall, at the junction of Faversham and Oare Creeks. It has one ancient pub, a boatyard and one private house. It is remote and there is no public transport.

The boatyard, where traditional wooden working boats are restored and repaired, is one of the many sites where Thames barges were built. With permission, a spare mud berth near the yard may be available, otherwise anchor off to the N and dinghy ashore.

The Shipwright's Arms has its own ghost, reputed to be a barge skipper shipwrecked one stormy night out in the Swale, who managed to get ashore and stagger to the pub door, but nobody heard him and he was found dead there next morning.

Entrance to Oare Creek – see text for best route in

Best water close to the port-side moorings

HOLLOWSHORE   **ME13 7TU**

Boatyard/moorings Hollowshore Moorings
☎01795 529033
www.hollowshoremoorings.co.uk

Services Moorings, water, electricity, covered slip, crane, full repairs

Sailmaker Paul Martin ☎01795 537936 or 07792 579210 www.paulmartinsailmaker.co.uk

Pub/restaurant The Shipwright's Arms ☎01795 590088 www.theshipwrightsathollowshore.co.uk

Transport Taxi ☎01795 536666, 591066

Oare Creek

If going far up Oare Creek, start at about HWN - 1½hr or HWS -2hr. The tide ebbs from the creek faster than it floods and it dries entirely after about half ebb. Watch the depth constantly as the gutway described below wanders from time to time.

Once past the craft moored in the first part of Faversham Creek, keep heading straight towards the pub (white building to left of large Hollowshore Moorings boatshed) and look for the end of a low fence that comes down to the shore from the sea wall to port. Look also for two buoys in the entrance to Oare Creek, N of the boatshed. When you judge that you are between the fence and the buoys, turn towards them and pass the first one close N of it. About 20m further on, leave the second, larger buoy close to port. It marks the end of a slipway from the boatshed.

The channel beyond is unmarked. Stand about 10m off the sterns of the boats moored on wooden jetties along the port shore for several hundred yards, jetties owned by Hollowshore Moorings. These end at Ham Wharf as the creek bends slightly to starboard, where you may find a large floating dry dock and moored barges. Pass as close to these as you dare for the best

The pontoons of Cylinder House Moorings

water, then for the next ¼mile continue upstream keeping a distance of about 10m off more jetties and pontoons until you reach a left hand bend whose right bank has an ancient wooden wharf. Reach mid-channel opposite the beginning of the wharf and continue mid-channel around the bend.

Around the left hand bend there's an old gunpowder dock to port and the channel moves across close to the pontoons of Cylinder House Moorings by the old red-roofed shed (known locally as the Cylinder House, once a saltpetre store). At these moorings a spare berth may be available if requested in advance. Power (uses tokens) and water is available here, but the nearest available toilets are at Youngboats, a short walk away at the head of the creek (see below).

Cylinder House Moorings ☎07905 106236
thecylinderhouse@yahoo.com

There are many more pontoon moorings at the head of the creek at Youngboats' yard. From the Cylinder

The upper reach of Oare Creek at LW

House onwards, the channel meanders, gets shallower and is marked by pairs of withies although these are not constantly maintained. Halfway along this final stretch the channel veers all the way to the port-hand shore then back to the middle. Keep to stbd of a line of vacant posts as you reach the first berths. Boats much over 10m LOA will be tricky to turn at the head of the creek. If in doubt, phone Youngboats for advice.

Also in Youngboats' yard is a cafe, and the HQ of Hollowshore Cruising Club, a small, welcoming club for the many boat owners in these creeks. It's open on Sundays at lunchtime, with a bar, and snacks are usually available.

Pontoon moorings at Youngboats

Oare village, also at the head of the creek, has two pubs, both of which serve food. There is an occasional bus service from Oare; the bus stop is by The Castle pub. Faversham itself is perhaps a 30-minute walk away.

OARE ME13 7TX

Access HW±1½hr

Boatyard Youngboats (Terry Young) ☎01795 536176 (Closed Sun-Mon) www.youngboats.co.uk, info@youngboats.co.uk

Services 8-T crane, berthing, storage

Water On pontoons

Electricity On pontoons (tokens from yard)

Scrubbing berth Max length 9m

Facilities WC, shower

Café on site, open most days

Club Hollowshore Cruising Club www.hollowshorecc.org

Pubs/restaurants The Castle ☎01795 533674 The Three Mariners ☎01795 533633 www.thethreemarinersoare.co.uk

Transport Buses

Taxi ☎01795 536666, 591066

17. THE SWALE

The Swale - Harty to Conyer

Continuing NW from Harty, the deep water channel runs past the Uplees NCB (Q) which marks a large wreck lying athwart the current, close beneath the surface. Just beyond, on the S shore are some scrubbing posts, although these have not been seen in use for a while.

The Swale now opens up into a much broader stretch of water, a row of narrow chimneys at a paper mill prominent 4M W, but at LW much of the water disappears.

On the N shore, beyond the Swale No.1 SHB (Fl.G.2s), is Windmill Creek, which generally dries although a very shallow draught boat might stay afloat in a hole near the junction with Bells Creek.

The Fowley Spit ECB (Q(3)10s) guards the end of Fowley Island and marks the entrance to South Deep, with Conyer Creek beyond.

South Deep

South Deep, particularly towards its W end inside Fowley Island, is a delightfully quiet and sheltered spot for an overnight stop and is also the main route from the E to the entrance to Conyer Creek.

Scrubbing posts on the S shore beyond Harty

Start close to port of the Fowley Spit ECB and aim for an unlit SHB off the E end of Fowley Island. Keep an eye on the depth - the channel tends to follow a curve closing on the S shore. Two cables beyond the SHB there are several large white waiting buoys laid by moorings operators at Conyer. Carry on past the charted sluice (R.Bn) on the S shore and after about 100m you should find a hole with 1·5m at LWS. Fowley Island is low lying, little more than saltings that virtually cover at HWS, and is a wildlife reserve where landing is prohibited. Beyond this secluded anchorage, the route W leads to an unlit PHB, then SW via a channel marked with small red and green buoys to an equally small ECB just inside the mouth of Conyer Creek.

Fowley Spit Westwards

After Fowley Spit ECB the channel W narrows considerably and is marked with lit PHBs (Fl.R.2s) as far as Elmley.

Boats drawing up to 1m can pass through this shallowest section of the Swale after LWS+1hr, provided the PHBs are followed meticulously. The No.8 PHB marks the last chance to turn S into Conyer or South Deep. At night, constantly check that you are heading for the next PHB in the sequence – with their identical light characteristics, it is possible to be misled. See aerial photo below.

CONYER CREEK

Conyer, which dries from half tide, can be approached from the E via South Deep (see above), the deeper route, or from the W via the Swale No.8 PHB. If routing via the No. 8, look for the charted islet of Little Fowley, N of the creek entrance. Little Fowley

Conyer Creek entrance near LW showing the two marked routes

Conyer Creek

In South Deep head W from the PHB before turning into the buoyed Conyer channel

Nearing the small Conyer Creek Marina

has eroded away in recent years so that it's still fully covered long after HW, but it is still marked with a small buoy. Near HW you should find 2m all the way from No.8 to a point between the islet and the W tip of Fowley Island, although depths change suddenly as you cross the gutways that meander across the flats.

There are two well marked routes for the final approach to the creek entrance. Either continue SE to the start of the E channel (30m W of the unlit PHB in South Deep), then following between the red and green buoys (you may find it shallow along this short stretch), or use a deeper W channel called the Butterfly.

If using the Butterfly Channel, find the first pair of marker posts for this about 300m NNW of the creek entrance, then follow between the posts, heading directly SW towards the sea wall, turning abruptly to port very close to the wall before meeting the E channel at the small ECB. This is clearly seen in the aerial photo on page 222.

From the ECB, the channel is marked by more small buoys leading close to two wrecks on the E shore, then gradually moving out between a mix of buoys and posts to the W side of the creek approaching a sharp left hand bend. Beyond the bend, where buoyage ends but posts continue at intervals, the channel is nearer to the centre and the village of Conyer comes into view.

The very small Conyer Creek Marina on the E bank is reached first. There may be drying pontoon berths available for visitors but call first (see Conyer details). Use the centre of the right-hand bend as you approach.

Once past this marina and the housing on the port bank, Blackden Moorings' drying pontoon berths lie directly ahead of you to port in Conyer Dock. They can only occasionally accommodate visitors, so phone ahead to check availability ☏01795 522833.

Turn to starboard opposite Blackden Moorings, taking a wide turn (do not cut the corner) into the large Swale Marina, providing 200 drying mud berths alongside pontoons and extending all the way to the head of the creek. Access all the way to the marina is about HW±1½hr – phone the harbour office

East Coast Pilot • 223

17. THE SWALE

Take the turn wide into Swale Marina

Swale Marina, with Blackden Moorings in the foreground

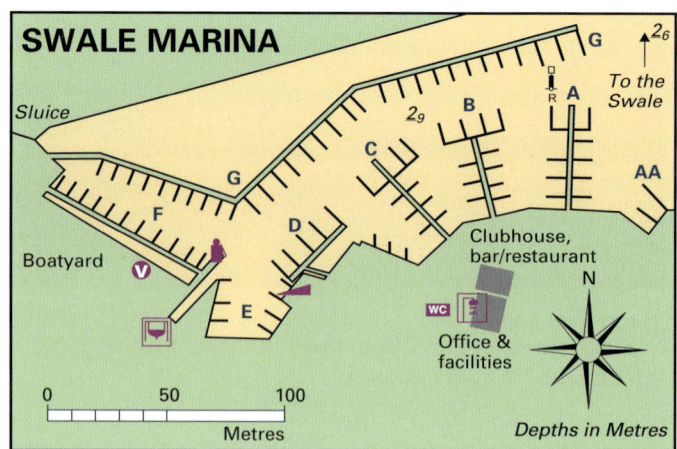

for advice. This well-kept marina has a boatyard with shipwright, a broad slipway, the usual facilities and a modern clubhouse for berth holders and visitors, with bar and catering, usually open at weekends.

As we went to press, the Ship pub had just closed, but the details are shown below should it reopen, and any updates will be at www.eastcoastpilot.com.

CONYER

Tides Sheerness

Access HW±2hr

Pub/restaurant Ship Inn on Conyer Quay
☎01795 520881
www.theshipinns.co.uk

Provisions Teynham village (bus or taxi)

Transport Buses (infrequent) to Teynham and trains from there to Ramsgate and Dover or London

Taxi ☎01795 426600, 444444.

CONYER CREEK MARINA   ME9 9HL

Contact ☎01795 521711
info@conyercreekmarina.co.uk
www.conyercreekmarina.co.uk

Facilities WC, showers

Water and Electricity On pontoons

SWALE MARINA   ME9 9HN

Contact Office ☎01795 521562
enquiries@swalemarina.co.uk
www.swalemarina.co.uk

Facilities WC, showers, chemical toilet disposal

Water and Electricity On pontoons

Fuel Diesel

Gas Ask in office

Boat repairs 30-T travel hoist, 25-T slipway, Coppercoat agent, shipwright on site

The Swale – Conyer Creek to Kingsferry

Heading W from the Swale No.8 PHB (Fl.R.2s), past No.10 PHB (Fl.R.2s) and the Elmley SHB (Fl.G.2s) near LW, the next feature is the disused ferry causeway at Elmley. (King James II is said to have fled the country from around here, hence the local name, Kingsferry.) The deepest water can be found slightly N of centre in the gap between two pairs of posts on the causeway. A buried gas pipe runs N-S just E of the causeway, so care should be taken not to anchor in the vicinity.

From the causeway, steer between the North Ferry SHB (Fl.G.2s) and the South Ferry PHB (Fl.R.2s). Depth will increase as you head in a curve for the Lilies SCB (VQ(6)+LFl.10s).

Milton Creek branches away S here. Once a busy trading waterway, it leads to Sittingbourne town centre, but a low-level road bridge (air draught 4·2m) now bars access in its lower reach.

Note At this point in the Swale, the direction of lateral buoyage reverses.

Beyond the Lilies, on the W side of the channel, is the Grovehurst Jetty frequently used by ships delivering bulk cargo. N of this jetty the channel is marked by lit SHBs (to be left to port when heading N), S11 (Fl.G.2s) then S10 (Fl(3)G.5s) in Clay Reach. At S9 (Q.G) it turns NW past S8 (Q.R) and widens into Ferry Reach with the Kingsferry lifting bridge in view less than a mile away. From here to Long Point, beyond the bridge, the speed limit does not apply and the stretch is used by fast powerboats.

In Ferry Reach there is a busy dock on the S shore, Ridham Dock, which takes frequent coaster traffic – you should learn of any imminent traffic by monitoring the channel for Kingsferry Bridge, VHF Ch 10.

Kingsferry Bridge and Sheppey Crossing

Kingsferry Bridge carries rail traffic and some local road traffic across a lifting span between two pairs of towers; the high level fixed road bridge (Sheppey Crossing) just W carries the bulk of road traffic between Sheppey and the mainland. If you need Kingsferry Bridge to lift (air draught when lowered is 3·35m at MHWS), it is best to call on VHF Ch 10 when you are an hour away, to ensure that the bridge keeper knows well in advance that you are approaching, and monitor Ch 10 thereafter.

The bridge is operated by Network Rail and does not open to a timetable, but it is required to lift on request if circumstances allow. In practice, although the bridge is manned continuously, the duty bridge keeper cannot open the bridge without permission from the railway signalman at Sittingbourne.

The train timetable allows for two lifts per hour, Monday to Saturday, at about H+10 and H+40. On Sundays there is a lift just once per hour, usually around H+15. The bridge is, however, said to be restricted to three lifts in two hours to allow the machinery to cool. In warmer weather, even on weekdays the bridge keeper may advise that only

Eastbound at LW, approaching the Elmley Causeway

A wide turn past the Lilies SCB towards Grovehurst commercial jetty

Yachts following a ship through Kingsferry Bridge, westbound

17. THE SWALE

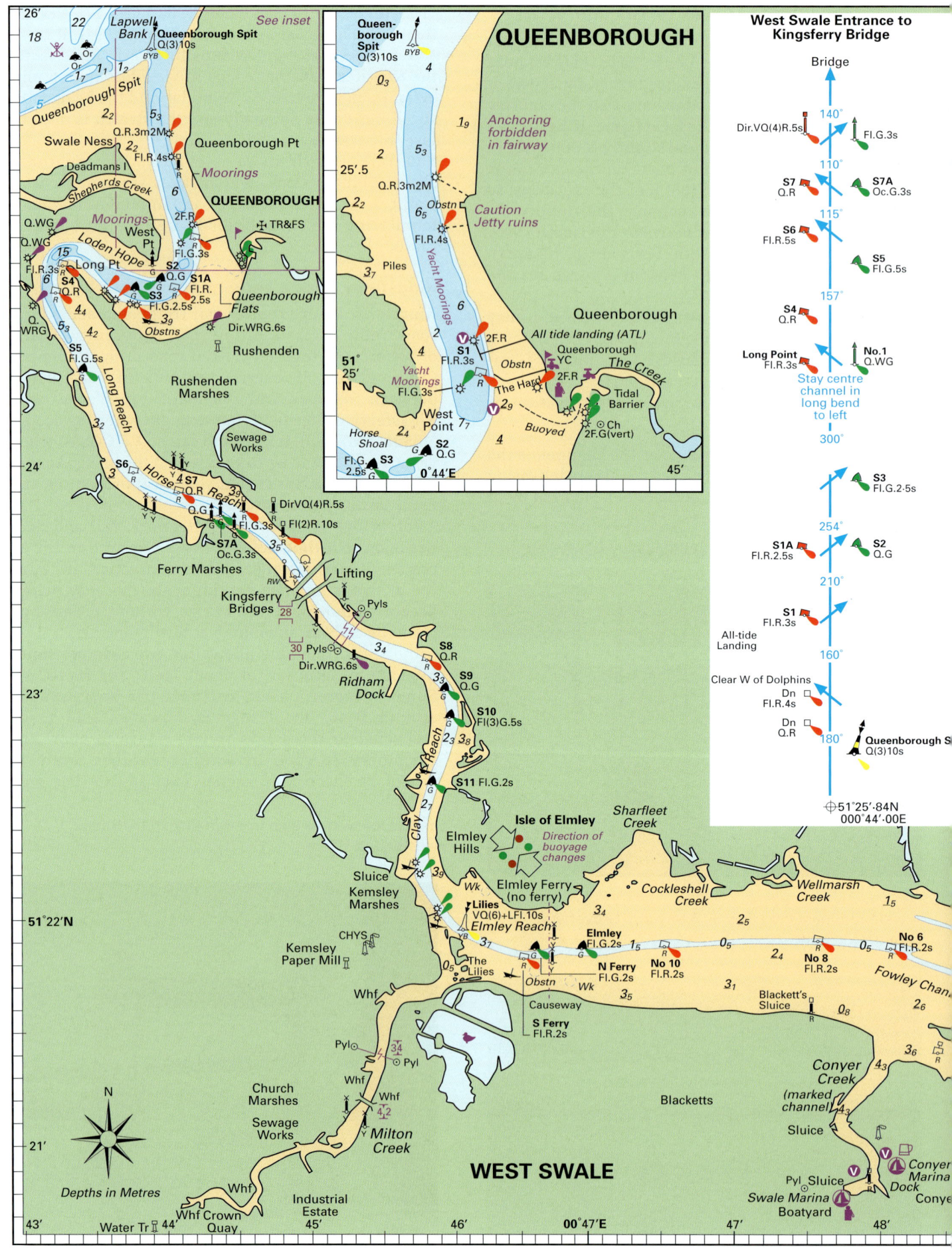

226 • East Coast Pilot

The Swale – Queenborough to Kingsferry

At Kingsferry, the lifting road/rail bridge in the foreground, the high-level road bridge beyond

one lift per hour is possible, to avoid overheating the elderly machinery whose replacement is long overdue. Normal courtesy and reasonableness when requesting a lift can only help ease your way through. If a lift for commercial shipping is due, it takes priority, but you will usually be allowed through immediately before or after a ship, as advised on Ch 10. In this situation do not assume anything – ensure that the bridge keeper tells the ship's pilot that you are waiting and that agreement is reached as to whether you lead or follow the ship through. The pilot will also be monitoring Ch 10.

If the lift is just for you and perhaps other leisure craft, help the bridge keeper reduce delays by keeping station close to the bridge at the time advised to you. The lift sequence starts with flashing R/G lights. Wait until a fixed G light is displayed before passing through. A loud horn sounds with the G light when the bridge is fully raised, as it always should be.

When planning a passage through the bridge, bear in mind that there can be circumstances when the bridge cannot be lifted. In very hot weather it is sometimes not lifted at all for fear of unequal expansion jamming the mechanism. Such failures, and also periods of scheduled maintenance, are usually advised in the MSI broadcasts by HMCG.

Note The stretch between Kingsferry and the Medway is descibed in the next section, starting from the Medway.

The Swale – Queenborough to Kingsferry

WEST SWALE

Entry waypoint
51°25'·84N 000°44'·00E Immediately NE of Queeborough
Spit ECB (Q(3)10s)

Tides Sheerness

Main Hazards

Ruins on E shore marked by dolphins. Some commercial traffic (large coasters).

Approaches

Approaches to the W Swale will be from seaward or down river from the Medway.

From seaward, follow directions for entering the Medway (see chapter 15) then, watching for commercial traffic, make for the W Swale entrance marked by the Queenborough Spit ECB (Q(3)10s).

Heading E down the Medway, the Queenborough Spit ECB can be hard to locate against the Sheerness shore and can be obscured by large tugs on moorings W of it. These tugs are active during shipping movements. Huge wind turbines stand on the shore behind.

KINGSFERRY BRIDGE

Contact
VHF Ch 10
Callsign *Kingsferry Bridge*
☏01795 423627

Lights
Alt Q R/G bridge lifting
F.G bridge open (28m MHWS)
Q.R bridge lowering, keep clear
Q.Y bridge out of action
No lights – bridge down (3·35m MHWS)

East Coast Pilot • 227

17. THE SWALE

Heading S in the Swale, leave the Queenborough Spit ECB to starboard and pass two large lit dolphins on the E shore (Q.R and Fl.R.4s) guarding dangerous remains of an old ferry terminal, which once hosted the 'Flushing Ferry' service to and from Vlissingen.

The hefty Queenborough Spit ECB marks the entrance to the W Swale

QUEENBOROUGH

Queenborough town is on the Isle of Sheppey at the entrance to the West Swale, a little under 2M S of Garrison Point at the mouth of the Medway. It offers a safe and, except in strong N through NW'lies, sheltered anchorage and almost always has visitor moorings available. The harbour is run by the Queenborough Harbour Trust.

Immediately S of the second dolphin, lines of moorings begin on both shores. Beyond the moorings on the E side, a long pontoon (2F.R) carrying the harbour office lies parallel to the shore, connected at its S end by a bridge to the hammerhead of the all-tide landing (ATL) floating jetty, which stretches across the mudflats from the E shore. Call *Sheppey One* on VHF Ch 08 for mooring instructions.

The Harbour Trust is constantly developing the facilities when funds allow. Check the ECP website, updates section, where we will show any significant changes.

Moorings that may be offered include alongside (possibly rafted) berths on the pontoon by the harbour office, and large multiple-occupancy buoys nearby.

SW of the ATL on the W side of the channel, a large concrete barge used to be available as a mooring and was popular for groups of boats cruising together. Unfortunately it was declared unsafe in recent years, although in 2023 it was being used again but only for commercial craft; any replacement is likely to be another barge or a pontoon in the same position.

Do not anchor in the fairway, because commercial traffic operates 24hr through the Kingsferry Bridge, but you may find a place to bring up under the N shore of Loden Hope.

The Harbour Trust runs a trot-boat service for those who are on buoyed moorings, trot-boat hours varying with season, with the price included in the mooring fee. If using your own dinghy to get ashore, be aware that the tides run strongly here.

The ATL has a gate at its shore end, which lets you ashore, but requires a code or purchased token to pass seawards again. The code is provided free by the harbour staff, or tokens to open the gate can be purchased from the two nearby pubs and from the Queenborough Stores in the High Street.

Queenborough YC welcomes visitors who may use its facilities when it's open. When the club is closed, there is a public toilet/shower block on the small green just behind the sea wall (see info panel).

To the S of the ATL is the long, sloping concrete Town Hard, usable by dinghy, which allows free access to and from the shore but is not clean.

Be sure to stay outside the two large dolphins when heading into or out of the W Swale

The large pontoon at Queenborough carrying the harbour office

Queenborough to Kingsferry Bridge

QUEENBOROUGH ME11 5AA

Tides Sheerness

Contact
VHF Ch 08
Callsign *Sheppey One*
Harbour office ☏07456 459754
info@queenborough-harbour.co.uk
www.queenborough-harbour.co.uk

Access 24hr ATL (pontoons) and public Town Hard (dinghies only)

Facilities Trot-boat; WC on pontoon; WC & showers in club, if open, or public facilities nearby, key from harbour staff or from Queenborough Stores in the main street. Scrubbing berth in creek.

Water On ATL

Electricity On pontoon, extra charge

Fuel From petrol station ½M in Queenborough Rd

Gas from petrol station

Repairs Jim Brett's yard in Queenborough Creek, with 8-T crane ☏01795 668263

Provisions Up the main street 100 yards, also large supermarket 20 mins walk

Pub/Restaurant Flying Dutchman ☏01795 667189 Old House at Home ☏01795 662463; Admirals Arm ☏01795 668598. Others in town, ask in harbour office

Club Queenborough YC ☏01795 663955 www.qyc.org.uk

Transport Buses; Trains to Sittingbourne for connections to London, Dover and Ramsgate

Taxi ☏01795 509999 or ask Hbr staff.

The creek at LW. The scrubbing berth is just beyond the rafted-out blue boat

Queenborough trot boat, a free service

Queenborough Creek

Along the south side of the town is the drying Queenborough Creek. Access (HW+/-1½) is across the mudflats closely following the small markers from the S1 PHB (Fl.R.3s) off the end of the concrete hard, then through the floodgate (usually open). The Town Quay on the N side of the creek can be crowded, but the bottom is flat and free from obstructions; the Harbour Office manages some of these spaces along the quayside. Also ask about use (at a small charge) of the scrubbing berth in the Creek, at the far end of the open quayside, where the bottom is a large concrete slab.

Flood gate activity is indicated by Control Lights as follows: 3F.R(vert) barrier closed; 3Fl.R(vert) closure imminent.

Queenborough to Kingsferry Bridge

The passage from Queenborough to the bridge is straightforward with good depth in the channel, plenty of lights at night and no unmarked obstructions. To help ships navigate at night, the channel is covered by sectored lights and leading lights.

Call the bridge keeper (VHF Ch 10, *Kingsferry Bridge*) before leaving the moorings at Queenborough to find out when the next lift will be. See bridge details on page 227.

The channel runs round a right hand bend into Loden Hope, past S2 (Q.G) and S3 (Fl.G.2·5s) SHBs. To port is an old wharf with cranes and occasionally vessels being broken up.

At the end of Loden Hope is a hairpin bend to port with best water midway between the banks all the way round. Do not cut this corner. There is a PHB (Fl.R.3s) off Long Point and two sectored lights (Q.WG) on the outside of the bend.

Once round Long Pt, Long Reach runs past S4 (Q.R) PHB and S5 (Fl.G.5s) SHB to S6 (Fl.R.5s) PHB where the channel bends to port past S7 (Q.R) PHB. Do not cut this corner either.

From S7, Horse Reach leads past S7A (Oc.G) SHB and lit beacons on either hand before the final stretch to the bridge on about 140°. There is a WRG sectored light located E of the bridge to guide shipping through and the port authority specifically warns against looking directly at this bright light.

The waters each side of the bridge are the only areas in the Swale without an 8kn speed limit and powerboats and PWCs are active there, especially at weekends. This stretch can be crowded in summer with leisure craft waiting for a bridge lift and sharing a fairly small area with much faster boats. Skippers may find it easier to wait NW of the fixed road bridge, as we do, rather than between the two bridges, especially on the flood tide.

18. NORTH KENT COAST

Margate at LW

18. NORTH KENT COAST

This chapter describes the coastal pilotage from Ramsgate to the Swale and Medway, including the ports of Broadstairs, Margate, Herne Bay and Whitstable.

BROADSTAIRS AND MARGATE HARBOURS

Contact
(Broadstairs and Margate harbours are managed by the Ramsgate HM)
Ramsgate Harbour office ☎01843 572100
Facilities Ad hoc berthing only

RAMSGATE TO NORTH FORELAND

On passage from Ramsgate N towards the Foreland, you can safely keep as close as ½M from the shore unless you have exceptional draught and it's near LW. Beware pot markers in the whole area. Apart from the very obvious steel dolphin (Fl.R.2·5s) ½M N of Ramsgate harbour, there are no charted individual hazards and you can enjoy the scenery of Thanet's chalk cliffs, soon giving way to the tiny haven of Broadstairs set around Viking Bay.

Broadstairs is a pretty little place and a bustling seaside resort in summer. The harbour, formed by a short stone arm at the N end of the bay, provides little

Inside Broadstairs tiny harbour near LW

shelter from onshore winds and dries completely to hard sand, and is perhaps not a proposition for a prolonged visit unless you have a sense of adventure, a suitable craft and the weather is settled. Two beacons mark the extremities of the sandy bay, only about 150m apart. A lunchtime anchorage stop for a swim a few hundred yards off or a row ashore for an ice

Broadstairs from the sea, stay between the two beacons on entry

Rounding N Foreland

232 • East Coast Pilot

North Kent Coast

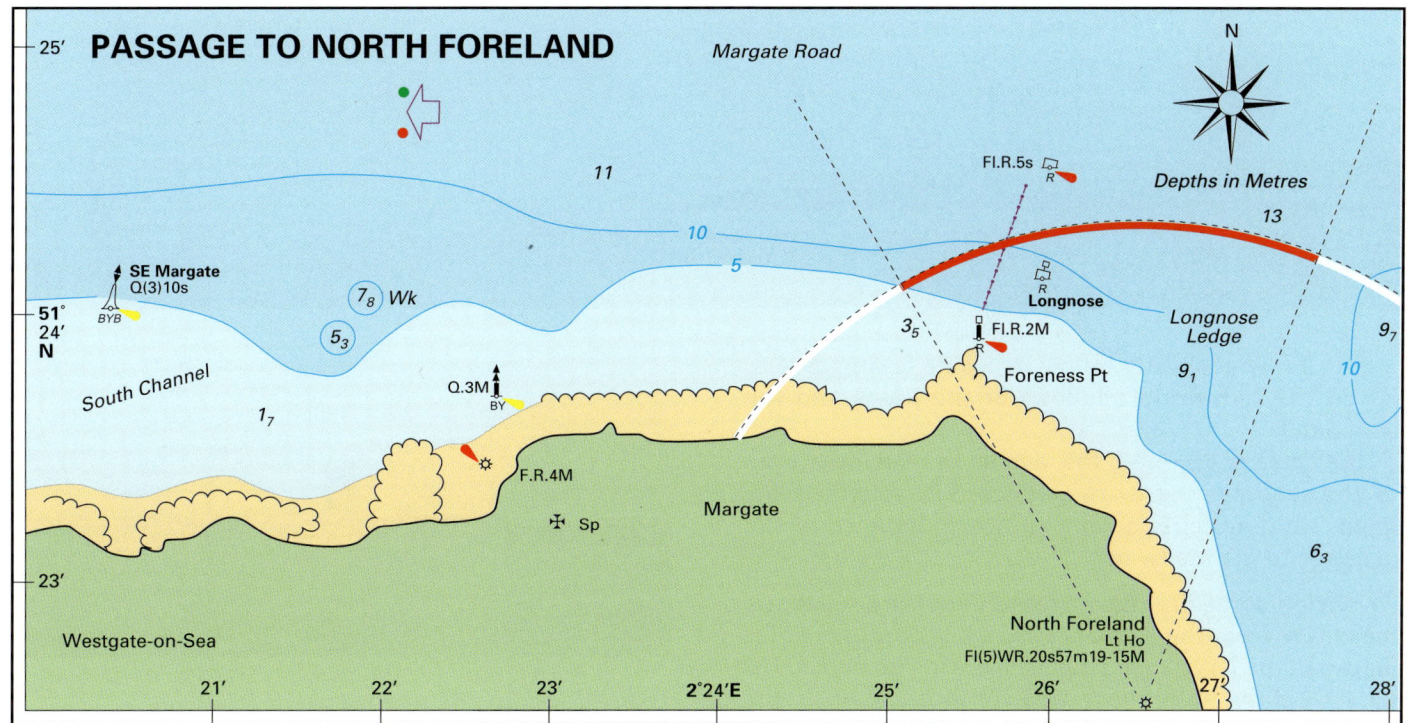

cream is something you might consider. The harbour is managed out of the Ramsgate Harbour office, where you can find advice if needed (see contact details above). Broadstairs SC runs dinghy races just offshore and occasionally hosts large events, which are best avoided by heading a little further out round them.

North of Broadstairs, the cliffs quickly rise again, surmounted by houses most of the way to the N Foreland lighthouse (Fl(5)WR.20s57m19-15M), which was notable for being the last in the country to be manned before it, too, became fully automated.

The cliffs reduce in height as you round the N Foreland and are punctuated by sandy bays. Off the Foreland itself, strong onshore winds can produce very rough conditions – it's the meeting place of two tidal streams, where the waters of the Thames Estuary meet the English Channel. In the prevailing SW'lies, however, it's usually well sheltered inshore, but be aware of the charted chalk ledges and also badly marked pots.

North Foreland westwards

Boats heading W have a choice here: to keep along the coast inshore of the mass of sandbanks that fills the Estuary (the 'overland' route) or to make N, turning NNW in the vicinity of the East Margate buoy (Fl.R.2·5s) for the Queens Channel (if heading for the Swale) or the Princes Channel if going to the Medway or Thames. Although the inshore route is the shortest, without local knowledge it should be treated with great caution in strong onshore winds and especially around LW, particularly through the shallows off Reculver.

The Princes Channel is a main shipping route and should be treated accordingly. Skippers of leisure

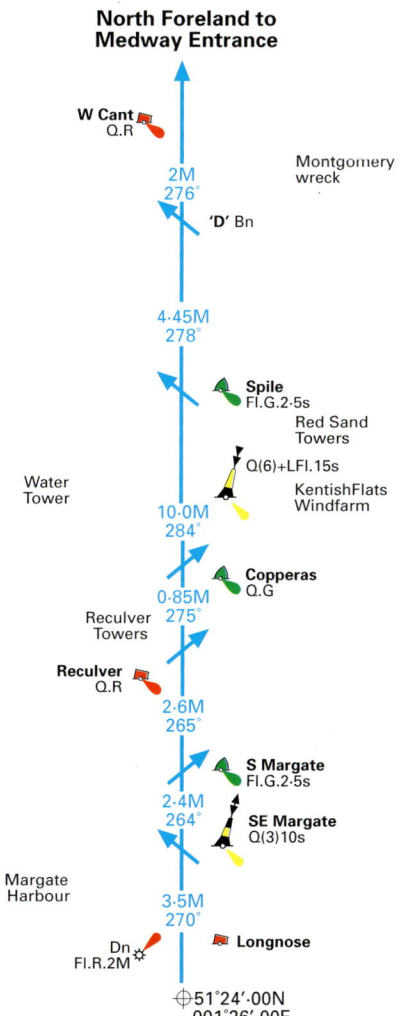

East Coast Pilot • 233

18. NORTH KENT COAST

Stay outside the large dolphin at Foreness Point

craft should generally follow its S side taking care to avoid the significant shallows of the Ridge and the Pan Sand.

The Queens Channel, too, avoids the Reculver area if the shallows there are a concern in your passage plan. Neither route adds significant distance to the passage to the Medway.

When following the inshore route along the Kent shore, head NW from the Foreland, rounding Foreness Point between the large steel dolphin marking an outfall (lit FL.R) and the unlit Longnose PHB three cables to the NE, and then on W through the South Channel. Again, pot markers can be a nuisance around Foreness Point.

Approaching Margate from the E, stay outside the large NCM

MARGATE

A little less than two miles W of the Longnose is the small drying harbour of Margate. If planning to take a closer look at it, be sure to avoid the hidden remains of the pier just E which was destroyed in a storm, its N end marked by a very large NCM (Q.3M). The harbour itself, with its single stone arm and stone lighthouse (F.R.4M) on its outer end, is sheltered from N through E but is totally open to the W, and dries at least 2m to mostly hard sand. From a distance, the harbour location is obvious from the N, but less so from the NW. HW is at about Sheerness -0035.

The Turner Contemporary gallery is close E of the harbour and a trip ashore to visit it, or perhaps the seafront delights of Margate, may be the only reasons to enter, although a suitable craft could certainly take shelter from winds in the sector from N through E to S. There is a broad slipway in the SE corner of the harbour and another narrower one outside, close E – do not obstruct these as they may be needed by the

The harbour dries completely to hard sand

Margate lifeboat. Fender boards are advisable against the wall – the best stretch of wall is perhaps between the first and second bends in, where there is more timber to lean on. The wall has several ladders.

Like Broadstairs, this harbour is also managed out of the Ramsgate Harbour office if needed (see contact

Margate seen from the NW

Lighthouse on end of harbour arm

Reculver westwards

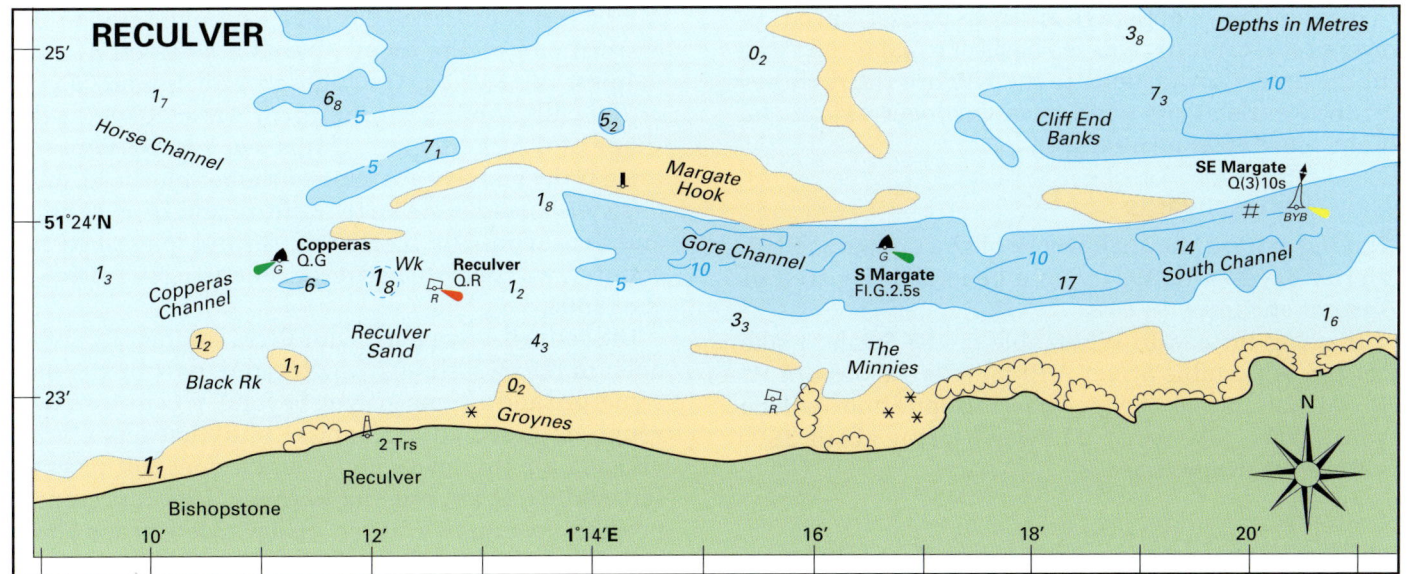

details at head of this chapter). Margate YC, mainly a dinghy sailing club, is just across the road at the foot of the hill.

Margate westwards

Heading on W, the shore beyond Margate rises as a low chalk cliff, which finally peters out again at Minnis Bay. The N side of the route on through the Gore Channel is marked by the SE Margate ECB (Q(3)10s), then S Margate SHB (Fl.G.2·5s); along here the deep channel is sheltered from the N by the Margate Hook Sand. Keep well S of the area around the S Margate buoy near LW as it's quite shallow in the vicinity. Beyond Minnis, the coastline sinks to barely more than a sea wall, blocking off the sea from what was once the Wantsum Channel which separated the Isle of Thanet from the mainland.

Reculver Towers are seen ahead. These two rectangular towers, linked together, are part of an ancient ruined church that stands inside the Roman 'Saxon Shore' fort of Regulbium, whose garrison guarded the N end of the Wantsum.

The old church at Reculver was built using materials from the Roman fort, but was largely demolished in the 19th century when it became clear that the sea would take it if unchecked, the materials being used

Reculver Towers, and the Reculver PHB – keep 100m N

to build a new church a mile inland. That the original Towers still stand today, on a low promontory protected just yards from the waves by a sea wall, is due in part to their importance to Trinity House as a landmark for mariners. From time to time the towers are floodlit until midnight.

Steering about 265° from the S Margate SHB, the Reculver PHB (Q.R) marking the start of the Copperas Channel is some 2·4M distant. The Margate Hook beacon is a prominent, unlit SCM on the sandbank to starboard and once housed a refuge for shipwrecked sailors.

Be aware that near LW the Copperas Channel route is suitable only for shoal draught boats. The Channel itself has good depth, but its approaches from the E seem to be progressively shallowing with perhaps only 1m at LW. The troublesome area is the last mile before the Reculver buoy, best approached on about a WSW heading. Leave the Reculver buoy itself at least 100m to port, then follow 275° for the Copperas SHB (Q.G). When about 250m past the Copperas, turn NW for the best water, watching the depth closely as you cross the tail of the Last Sand, and continue for at least ½M before resuming a W'ly heading across the Kentish Flats. Note particularly the unmarked Black Rock, SW of the Copperas buoy, which dries at LWS.

East Coast Pilot • 235

18. NORTH KENT COAST

Incidentally, copperas, or iron pyrites, used in dyeing and tanning, was the basis of a major industry in the area. Conspicuous to the NW are the turbines of the Kentish Flats wind farm, just over 4M off the Kent shore at its nearest point.

Reculver westwards

Having skirted the shallows W of the Copperas SHB, Herne Bay lies WSW, across a generally flat area of further shallows.

If going instead to Whitstable or the Swale, make for the Whitstable Street PHB (Fl.R.2s), about 6M W. If you plan to go to the Medway, the Spile buoy will be your target, just over 10M away bearing about 280° via the 'Overland Passage'.

APPROACHES TO HERNE BAY FROM EAST

Main hazards
Entire approach is across flat shoals.
Disused pierhead (Q.18m4M) 0·6M NNW
Steel dolphin (Fl.Y 5s) 0·95M ENE
Area used by fast powerboats and PWCs.
Very soft mud in harbour.

HERNE BAY   CT6 5JG

⊕ **Landfall waypoint**
51°22'·70N 001°07'·20E

Charts
Imray 2100, C1
Admiralty SC5606, 1607

Tides
HW Sheerness -0025

Contact
Foreshore manager ☏01227 266719
foreshore.services@canterbury.gov.uk

Access HW±2hr

About ½M N of Herne Bay SC (the dinghy club at the eastern end of the town) there's a substantial steel dolphin, lit Fl.Y 5s. On high ground inland, due S of the club, there is a prominent water tower in the shape of a cocktail glass. Out at sea ¾M NNW of the town is the massive abandoned timber pierhead, once busy with paddle-steamer traffic to and from London and Southend. The pier itself, second longest in the country, was demolished after collapsing in storms in the 1980s.

The council-owned harbour dries completely and is open to the W, although sheltered in part by the pier structure and a stone groyne beyond. It is formed by a rough stone arm (its root at its E end) that acts as a sea defence for the town. The Council does not provide for visitors at all, but the harbour does represent a possible emergency haven or an adventurous short visit for shoal draught craft that can take the ground. In strong onshore winds at HWS the place should be avoided if at all possible, because waves will overtop the harbour arm.

Approach to the harbour is not dictated by any particular deeper route - the bottom is hard flat sand from some distance out and the harbour entrance is close to a conspicuous block of flats. Yellow buoys parallel to the shore define an 8kn inshore speed limit. The entrance is about 50m wide, the W side is the shore end of the old pier, lit 2FG(vert), being a flat platform on piles carrying fairground items (like a helter-skelter) from time to time. The W end of the arm, on your port side, is lit 2FR(vert). Turn E as soon as you pass the end of this arm to find the deepest water, which follows close inside the arm.

The harbour dries completely to very soft deep mud over clay. Several local fishing boats and other craft are moored here, but there are no visitor moorings provided, although you might find a spare one. If anchoring, it could be best to choose a spot at the W end and it would be wise to buoy your anchor. There is no need to inform the Council for a short stop.

Around HW you could lie briefly in at least 2m alongside the S edge of the broad public slipway inside the E end of the harbour which, in season, can be busy with powerboat launching and recovery. Until perhaps HW+3 you can land by dinghy on this slipway

Approach Herne Bay harbour from the N, the tower block is a useful landmark

236 • East Coast Pilot

Herne Bay westwards to Whitstable

The drying harbour near LW — Slipway, Deepest water inside the arm, Lines of moorings

The harbour at half tide, slipway in the distant corner

or on the beach, but do not even think of trying to wade ashore through the mud. Its treacherous nature is such that HM Coastguard uses the harbour for national training in mud rescue!

Herne Bay westwards to Whitstable

Between the old Herne Bay pierhead and Whitstable is a popular area for pots, not all of which may be properly marked.

The Whitstable Street shingle bank bars the way W and dries for almost a mile from shore at LWS. The Whitstable Street PHB (Fl.R.2s) at its N end, 2M from the shore, is the normal turning point for craft approaching the town.

East Coast Pilot • 237

18. NORTH KENT COAST

WHITSTABLE

Main hazards
Shallows in approach
'The Street' shingle bank to E
Some commercial traffic

Whitstable is the third refuge harbour along this stretch of coast, but is again not commonly visited. The town is very much an East Coast place, much more like the coastal towns of Essex and Suffolk than its neighbours in Kent and can be worth a visit if you are prepared to anchor or moor offshore and use the dinghy. The town has become fashionable in recent years and local prices can reflect this. There are many small specialist shops and art galleries and a number of good restaurants. Fresh fish is usually available from the quayside.

It's very much a working port, home to the local fishing fleet, and coasters carrying aggregates or timber frequently call. The harbour dries to soft mud at LWS and is not a yacht-friendly place. In an emergency it would be available, but try to contact the HM before attempting to enter (note that the VTS only operates during shipping movements). The walls are high and unforgiving and fender boards are needed, unless you can raft alongside. There is a pontoon in the SE corner but this is normally fully booked for regular day-trip traffic. In onshore winds there can be a considerable swell in all parts of the harbour.

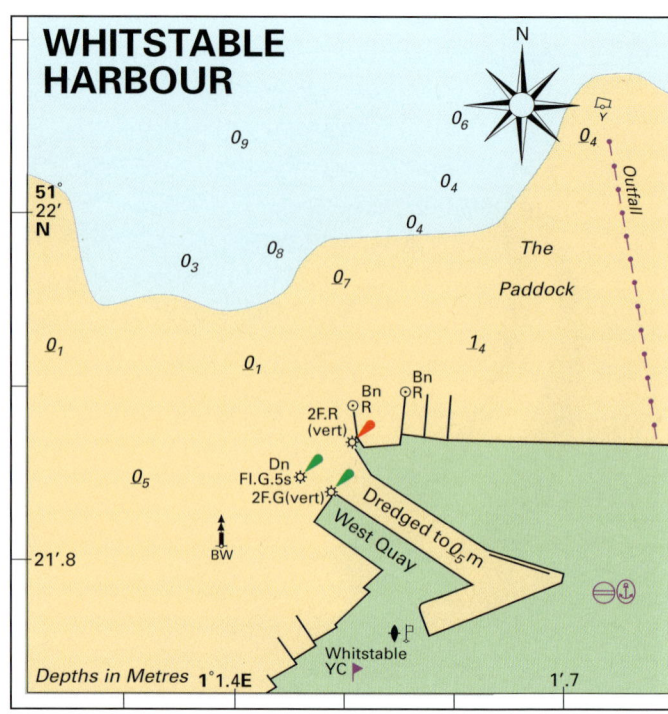

Whitstable Harbour seen from the Oyster PHB

The harbour entrance, looking NW from inside

WHITSTABLE   CT5 1AB

Landfall waypoint
51°22'·70N 001°01'·20E

Charts
Imray 2100, C1
Admiralty SC5606, 1607

Tides
HW Sheerness -0010

Contact
VHF Ch 09 Whitstable Harbour Radio (monitored only during shipping movements)
Harbour Manager Whitstable Harbour Office ☏01227 266719

Access HW±3hr

Slipway Public timber ramp between YC and W arm of harbour

Club Whitstable YC ☏01227 272942 (Mon-Fri, 1000-1400), office@wyc.org.uk, www.wyc.org.uk

Chandler and outboard engineer Whitstable Marine ☏01227 262525 www.whitstablemarine.co.uk

Rigger At chandler above

The harbour entrance is difficult to make out even in clear weather. It is lit at night, but in daylight the town behind is fairly featureless. Look for a long low roof (visible well out to sea) and a tall silo, both just E of the harbour.

The harbour approach is across shallows. At night, locate the lit Oyster PHB (Fl(2)R.10s) and a SHM dolphin (Fl.G·5s) close to the West Quay head. The two pierheads display 2F.R(vert) and 2F.G(vert) respectively.

The beach immediately W of the harbour has two slipways – the one closest to the harbour wall is

Whitstable

HM's office
Pontoon
RNLI launch and recovery area
Public Slipway

Whitstable Harbour

Looking E in the harbour, the pontoon at the far end

18. NORTH KENT COAST

public, the other belongs to Whitstable YC, but stay off the RNLI launching area of beach between the two (see aerial photo). The yacht club is just W of the RNLI boathouse and, although predominantly a dinghy club, it has a small cruising section and may have a spare mooring on enquiry from the secretary. The bottom of the beach in front of the club and for 150m W is firm, flat shingle compacted on mud (it was a Thames barge hard) and is an ideal spot for a scrub or below-waterline maintenance in quiet weather – as a guideline, a boat with 1·2m draught will ground at about half tide. Close by there is a chandler where help may be available for rigging or outboard problems.

A few hundred yards further west there is a large and expanding area of flags, posts and buoys guarding numerous metal trestles for raising shellfish. The area is expanding NW-wards, is extremely hazardous to small craft and swimmers, and must be avoided.

Further southwest in Whitstable Bay are more charted oyster beds, again limiting anchoring possibilities.

There is no shelter in Whitstable Bay in strong SW through N winds, when a far better option is to make for the Swale. A NW'ly in particular can make life very uncomfortable with a vicious, steep chop quickly building up across the shallows.

Reculver to The Medway

On passage from the Copperas Channel to the Medway, passing outside the Isle of Sheppey, shape a course of about 280° to the Spile SHB (Fl.G.2·5s) at the W end of the Four Fathoms Channel, just over 10M distant.

This takes you along the Overland Passage, an ancient name still shown on charts and referring to the shallow water where least charted depth is around 2·5m. Just N of the rhumb line from the Copperas SHB to the Spile SHB, note the charted buoyed exclusion area marking shallows (0·9m at LAT) where wind farm export cables cross each other on the sea bed and are protected by piles of rock armour. Three of the four buoys are lit Fl.(4)Y.10s, while the fourth and southernmost is a SCB lit Q(6)+LFl.15s. It is possible that this area will grow in future years as more cables are added.

Off Whitstable, another old name takes over, the Four Fathoms Channel, which on some charts has the legend 'at HWS' wisely added after it. If passing through at less than half tide, avoid going too close inshore off NE Sheppey where there are several shallow patches only visible on large scale charts.

W of the Spile, the route crosses an area of continuing shallows called the Cant. The chart warns of 'numerous pieces of wreckage, some of which dry at LWS' across the Cant, but despite this there is much fishing and trawling activity and the area is heavily used by small craft without problems.

The Cant has various substantial charted posts dotted across it, but these do not mark hazards. Obstructions stretch N from the shore towards the old Mid Cant post but these stop three cables short of the post itself.

If depth is not an issue, head 278° from the Spile to the Mid Cant post and then 275° towards the West Cant PHB (Q.R) on the SE side of the Medway approach channel. Otherwise stay further out to round the Cheyney Spit, which extends to the N of the unlit 'D' beacon, which is topped with an orange diamond.

The infamous wreck of the *Richard Montgomery* lies on the Sheerness Middle Sand, NW of the buoyed shipping approach channel, with her masts still visible. A Liberty Ship on her maiden voyage in 1944 with a cargo of munitions bound for Normandy, she was at anchor when she swung onto the sands and broke her back; she was partly unloaded soon afterwards, but a huge quantity of bombs and other munitions still lie there. The wreck is regularly surveyed, but the cargo has always been considered too dangerous to touch and the wreck is surrounded by an exclusion zone defined by lit yellow buoys.

Medway entrance, off Garrison Point and looking across towards the west side and the Recommended Yacht Track

Reculver to The Medway

In 2023 plans were being considered to remove the masts to negate any danger of them falling, which would leave only the obvious buoyage around it.

When approaching the Medway, listen on Ch 74 to Medway VTS for shipping movements and maintain a good lookout astern. Note that smaller ships do use the buoyed secondary channel that runs along the S edge of the main Medway Channel. There is a charted Recommended Yacht Track for entering or leaving the Medway, which runs along the western edge of the entrance – it is safer to use this rather than enter close to Garrison Point where you may meet an outbound ship. For full details of the Medway entrance, see Chapter 16.

D Beacon, on the N end of Cheyney Spit, 2 miles E of Garrison Point

The wreck of the *Richard Montgomery*, its masts may be removed

East Coast Pilot • 241

19. RAMSGATE

⚓ **Landfall waypoint**
51°19'·53N 001°30'·27E (Immediately S of 'RA' SCB)

Charts
Imray 2100, C1, C8
Admiralty SC5606, 5605; 323, 1828, 1827

Tides
HW Dover +0030

Contact
Ramsgate Port Control VHF Ch 14, ☎01843 572112
Callsign *Ramsgate Port Control*
Harbourmaster ☎01843 572100 or 07919 211143
www.ramsgateroyalharbour.co.uk

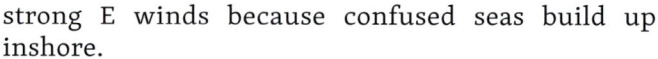

Main hazards

The N section of the Goodwin Sands lies only 4M from the harbour entrance and any passage N of this area, heading E or W, must be undertaken with extreme caution, particularly on the flood tide, which sweeps SW onto the sands and will readily catch out the unwary.

Shallows lie S of the harbour entrance, the Quern Bank being closest, and the Cross Ledge further S. To the N, the shallows shelve gently with no uncharted hazards, but stand well off the North Foreland in strong E winds because confused seas build up inshore.

Ramsgate is a busy base for wind farm construction and maintenance, and for Border Force patrol craft, fishing boat and fast pilot boat traffic. Cross-Channel car-ferry traffic ceased in 2013, although at the time of writing the local authority which owns the harbour is seeking a port operator for the outer area including the old ferry terminal, so it is entirely possible that a ferry service might re-start during the lifetime of this edition of ECP.

There is a dredged approach channel running E-W but small craft should use the Recommended Yacht Track that lies parallel to the S side of the channel.

Ramsgate's outer breakwaters are low lying, built of rubble and can be difficult to make out from the E. The N pier head has a G beacon (Q.G 10m5M); the S has a R beacon (VQ.R 10m5M).

The tide sweeps across the entrance at up to 2kn, roughly NE-SW, with the N-going ebb running from HW-1¼ and HW+4hr (local).

Ramsgate Harbour is immediately below the flightpath of nearby Manston Airport, which at the time of writing is currently closed, but where years of attempts to resume flying operations look as though they might finally succeed.

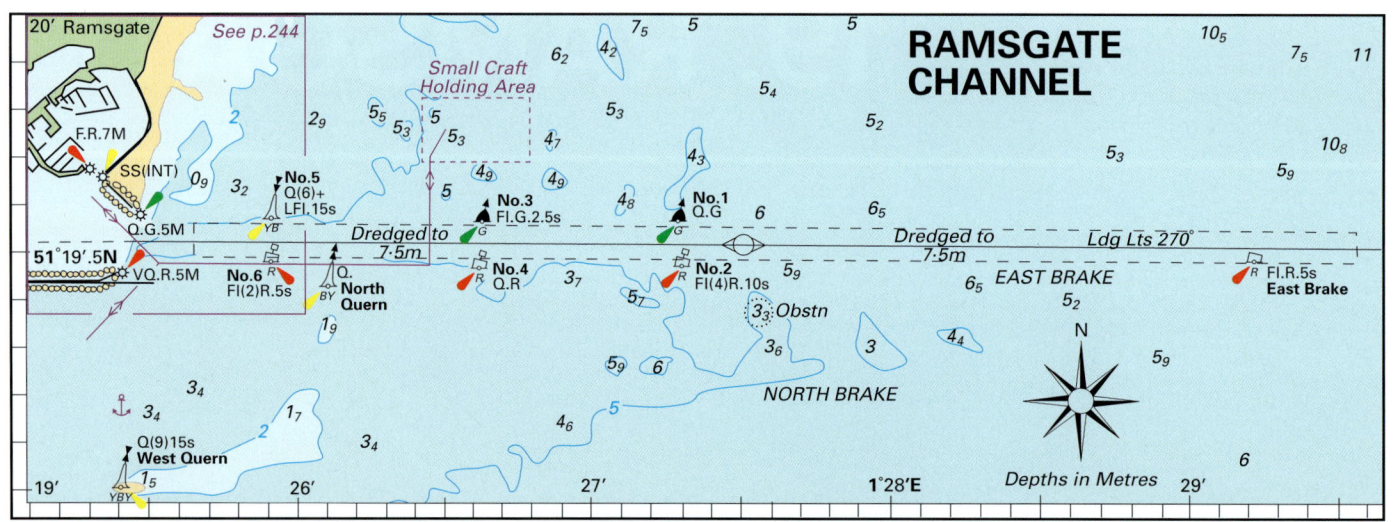

Ramsgate outer harbour entrance, between stone pierheads - only enter with permission, and under power, not sailing

Ramsgate

Final turn to approach the entrance to the Royal Harbour. Maintain listening watch on Ch 14 until round the pierhead

Approaches

From N Follow the coast S from North Foreland keeping ½-1M offshore. There is a Small Craft Holding Area a short distance N of the approach channel No.3 SHB (Fl.G.2·5s) and a track S from there crosses the channel just W of No.3 SHB and No.4 PHB (Q.R) to join the E–W Recommended Yacht Track.

Exercise great care crossing the approach channel and if in doubt, check with Port Control before doing so. Alternatively, with care, small craft can arrive close N of the No.5 NCB (closest to the entrance) before calling Port Control (see 'Entry' below).

From E In daylight, first sighting will be the chalk cliffs of the Foreland, N of the harbour. By night, North Foreland light (W sector) should be identified. Approach the 'RA' SCB (Q(6)+LFl.15s) then join the Yacht Track on the S side of the channel. Keep a sharp lookout for commercial traffic.

From SE Approach outside the Goodwins, keeping clear of the Goodwin Knoll, to arrive at the 'RA' buoy. Do not risk turning NW across the N end of the Knoll, especially when the flood tide is setting hard onto the bank. Every year, unwary skippers are caught out here and provide work for the local RNLI crew.

From S From the S, either follow the Gull Stream NE from Deal Pier, turning N towards the No.4 approach channel buoy once past the Brake PHB (Fl(4)R.15s) or stay close inshore through Ramsgate Channel to W of the Brake and Cross Ledge banks.

The inshore route requires extreme caution, especially close to the B2 SHB (Fl(2)G.5s), which is small and difficult to locate. It guards the Cross Ledge bank, which shifts frequently and must be left well to starboard. Once past, continue in a wide arc W to pass well W of the West Quern WCB (Q(9)15s) to arrive close S of the harbour entrance. This route is not advised at night, nor near LW.

There is a Small Craft Holding Area immediately off the S breakwater (see the harbour chartlet on p. 244).

Entry

Note that sails should be dropped before entering the harbour - if you cannot do this for some reason, seek permission from Port Control first.

From the No.4 channel PHB, follow the charted Recommended Yacht Track. Pass close N of the North Quern NCB (Q) to clear shallows.

It is essential that skippers call *Ramsgate Port Control* on Ch 14 and ask for permission to enter the harbour. Control lights are displayed (3.vert.G clear to enter; 3.vert.R no entry) on the cream painted Port Control building at the root of the N breakwater. They can be difficult to identify against town lights at night. When a light (Fl.Or) is displayed there, it means a ship is manoeuvring and you must not enter or leave harbour.

On receiving permission to enter, proceed under power through the outer entrance. If required to wait, use one of the charted holding areas. Port Control will usually instruct you to stay on Ch14 until you enter the Royal Harbour and have the marina in view, only then switching to Ch80.

Ramsgate Entrance to Ramsgate Marina

Maintain a listening watch on Ch 14. From the outer harbour, the marina lies to the N in the Royal Harbour behind high stone walls. Leave the Harbour SHB (Q.G) to starboard and light (F.R) on end of W Pier close to port. There may be a seasonal PHB (Fl.R.2s) paired with the Harbour buoy. Beware the drying bank on starboard (E) side and watch out for boats leaving - never assume that a vessel will not suddenly appear round the pierhead in contravention of Port Control's instructions. Once round the pierhead, call *Ramsgate Marina* on Ch 80 to request a berth (0700-2100 in summer, 0700-1900 in winter). Outside hours, Port Control may advise.

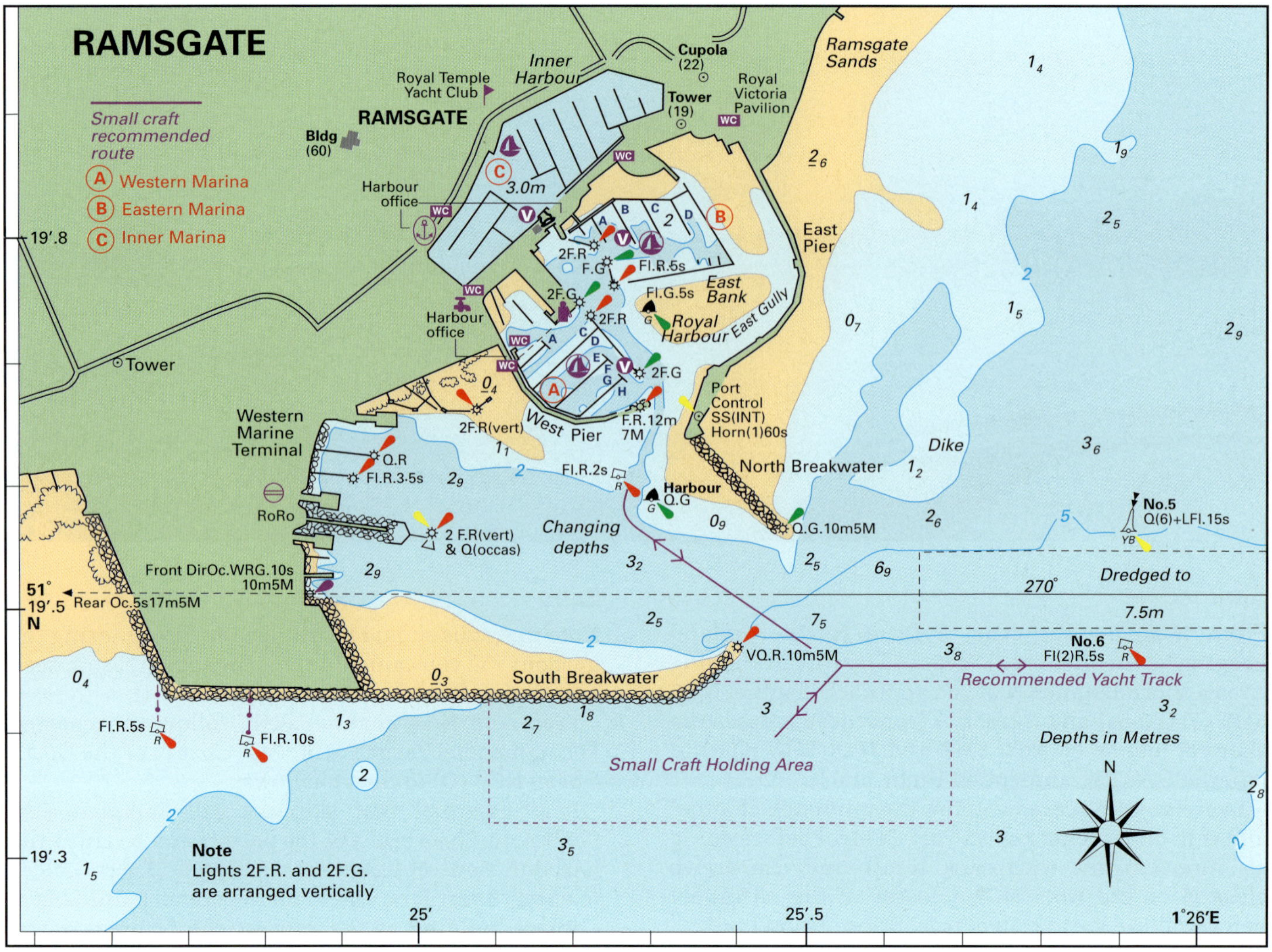

19. RAMSGATE

Ramsgate Marina

There are actually three parts to the marina – West, East and Inner. Leisure craft use the West Marina, immediately to port inside the Royal Harbour entrance. The East Marina lies N from the entrance and is entered between two lit dolphins at its W end. Beware the drying East Bank to starboard guarded by a SHB (Fl.G.5s), which is moored actually over the bank. The East Marina is mainly used by commercial craft and it is very unlikely that leisure craft would be directed there.

Visitors' berths in the West Marina are usually plentiful, except during large events, like Ramsgate Week, although it can get quite full by early evening with craft having just crossed the Channel and en route elsewhere. By day in summer, you may be allocated a specific berth, but generally you will be advised to find an empty one on a choice of pontoons, where no 'Reserved' notice is displayed. The outside of the long N-S pontoon is usually kept free for large craft and those waiting for inner marina access. The W Marina is usually dredged to about 2·5m, but harbour staff suggest you should mention your draught when calling up, especially if over 2m, so you can be directed to a suitable area.

In strong winds from N through E and S or even SW, the harbour can be affected by swell, the E Marina more so than the W, but you will normally be in the W Marina anyway. The further into the marina you go, the less this is likely to affect you.

For long term stays only, and only by previous arrangement, you may be able to berth in the Inner Harbour. This is entered through a lifting bridge and a single gate, NW beyond the W Marina, and open free-flow approx HW±2hr. Signal lights on the Dock Office control movements in and out, but always call *Dock Office* on Ch 14 for clearance to proceed.

The useful scrubbing berth in the NW corner of the W marina

246 • East Coast Pilot

Ramsgate Marina

Ramsgate W marina

Royal Temple YC

The Marina Office is a wooden building immediately W of the lifting bridge, but most visitors will use the secondary office which is at the top of the NW ramp out of the W Marina. Access to the pontoons and toilet buildings is protected by key codes issued when you check in. There is also a small unsecured toilet block on the W Marina pontoons, near the base of the NW ramp. A waste tank pump-out point is also located here.

There is a large drying area, an old slipway, in the NW corner of the W Marina which can be used for scrubbing and below-waterline maintenance. There are steps down to it from the back of the W toilet block, where there is also power and water available.

Remember to call Port Control on Ch 14 for permission to depart the harbour before leaving your berth.

The Royal Temple YC overlooks the harbour with fine views and is friendly and welcoming to visiting yachtsmen. Ramsgate is not only a busy stopover for leisure craft, it has varied eating, shopping and provisioning, 'probably' Britain's largest pub (the Royal Victoria Pavilion), an interesting maritime museum by the clock tower (NE corner of the inner harbour www.ramsgatemaritimemuseum.org), and is a short bus ride away from historic Canterbury, Sandwich, and Broadstairs. Aircraft enthusiasts will enjoy the famous Spitfire Museum at Manston ☏01843 821940 www.spitfiremuseum.org.uk, No.48 bus.

RAMSGATE MARINA CT11 9LQ

Contact
VHF Ch 80
Callsign *Ramsgate Marina*
Marina berthing office / Harbourmaster
☏01843 572110
Duty Dockmaster ☏07919 211143
harbouradmin@thanet.gov.uk
www.ramsgateroyalharbour.co.uk/

Access 24hr

Fuel Red & white diesel and petrol from fuel barge by Commercial Jetty pierhead at N side of W Marina

Facilities WC, showers, launderette, WiFi, pump-out (inner harbour), 32-T boat hoist

Water On pontoons (use own hose)

Electricity On pontoons

Gas Marlec Marine (see below)

Chandler Marlec Marine ☏01843 852452 www.marlecmarine.com; Bowman ☏01843 447300 or 07900 562111

Engineer M-Sea Marine ☏07784 104861; Ramsgate Marine ☏07772 003385 ramsgatemarineltd@icloud.com

Rigger, sailmakers Northrop Sails ☏01843 851665 www.northropsails.com
(All above businesses are in the 'arches' behind the inner harbour)

Slipways Two – one in inner harbour near chandler, the other by the E Marina. Both 5-T limit. Use by prior arrangement only – contact marina berthing office (see above).
Larger slipways, repairs and maintenance behind E Marina – Ramsgate Slipways ☏07940 731558 www.eap-ltd.co.uk/ramsgate/

Provisions in town

Post Office, banks in town

Pubs/restaurants Many around the harbour and in town

Yacht club Royal Temple YC ☏01843 591766 (food usually available). info@rtyc.com www.rtyc.com

Transport Trains – mainline station with frequent services to London and Dover. Buses – useful frequent 'Thanet Loop' service stops opposite Inner Marina

Taxi ☏01843 601601, 581581

20. Thames Passages

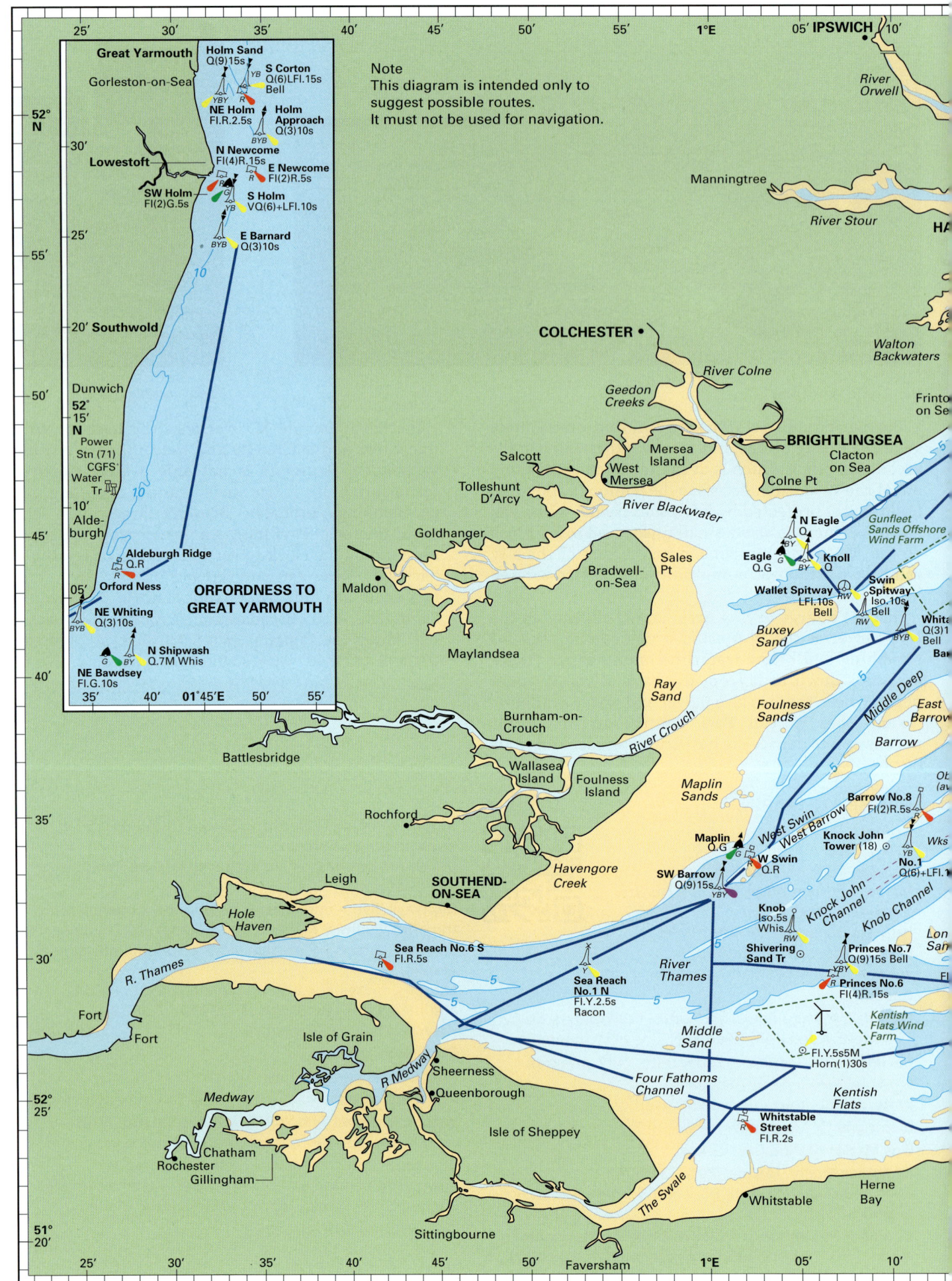

248 • East Coast Pilot

Thames Estuary passages

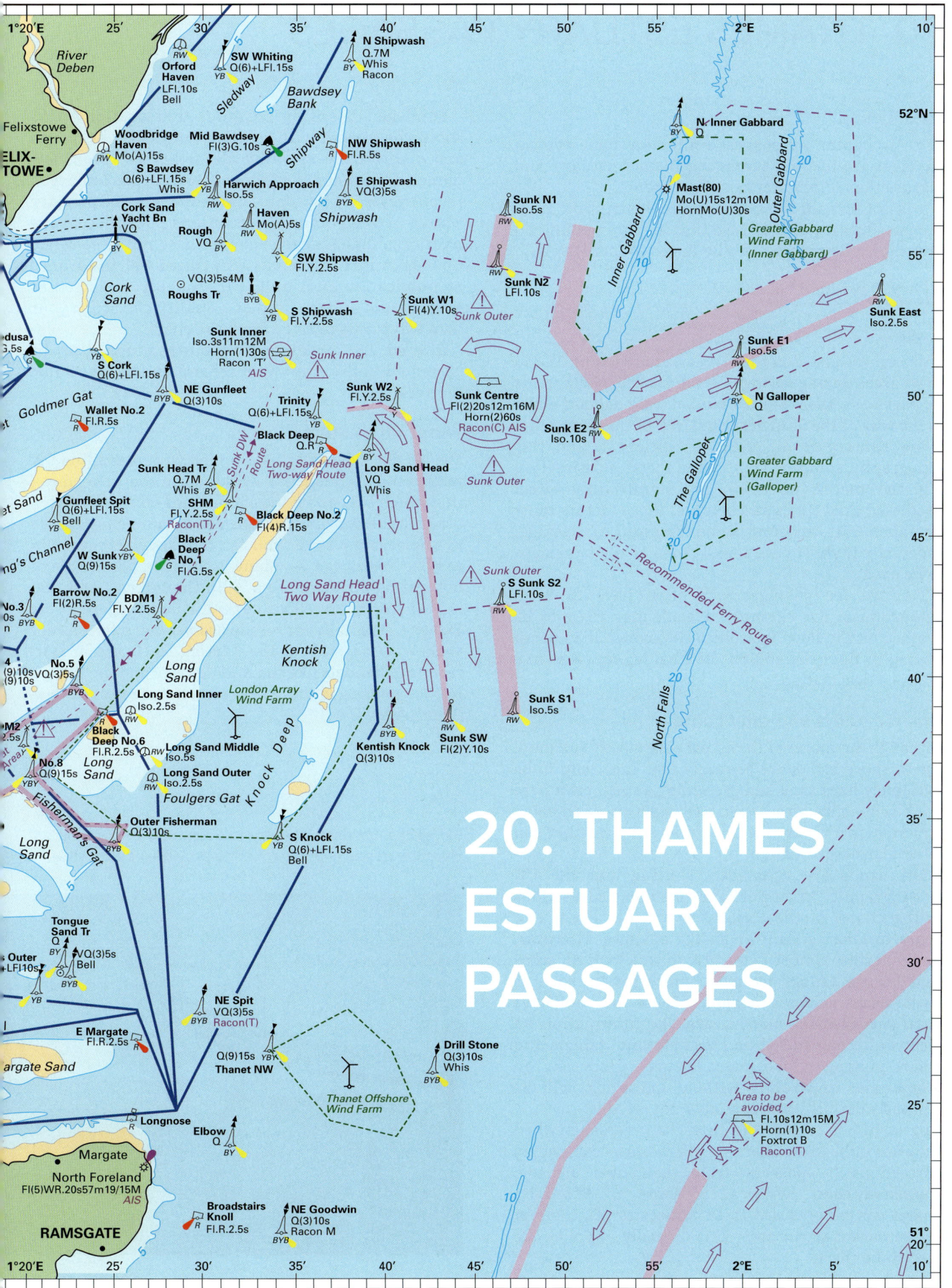

East Coast Pilot • 249

20. THAMES ESTUARY PASSAGES

Introduction

In this chapter we suggest routes for some typical passages around and across the Thames Estuary, and discuss the factors that can affect them.

It is not intended to be a detailed description of all the possibilities. For that we thoroughly recommend *Crossing the Thames Estuary* by Roger Gaspar (Imray).

HAZARDS

Tides

Tides can run hard in the estuary, approaching 3kn in some areas during springs – see tidal stream diagrams on pages 6-8. There's also a kind of 'roundabout' effect in the area of the Shingles banks, SW of the Long Sand.

The Estuary is, in effect, a bottleneck and this topography, combined with wind speed and direction and barometric pressure, can significantly affect predicted tidal times and heights. These factors must be taken into account when planning a passage, especially if short cuts across some of the banks are to be used.

Timings for passages will often have to be a compromise. For example, a bank may need to be crossed on the flood near local HW, which may mean having to fight the ebb on the final leg up river to a planned destination.

Charted buoys and sand banks

Although the shores of the Estuary are mostly soft mud, the offshore banks are certainly not. They tend to be extremely hard sand and grounding a small craft here on the ebb in rough seas can be dangerous. Even being stranded on a rising tide in deteriorating weather can be an alarming situation.

The sands are constantly shifting and the UK Hydrographic Office publishes frequent corrections to the charts of the Estuary as often as every two years to take account of all the changes. However, new surveys almost certainly do not look at areas that leisure sailors are most interested in, such as swatchways across sandbanks. These may not have been surveyed for many years. The information on electronic charts used on chart plotters, tablets and smart phones, which many leisure sailors rely on (sometimes apparently without question), will be similarly doubtful and arguably not reliable.

Our advice is to buy the new chart versions when they are published. Chart suppliers Imray can supply corrections by post or from their own website, www.imray.com, while corrections to Admiralty charts can be obtained from Notices to Mariners at www.nmwebsearch.com. This equally applies to electronic charts.

Published lists of the positions of navigation marks should be treated with caution. Buoys may be moved and occasionally removed altogether or given new names, as has happened several times in the Estuary in recent years. A up to date chart should be the primary source of waypoints. The positions published in the nautical almanacs each year are also not to be relied upon because these books are printed well in advance of publication and, unless thoroughly corrected as well, should only be used as a 'reality check' for your own waypoints derived from the chart.

Altered or updated waypoints must also be corrected in the ship's GPS set and on any electronic plotters.

Wind and weather

The NE-SW tidal streams, coupled with prevailing SW winds and frequent NE winds over the area, mean that rough seas and wind against tide conditions often occur in the Estuary. The 'Thames Estuary chop' can be as unpleasant a sea as you can find anywhere, even in as little breeze as a F4. Many yachtsmen have a rule of not setting off if there's a '6' in the forecast and that is probably an excellent general rule to follow in the Estuary, especially for windward passages across very shallow areas, such as the Kentish Flats, and in fast-running channels like the Middle Deep and the Wallet. Not for nothing is the Wallet sometimes referred to as 'Vomit Alley'!

Skippers must use all means to keep clear of shipping. Here the genoa is partly rolled to provide a better view

Thames Estuary passages

As ever, landmarks can be useful. Here Herne Bay's water tower is visible, 11 miles from the West Swin, through the Kentish Flats windfarm

Traffic

The whole Estuary is busy with commercial shipping, some of it very large and fast moving and almost invariably 'Constrained by Draught'. A good lookout is essential, as is a listening watch on VHF Ch 16 and 69 (the Port of London Authority (PLA) channel for the outer Thames). Be aware of the charted 'Precautionary Areas'. The Oaze area in particular can be tricky to cross N/S because it contains the junction of several channels – ships approaching in the distance will probably not hold the fixed course you see at any point in time on radar or AIS, so beware of making assumptions based on such information. Be aware that, if you are transmitting AIS, and leisure sailors increasingly do, the PLA may call you on VHF Ch 69 to check your intentions, as the authors have learnt personally!

Tidal heights

When navigating the Thames Estuary it's worth remembering that current tidal heights at gauges at Walton, Margate, Shivering Sands and Southend are broadcast every half hour (H+15 and H+45) by London VTS on VHF Ch 69. This information can help you make routing decisions if you are considering taking a shortcut. Tide tables only contain predictions - tidal heights and timings can be dramatically affected by the weather.

Wind farms

The Gunfleet, Kentish Flats, Thanet, and London Array wind farms are now fully operational, and it is entirely possible that some of these may be expanded and new ones constructed. Cable laying during construction, in some cases across long distances, is another typical modern hazard we must contend with, together with continuous ongoing maintenance.

Before planning a passage across the area, it is wise to get the most up-to-date information about the wind farms and to plan accordingly.

General advice

Work up a comprehensive passage plan before you start, including detailed tidal information for points on your journey. The Admiralty Tidal Atlas can be a great help in doing this.

Do not attempt shortcuts in bad weather. Shortcuts across sandbanks will, by their nature, offer little water under the keel and in rough seas there will be increased danger of grounding in the troughs. Unless certain of adequate depth, the prudent navigator will take the long way round and have contingency plans for using an alternative route or even abandoning the passage.

The estuary is littered with old beacons – the Whitaker, the Barrow and the Pan Sand are three examples – that are useful reference points, but are reaching the end of their lives. Most were erected long ago by an Admiralty Hydrographic Training Unit, possibly to aid surveys of the estuary, but they are not maintained and they are not being marked

20. THAMES PASSAGES

The Naze Tower stands out well as another landmark for position fixing if needed

when they collapse. There are other marks usually visible in good weather, such as the WWII forts at Red Sand, Shivering Sand, Knock John and Roughs, all of which can be useful position fixing aids but again all getting old and won't be there for ever.

Use every opportunity and device to maintain an up-to-date position on the chart. During a passage across the Estuary, decisions and course changes will be frequent and each will demand precise knowledge of the vessel's position. Such position fixing has been made considerably easier for most navigators with the widespread use of GPS and electronic plotters, but nevertheless maintain the log, as often as every 15 minutes in poor visibility, recording each buoy or beacon identified and passed. Do not ignore the chance to confirm a GPS position by visual identification or hand-bearing fixes. Everything will be of use should the electronics fail, as indeed they can.

ROUTES

Along the coast

Passages between the area of the Medway and Swale in the S and the Essex and Suffolk rivers in the N will follow the 'coastal' route and be able to take advantage of the tide.

A passage from the E Swale to the Blackwater or beyond, for example, might start from Harty Ferry just before local HW, push the last of the flood down to the Columbine or Columbine Spit buoys, then head N (with an appropriate W component to allow for tide) to pass the Middle Sand SWM and the Red Sand Towers and across shipping lanes before turning NW into the W Swin at the SW Barrow WCB as the ebb gathers pace.

From the Medway the passage to this point is straightforward, albeit needing similar close attention when crossing shipping channels to reach the Essex shore.

The route would then pass the Maplin SHB, cross into the Middle Deep between the Maplin Edge SHB

The Maplin SHB stands at the SW end of the West Swin

The Swin Spitway SWB

and Maplin Bank PHB, and continue NE to pass the E Maplin PHB and Maplin Approach SHB. This buoy is some 18M from the Columbine and the passage will have used at least 3hr, perhaps 4hr, of ebb out of a total of little more than 5hr of ebb tide available on this down-tide route. Note that sections of the East Swin fall within the Shoeburyness Firing Danger Area, which was the reason for the buoyage being moved to the Middle Deep some years ago.

Thames Estuary passages

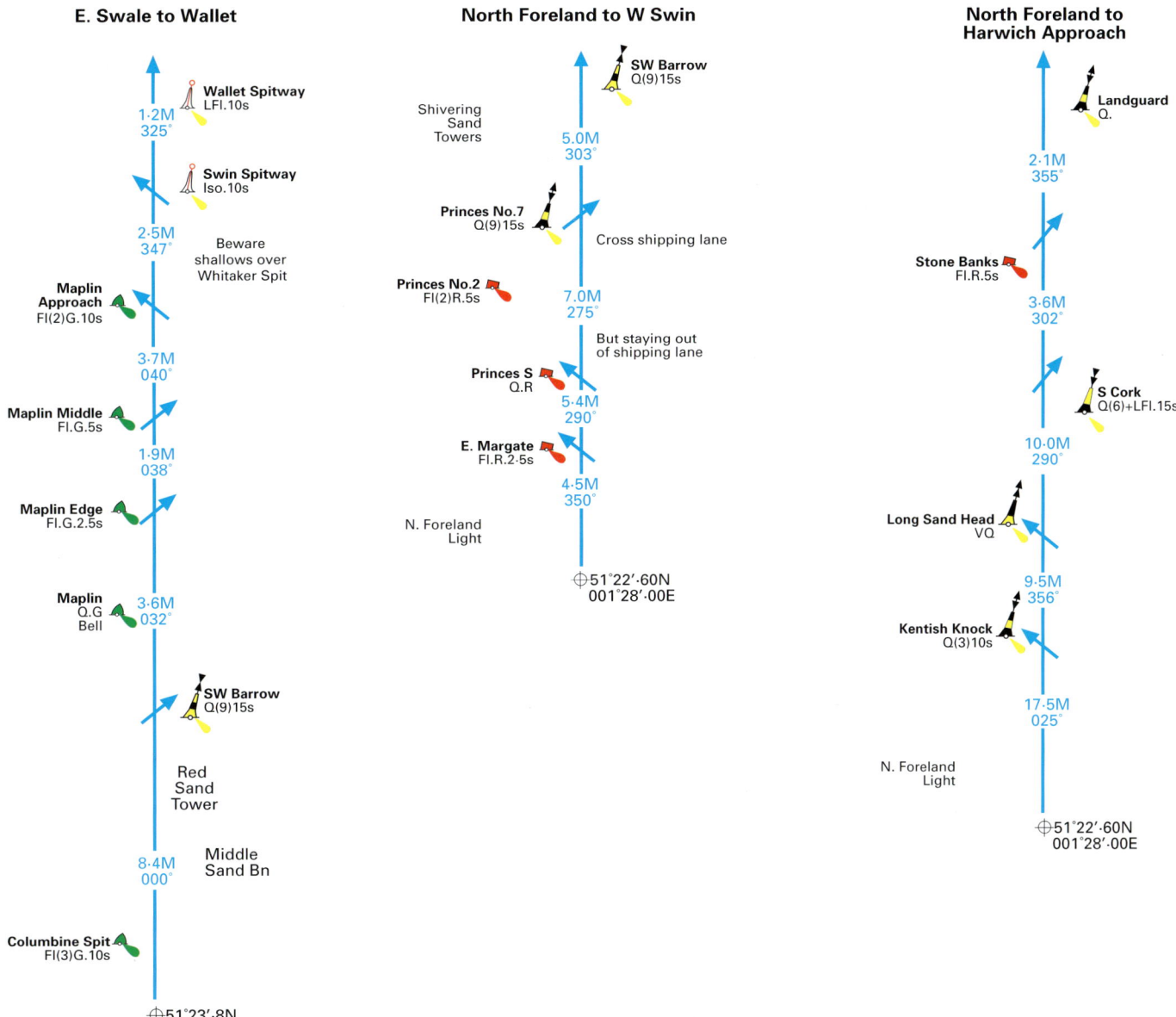

From the Maplin Approach SHB, if the Crouch is your destination, head NW towards the Inner Whitaker SCB (being careful of the depth over the Whitaker Spit), then SW into the Crouch. Otherwise, this coastal route heads NNW to the Swin Spitway SWB, crossing the Buxey Sand to the Wallet Spitway SWB. From here, head NW for the Blackwater and Colne, or NE for the Orwell area or beyond. If the latter then the Wallet is the best route even if you have to cross the Spitway near local LW, because the early flood runs hard SW on the S side of the Gunfleet, while the streams in the Wallet are weaker.

This inner northern Estuary route is readily reversible, timing a departure S from the Whitaker area to ensure enough depth at the planned destination. As with the down-tide route described above, due care must be taken with timing at the Spitway as again you may well be around there near LW.

Skippers on passage SW on this inner route from the Ore, Deben or Orwell areas are recommended to time their departure to reach the Whitaker as suggested above. They will be at sea during most of one ebb and one flood tide and it is preferable to fight the ebb in the Wallet and carry the flood in the Middle Deep and beyond. If bound for the N Foreland via this inshore route, perhaps because of poor weather, time your departure to arrive at the SW end of the West Swin near HW Sheerness, then cross to the Kent coast and carry the ebb down towards Margate – the Kent coastal sector being described in detail in Chapter 18.

East Coast Pilot • 253

20. THAMES PASSAGES

The WWII Red Sand Tower still stands brooding at the S edge of the Oaze Deep

Round the outside

Between N Foreland and Harwich, given a favourable wind, the simplest route is one that goes around the outside of most of the banks.

Leave N Foreland at around HW Dover -1hr and head for the Long Sand Head. You can sail down the Knock Deep, passing through the London Array wind farm, or go outside the Kentish Knock Sand. On this outside route, note that the 'Long Sand Head Two-Way Route' runs E of a line joining the Kentish Knock ECB and the Long Sand Head NCB. Stay W of this line, turning just inside the Long Sand Head buoy to track NW across the SW portion of the Sunk Inner Gyratory System, making either for the Medusa Channel or the Roughs Tower and the Cork Sand Yacht Bn, and then on into Harwich. You should be able to carry a favourable tidal component until about HW Dover -6hr which should then mean entry to the Orwell in the first hours of the flood.

In reverse, a departure from the Orwell on the last of the ebb would give about 6hr of SW-going stream, but the ebb from the English Channel starts heading N off the Foreland at about HW Dover -1hr.

Across the middle

When taking passage as direct as possible between North Foreland and the Essex or Suffolk Rivers, the Long Sand, the Sunk Sand and two channels have to be crossed. Craft of less than 6m draught are discouraged by the PLA from routing along the Barrow Deep and Black Deep.

1. Crossing the Long Sand

The N Edinburgh Channel across the Long Sand is not buoyed and is really not useful to us anyway. Fisherman's Gat is a preferred route for small craft, hardly if ever used by commercial shipping now, and leisure craft skippers also use Foulger's Gat, even further to the NE.

Fisherman's Gat offers an easier passage – generally less stressful than using Foulger's, and you are unlikely to need to keep clear of any shipping.

Foulger's Gat is now enclosed within the boundaries of the London Array wind farm, but its layout allows a route through it marked by the Long Sand Inner, Middle and Outer SWBs. However, there may be occasional short-term closures during maintenance and when wide exclusion zones are enforced around turbines. In such circumstances there are usually guard boats, which may contact you on VHF if you have not already asked for permission to pass. Refer to www.eastcoastpilot.com for the latest information. Beware of strong cross-tides at each end of the Gat, be aware that the SWBs can be hard to make out from a distance and, because the route is a dogleg, you may not be able to see the next buoy hidden behind turbines. It is possible, too, to become disorientated with so many identical turbines around you, unless you pay special attention to maintaining your heading. We do think that Fisherman's Gat is a better bet.

2. Crossing the Sunk Sand

Having crossed the Long Sand, there are no helpful marks for crossing the Sunk Sand to the Barrow Deep, and it's important to refer to the latest information. Commercial surveying of the Sunk Sand is seldom regular but the PLA does conduct 'Check Surveys' from time to time. It's vital that your charts, both electronic and paper, are bang up to date. North of the Sunk Sand, the Barrow Deep does carry commercial shipping but the volume of traffic is much less than in the Black Deep.

The SW Sunk is the most direct route to and from the Essex Rivers. The tide can run quite quickly in the swatchway and a tide rip can be seen around the edge of the SW knoll in the last two hours of the flood. But there is ample room to stay clear as the west entrance is deep. North from the swatchway, passage to or from the Essex Rivers can skirt the E side of the East Barrow Sand taking note of a shallow 'finger' on the NE tip. Further North, due regard needs to be taken if arriving at the Spitway at low water.

Crossing the Middle Sunk appears very convenient for either the Essex or Suffolk Rivers, the gap being roughly north of the No 8 ECB at the NW end of the Fisherman's Gat, taking care to keep clear of the unmarked sunken wreckage of the Sunk Bn. However, no comprehensive survey has been conducted there for many years, it's a shallow route – beware too that the NE corner of the Middle Sunk is extending NE-wards and has seen several small craft groundings. **Frankly this Middle Sunk route is considered too risky to use at the present time, and we do not recommend it.**

A route across the Little Sunk has better water, crossing a deeper section found on a heading WNW towards the Barrow No.2 PHB, after which a diagonal course leads to the end of the Gunfleet Sands without hindrance, picking up the Medusa Channel towards Harwich or via the Cork Sand Yacht Beacon to the Deben and beyond.

Again, the navigator must exercise due caution if using any of these crossing points and refer to *Crossing the Thames Estuary* (Imray) for the latest guidance. To avoid navigating across the Sunk Sand at all, you may choose to make NE to the Sunk Head Tower NCB and from there NW to pick up the Medusa Channel towards Harwich and the rivers beyond. Remember though that the PLA discourages yachts in the Black Deep and you must stay well clear of traffic.

On a passage from the N Foreland towards Essex, the timing is difficult overall, potentially fighting the start of the ebb in the Crouch or Blackwater on arrival. Equally, when departing from either of these rivers you may be faced with arriving at the Sunk on a falling tide. Shallow draught certainly increases your options and with good weather the trip from the Foreland to the Crouch may be better accomplished by starting at around HW Dover +2½hr, reaching the Barrow Deep at LW Dover, nicely positioned to carry the new flood to your destination.

Alternatively you could choose not to take the shortcuts at all, but to use the Middle Deep and W Swin and the Princes Channel, cutting across the shipping lanes between the SW Barrow WCB and the Princes No.7 WCB. This route is longer if going from or to the Crouch or the Blackwater and carries its own tidal considerations, but in poor conditions it would perhaps be the best option.

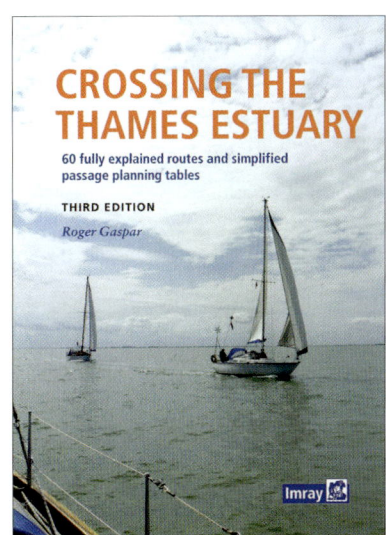

Crossing the Thames Estuary

The authors thoroughly recommend Roger Gaspar's excellent book *Crossing the Thames Estuary* (Imray) as an aid to passage planning and believe it should be a companion to *East Coast Pilot* at your chart table.

Roger's book has a useful supporting website at **www.crossingthethamesestuary.com**, which includes details of his own most recent surveys, not available elsewhere.

All sorts of traffic uses routes in the Estuary

INDEX

A

Abbreviations xi
Ada Point 132
Aldboro Point 99
Aldeburgh 37, 38
Aldeburgh YC 36, 37
Alde River 33, 36, 37, 39
Allington 201
Allington Lock 208, 209
Allington Marina 209
Alresford 99
Alresford Creek 100
Alresford Grange 100
Althorne 133
Althorne Creek 132
Anglia One wind farms 13
Arthur Ransome's Walking Trail 67
AW Marine 'The Marina' 156
Aylesford 204, 206, 208
Aylesford Priory 207

B

Babergh PHB 54, 62, 64
Ballast Hill 78
Baltic Wharf 78, 79, 132
Bargander Sand 157
Barling Ness 147, 148
Barling Quay 148
Barnard ECB 13
Barrow Deep 255
Barthorp's Creek 33
Bartlett Creek 191
Bartonhall Creek 148
Bass' Dock 48
Batchelor Spit 107
Bathside Bay 57
Battle of Maldon 119
Battlesbridge 136, 137
Bawdsey 42, 44
Bawdsey bank 42
Bawdsey Cliffs 32, 37
Bawdsey Manor 42, 44
Bawdsey shore 42
Beacon Marina 72
Beaumont Quay 89
Bedlams Bottom 189
Bell Wharf 153
Bench Head 92, 107, 108
Bench Head Shoal 94
Benfleet 152
Benfleet Creek 156, 158
Benfleet YC 152, 156, 157, 158
Besom Fleet 109
Bishop Spit 190
Blackedge 148
Blackman's Breakwater 55

Black Point 132
Blacktail West 144
Blackwall Basin 172, 174
Blackwater Marina 117, 119
Blackwater River 82, 93, 94, 106, 107, 108, 113, 116, 121, 126
Blackwater SC 120
Blue Bridge 173
Blyth River 26, 28
Boyton Dock 34
Bradwell 106, 113
Bradwell Beacon 113
Bradwell Creek 113
Bradwell Marina 115
Bradwell Power Station 108, 113
Bradwell Quay 114
Bradwell Quay YC 114
Bradwell Waterside 115
Bramble Creek 89
Bramble Island 89
Brandy Hole 136
Brandy Hole Bay 136
Brandy Hole Moorings 136
Brandy Hole Reach 136
Brandy Hole Yacht Club 136
Branklet 140
Branklet Spit 140
Bread Street Kitchen 178
Breydon Bridge 12, 14, 15
Breydon Water 12
Bridge Keeper 144
Bridgemarsh 132
Bridgemarsh Creek 133, 134
Bridgemarsh Island 133, 134
Bridgemarsh Marina 132, 133
Brightlingsea 94, 98, 99
Brightlingsea Creek 95
Brightlingsea SC 96
Brinkman's Wharf 155
Bristol 77
Broads 12, 14, 23
Broadstairs 232
Broomway 143
Brush Bend 13, 14, 15
Brush Bend Lights 13
Bugsby's Reach 172
Bullman's Wharf 146
Burham Marshes 206
Burnham-on-Crouch 128, 132, 136
Burnham Week 128
Burnham Yacht Harbour 130, 131
Butley River 34, 35
Butterfly Channel 223
Butterman's Bay 65
Buxey Edge 128
Buxey Sand 92, 106, 126
Buxley 126, 128

C

Caister Roads 13
Canary Wharf 172
Canvey Island 152
Carlton Railway Bridge 23
Carlton Road 22
Cathouse Hard 68
Chainrock Jetty 159
Chatham 166, 192
Chatham Marina 199
Chatham Maritime Marina 198
Chatham Naval Dockyard 196
Chatham Ness 200
Chatham Ness Shoal 201
Chelmer River 121
Chelmondiston 67
Chelmsford 120
The Chequers Inn 116
Cheyney Spit 241
Church End 142
Cindery Creek 97, 98
Cindery Island 96, 98
Clamp House 66
Clementsgreen Creek 136
Cliff Foot Rocks 55
Cliff Quay 69, 71
Cliff Reach 132
Coalhouse Point 165
Cob Island 38, 39
Cobmarsh Island 109
Cockham Reach 197
Cockham Woods 196
Colchester 102
Colchester Borough Council 103
Colchester Oyster Fishery 99
Colliers Reach 38, 120
Collimer 65
Collimer Point 64
Colne Bar 107
Colne Channel 94
Colne River 92, 94, 99, 101, 102, 106, 107, 126
Colne Smack Preservation Society 98
Colne YC 96, 98
Colton Creek 65
Constable country 79
Conyer 222, 224
Conyer Creek 222, 225
Conyer Creek Marina 223
Cork Sand Bn 56
Cork Sand Yacht Bn 56
Corton Roads 19
Crayfordness 169
Creeksea SC 129, 132
Cross Ledge 244
Crouch 82, 253

Crouch River 93, 106, 126, 127, 128, 130
Cuckolds Point 178
Cutty Sark 174
Cuxton Marina 204

D

Dagenham 169
The Dardanelles 84
Darnet Ness 192
Debbage Yachting 73
Deben River 42, 45, 50, 51, 253
Deben YC 48
Decoy Point 116, 119
Dedham Vale 79
Deer Park Lodge 69
Dengie Flats 126
Dennington 33
Devil's Reach 142
Dovercourt Bay 56
Dovercourt SC 57
Downham Reach 69

E

East Canvey 152
East Dock 182
East Mersea Stone 94, 98
East Suffolk Water Ski Club 44
Edinburgh Channel 254
Elmhaven Marina 205
Elmley 212
Embankment Marina 166
Erith 168, 170
Erith YC 169, 170
Erwarton 77, 78
Erwarton Bay 76, 77
Erwarton Ness 54, 77
Essex Marina 131
Exchem 89

F

Fagbury 54, 62
Fagbury Point 63
Falkenham Marsh 45
Fambridge 133, 134
Fambridge Yacht Haven 135
Faversham 216, 219
Faversham Creek 214, 216, 220
Felixstowe 54, 57, 65, 82, 83
Felixstowe Container Port 54
Felixstowe Ferry 42, 44, 45
Felixstowe Ferry Boatyard 44
Felixstowe Ferry SC 42, 44
Felixstowe South Quay 54
Fellowship Afloat 112

256 • East Coast Pilot

Index

Fenn Creek 136, 137
Ferry House Inn 214
Ferry Point 42
Ferry Reach 225
Fiddler's Reach 169
Fingringhoe 99, 100, 101
Fingringhoe Creek 101
Folly Point 192
Foreness Point 234
Foulness Island 140
Foulness Sand 126, 127, 128
Foundry Reach 84, 85
Foundry Spit 84
Four Fathoms Channel 240
Fowley 212
Fowley Island 222
Fox's Marina 69, 70
Framlingham 33
Frank Halls boatyard 86
Frinton 88
Front Brents Jetty 218
Fullbridge 121
Funton Reach 189

G

Gabbard 13
Gabriels Wharf boatyard 208
Gallions Point Marina 170
The Galloper 56
Ganges 59, 76
Garnham's Island 89
Garrison Point 186
Gashouse Creek 57
Gedgrave Cliffs 35
Geedon Channels 99
Gillingham 194
Gillingham Marina 192, 193, 195
Gillingham Pier 196
Gipping River 73
Goldhanger Creek 116, 119
Goldhanger Spit 116
Goodwin Sands 244
Gorleston 12
Gorleston Pier 12, 13, 14
Grain Spit 164
Grain Tower fort 186, 241
Grain Tower Fort 188
Granary Reach 48
Granary Yacht Harbour 50, 51
Gravesend 164, 166, 168
Gravesend Pontoon 167
Gravesend Reach 165
Gravesend SC 166
Great Cob Island 110
Great Oakley Dock 89
Great Yarmouth 12, 13
Great Yarmouth Harbour 12
Greenland Dock 175
Greenland Pier 175
Green Point 45
Greenwich 162, 174
Greenwich YC 171, 172
The Grindle 66
Gulliver 18
Gulls 35
Gull Wing bridge 21
The Gunfleet 251
Gunfleet Sands 92

The Gut 109
Gyppeswick 73

H

Hadleigh Ray 152, 153, 154, 156, 157
Halfpenny Pier 57, 58
Halling 206
Hall Point 67
Hall Quay 14, 15
Halstow Creek 189
Hamford Water 83, 88, 89
Hamilton Docks 20
Ham Ooze 188
The Hams 47
The Hard 98
Harlow 117
Harty 222
Harty anchorage 215
Harty Ferry 214
Harwich 18, 55, 56, 57, 62, 82, 94, 255
Harwich & Dovercourt SC 56, 58
Harwich Harbour 54, 56, 58, 62
Harwich Harbour Control 54
Harwich Haven Authority 54, 56
Harwich International Port 76
Harwich Shelf 54, 55, 56
Harwich Town 54, 56
Harwich Town SC 57
Haven Bridge 14, 15
Havengore 146
Havengore Bridge 140, 143, 144, 145, 146
Havengore Creek 143, 144, 145
Haven Point 145
Haven Ports YC 65
Havergate Island 33, 34, 35
Hawkwood Stone 206
Hemsby 13
Heritage Community Mooring 180
Hermitage Community Moorings 179, 181
Herne Bay 236, 237
Herring Point 119, 121
Heybridge 120, 121
Heybridge Basin 120, 121
Hilly Pool Point 120
HM Chandleries 64
HMS Beagle 143
Holborough Reach 206
Holbrook Bay 78
Holbrook Beacon 78
Holbrook Creek 78
The Hole 157
Holehaven 152, 159, 163
Holehaven Creek 158, 165
Hollesley Bay 32, 33
Hollowshore 217, 220
Hollowshore Cruising Club 221
Hollowshore Moorings 220
Holm 19
Holm Channel 13
Holm Sand 13

Honey Island 89
Hoo Marina 196
Hoo Ness YC 196
Horse Sand 44, 214
Horse Shoal 128
Horseshoe Point 188
Horsey Island 84, 88
Horsey Mere 85, 87, 88, 89
Hullbridge 136
The Hythe 102
Hythe Quay 121
Hythe Quay Yacht Moorings 123

I

IALA 14
Iken Church 39
Inner Bench Head 94
Inner Whitaker 127
Ipswich 62, 65
Ipswich River 62
Ipswich Wet Dock 62, 71
Iron Wharf 217, 218
Island Point 83, 89
Island Reach 38
Island YC 154, 156
Isle of Harty 214
Isle of Sheppey 212
Islet of Little Fowley 223

J

James Lawrence Sailmakers 98
Jenningtree Point 170

K

Kentish Flats 251
Kethole Reach 188, 190
King Edward Quay 102
King's Boatyard 66
Kingsferry 225, 227
Kingsferry Bridge 212, 225, 227, 229
King's Head 36
Kingsnorth Power Station 191
Kirby Creek 88, 89
Kirby Quay 88
Kirton marshes 46
The Knoll 92, 93, 106
Knoll Spit 42
The Knuckle 27, 28
Kyson Point 47

L

Lake Lothing 21, 23
Landermere Creek 89
Landermere Quay 89
Landfall Waypoint 54, 55, 56
Landguard 54, 56
Landguard Beach 54, 57
Landguard Fort 54
Larkman 50
Lawling Creek 117
Leigh Creek 152, 153, 154
Leigh Marina 153, 154

Leigh Motor Boat Club 153, 154
Leigh-on-Sea (Leigh) 152
Leigh SC 153
Leigh Station 157
Levington 57, 65
Levington Creek 64, 65
Leysdown 213
Limehouse 178
Limehouse Marina 173, 176, 177, 178
Limehouse Reach 201
Lime Kiln 50
Lime Kiln Quay 51
London Bridge 163
London Coastguard 163
London Gateway Container Port 158
London VTS channel 163
Long Gull 35
Long Reach 34, 65, 66
Long Sand 250, 254
Lower Gull 34
Lower Halstow 189
Lower Halstow YC 190
Lower Pool 178
Lowestoft 12, 13, 18, 20, 22, 54
Lowestoft Beacon Marina 22
Lowestoft CC 22
Lowestoft Harbour 20
Lowestoft Marina 23
Lowestoft Ness 13, 19
Lowestoft Port Control 18

M

Maldon 106, 120, 121, 122
Maldon Little Ships Club 123
Maldon YC 121
Maltings 39
Manningtree 78, 79
Maplin Sands 140, 143, 144
Marconi SC 116
Margaret Ness 171
Margate 234
Margate Harbours 232
Margate Hook Sand 235
Margate YC 235
Marsh End Sand 152
Martello Tower 36
Martlesham Creek 47
Martlesham Creek Boatyard 47
Maybush 46
Maylandsea Bay BC 119
Maylandsea Bay SC 118
MBC Marina 51
Medusa Channel 56, 82, 255
Medway 164, 188, 227, 252
Medway Bridge Marina 203
Medway Canal 166
Medway Cruising Club 193
Medway River 186, 187
Medway & Swale Boating Association 186
Medway VTS 186
Medway YC 197
Melton 46, 48, 50
Melton Boatyard 50
Mersea 109, 110
Mersea Flats 92, 94

INDEX

Mersea Fleet 109
Mersea Island 99
Mersea Quarters 108, 109
Mersea Quarters and Tollesbury 108
Mersea Stone 99
Methersgate 47
Methersgate Quay 47
Middle Creek 192
Middleway 146
Mill Beach 119, 120
Millwall Docks 174
Milton Creek 225
Minnis Bay 235
Mistley 78, 79
Mistley Marine 79
Mistley Quay 76, 78
Mundon Pt 117
Mundon Stone Point 117
Mussel Scarfe 84
Mutford Lock 23
Mutford Road Bridge 23

N

Nacton Foreshore 65
Nacton Quay 65
Narrow Cuts 146, 147
Narrow Street 178
Nase Point 140
Nass Beacon 110
National Coastwatch Institution 155
Naze Tower 82, 252
Neptune Marina 71, 72
Ness 33
New Cut 73
The New Cut 73
New England Creek 146
Nore Swatch 163
Norfolk Broads 14
Norman Keep 35
North Double 119
North Eagle 107
Northey Island 120
North Fambridge Yacht Station 134
North Fambridge YC 134
North Foreland 232, 233
North Training Wall 13

O

Oakley Creek 89
Oare 215, 221
Oare Creek 215, 220
The Old Packing Shed 109
Old Brickyard Dock 38
old Herne Bay 237
Ore River 32, 33, 34, 35, 36, 253
Orford 32, 35, 36, 37
Orford Haven 32, 33
Orford Haven SWB 33
Orford Ness 32, 34, 36, 37
Orinoco Channel 192
Orwell 59, 62, 253
Orwell Bridge 65, 67, 69
Orwell River 54, 57, 62

Orwell YC 69, 70
Osea 106, 117, 119
Osea Island 115, 116, 120
Ostrich Creek 69, 70
Otterham Creek 191
Oulton Broad 23
Oxley 33

P

Packing House Island 109
Packing Marsh Island 109
Paglesham 140, 143, 147, 148
Paglesham Creek 142
Paglesham moorings 140
Paglesham Reach 142
Palmerston Fort 193
Pan Sand 234, 251
Parkeston 77
Parkeston Quay 76
Peel Ports Group 12
Pepys 62
Peter's Bridge 206
Pewit Island 89, 99
Pigpail Sluice 36
Pin Mill 65, 66
Point Clear 95, 98
Poplar Dock 172
Poplar Dock Marina 173, 174
Port Medway Marina 204
Port of Brightlingsea 96
Port of London Authority (PLA) 162
Port Traffic Signals 14
Port Werburgh 192
Potter Reach 67
Potton Creek 146
Potton Island 142
Potton Point 142, 146
Prettyman's Point 46
Prince Philip Lock 71
Princes Channel 233, 255
Pye Channel 83, 89
Pye End 56, 62
The Pyefleet 99
Pye Sand 82

Q

Quarters Spit 109
Queenborough 163, 164, 186, 212, 228, 229
Queenborough Creek 229
Quern Bank 244

R

Radio Caroline 36, 116
Rainham Marshes 170
Ramsey 76
ramsgate 244
Ramsgate 232
Ramsgate Entrance 245
Ramsgate Harbour 233, 244
Ramsgate Marina 245, 246, 247
Ramsholt 45, 46
Ramsholt Arms 45
Ramsholt Woods 46
Rat Island 99

Ratsey and Lapthorn 98
Ray Channel 109
Ray Gut 152
Ray Sand 126, 127
Raysand Middle 127
Raysand North 127
Reculver 240
Reculver Towers 235
Redoubt Fort 56
Red Sea 89
Regent Road 14
Ridham Dock 225
River Colne 82, 99
River Deben 77
River Medway 186
River Stour 54, 57
River Swale 212, 213
Roach River 128, 140
Roach Sailing Association 143
Robertson's Boatyard 50, 51
Rochester 186
Rochester Bridge 196, 200, 201
Rochester Oyster Fishery 206
Rochester Sailing Club 202
Rochford 140, 148
The Rocks 46
Roman River 101
Rotherhithe peninsula 176
Rotherhithe road tunnel 178
Rowhedge 98, 101, 102
Royal Burnham YC 129
Royal Corinthian YC 128, 129
Royal Engineer Yacht Club 198
Royal Harwich YC 67, 68
Royal Naval Dockyard 186
Royal Navy 197
Russia Dock Woodland 176

S

Salcote SC 120
Salcott Channel 109
Salcott Creek 109
Saltpan Reach 188, 190
Saunders Ness 174
S Corton 13
Scroby Sands 13
Sea Reach 162
Secret Water 82, 88
Segas SC 193
Sharfleet 188
Sharfleet Creeks 188
Sheerness 163, 186, 187
Sheerness Docks 186
Sheerness Middle Sand 241
Shell Ness 214
Shingle Street 32, 37
Shivering Sand 252
Shoebury 144
Shore Ends 127, 128
Shotley 56
Shotley bank 63
Shotley Horse 62
Shotley Marina 56, 57, 58, 59, 62, 64
Shotley spit 58
Shotley Spit 54, 57, 62
Shotley Spit SCB 54
Skeleton Works 13, 14

Skipper's Island 89
Slaughden 36, 38
Slaughden Quay 36, 37, 38
Slaughden SC 37
Smallgains 152
Smallgains Creek 154
Smith Shoal 78
Snape 39
Snape Bridge 33
Snape Maltings concert hall 33
Snodland Church 206
South Channel 110
South Deep 222
South Dock lock 175
South Dock Marina 175, 176
Southey Creek 119
Southwold 26, 28, 29
Southwold ferry 29
Southwold Harbour 29
Southwold Port Radio 26, 29
South Woodham Ferrers YC 137
Spitway 126
The Spitway 106
Stanford Channel 13, 19
Stangate 116, 188, 190
Stangate Creek 163, 188, 189
St Clement's 169
St Katharine Docks 164, 183
St Katharine Docks Marina 180
St Katharine's Pier 181
St Lawrence Bay 116
St Mary's church 121
St Mary's Island 196
St Mary the Virgin 123
Stoke Saltings 190
Stoke SC clubhouse 69
Stone 116
Stone Banks 56
Stone Heaps 64
Stone Point 83, 84
Stone Sailing Club 116
Stonner Island 46, 47
St Osyth 98
St Osyth Boatyard 98
St Osyth Creek 97
Stour 76
Stour River 56, 76, 77
Stour SC 79
Stow Creek 134, 135, 136
Stratton 64
Strood 166
Strood Channel 99, 109
Strood YC 202
The Stumble 116
Stutton Ness 78
Suffolk Broads 22
Suffolk Yacht Harbour (SYH) 62, 64, 65
Sunken Buxey 127, 128
Sunken Island 109
Sunken Pye 82
Sunk Gyratory System 56
Sunk Sand 254
Sun Pier 200
Surrey Docks 176
Sutton Hoo 48
Sutton Wharf 149
Swale 212, 216, 236, 252

Index

Swale Marina 224
Swallowtail 128
Swin Spitway 126
Swire Hole 107, 127
small craft symbols xi
symbols used on charts x

T

Thames Barges 62
Thames Barrier 163
The Thames Barrier 170
Thames Barrier Navigation Centre (TBNC) 171
Thames Estuary 88, 93, 233
Thamesport 190
Thames River 127, 162
Thanet 251
The Medway 240
The Queens Channel 234
The Royal Temple YC 247
Thirslet Spit 115, 116
Thorn Fleet 109
Thunderbolt Pier 200
Thurrock YC 168
Tidal heights 251
Tide Mill 50
Tide Mill Harbour 48
Tide Mill Marina 50, 51
Tide Mill Yacht Harbour 50
Tilbury ferry 167
The Tips 47
Titchmarsh Marina 84, 85, 87, 88
Tollesbury 110
Tollesbury Marina 112
Tollesbury Pier 115
Tollesbury South Channel 111
Tower Bridge 162, 175
Town Quay 218
Training Wall 14
Trawl dock 20, 21
Trimley 64
Trimley Bay 64
Trimley Marshes 64
Trinity 54, 62
Trinity Berth 62
Trinity Buoy Wharf 172
Trinity House 42, 56, 57
Trinity Quay 54, 57, 62, 63, 64
Troublesome Reach 47
The Twizzle 85, 87
Twizzle Creek 84, 87
Two Tree Island 156, 157

U

Ufford 50
Upnor Reach 197
Upnor SC 197
Up River YC 137

V

Victoria Wharf 153
Victory Moorings 200
The Violet 147

W

The Wade 88
Wadgate Ledge 56
Wakering Boatyard 146
Wakering YC 149
Walberswick 28, 29
Waldringfield 42, 46, 47
Waldringfield Boatyard 46
Waldringfield SC 45
Wallasea 131
Wallasea Bay 132
Wallasea Island 128
Wallasea Ness 128
The Wallet 82, 92
Wallet channels 106
Wallet Spitway 107
Walter Cook's yard 122
Walton 84, 88
Walton Backwaters 82
Walton Basin 86
Walton Channel 83, 84, 85, 87
Walton & Frinton YC 85, 86
Walton-on-the-Naze 56, 82, 87
Walton Pier 82
Walton Yacht Basin 86
Wantsum Channel 235
Waterside 96
Waterside Marina 96
Waveney 20
Waveney Dock 18
Weir Point 33
West Dock 64
West India Dock 172, 173, 174
West India Marine Control 174
Westmarsh Point 95
West Mersea 108, 110
West Mersea YC 108
West Point 116
Westrow Point 38
West Swale 188, 227
Wet Dock 72
Wherstead Road Bridge 73
Whisstock's Boatyard 48
Whisstock's Place 49
Whitaker Beacon 126
Whitaker Channel 126, 127
Whiting Bank 33
Whitstable 236, 237, 238
Whitstable YC 240
Whitton Marine 192
Wickham Point 202
Wilford Bridge 48, 50, 51
Wind farms 251
Witch's Quay 89
Wivenhoe 98, 100, 101
Wivenhoe barrier 101
Wivenhoe SC 100, 101
Wivenhoe SC moorings 101
Woodbridge 42, 47, 48
Woodbridge CC 42, 48
Woodbridge Haven 42
Woodrolfe Creek 111, 112
Woolverstone 62, 67, 69
Woolverstone Marina 67, 68
Woolwich 162, 170
Woolwich Ferry 170
Wouldham 205
Wouldham Church 205
Wrabness 78

Y

Yantlet Flats 164
Yarmouth 13
Yarmouth Radio 12, 14
Yokesfleet Creek 142, 146